Internet Business Models and Strategies:

Text and Cases

Internet Business Models and Strategies:

TEXT AND CASES

Allan Afuah
University of Michigan

Christopher L. Tucci
New York University
Stern School of Business

McGraw-Hill
Irwin

Boston   Burr Ridge, IL   Dubuque, IA   Madison, WI   New York   San Francisco   St. Louis
Bangkok   Bogotá   Caracas   Lisbon   London   Madrid
Mexico City   Milan   New Delhi   Seoul   Singapore   Sydney   Taipei   Toronto

McGraw-Hill Higher Education

A Division of The McGraw-Hill Companies

INTERNET BUSINESS MODELS AND STRATEGIES: TEXT AND CASES
Published by McGraw-Hill/Irwin, an imprint of The McGraw-Hill Companies, Inc. 1221 Avenue of the Americas, New York, NY, 10020. Copyright © 2001, by the McGraw-Hill Companies, Inc. All rights reserved. No part of this publication may be reproduced or distributed in any form or by any means, or stored in a data base or retrieval system, without the prior written consent of The McGraw-Hill Companies, Inc., including, but not limited to, in any network or other electronic storage or transmission, or broadcast for distance learning.

Some ancillaries, including electronic and print components, may not be available to customers outside the United States.

This book is printed an acid-free paper.

1 2 3 4 5 6 7 8 9 0 FGR/FGR 0 9 8 7 6 5 4 3 2 1 0

ISBN   0-07-239724-1

Vice president/Editor-in-chief: *Michael W. Junior*
Executive editor: *Jennifer Roche*
Editorial assistant: *Tracy L. Jensen*
Marketing manager: *Ellen Cleary*
Project manager: *Laura Griffin*
Production supervisor: *Michael R. McCormick*
Senior designer: *Jennifer McQueen Hollingsworth*
Media technology producer: *Barb Block*
Compositor: *Lachina Publishing Services*
Typeface: *10.5/12 Times Roman*
Printer: *Quebecor Printing Book Company/Fairfield*
Cover image: *Copyright 2000 PhotoDisc, Inc. All rights reserved.*

Library of Congress Cataloging-in-Publication Data

Afuah, Allan.
    Internet business models and strategies : text and cases / Allan Afuah, Christopher L. Tucci.
        p.   cm.
    ISBN   0-07-239724-1 (alk. paper)
    Includes index.
        1. Business enterprises -- Computer networks.   2. Electronic commerce.   3. Internet
(Computer network)   I. Tucci, Christopher L.   II. Title.
HD30.37.A33   2001
658.8'4dc--21   00040692

www.mhhe.com

Contents

Preface

The impact of the Internet on industries, businesses, and firms' competitive advantage has been phenomenal. At the same time and reflecting its importance, the phrase "business model" has also found its way into the vocabulary of just about everyone who must manage or work in businesses with an Internet content, from venture capitalists to CEOs. Despite the enormous importance of the Internet and business models to firms, and the explosive interest in both subjects, there are no business school texts that address the impact of the Internet on firm performance.

In *Internet Business Models and Strategies: Text and Cases,* we draw on research in strategic management and the management of technology to develop an integrative framework that allows readers to put their minds around what determines firm performance and the central role that business models play in the face of the Internet. We offer concepts and tools that students of management need to analyze and synthesize business models, especially Internet business models. The framework developed in the book allows its users to make more informed concept- and theory-grounded arguments about Internet start-ups, bricks-and-mortar firms that must face challengers, the relative merits of formulating and implementing Internet business models and strategies, and how much start-ups might be worth.

In the first part of the book, we explore the concepts on which Internet business models rest, and the tools that can be used to analyze and appraise them. In addition to building a conceptual framework, the chapters include discussion questions and key terms to engage readers further with the subject matter. The second part of the book offers cases of both pure-play Internet firms as well as bricks-and-mortar firms that must formulate and execute successful business models and strategies in order to gain, defend, or reinforce a competitive advantage in the face of the Internet.

To the best of our knowledge, no other book addresses the central issues of the impact of the Internet on business performance. This is not to say that there are no books on e-commerce or the impact of the Internet from a functional perspective, simply that they do not centrally address business issues, particularly the impact of the Internet on business models and firm performance.

INTENDED AUDIENCE

The book should be of particular interest to those who are interested in managing a business with an Internet component. It is designed for those who want to pursue ventures in e-commerce, manage such ventures, compete with such ventures, or interact with them. This includes individuals who plan to work for venture capital firms that must understand the viability of the business models they are financing, Internet start-ups, bricks-and-mortar firms that must adopt the Internet to fend off challengers or reinforce an existing competitive advantage, consulting firms that must undertake Internet-related assignments for clients, investment bankers who must value Internet businesses, and even those in government who must formulate policies that influence firm performance in the face of the Internet. Thus, students and managers alike will find this book useful. These potential users can refer to this book at different stages of their careers.

Graduate Business School Programs

There are four different contexts in which the book can be used in business schools: It can be used (1) in a stand-alone e-business strategy course in a strategy group, marketing department, entrepreneurship area, or any of the functional departments that contribute to an e-commerce track, (2) as a module in a core strategy course where as much attention must be given to Internet business models as traditionally has been given to business strategy, (3) as a module in management information systems (information technology, computer information systems) courses that provides a link between the Internet as an information technology and firm performance—that is, a module that emphasizes profiting from an information technology; and (4) as an Internet business models elective in one of the many e-commerce tracks, concentrations, departments, and degree programs that are being introduced in business schools.

Undergraduate Programs

Undergraduates are increasingly sophisticated about the Web. Moreover, many of them graduate to take jobs that have an Internet or business model content. Many of them will start their own Internet businesses while in college or right after they graduate. A large number of the Internet courses taught to undergraduates usually dwell on the technology, transactions, and connectivity, and pay little or no attention to the link between these technologies and firm performance. This book helps readers focus on profiting from the Internet. Thus the material can be useful in undergraduate courses offered in the fields of strategy, e-commerce, computer/ management information systems, information technology, entrepreneurship, or marketing.

Practicing Managers

Any manager or functional specialist who must contribute to formulating and executing Internet business models and strategies should find the book useful. It may also be appropriate for those, such as consultants and venture capitalists, who must analyze, appraise, and sometimes synthesize business models and strategies for start-ups or bricks-and-mortar firms.

Our interest in the Internet, management of technology, and the strategic issues on which profiting from technological change rests, has built up over the last twenty years. That interest kicked off when we worked at different times in Silicon Valley before meeting at MIT as PhD students in the Management of Technological Innovation Area. Subsequently, Allan went to the University of Michigan Business School to teach Technology & Innovation Management as well as Strategic Management, while Chris went to the NYU Stern School of Business to teach Technological Innovation & New Product Development, Strategic Management, and Operations Management. We hope that you, the reader, will share our passion for this timely subject! We welcome your thoughts and suggestions as well at our website, www.mhhe.com/afuahtucci.

Allan and Chris
Ann Arbor and New York City

From the Publisher

INSTRUCTOR SUPPORT MATERIAL

Instructor's Manual Online

The instructor's manual, prepared by the authors, contains teaching suggestions, case notes, sample syllabuses, and additional helpful materials. It can be accessed through the book's companion website at www.mhhe.com/afuahtucci.

Website: www.mhhe.com/afuahtucci

Instructor resource materials are contained at this website and include an opportunity for instructors to contact the authors, to post and share syllabi, resources, and other materials in addition to gaining access to relevant e-commerce education links. Please contact your McGraw-Hill/Irwin sales representative for the password to this protected material.

Customized Publication and Updated Cases Available through Primis

The content of this text is also available through Primis Online, a large and growing database that provides you the flexibility of choosing only the material that matches your course. You can easily build a custom version of this text at mhhe.com/primis/online. In addition, you will find updated cases that accompany this text.

PageOut: Your Own Course Website for Free

With PageOut you will receive a unique website address that is home for all of the courses you teach. It requires no prior knowledge of HTML, no long hours of coding, and no design skills on your part. Easy to follow templates help you create your site quickly with a professional design. The PageOut interactive syllabus offers a place where you can add your own content, create Web links, and post assignments. PageOut also has an online gradebook and discussion area.

PageOut is hosted by McGraw-Hill and, best of all, is free with the adoption of a McGraw-Hill title. To learn more, please contact your McGraw-Hill/Irwin sales representative.

STUDENT SUPPORT MATERIAL

Website: www.mhhe.com/afuahtucci

There is a companion website for this text that provides students with access to study tools, an opportunity to contact the authors, to review relevant e-commerce and e-strategy links, and more.

Acknowledgments

This book has been a collective task, and we would like to express our gratitude to several people who contributed to it. First, we are basing many of the frameworks and concepts of this book on several streams of literature, including those of strategic management, management of technology, economics, and organizational behavior. We would like to thank those academics, consultants, practicing managers, and other researchers whose work we have cited throughout the book. We also owe a debt of gratitude to our mentors in the Management of Technological Innovation group at MIT, especially Michael Cusumano, Rebecca Henderson, Ed Roberts, and James Utterback.

We heartily thank our students at the University of Michigan Business School and the New York University Stern School of Business. Many of the ideas in the book were pretested on them, and all the cases in the last part of the book were written by them under our supervision. Our stimulating interactions in the classroom gave us energy for the project and also led us to believe that there was deep interest in a textbook that focused on the strategic implications of the Internet. Two of our students deserve special mention. Denise Banks was an expert reader, making many nuanced suggestions for the manuscript. Alison Matochak was an incredible research assistant who made many helpful comments on the manuscript and drafted chapter summaries, key words, and discussion questions.

The book was refereed in a peer-review process and we are grateful to the referees for their helpful suggestions, insightful comments, and constructive criticism of the drafts. We would like to thank Anthony F. Chelte (Western New England College), Stéphane Gagnon (McGill University), Benjamin Gomes-Casseres (Brandeis University), Brian Lindquist (University of Phoenix), Timothy Mills (University of Phoenix), B.P.S. Murthi (University of Texas at Dallas), d.t. ogilvie (Rutgers University), Ralph Oliva (Pennsylvania State University), Mihir Parikh (Polytechnic University and Institute for Technology & Enterprise), Kenneth Sardoni (University of Phoenix), and four anonymous reviewers.

Jennifer Roche was the executive editor in charge of this book and she has taken up this task with aplomb, shepherding the project through the various stages in a professional, fair, and enthusiastic way. It was clear from our early interactions with Jennifer and with Mike Junior, the editor-in-chief, that McGraw-Hill/Irwin "got it" in terms of their thinking about the Internet and its impact on the educational curricula of business schools. In addition to our main contacts, there was an entire production team behind the publication of the book, including Barb Block, Ellen Cleary, Elizabeth Degenhard, Laura Griffin, Tracy L. Jensen, Michael R. McCormick, and Jennifer McQueen Hollingsworth. We have been quite impressed by their professionalism and ability to make things happen.

Finally, we would like to express our warmest thanks to Chris's wife, Carolyn, who went well beyond the call of duty, not only for obliging our (and her) hectic work schedules, but also for lending her own editorial prowess to the manuscript.

The Internet

CHAPTER 1

Introduction and Overview

Most firms are in business to win, to outperform their competitors. They are in business to make money. They adopt new technologies to fend off new competitors, reinforce an existing competitive advantage, leapfrog competitors, or just to make money in new markets. Performance is critical. If performance is so significant to firms and their managers, an important question is: What determines performance to begin with? Only by understanding the determinants of business performance can firms better formulate their business models—how they plan to make money over the long term. By understanding the determinants of **firm performance**, firms are in a better position to comprehend how a technology such as the Internet impacts that performance and how firms can exploit the new technology. In this chapter, we briefly describe the determinants of firm performance and the role played by business models, especially Internet business models. We sketch the framework on which the book is built.

DETERMINANTS OF PERFORMANCE

There are three major **determinants of business performance**: business models, the environment in which businesses operate, and change (see Figure 1.1).[1] Before delving into these determinants, we need to define what performance means in this book. What exactly constitutes firm performance can be the subject of passionate debate and even controversy. One can make a strong argument for defining performance as profits, cash flow, economic value added (EVA), market valuation, earnings per share, sales, return on sales, return on assets, return on equity, return on capital, economic rents, and so on. Throughout this book, except where noted, performance means accounting profits. Now, let's return to the determinants of performance.

Business Models

The first determinant of a firm's performance is its **business model**. This is the method by which a firm builds and uses its resources to offer its customers better

FIGURE 1.1 Determinants of Business Performance

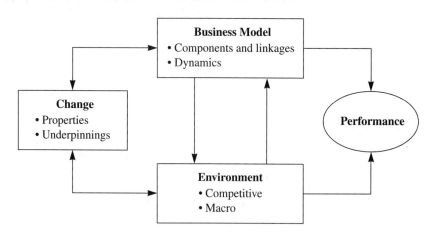

value than its competitors and to make money doing so. It details how a firm makes money now and how it plans to do so in the long term. The model is what enables a firm to have a sustainable **competitive advantage**, to perform better than its rivals in the long term. A business model can be conceptualized as a system that is made up of components, linkages between the components, and dynamics.

Components and Linkages

A business model is about the value that a firm offers its customers, the segment of customers it targets to offer the value to, the scope of products/services[2] it offers to which segment of customers, its sources of revenue, the prices it puts on the value offered its customers, the activities it must perform in offering that value, the capabilities these activities rest on, what a firm must do to sustain any advantages it has, and how well it can implement these elements of the business model. It is a system, and how well a system works is not only a function of the type of components, but also a function of the relationships among the components. Thus, if the value that a firm offers its customers is low cost, then the activities that it performs should reflect that. Take the bricks-and-mortar example of Southwest Airlines. In the 1980s and 1990s, it offered its customers low-cost frequent flights.[3] Two of the activities that the firm performed—no meals on its flights and flying only out of uncongested airports—were consistent with this low-cost strategy. In addition to the relationships among the components of a firm's business model, there is the relationship between the business model and its environment. A good business model always tries to take advantage of any opportunities in its environment while trying to dampen the effects of threats from it.

Dynamics

The right business model components and linkages do not last forever. Managers often have to change some components or relationships before competitors do it for them. In some industries, firms have to keep reinventing their business models. They have to cannibalize themselves before someone else does. It is these actions associated with change, whether initiated by a firm to preempt competitors or to fend them off, or in response to any other opportunities and threats, that we refer to in this text as **dynamics**. In the 1990s Dell Computer was often cited as a firm that was good at reinventing its business model.

Environment

Competitive Environment

Firms do not formulate and execute their business models in a vacuum. They do so in a **competitive environment**. They face competitors who have their own business models, who are just as interested in making money, and who may be equally capable of offering the same level of value to customers. They also face suppliers and customers who may be just as interested in maximizing their own profits as the firms are.

A firm's competitors can, and often do, force down the prices that a firm can charge for its products or force it to offer higher value to customers at a smaller price premium.[4] The lower the prices or the higher the costs, the lower the profits that a firm can make. Rivals do not compete only in the value that they offer customers. They also compete for talent and other resources. Although suppliers can be partners or allies, they are in a sense competitors because their actions can increase a firm's costs and lower the prices that the firm can charge its own customers. Powerful suppliers can extract high prices from a firm, thus raising its costs. They may even force a firm to take lower-quality products, making it difficult for it to offer the kind of value that it would like to offer customers. Similarly, although customers can be loyal allies, their actions often have the same results as those of competitors. If customers are very powerful, they may be able to extract lower prices from a firm or force it to ship products of higher quality than the price warrants. If the market in which a firm is operating is easy to enter, then the firm faces the constant threat of other firms entering its competitive space. This puts a lot of pressure on the prices that a firm can charge because higher prices tend to attract more entrants. Of course, the higher the number of substitute products, the more difficult it is for the firm to make money since higher prices or lower quality will drive customers to substitute products. Finally, the type of technology on which industry products and activities rest also has an impact on firm performance.

Macro Environment

Beyond the competitive environment is the overarching **macro environment** of government policies, natural environment, national boundaries, deregulation/regulation, and technological change. In other words, industries themselves do not operate in a vacuum.[5] The government plays one of the most important roles of the macro environment in terms of firm profitability. Without the government, for example, there would be no Internet. Moreover, government policies worldwide will go a long way in determining the extent to which the Internet thrives and to which firms within their domains profit from the new technology.

Change

The last determinant of firm performance is change. Its role is more indirect than direct. Change impacts business models or their environments, which can translate into higher or lower profitability. Change can come from competitors, suppliers, customers, demographics, the macro environment, or the firm itself. It can be present in firm strategies, demographics, demand and supply, government regulation/deregulation, or the technologies that underpin an industry's products. For example, the microprocessor and personal computer (PC) transformed a computer industry once dominated by makers of mainframes like IBM and makers of minicomputers such as Digital Equipment Corporation into one in which PCs and workstations/servers dominated. Better still, witness the change brought about by the Internet that we explore in this book.

The impact of change on a firm's business model or industry is a function of the type of change. Radical or disruptive change can render existing business models obsolete and drastically alter the competitive landscape in existing industries or create entirely new industries while killing old ones. It can result in what the economist J. A. Schumpeter (1883–1950) termed "creative destruction" when it gives rise to new entrepreneurial firms creating wealth and old, established incumbents dying off.[6] The Internet may be doing just that to many industries.

The Internet

The Internet is a technology with many properties that have the potential to transform the competitive landscape in many industries while at the same time creating whole new industries. The **Internet** is a low-cost standard with fast interactivity that exhibits network externalities, moderates time, has a universal reach, acts as a distribution channel, and reduces information asymmetries between transacting parties. These properties have a profound impact on the 5-Cs of coordination, commerce, community, content, and communications. Since nearly every firm's activities rest on some subset of the 5-Cs, one can expect the Internet to have a profound effect on all firms. It plays a critical and profound role in the way firm activities (internal or external) are coordinated, how commerce is conducted, how people and machines communicate, how communities are defined and how they interact, and how and when goods are made and delivered. The Internet has the potential to disrupt established ways of conducting business while creating new ones and new businesses.

INTERNET BUSINESS MODELS

Given such landscape-transforming properties of the Internet, the question is, How can a firm take advantage of them and make money? An **Internet business model** spells out how. It is the method by which a firm plans to make money long term using the Internet. The Internet business model is the system—components, linkages, and associated dynamics—that takes advantage of the properties of the Internet to make money. It takes advantage of the properties of the Internet in the way it builds each of the components—value, scope, revenue sources, pricing, connected activities, implementation, capabilities, and sustainability—and crafts the linkages among these components. For example, the Internet's universality and time-moderation properties allow employees of a firm located in different parts of the world to collaborate on product development, thus decreasing the time needed to bring a product to market. They also allow retailers to stay open 24 hours a day to shoppers, in the privacy of their homes, from different parts of the world.

For expository purposes, Internet business models can be categorized as pure play or clicks-and-mortar. A firm is said to have a pure play Internet business model if, at the model's conception, the firm did not have an existing bricks-and-mortar business model. With a clean slate, a firm can conceive and execute a business model that is free of some of the baggage that old ways of doing things can carry. A clicks-and-mortar model is an Internet business model conceived when a bricks-and-mortar model is already in place. A firm with such a model must deal with the impediments of its past models. Which components and linkages of a firm's bricks-and-mortar business model are impacted by the Internet is a function not only of those components and linkages but also of the type of competitive and macro environments in which the firm operates.

Internet business models, whether pure play or clicks-and-mortar, come in all forms. They include brokerage, advertising, infomediary, merchant, manufacturer, affiliate, community, subscription, and utility.[7] All, however, have one goal: to make money. Each model's ability to achieve this goal rests on its components and the linkages between them and its resilience, flexibility, and ability to take advantage of change.

INTERNET BUSINESS MODELS AND STRATEGIES

This book is about Internet business models and strategies and what it takes for them to allow firms to make money. There are five parts to the book (see Figure 1.2). Part I explores the Internet—the technology and its properties. Part II examines the components, linkages, dynamics, and valuation of a business model. Part III turns to the role of the competitive and macro environment in firm profitability. Part IV considers applications of the concepts, models, and tools discussed in the text. Part V presents the cases.

Part I: The Internet

An important part of profiting from an innovation is understanding where one is located or should be located in the innovation value-added configuration. In Chapter 2 we explore the Internet value-added network. We examine infrastructure providers, Internet service providers (ISPs), applications service providers (ASPs), suppliers (of hardware, software, and content) to the Internet infrastructure, complementors, and end users. We pay attention to the relationships between the different members of the configuration and the evolving terminology.

In Chapter 3 we explore those properties of the Internet that promise to transform the competitive landscape in many industries. In particular, we examine 10 properties: mediating technology, universality, network externalities, distribution channel, time moderator, information asymmetry shrinker, infinite virtual capacity, low cost common standard, creative destroyer, and reducer of transaction costs. We pay particular attention to how these properties impact the 5-Cs of coordination, commerce, community, content, and communications. We also discuss the

FIGURE 1.2 Conceptual Framework: Where Chapters Fit in the Context of Business Performance

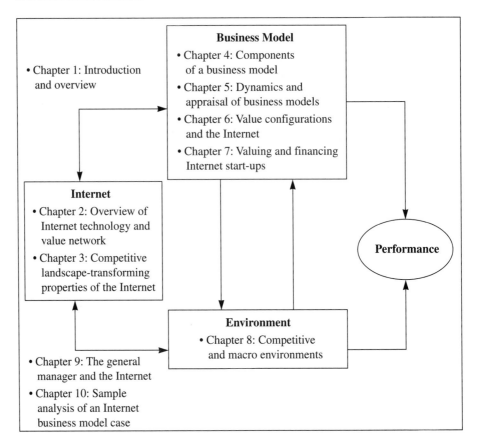

limits to the Internet because any good business model must recognize the limitations of the driving force on which it rests.

Part II: Components, Linkages, Dynamics, and Evaluation of Business Models

Having examined the Internet and its properties, we move on to explore Internet business models. In Chapter 4 we examine the components of a business model and the linkages among them. In particular, we discuss the value, scope, revenue sources, price, connected activities, implementation, capabilities and sustainability, and relationships among them, all of which determine the impact of a business model on firm performance. In Chapter 5 we recognize that the elements of a business model are not static but dynamic as firms initiate or respond to both exogenous and endogenous changes. We explore some of a firm's actions and reactions to attain and maintain a profitable business model in the face of change. We also offer a method for appraising a business model, a method for determining the attractiveness of a business model.

An important part of offering superior customer value is performing the activities that underpin the value. In Chapter 6 we examine the three different value configurations on which value rests: the value chain, the value shop, and the value network. Each has its own characteristics; treating an industry that has a value network as if it had a value chain can be misleading. Understanding these configurations also provides a strong basis for comprehending the extent to which the Internet impacts bricks-and-mortar models and the viability of clicks-and-mortar models.

In Chapter 7 we confront two interesting questions: how to value a start-up company and how to finance it. We explore different methods of valuing a firm or Internet business model: price/earnings (P/E) ratio, price/earnings/growth (PEG) ratio, cash flows, and business model attributes. We also explore the role of intellectual capital in valuations, and examine different methods of financing entrepreneurial activity.

Part III: The Role of Competitive and Macro Environments

In Chapter 8 we recognize that business models do not operate in a vacuum and examine the role of a firm's competitive and macro environments as determinants of profitability and as influencers of business models. We also explore how these environments impact and are impacted by the Internet.

Part IV: Applying the Concepts, Models, and Tools

Chapter 9 takes the point of view of a general manager who must conceive and execute a business model. It walks through some of the things to which the manager must pay attention in formulating and executing business models and strategies. This is a summary of the book from a practitioner's point of view with the addition of a few corporate-level examples. The chapter also explores some of the differences between bricks-and-mortar firms and pure play Internet firms. In Chapter 10 we present an example of how to analyze cases with the focus on an Internet business model case.

Part V: Cases

Relationship between the Text and Cases

The text part of this book explores those concepts, theories, tools, and models that allow students and managers to understand how to gain and maintain a competitive advantage using the Internet. The cases present some of the complex contexts in which managers often must make decisions. Thus, such decisions often require more than one concept, tool, or model. As such, a good analysis of each of the cases in Part V usually requires an understanding of the material from more than one topic.

SUMMARY

Firms are in business to make money. A business model plays a critical role in achieving that goal. The type of environment in which a firm operates and the type of changes that it faces also play important roles. The Internet stands to establish new game strategies for business as it renders existing bricks-and-mortar strategies obsolete while creating opportunities for wealth creation. To take advantage of the

Internet entails conceiving and executing a good Internet business model. Such a model must not only have the right components, but also the right linkages between them and its environment. It also must have the resilience and flexibility to take advantage of change. This book explores all these factors.

KEY TERMS

business model   3

competitive advantage   4

competitive environment   5

determinants of business performance   3

dynamics   5

firm performance   3

Internet   6

Internet business model   6

macro environment   5

DISCUSSION QUESTIONS

1. By including customers and suppliers in the competitive environment, we imply that they are competitors. Why might we think of suppliers and customers as competitors?

2. It has been argued that the extent to which each determinant of performance impacts a firm's performance is a function of the measure of performance. Do you agree or not? Support your answer with examples.

3. The arrows in Figure 1.1 suggest that a firm can, through its business model, influence both its competitive and macro environments. Do you agree or not? Does the type of industry make a difference? the type of environment?

4. What is the difference between business models and Internet business models?

REFERENCES

1. A firm's performance is determined by its firm-specific resources and capabilities, the type of activities in which it is engaged, the type of industry, and the type of regional or national environment in which it lies. See R. Rumelt, "How Much Does Industry Matter?" *Strategic Management Journal* 12 (1991), pp. 167–85; R. R. Nelson, "Why Do Firms Differ, and How Does It Matter?" *Strategic Management Journal,* Winter Special Issue 12 (1991), pp. 61–74; B. Wernerfelt, "A Resource-Based View of the Firm," *Strategic Management Journal* 5 (1984), pp. 171–80; M. E. Porter, *Competitive Strategy: Techniques for Analyzing Industries and Competitors* (New York: Free Press, 1980); M. E. Porter, *The Competitive Advantage of Nations* (New York: Free Press, 1990).

2. Unless specified otherwise, the word "product" means "product or service" throughout this book.

3. M. E. Porter, "What Is Strategy?" *Harvard Business Review,* November–December 1996, pp. 61–78.

4. Porter, *Competitive Strategy.*

5. Porter, *The Competitive Advantage of Nations.*

6. J. A. Schumpeter, *The Theory of Economic Development* (Boston: Harvard University Press, 1934), a translation from the German, *Theorie der Wirtschaftlichen Entwicklung* (Leipzig: Duncker & Humboldt, 1912).

7. Michael Rappa, "2000. Managing the Digital Enterprise: Business Models," ecommerce.ncsu.edu/topics/models/models.html.

CHAPTER 2

Overview of Internet Technology and Value Network

DEFINITION AND HISTORY

What Are the Internet and the World Wide Web?

This book is about Internet business models and how to analyze them. So far, we have only briefly discussed the Internet and said nothing about the World Wide Web. In this chapter, we fully explore both. The Internet is a vast collection of networks of computers that are interconnected both physically and through their ability to encode and decode certain specialized communications protocols called the Internet Protocol (IP) and the Transmission Control Protocol (TCP).[1] A *protocol* in this sense is simply a specification of how computers exchange information. IP describes how information to be transmitted should be broken down into small *packets,* while TCP describes how a "stream" of packets should be reconstructed at the other end and what to do, for example, if a packet is missing.[2]

The Internet infrastructure consists of five major components: the backbone, routers (digital switches), points of presence (POPs), computer servers, and users' connected computers (see Figure 2.1).[3] This system allows authorized users connected to the network anyplace in the world to have access to data stored on computers anywhere else in the world.

The **backbone** is a collection of high-speed telecommunications lines (what used to be called "trunk lines" or simply "telephone lines" but now have a much higher capacity) that are connected by high-speed computers. It is made up of fast fiber-optic lines that allow computers to transfer data at very high speeds. The **bandwidth** of the telecommunications line refers to the capacity or speed of data transfer: the amount of information—the digital 1s or 0s that are called **bits**—the line is capable of carrying per unit time, usually expressed in the number of bits per second (bps) or millions of bits per second (Mbps) or, for very high-capacity lines, billions of bits per seconds (gigabits per second, or Gbps). Thus the backbone of the Internet is made up of high-bandwidth lines that crisscross North America and extend throughout the world. For example, in 1999 MCI Worldcom's backbone lines from New York to Detroit to Chicago to Salt Lake City to

FIGURE 2.1 Internet Components

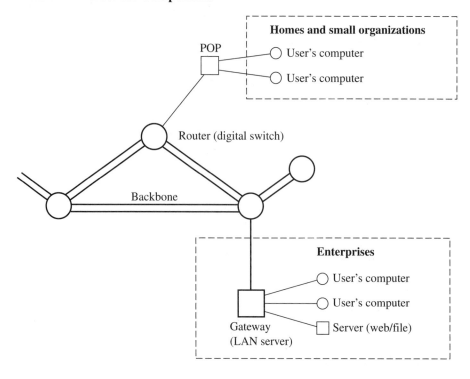

the San Francisco Bay Area had a capacity of 2.488 Gbps (2,488 Mbps or 2.488 billion bits per second).[4] In 1999, forty backbone carriers transported almost all of the long-distance traffic.[5]

Connecting each backbone line to another is a high-speed **digital switch** such as an asynchronous transmission mode (ATM) switch. These switches are actually very fast dedicated computers that move "traffic" (information) along the backbone lines. The switches take the information and pass it along to the next backbone line. Switches that perform a "routing" function, deciding on which direction to pass traffic, are called **routers**. For example, suppose you request information from a computer in a different part of the country. This generates "**traffic**" in the form of a request to a remote computer and a response from that computer, if the information is available.[6] We will shortly discuss what happens at each end of this transaction. In between the two ends, the information "flows" along the backbone lines as it is forwarded from one digital switch to the next. Many of these intermediate switches are connected to more than two backbone lines. Based on the destination and the congestion along the lines, they decide which line information should be "routed" (forwarded).

To gain access to this network requires other specialized computers. The three most common types of end users are (1) individuals, (2) small- to medium-sized organizations, and (3) large organizations or "enterprises." Individuals and small organizations are often grouped together because their access is usually identical. They gain access to the Internet by means of an Internet service provider's (ISP) **point of presence (POP)**. A POP is simply a point of access to the network and consists of a switch (computer) that knows how to route traffic to the end users connected directly to it.[7]

Large enterprises connect to the Internet by means of a similar kind of switch called a *gateway* or **local area network (LAN)** server, which may or may not be behind a "**firewall**"—a combination of specialized hardware and software that provides protection from users and requests outside the LAN. LANs consist of various types of hardware devices and other resources that organizations can share. Large LANs such as those that serve enterprises are usually connected directly to a high-speed switch through the LAN server, which also knows how to route local traffic to end users on the LAN (see Figure 2.1). All computers that can interconnect with the Internet are considered part of the Internet.

The **World Wide Web** (WWW or the Web, for short) is the collection of computers on the Internet that support a certain hypertext function. **Hypertext** is different from "normal" text in that it does not follow a linear path from top to bottom; instead, one can follow items of interest in a nonlinear fashion by selecting words or pictures of interest and immediately gaining more information on the items selected. Not all potential items (words or pictures) can be selected, so how does the user-reader know which items are available? The *author* of the page decides which items are worthy of more information and creates a special link from the current page to the page (or pages) that has additional information. The pages are also called the **content**; thus, the author is often referred to as the *content creator.* In the language of the World Wide Web, a user *clicks on* (selects) the link to gain the desired information.

For example, imagine that you wish to post your resume online to improve your chances of getting a job. When you contact recruiters, you tell them to go to your Web page to see the latest version of your resume. There are many tools available to translate your document into HTML (HyperText Markup Language), which will be discussed shortly. Simply posting the text of the resume is entirely possible. Recruiters will see only the text of the resume and will not be able to follow links to other sites. However, you decide that it is appropriate to provide more information in two areas. First, your university, Best University, has its own website, so on your resume you create a link between the words "Best University" and the website, http://www.best.edu. Therefore, users viewing your resume see the link underlining Best University; when they click on it, they are connected to the Best University website. As the author, you determine which links are "clickable."

The above link was to an external source of the additional information. However, you may want to develop some further content. For example, in the section under Additional Information, you may want to have a picture of you at age 12 shaking hands with Bill Gates. Let's say that you do not want that picture, which you have scanned into a file, to be on your resume, but you do want anyone who wants to look at the picture to be able to gain access to it from your resume. So, in the Additional Information section on your resume, you link the words "shook hands with Bill Gates" to the new file. Thus, you now have two links in your resume, one to content created and maintained by someone else (the university website), the other to content created, or at least maintained, by you (the picture). This is part of the process that content authors go through whenever they design content for the Web.

The World Wide Web works because the Internet infrastructure is in place to support it. Thus, the WWW performs a function (hypertext) that is a subset of all the functions available on the Internet (e.g., file transfers, remote login, electronic mail—see the appendix to this book for more details). Because the WWW is the most famous function of the Internet, many people use the terms interchangeably; as we have seen from the above discussion, this is slightly inaccurate.

A Brief History of the Internet and the World Wide Web[8]

During the Cold War the United States military and its think tanks such as the RAND Corporation were faced with a problem. The threat of nuclear attack loomed in the minds of military strategists: specifically, any centralized "control center" would be a prime target in a nuclear attack. This problem gave birth to the idea of a decentralized "network" with redundant connections. The research was sponsored for many years by the Advanced Research Projects Agency (ARPA), a government agency affiliated with the Department of Defense. When a few computers (e.g., one at UCLA and another at the Stanford Research Institute—SRI) were connected in the late 1960s and early 1970s, the precursor of the Internet, the **ARPAnet**, was born.

By design, the system was intended to be redundant; that is, it would have many paths of delivering data so that if one part of the network were disabled, other paths could be found automatically. In this decentralized environment, the network grew from a handful of U.S. universities to practically all universities in the United States and many overseas, in addition to many research institutes and some companies, usually defense-oriented companies with some affiliation with DARPA (Defense Advanced Research Projects Agency, as ARPA became known). At one point, the National Science Foundation took over responsibility for providing the backbone (high-speed trunk line) services. As the number of commercial users grew from year to year and it became clear that users were willing to pay for such services, private telecommunications companies stepped into the void and began providing their own high-speed lines, the use of which they rented or sold to companies wanting access.

Most of the traffic in the early days of the Internet, as the network eventually became known, was generated by just four applications. The most widely used service was *electronic mail,* or e-mail. E-mail service allowed a user at one end-user computer (also known as a *host*) to send a text message and have this message stored for delivery at the recipient's host for retrieval by the recipient when convenient. In addition to e-mail, *discussion lists* and *newsgroups* became popular. Users posting messages to a newsgroup or a discussion list had their messages copied to all other subscribers of the list. Another popular application, especially among the scientific community, was **file transfer protocol (ftp)**. With a file transfer, one could either send a file to or retrieve one from a remote host. The advantage of this was that a user could move large blocks of data very quickly, much more quickly than backing up a file on tape and carrying or mailing it to the remote site. Finally, a highly useful application was **telnet** or *remote login* capability. This allowed the user to log in to a remote host and perform functions on the remote computer as if the user were connected to the host on-site. For example, a user in California could log in to a computer in Korea and be indistinguishable from a user sitting at a terminal in Korea.

These four applications were popular enough to drive the growth of the Internet for many years. The Internet infrastructure—the backbone, digital switches, computer servers, POPs, users' computers, software, and protocols—was created to help users gain access to information on computers anywhere in the world. The problem in the early days was that to find information on the Internet, a user had to specify the address of the computer on which the information resided. This made finding information on different computers tedious and limited to those with computer science skills.

Tim Berners-Lee, a researcher at CERN,[9] the particle physics laboratory near Geneva, Switzerland, would change all of that. The scientists who worked at CERN came from all over the world and had immense problems exchanging incompatible documents and e-mail messages from their own proprietary systems. Berners-Lee revived an earlier idea of his from 1980 that was a precursor to a hypertext storage and retrieval system. He proposed that CERN's scientists could combine their knowledge by linking their documents contextually. He developed a language called **HyperText Markup Language (HTML)** that he could use not only to create links to different computers, but also to display graphics associated with some files. To the user, such links, or hypertext, are highlighted; all the user needs to do to gain access to the information associated with the link is to click on it. These hypertext links and the associated information stored on the Internet nodes became known as the World Wide Web. CERN made the source code for the first WWW browser and server freely available, which spurred growth in their development as programmers from all over the world began contributing to the infrastructure of the WWW.[10]

THE INTERNET VALUE NETWORK

Associated with each of the components of the Internet is an industry or group of firms that market similar or related products. In this section, we describe the various sectors of the Internet economy and give the names of the largest companies in each sector. We call this the "**Internet value network**" because in the broadest sense, all the components described below and their interrelations create value for the end users, the customers, and organizations that actually use the network.[11]

Generally speaking, we propose that the Internet value network can be divided into three major groups: users, communications service providers, and suppliers. This division into three groups is an abstraction; many firms are both users and suppliers, or users and communications service providers, or communications service providers and suppliers. For example, Cisco Systems is a supplier of communications equipment *and* a large user (a Web merchant) in its own right; that is, Cisco not only makes routers that Internet service providers (ISPs) buy but also sells directly to those ISPs over the Internet.

In addition, some segments might just as easily be classified as both suppliers and users. To give a specific case, media and content companies supply editorial content to firms as well as run "**portals**," which are entry and focal sites for consumers and businesses. For this reason, we have included a category under both users and suppliers. Thus, the categorizations of any one firm or even subsegment are slightly arbitrary; however, the broad trends will be evident as we discuss the logic of each group and segment.

The three large groups—users, communications services, and suppliers—can be further subdivided into segments. We will examine each group in turn and provide examples of 5 to 10 of the largest companies in each segment (see Table 2.1).

TABLE 2.1 The Largest Companies in Each Value Network Segment

Segment	Company	Revenues (in millions), Market Share, and Users
1. E-commerce		
	1. Cisco Systems	$9,100 (online)
	2. AOL*	5,700
	3. Intel	5,600
	4. Dell Computer	4,500
	5. IBM	3,500
2. Content aggregators		
	1. AOL*	$5,700 (online)
	2. Yahoo!	400
	3. Excite	200
	4. CNET	200
	5. Lycos	100
3. Market makers		
	1. Charles Schwab	$1,100 (online)
	2. Citigroup	800
	3. E*Trade	400
	4. Sabre Group	300
	5. eBay	300
4. Service providers		
	1. IBM	$87,500 (including non-services)
	2. EDS	18,500
	3. Computer Sciences	7,700
	4. EMC	6,700
	5. Pitney Bowes	4,400
5. Backbone operators		
	1. MCI Worldcom*	33.0% (market share)
	2. Sprint*	9.7%
	3. Intermedia	7.7%
	4. Cable & Wireless	6.4%
	5. Electric Lightwave	5.3%
6. ISPs/OSPs		
	1. AOL	22.2 M (users)
	2. NetZero	3.8 M
	3. Earthlink	3.3 M
	4. CompuServe	2.7 M
	5. MSN Internet	2.5 M
7. Last Mile		
	1. AT&T	$62,400
	2. SBC Communications	49,500
	3. MCI Worldcom	33,300
	4. Bell Atlantic	33,200
	5. GTE	25,300
8. Content creators		
	1. Time Warner*	$27,000
	2. Walt Disney	24,500
	3. Knight Ridder	3,300
	4. Dow Jones	2,100
	5. Ziff-Davis	700

*Merger/acquisition activity in 2000

(continued)

TABLE 2.1 *(continued)*

Segment	Company	Revenues (in millions), Market Share, and Users
9. Software suppliers		
	1. Microsoft	$19,700
	2. Oracle	8,800
	3. NCR	6,200
	4. Computer Associates	5,300
	5. SAP (America)	5,000
10. Hardware suppliers		
	1. IBM	$87,500
	2. Hewlett-Packard	42,400
	3. Lucent Technologies	38,700
	4. Compaq	38,500
	5. Motorola	31,000

Source: Internet World, Network World, Red Herring, Business2.0, Boardwatch Magazine, and Telecommunications Reports International.

FIGURE 2.2 Value Network Segments with Largest Companies

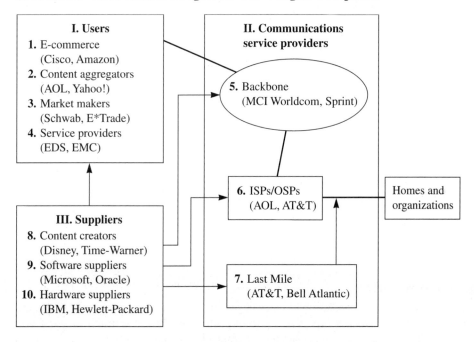

I. Users

Users are companies that use the Internet intensively in the core of their business. We exclude from consideration here large companies that use the Internet intensively but only at the periphery of their business (see Chapters 5, 6, and 9). Users may be subdivided further into four categories (see Figure 2.2): (1) *e-commerce,* those companies that sell goods over the Internet; (2) *content aggregators,* those that gather content from multiple sources and display that content on their sites; (3) *market makers* which act as intermediaries or brokers, or run electronic markets; and (4) *service providers* that furnish all other Internet-based services.[12] Technically, individuals and non-Internet organizations (e.g., automobile manufacturers) are also "users," but they will not be discussed here because our main concern in this chapter is to describe the interrelations that comprise the Internet infrastructure.

1. E-commerce Companies

E-commerce (electronic commerce) companies exchange "real products for real money through online channels."[13] While some people refer to e-commerce as any business having anything to do with the Internet, we will be more precise in our classification and limit ourselves only to those companies that sell over online channels. Some companies manufacture or assemble the goods themselves; others simply resell goods made by other companies. The largest companies in this space sell over the Internet products that they manufacture themselves (see Table 2.1). As mentioned above, Cisco Systems manufactures communications equipment (mainly routers) and sells them directly over the Internet to ISPs. Some e-commerce companies sell only over the Internet; others sell both over the Internet and in standard bricks-and-mortar distribution channels. When the downstream buyers' (not those of the end-user customers) needs conflict with the Internet channel, it is called *channel conflict*. Many companies are involved in multiple segments, especially the e-commerce segment, where companies can compete in any other segment and take orders over the Internet. For example, Intel is one of the largest hardware components manufacturers, but it also sells a few billion dollars worth of those components online. America Online (AOL) is the largest online service provider (OSP), and it books all of its revenues online. Thus, the e-commerce segment is a catch-all for any segment selling online and can be treated in tandem with the other segments.[14]

2. Content Aggregators

The next category of users encompasses *media companies* and *content providers*. Note that media companies and content providers are listed under both users and suppliers because most of them are intensive users of the Internet as well as suppliers (of information) to other users. In this section, we discuss the companies whose business revolves around intensive use of the Internet, such as America Online, Netscape (which was acquired by AOL in 1999), Yahoo, and Excite. These companies, while they are content providers, are mainly information aggregators and portals.

3. Market Makers

In contrast to expectations, many of the biggest names in Internet business are *intermediaries*. We say "in contrast to expectations" because much of what you read in the business press is how the Internet *reduces* intermediation (i.e., reduces the possibility of being an intermediary). As we will see in Chapter 6, this is not quite true; indeed, the Internet may actually *increase* intermediation. The Internet allowed and continues to allow a new class of intermediaries who bring buyers and sellers together and make money by charging one or the other party a small transaction fee. Thus, we see a large number of brokerages (buyers and sellers of securities), banks (borrowers and lenders), and travel agents (buyers and sellers of travel services) using the Internet. We call attention to market makers like Charles

Schwab, which has grown from a bricks-and-mortar discount stock brokerage, where clients visited branch offices or telephoned their orders in, into the largest Internet market maker because of the migration of orders to the Internet. This segment also includes companies that run or set up electronic markets, such as electricity markets, and electronic auctioneers, such as eBay. They all have the same logic of bringing buyers and sellers together.

4. Internet Services

Internet services include support services such as consulting, outsourcing, website design, electronic data interchange, firewalls, and data storage backups. Any service beyond communications services belongs in this category.[15] Thousands of companies perform these services, but the companies in this segment tend to be very small. Five of the largest service companies are listed in Table 2.1. These companies make money by selling their services or their expertise on a fee-for-service basis. Electronic Data Systems (EDS), for example, has made a name for itself in the outsourcing of information technology services. When a company in a noncomputer industry grows tired of managing its own data processing (e.g., databases, payroll, hardware upgrades, software upgrades), the original firm may decide to hire another firm to completely run its own data processing, freeing up management to run its original business. This is referred to as **outsourcing**. Some of these services offered by EDS and other companies have now begun migrating to the Internet; for example, EDS can completely manage the software upgrade process for an entire company over the Internet.

II. Communications Services

Communications service providers may also be divided into several segments: backbone service providers, ISPs/OSPs, and Last Mile providers. **Backbone service providers** are those companies that maintain their own backbone lines, as described at the beginning of this chapter. An **Internet service provider (ISP)** delivers access to consumers and small- to medium-sized organizations, while **online service providers (OSPs)** do the same but also provide content to subscribers. **Last Mile providers** develop, maintain, and provide the physical connection (e.g., the telephone, cable, or wireless connections) to consumers and small- to medium-sized organizations. The companies in this group all provide telecommunications services to each other, to the users' segment, and to consumers. They develop communications networks that enable the connectivity of their customers. Their key expertise is in designing and developing new products (e.g., *69, ISDN, DSL, cable modems) developing sophisticated billing systems, and maintaining equipment and lines. They also all face a similar problem: recovering fixed costs.

Anyone who has used a telephone in recent years has probably noticed that long-distance rates have fallen dramatically from 28 cents per minute to 15 cents (remember 10-cent Sundays?) to 10 cents per minute, 24 hours a day, seven days a week. In 2000 the rate is pushing down further to 5 cents a minute and lower! How do we explain this relentless price movement? The problem for the companies, not for the consumer, is that the fixed cost of buying and installing a switch and developing a billing system is very high, but the marginal cost of connecting an additional telephone call is essentially nil. This was not much of an issue when one telephone company, AT&T, dominated the telephone industry. It simply charged enough to recover its fixed costs and make a profit. But after the long-distance market was opened to competition, any company that had made the high fixed investment was—and continues to be—in a battle for revenues; hence the price competition and the "race to the bottom." This is an extreme example of a more general problem in so-called knowledge-based industries which we will discuss further in Chapter 4.

In any case, the telecommunications service providers in the Internet sphere have not had to face this problem yet, perhaps because of the tremendous growth of the market, perhaps because many of them still hold monopolies in local telephone service. Most of the companies in the communications services segment rely on a subscription-based model for making money.

5. Backbone Operators

The first segment of the Internet infrastructure is the companies that run the backbone. The companies in this segment control large-bandwidth lines and are able to handle a large volume of digital traffic. Table 2.1 shows the market share of the five leading companies in the industry. MCI Worldcom dominates with one-third of the market, followed by Sprint at almost 10 percent. MCI Worldcom (which was itself formed by the merger of MCI and Worldcom) attempted to acquire Sprint in 2000. These companies make money by selling Internet connectivity services to Internet service providers and large companies on a subscription basis. For information purposes, the median charge in 1999 for tapping into the network through the backbone operators was about $1,800 per T1 line (1.544 Mbps) per month.[16]

6. ISPs / OSPs

How do individuals or small organizations without LANs access the Web? A group of firms called Internet service providers (ISPs) provide the hardware and software that enable individuals to gain access to the Web. ISPs have their own servers, switches, and software to connect individuals to the Internet. ISPs include firms such as AT&T, MCI Worldcom, Sprint, UUNet, Netcom, Online, PSI, and others. In addition to ISPs that offer their customers access to the free content of the Internet, proprietary online service providers (OSPs) not only offer their subscribers access to the Internet but also, for a fee, offer access to a private, closed network whose content is only for fee-paying members. OSPs include America Online (AOL), CompuServe, Prodigy, and Microsoft Network. Table 2.1 lists the companies by the number of subscribers each ISP/OSP serves. These companies make money by providing Internet access through their points of presence (POP) to small organizations and to individuals, usually for a flat monthly fee.

7. Last Mile

The connection to consumers is sometimes known as the Last Mile because it represents the physical connection between the POP—which is usually considered to be local, such as the local telephone switch—and the end user. These connections can take many forms, such as telephone wire ("twisted pair"), fiber optics, cable, and wireless. More generally, the Last Mile is the category of the industry supporting these types of communications services. As shown in Table 2.1, this segment is dominated by telecommunications companies, mainly local phone companies. We would have to move all the way down to #12 before we even get to a cable company. Also note the sheer size of the companies in the Last Mile category, which is much bigger on average than any of the other segments. Most of these companies grew to their vast size as a result of the monopoly they had as local telephone companies. Now they make money by investing in local lines and selling access to these lines on a subscription basis.

Many researchers believe that controlling the Last Mile is a battle in its infancy. The former AT&T local telephone monopolies (the Regional Bell Operating Companies) have done a creditable job of maintaining their control over the Last Mile, perhaps through their development of new products or their influence on the regulatory process.[17] Two developments over the last decade that count as new products are Integrated Services Digital Network (ISDN) and the Digital Subscriber Lines (DSL). Both technologies allow for higher-bandwidth transfers, using the normal twisted-pair telephone wiring, and enable the end user to talk on the telephone while sending and receiving digital data at rates higher than those available from a modem.

AT&T itself, though, has chosen a two-pronged approach to wrest control of the Last Mile from the regional Bell operating companies. The first is a "wireless" strategy (e.g., giving away cellular telephones, promoting flat rate long-distance service from cellular telephones, eliminating roaming charges, providing complimentary services such as traffic reports) that attempts to supplant the wireline telephone from its primacy in the hearts of consumers. AT&T's second approach relates to the use of cable television lines as an alternative Last Mile conduit. Cable lines can provide high-speed Internet access. Therefore, in 1999 AT&T acquired MediaOne—one of the largest cable television companies—with the intention of providing an alternative to the regional Bells. In addition, other media firms that own cable companies, such as Time Warner, have been developing products based on high-speed Internet access over the cable. Even electric utilities have contemplated entering this market, using the electricity lines they have already installed and maintained!

Why do these companies care so much about the Last Mile? There are several reasons for this intense interest. The first is control over strategic resources. Just about every page served, every commerce transaction, and every download will pass through that Last Mile, so it is natural that certain firms do not want to leave to chance or historical accident who controls that Last Mile. In the past the regional Bell operating companies controlled that last mile, which turned out to be immensely profitable. Thus, the Last Mile has attracted entry precisely because of its profitability. This entry represents the first time the regional Bells have faced any serious competition; it was only a matter of time before other companies with a different technology jumped in to shave off a piece of that gigantic market. As mentioned above, all consumers go through a Last Mile provider before attaining access to the Internet, and it seems that consumers are quite willing to pay for high quality/bandwidth in the Last Mile.[18]

III. Suppliers

Finally, suppliers can be divided into three segments: (1) content creators, (2) software suppliers, and (3) hardware suppliers. These segments belong with "suppliers" because they typically supply upstream products or services to users and communications service providers, and in some cases to each other. Content creators are in the business of developing news- and entertainment-oriented content in many forms, including text, music, and video. Computer software suppliers develop the software, usually in packaged form, and sell the software that runs on consumer and enterprise computers, including personal computers and engineering workstations. Computer hardware companies manufacture the desktop computers, workstations, servers, telecommunications, and switching hardware that end users and communications service providers need. Hardware suppliers also manufacture components such as the internal devices that control or interact with computer hardware systems.

8. Content Creators

Media/content suppliers are the developers and owners of intellectual capital. They produce such works as music, games, graphics, video/motion pictures, and text (articles, news, and other sorts of information). The two largest companies, Disney and Time Warner, are fully integrated in the content business, producing and developing all of the above, such as motion pictures, videos, music, games, and news in their business units. In contrast to the bricks-and-mortar economy, this category of the Internet economy has been the most in flux with no dominant model of making money. The subscription model applies to few content creators, mainly those dispensing financial information. For example, Dow Jones supports its Wall Street Journal Interactive Edition with subscriptions from *The Wall Street Journal* subscribers and even nonsubscribers, who are charged more for the content.[19] Fee-for-service is another model pursued by some of these companies, although users are apparently unwilling to pay for most intellectual content (with the exception of pornography).

Part of the problem is that it is extremely inexpensive to reproduce digital media, thus making it very difficult to enforce intellectual property ownership of media content. We will discuss this further in Chapter 3, but for now most media/content suppliers have been satisfied to give away their content for free, raise the number of "**eyeballs**" (the number of unique viewers), and pin their hopes on an advertising model. Some sell complementary goods and make money from that rather than the content. For example, Sony sells gaming hardware that is Internet-enabled so that consumers can play games with other Internet users. While there is nothing (or little) to prevent the copying of the gaming software, the hardware itself is more difficult to imitate.[20]

9. Software Suppliers

Software suppliers provide software products, such as word processing or spreadsheet applications, operating systems, printer drivers, databases, electronic commerce software, and so on. These companies operate on the principle of selling software products to end users or to companies interested in starting or maintaining an Internet presence. They are like manufacturers, investing in software development and marketing and selling products, presumably for a profit. While fixed-cost recovery and easy replication are also theoretically issues—and may be so in the future—the insatiable appetite of the public for increased features (coupled with Microsoft's dominant position) keeps the industry growing.[21] Microsoft is the largest of these companies; it is the software company of choice for desktop personal computers and, in the late 1990s, some servers. Oracle has made the transition from database company to Internet-database company and has maintained its position as the second-largest software company.

To provide a taste of some kinds of Internet-based software suppliers, consider electronic commerce (e-commerce) software. Electronic commerce software companies produce software that enables e-commerce, which can be one of several different types. Prior to the advent of the Internet, the most important and popular kind of e-commerce was electronic data interchange (EDI). EDI allowed companies to exchange ordering and inventory information up and down the supply chain; for example, when a distributor ran low on inventory for a certain product, an EDI system passed that information to the manufacturer. In the past EDI was implemented on private data networks; in the late 1990s this technology has migrated to the Internet.[22]

There are a variety of other e-commerce applications having to do with retailing products on a website, such as "shopping cart" technology, order/payment processing, and "micro-payments."[23] Shopping cart technology keeps track of purchases that consumers make. While this might sound like a trivial task, most people do not realize the complexity of tracking such information from page to page on a website. It operates on the principle that the Web server for the retailer does not know who you are when you make repeated shopping selections without some form of identification. The companies that make the browsers allow an identification number of sorts to be stored on your computer, which can be passed to the retailer every time you interact with it.[24] In this way you can keep adding items to your shopping cart and the retailer always knows that it is you placing the order.

Order/payment processing software is designed to track orders, track inventories, and, most importantly, process credit card transactions. As you can imagine, the security considerations of processing payments are immense. Most of the effort in this area has been to design systems that prevent credit card numbers from falling into the wrong hands through the use of encryption.[25] Micropayment or microcash software is designed to handle very, very small transactions. For example, imagine that you wanted to listen to a piece of music only once over the Internet. The recording studio would like to charge you a royalty fee of 1/20¢ (i.e., if you listened to it 20 times, you would owe 1 cent). How can companies keep track of such small payments? Micropayment systems are designed to do just that.

In 1999 a new type of software business sprang up: the **application service provider (ASP)**. The ASP service, also referred to as an "app-on-tap," provides a centralized repository for software applications which individuals can "borrow" or "rent" to run on their own desktop personal computers. This end-user system is called a **thin client** because the applications no longer reside on the end-user system. The applications are delivered over the Internet to the thin client on demand. Applications envisioned for this type of service span the full range from database software packages to word processing applications to corporate business process analysis programs. Large enterprises also appreciate the ASP system because it enables the centralized information technology (IT) function to regain control over employees' desktop software. In recent years, as corporate computer systems have become more decentralized, it has become more difficult for companies to control the versions of software that employees store on their own personal computers.

10. Hardware Suppliers

The hardware category comprises three interrelated areas: communications equipment manufacturers, computer equipment manufacturers, and hardware component manufacturers. The *communications equipment* manufacturers are the producers of the various kinds of routers and other digital switches. Lucent Technologies (formerly part of AT&T) dominates this industry, although 3Com and Cisco are also well known for their communications equipment. Motorola, while very large, also gains much of its revenue from cellular telephones and semiconductors. These companies make money by selling their manufactured products, which are hardware/software systems that enable the Internet to move data traffic. The customers of these companies include backbone operators, ISPs, and large organizations that have their own internal networks.

Computer hardware contains both client and server hardware—that is, end-user computers (personal computers and workstations) and server devices (Web servers, file servers, e-mail servers, LAN servers).[26] The largest computer hardware company is undoubtedly IBM, which brought in more than $87 billion dollars in 1999, much of which came from hardware sales. Other large computer manufacturers include Hewlett-Packard and Compaq. These companies also produce servers, as does Sun Microsystems, which is one of the largest server manufacturers. These companies sell their hardware to end users and to other businesses. They are the main customers of the *hardware components* companies, which sell computer chips and peripherals such as disk drives to the computer hardware companies and the communications equipment companies. The hardware components segment also operates under the producer model where the largest companies are Motorola and Intel (processor and other semiconductor chips) and Seagate (disk drives).

SUMMARY

This chapter has provided a brief introduction to the history and terminology of the Internet along with the key segments of the Internet industry. The Internet and the World Wide Web, often used interchangeably, are not the same. The Internet is a vast system of computers that are connected by high-speed communications lines and can understand the IP/TCP protocols. The WWW is linked content that is accessible through the Internet, written in HTML and viewed through a browser. In addition to the WWW protocol (http), the main four applications on the Internet are e-mail (electronic mail), discussion lists/newsgroups, FTP (file transfer protocol), and remote login (telnet). Companies in the Internet infrastructure are found in 1 of 10 market categories, grouped into three segments: users, communications service providers, and suppliers. Users are divided into e-commerce companies, content aggregators, market makers, and service providers. Communications service providers are divided into backbone operators, ISPs/OSPs, and Last Mile providers. Finally, suppliers can be divided into content creators, software suppliers, and hardware suppliers.

KEY TERMS

application service provider (ASP) 23	**bandwidth** 11
ARPAnet 14	**bits** 11
backbone 11	**content** 13
backbone service providers 19	**digital switch** 12

DISCUSSION QUESTIONS

1. Step by step, draw a map of what happens when you buy a new widget online. Start with pressing the "Add to Shopping Cart" button on the vendor's website. End with the vendor packing your order. Who makes money in this transaction? Where is value added?

2. Discuss the benefits and pitfalls of being in the content creation business. Name a content creation company and describe the weaknesses in its business plan.

3. Is an Internet service provider different from a backbone operator? How?

4. Looking at a company such as Amazon.com (see Chapter 10), would you classify it as an e-commerce company, a content aggregator, a market maker, or a service provider? Why? How about a company such as eBay (see the eBay case in Part V)?

5. Think of another industry besides telecommunications where fixed-cost recovery is an important challenge.

REFERENCES

1. These protocols are almost always used in tandem, hence the terms IP/TCP and TCP/IP. Technically, a computer does not have to be able to understand IP/TCP itself; it simply has to be connected with a gateway computer that does.

2. See the appendix to this book for more detail on these protocols.

3. See Haim Mendelson, "A Note on Internet Technology," Stanford University Graduate School of Business #S-OIT-15, January 1999; see also www.whatis.com/tourenv.htm; finally, refer to Charles W. Hill, "America Online and the Internet," in C. W. Hill and G. R. Jones, *Strategic Management*, 4th edition (Boston: Houghton Mifflin, 1999), pp. C92–C106.

4. *Boardwatch Magazine's Directory of Internet Service Providers* (Golden, CO: Penton Media, 1999).

5. The backbone carriers do not carry all of the traffic for several reasons: local area networks (LANs) carry local traffic; some large companies have their own networks, usually based on IP/TCP (called *intranets* if operating solely within one company and *extranets* when outside organizations have direct access); and the existence of alternate media controlled by other companies, such as microwave and satellite service.

6. The technical details of how this works are given in the appendix.

7. POP should not be confused with POP3, which stands for Post Office Protocol and is used for electronic mail delivery. See the appendix for further details.

8. See Stephen Segaller, *Nerds$^{2.0.1}$: A Brief History of the Internet* (New York: TV Books, 1999); Mendelson,"A Note on Internet Technology"; and info.isoc.org/guest/zakon/Internet/History/HIT.html.

9. Conseil Européen pour la Recherche Nucléaire, also known as the European Laboratory for Particle Physics.

10. For more details, see Segaller, *Nerds*[2.0.1], pp. 284–89, or Tim Berners-Lee and Mark Fischetti, *Weaving the Web: The Original Design and Ultimate Destiny of the World Wide Web by its Inventor* (San Francisco: Harper Collins, 1999).

11. The "Internet value network" is a broad term for all the components and their interrelations. In Chapter 6, we will explore the term *value network* that is one of three generic value configurations. Thus, within the sphere of the broader Internet value network, there can be many, smaller value networks.

12. This is not to be confused with Internet service providers (ISPs), which provide homes and small organizations with Internet connectivity. ISPs are described under communications services.

13. Jeffrey F. Rayport, "The Truth about Internet Business Models," *Strategy and Business* 16 (3rd quarter 1999), pp. 5–7.

14. Some companies will be categorized only as e-commerce: those that purely sell (retailers or resellers) and those that compete in non-Internet businesses that also sell online.

15. Communications services are not considered part of this category; as the Internet is a communications medium, the communications service provider segment is large enough to rate its own segment as described in the next section.

16. *Boardwatch Magazine's Directory of Internet Service Providers.*

17. In Chapter 9 we will briefly discuss the role of government and regulation and how it relates to the external environment.

18. Subscriptions for telephone DSL and high-speed cable access lines were being billed out at approximately $50 per month in 2000.

19. Dow Jones & Company, Inc., Quarterly Report, SEC Form 10-Q, November 12, 1999.

20. At least one company has manufactured a Sony-compatible gaming device by reverse-engineering it.

21. Some have argued that illegal copying of software is not harmful to software producers because copying builds up the installed base of users, thus exploiting network externalities evident in the industry. See Chapter 3 for more information.

22. See Ravi Kalakota, Marcia Robinson, and Don Tapscott, *E-Business: Roadmap for Success* (Reading, MA: Addison-Wesley, 1999).

23. This is just a smattering of e-commerce software applications, see Ravi Kalakota and Andrew B. Whinston, *Electronic Commerce: A Manager's Guide* (Reading, MA: Addison-Wesley, 1997); see also Marilyn Greenstein and Todd Feinman, *Electronic Commerce: Security, Risk Management, and Control* (New York: Irwin/McGraw-Hill, 2000) for more information on commerce applications.

24. This information is stored in a so-called *cookie* on your computer. The cookie contains three main pieces of information: the information the retailer wants to store (IDs, etc.), the domain name of the retailer (i.e., who has authorized access to that piece), and the expiration of the information. See home.netscape.com/newsref/std/cookie_spec.html for the exact specification.

25. See Greenstein and Feinman, *Electronic Commerce,* for more information on Internet security and how it relates to e-commerce.

26. See the appendix for more details on the client-server model.

Competitive Landscape-Changing Properties of the Internet

In Chapter 2 we examined the Internet value network and the roles of different players in adding customer value. While that examination tells us who is located where in the configuration and what each group of players does and the relationship between them, it still leaves two very important questions unanswered: What makes the Internet a better technology than its predecessor technologies? Does it really have the potential to transform competitive landscapes? Answering these questions is critical to conceiving and executing business models that exploit the Internet. We will focus on those properties that have the potential to impact business models and industry profitability and examine their impact on the 5-Cs of electronic transactions—be they commerce, business, or otherwise. Many business models rest on elements of the 5-Cs, so by understanding the impact of the Internet on them, we can better understand how Internet business models can be conceived and executed, and how they impact existing bricks-and-mortar models.

PROPERTIES OF THE INTERNET

The Internet has many properties, but 10 of them stand out: mediating technology, universality, network externalities, distribution channel, time moderator, information asymmetry shrinker, infinite virtual capacity, low cost standard, creative destroyer, and transaction-cost reducer.

1. Mediating Technology

The Internet is a **mediating technology** that interconnects parties that are interdependent or want to be.[1] The interconnection can be business-to-business (B2B), business-to-consumer (B2C), consumer-to-consumer (C2C), or consumer-to-business (C2B). It can also be within a firm or any other organization, in which case it is called an intranet. In either case, the Internet facilitates exchange relationships among parties distributed in time and space. In some ways, it is like the technology that underpins bricks-and-mortar bank services. A bank acts as a medium for lenders and borrowers, taking money from some customers and lending it to others. In other ways, the Internet is like print, radio, and TV media which mediate between their audience and paying advertisers. The Internet's interactivity gives it some unique advantages over these media as parties can interact, asking and answering questions rather than one party sending and another only receiving messages. Most important, anyone connected to the Internet has the power to broadcast information to anyone on it. In the older media, broadcasting is limited to a select few.

2. Universality

Universality of the Internet refers to the Internet's ability to both enlarge and shrink the world. It enlarges the world because anyone anywhere in the world can potentially make his or her products available to anyone anywhere else in the world. For example, a musician in Ann Arbor, Michigan, can make his music available to the rest of the world by posting it on the World Wide Web. A software developer in Egypt can sell her software to customers all over the world simply by posting it on a website in Alexandria. A steelmaker in Korea can post the prices, availability, and quality of its steel on a website in Seoul. People anywhere in the world can access these varied postings on the Web. Ford Motor Company can put bids for the new components that it needs for its cars on its website, allowing anyone in the world with the capabilities to supply the component to bid for their supply.

The Internet shrinks the world in that a skilled worker in South Africa does not have to move to California to work in the Silicon Valley. Software developers in the Silicon Valley can have access to programming skills in a country as far away as Madagascar. As we will see throughout this book, this property has many implications for many industries. For example, it suggests that we can expect more software firms to enter the software industry and salaries for certain skills to be more competitive, no matter where the owners of such skills are located.

3. Network Externalities

A technology or product exhibits **network externalities** when it becomes more valuable to users as more people take advantage of it.[2] To understand what this means, the reader might think of owning a telephone in a system that is connected only to the authors of this book. Such a phone would be much less useful to the reader than if it were connected to members of the reader's family and the rest of the world. Clearly, the more people who are connected to a telephone system, the more valuable it is to its users. The Internet clearly exhibits this property: The more people connected to it, the more valuable it is. The more people that are connected to a network within the Internet, the more valuable that network is. Suppose a collector wants to auction off a rare work of art. The auction firm that she selects is more valuable to her only if the firm has a large number of clients since she will then have a large set of bidders for her work of art. If she instead wants to buy a work of art, she is still better off going to the firm with the large network; the larger the auction firm is, the better the selection and her chances of finding what she wants. For individuals looking for a chat group, the larger the network, the better the chances of finding others with similar tastes with whom they can share ideas and further their sense of community. Since a network is more attractive the more members that it has, one can expect larger networks to gain new members at a faster rate than smaller ones; that is, the larger a network, the larger it is going to become. This is the positive feedback in which a firm—once it finds itself ahead in network size—is likely to see its lead increase rather than decrease.[3] The question is, When does this snowballing stop? It usually ends when a change, especially a technological change, comes along that renders the basis for the advantages of the network obsolete.

29

CHAPTER 3
Competitive
Landscape-
Changing
Properties of the
Internet

At least two estimates of the value of network size have been offered. Bob Metcalfe, founder of 3Com and inventor of the Ethernet, advanced what is now called **Metcalfe's law**: The value of a network increases as the square of the number of people in the network.[4] That is, value is a function of N^2, where N is the number of people in the network. It has also been argued that the increase in value from size is exponential.[5] That is, the value of a network increases as a function of N^N.

The phenomenon of network externalities is not limited to connected networks like telephone systems and the Internet. It also applies to products whose value to customers increases with complementary products. Computers, even stand-alone ones, are a good example. Software is critical for their use, so the more people who own computers of a particular standard, the more likely that software will be developed for them. And the more software that is available for them, the more valuable they are to users since users have more software to choose from. And the more computers, the more people who are willing to develop software for it. These events lead to the positive feedback effect. We will suggest in later chapters that one goal of a firm may be to build a large network early because the size of the network can act as *switching costs* for members of the network while attracting others at a faster rate than smaller networks.

4. Distribution Channel

The Internet acts as a **distribution channel** for products that are largely information—bits (zeros and ones). Software, music, video, information, tickets for airlines or shows, brokerage services, insurance companies, and research data can all be distributed over the Internet. When the product itself cannot be distributed by means of the Internet, information on its features, pricing, delivery times, or other useful information about the product can. The Internet has two kinds of effects on existing distribution channels: replacement or extension. There is a **replacement effect** if the Internet is used to serve the same customers served by the old distribution channel without bringing in new customers. The replacement of travel agencies in distributing airline tickets is a good example.[6] Few customers will start flying simply because they can buy airline tickets over the Internet. On the other hand, investors who ordinarily cannot afford to buy stocks from stockbrokers can use the Internet to participate in the stock market where they can afford the lower online brokerage fees. This is the **extension effect**. Very often, the extension effect is also accompanied by some replacement effects. Some investors who previously went to stockbrokers to buy their securities have likely switched to doing it themselves over the Internet.

5. Time Moderator

The fifth property of the Internet is **time moderation**, or its ability to shrink and enlarge time. For example, it shrinks time for a potential customer who wants information on a new car or the way houses look in a particular neighborhood in the

Netherlands; the customer can get it instantaneously using the Web. It enlarges time for a customer who might not be able to attend an auction held from 12:00 noon to 3:00 P.M. on a Saturday, but who will find the material is auctioned on the Internet 24 hours a day, seven days a week, to anyone anywhere in the world. Work can continue on a microchip design 24 hours a day: Engineers in Japan work on the chip and at the end of their workday, turn it over to engineers in Israel who, at the end of their own workday, turn it over to engineers in the United States and back again to Japan.

6. Information Asymmetry Shrinker

An **information asymmetry** exists when one party to a transaction has information that another party does not—information that is important to the transaction. Such asymmetries, for example, were a source of advantage for car dealers. They often knew the costs of the cars they were selling while the average buyer did not. The Web reduces some of these information asymmetries. Since an automobile manufacturer's suggested prices are easily obtainable from the Web, customers can go to a car dealer armed with the same information that the dealer has about the car.

7. Infinite Virtual Capacity

More than 30 years ago, Gordon Moore of Intel predicted that every 18 months, computer processing power would double while the cost would stay about the same. As of 2000, his prediction has proved true. While these outstanding technological advances have boosted processing speed, similar advances have been made to storage and network technologies. Using these technologies, the Internet often gives customers the feeling that it has **infinite virtual capacity** to serve them. If you want to buy a stock or book, you do not have to wait on hold or in a long line. Suppliers and vendors now have more memory and computing power. Therefore, they can collect more data on customers, enabling them to offer personalized service to better help customers discover their needs. Virtual communities like chat houses have infinite capacity for members who can talk anytime of the day for as long as they want.

8. Low Cost Standard

Firms could not exploit the properties of the Internet if they did not adopt it. For two reasons, adoption has been easy. First and most important, the Internet and the Web are standards open to everyone everywhere and are very easy to use. Whether users are in a jungle in the Congo or in New York City, they use the same point-and-click and create a Web page that can be accessed anywhere in the world. Information is transmitted and received using the same protocol. Second, the cost of the Internet is a lot lower than that of earlier means of electronic communications such as proprietary electronic data interchange (EDI).[7] The U.S. government underwrote much of the development costs for the Internet. Many of the remaining costs are shared among the millions of users since it is a standard. If instead of one standard Internet, many proprietary networks that do not talk to each other existed, then users would be paying for the many networks instead of the one network. That's more costly. Firms still have to invest in adopting the Internet, but the costs are considerably lower than they would have been had the Internet not been an open standard and had most of the costs not already been underwritten by the U.S. government.

9. Creative Destroyer

31

*CHAPTER 3
Competitive
Landscape-
Changing
Properties of the
Internet*

These properties of the Internet have enabled it to usher in a wave of what J. A. Schumpeter called "**creative destruction**" in many industries.[8] Newspapers, for example, offer their readers editorials, news, stock prices, weather forecasts, classified and want ads, advertising, and promotions.[9] Offering this value to customers requires an investment in a printing press, distribution network, content, and brand name. This investment constitutes a barrier to entry to potential new entrants. The Internet is a low cost standard printing press of sorts and a distribution network with unlimited capacity that reaches more people than any newspaper could ever hope to reach. This tears down a large part of the barriers to entry that exist in the newspaper business. Furthermore, this network allows instantaneous, low cost interactive communication. With such low entry cost, flexibility, and virtually unlimited possibilities, one does not have to bundle editorials, news, stock prices, weather forecasts, classified and want ads, advertising, and promotions together to make money. Entrepreneurs can focus on each. For example, a firm can focus on auctioning what used to be in the want ads. This is creative destruction for the newspaper industry—the old giving way to the superior new. In general, creative destruction is taking place in three forms. First, brand-new industries have been created. Suppliers of Web software (e.g., browsers) or services [e.g., those provided by Internet service providers (ISPs)] have the Internet to thank for their business. Second, the Internet is transforming the structure, conduct, and performance of other industries, in many cases rendering the basis for competitive advantage obsolete. Travel, newspapers, and insurance are the tip of an iceberg of industries that are destined for creative destruction. As we will see later, these are industries whose basis for offering value to customers is overturned by one or more of the properties of the Internet. Third, the basis for competitive advantage in other industries has been enhanced. A firm like Intel, which has always pushed the frontier of semiconductor technology, finds the demands a match for its technological prowess and strategies in an industry that is critical to the Internet.

10. Transaction-Cost Reducer

The Internet also reduces transaction costs for many industries—thanks in part to the universality, distribution channel, low cost standard, and information asymmetry reduction properties. **Transaction costs** are the costs of searching for sellers and buyers; collecting information on products; negotiating, writing, monitoring, and enforcing contracts; and the costs of transportation associated with buying and selling.[10] Firms often must conduct searches to find the right suppliers to provide the components they want. Buyers must learn about suppliers' reputations, product features, and prices. Sellers must learn about buyers' financial standing and other characteristics of a good customer.[11] Buyers and sellers must negotiate contracts, sign them, monitor their execution, and enforce them. All these activities cost money. The Internet reduces these transaction costs. It reduces search costs because information on buyers, sellers, and products can be obtained more easily through the Web. The ability of the Internet to shrink information asymmetry also means a reduction in the cost of contract negotiation, monitoring, and enforcement. For products like software, music, and video that are in digital form, transportation costs are also greatly reduced since they can be "shipped" over the Internet. We will see later in this book that the reduction in transaction costs has some implications for the boundaries of the firm.

Conceiving and delivering value to customers entails the performance of many activities that rest on information exchange. Five of these activities are coordination, commerce, community, content, and communication. We will call them the **5-Cs**. The properties of the Internet just described potentially have a huge impact on these 5-Cs in intrafirm, business-to-business (B2B), business-to-consumer (B2C), consumer-to-consumer (C2C), and consumer-to-business (C2B) transactions (see Figure 3.1).

Coordination

For just about every firm, performing a task T often requires the performance of interdependent subtasks A, B, and C which may require common resources R. The **coordination** of these tasks entails ensuring that each of the subtasks are performed, that information from A needed to accomplish B or C does indeed get to each of them and does so on time and efficiently, and that resources R are available for A, B, and C when needed with little waste. Coordination—whether of the schedules of three people who want to attend a meeting, the design and development of a Pentium III, or the design and building of a Boeing 777—can be critical. The cost, completion time, features, and quality of the final task rest on the coordination of subtasks and resources. In adding value along its value configuration, a firm often has to coordinate many activities between groups within the firm and groups from outside. Most of what is exchanged in the coordination is information, and the Internet, as an information technology, can help tremendously. The construction industry narrated in Illustration Capsule 3.1 points to the importance of coordination and the enormous role that the Internet can play in coordinating activities. With the help of the Internet, much of the $200 billion lost annually in the industry to inefficiencies, mistakes, and delays could be recovered by better coordination of the activities of the dozens of businesses involved. The mediating and interactivity property of the Internet means that the thousands of transactions recorded on paper in the bricks-and-mortar world can be recorded electronically and any changes made during construction are immediately available to architects, engineers, and contractors. Blueprints and thousands of other documents do not

FIGURE 3.1 Properties of the Internet and the 5-Cs

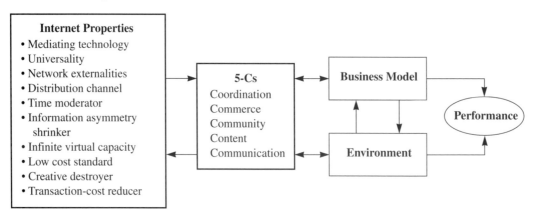

have to be shipped over long distances overnight, saving some of the $500 million spent each year to transport them. Mistakes are reduced, cutting down on costs, delays, and possible litigation.

33

CHAPTER 3
Competitive
Landscape-
Changing
Properties of the
Internet

The Internet can be equally valuable during product development. Automobile product development, for example, entails the coordination of thousands of people within the automaking firm and dozens of suppliers outside the company. The Internet can greatly simplify the process. Potentially, automakers can implement the type of build-to-order processes that PC makers such as Dell Computer employ in building computers. By choosing what they want in their cars, customers do not have to, for example, take heated seats and power mirrors just because these features come with the antilock brakes that customers want. Fewer components can mean lower cost and better reliability. Moreover, Daimler-Chrysler engineers located in Europe and the United States developing a new car do not have to travel to Detroit or Stuttgart. They can use the Internet or intranet to coordinate their activities. The properties of time moderation and universality suggest that these engineers do not have to work on the car at the same time either. Engineers working on a car today can share in the knowledge accumulated in previous projects and stored in the firm's databases that can be made available over an intranet. Moreover, as development is going on, the purchasing group and suppliers

---

Illustration Capsule 3.1
Building Construction and the Internet

The Economist had this to say about the impact of the Internet on the building and construction industry:

Anyone who has ever hired a builder knows that even the simplest job tends to be plagued by cost overruns and delays. And the bigger the project, the bigger the problems: according to one estimate, inefficiencies, mistakes and delays account for $200 billion of the $650 billion spent on construction in America every year. It is easy to see why. A building project, whether it is a hotel or a cement plant, involves dozens of businesses—architects, engineers, material suppliers—working together for months or years. Each project entails thousands of transactions, all of them currently recorded on paper. A typical $100m building project generates 150,000 separate documents: technical drawings, legal contracts, purchase orders, requests for information and schedules. Project managers build warehouses just to store them. Federal Express reputedly garnered $500m last year just shipping blueprints across America. Worse, construction is a slow affair, regularly held up by building regulations, stroppy [belligerent] unions and bad weather. Owners, architects and engineers must physically visit sites. With everything still done by fax or telephone, requests for the size of a roof tile can take weeks and seemingly minor changes can lead to long delays as bits of paper wind through approval processes. Even then, mistakes are common. Wrong supplies arrive and bills go unpaid. Given onerous shipping costs and the high value of commercial contracts, mistakes matter. Building is one of the world's most litigious industries.

Help is at hand. A group of new business-to-business companies plan to turn all construction into an efficient virtual process. Daryl Magana, chief executive of Bid.com, says his company creates a separate website for every building project for clients including the city of San Francisco, The Gap and General Electric. Everyone involved from the architect to the carpenters can then have access to this site to check blueprints and orders, change specifications and agree on delivery dates. Moreover, everything from due dates to material specifications is permanently recorded.

Clients love this approach. Harlan Kelly, city engineer at the city of San Francisco, says Bid.com has cut project time by six months: "We can do things quicker, faster and better and there are fewer arguments about whether information has reached people." Charlie Kuffner, Northern California business manager for Swinerton & Walberg Builders, a large contractor, says that using Bid.com has reduced by two-thirds the time needed to deal with requests for information . . . The scale economies are potentially enormous . . .

can monitor development progress, taking note of any changes that they may have to make in the design of components.

Commerce

There are many advantages to purchasing and selling goods and services over the Internet—or performing e-commerce. The low cost standard and universality properties, for example, suggest that firms and individuals who engage in **commerce** over the Internet have potential access to customers all over the world since customers everywhere potentially have access to the Internet. E-commerce can be business-to-business (B2B), business-to-consumer (B2C), consumer-to-consumer (C2C), or consumer-to-business (C2B).

Business-to-Business

In **business-to-business (B2B)**, businesses buy and sell goods and services to and from each other. In 1999 B2B commerce was estimated to be about $1.3 trillion by 2002.[12] The universality property suggests that buyers can put out requests for new bids for supplies on their websites and sellers from all over the world have a chance to bid. And the network externality property suggests that the more buyers there are, the better off sellers will be and vice versa. More buyers means sellers have more customers for their goods. More sellers means more choices for buyers. The more sellers, the better things can be for all sellers. This is the case especially when sellers can learn from each other or produce complementary goods.

A problem arises when sellers and buyers are highly fragmented; that is, there are a great many small sellers and buyers. Because buyers are fragmented, a seller may not even know who all the buyers are. The buyer may not know who all the sellers are either. Each supplier has to search through the Web pages of all buyers to find out what they want, give them the product descriptions that they need, find out about their creditworthiness, complete the buyer's requests for quotation (RFQs), and so on. Thus, the more sellers and buyers and the more fragmented both are, the higher the transaction costs. To see why, consider Figure 3.2. Figure 3.2(a) shows only two sellers S_1 and S_2, and two buyers B_1 and B_2. It takes each of the two sellers just two searches for a total of four contacts with buyers. When the number of sellers and buyers goes up to four each, the number of contacts that sellers have to make goes up to 16 as each of the four sellers must look for the four buyers as shown in Figure 3.2(b). Thus, the costs of sellers and buyers undertaking transactions with each other increases rapidly as the number of buyers and sellers increases. This is where **B2B hubs**—also known as B2B intermediaries or **B2B exchanges**—come in. They provide a central point in the value system where sellers and buyers can go to find each other. Figure 3.2(c) shows Figure 3.2(b) with a B2B hub added. Now, instead of 16 contacts (N^2), only 8 ($2N$) are needed. The four sellers make four postings on the hub's website and four buyers view the postings for the total of eight. Thus, sellers enjoy the benefits of a network of size N^2 but only have to make $2N$ contacts. More importantly, the hubs can offer software to further reduce the number of contacts.

Two types of hubs have been identified: vertical and functional.[13] **Vertical hubs** usually focus on an industry or market and provide content that is specific to the industry's value system of sellers, buyers, and complementors. This allows them to develop industry-specific capabilities. Examples include e-Steel which acts as an

FIGURE 3.2 B2B Networks

35

*CHAPTER 3
Competitive
Landscape-
Changing
Properties of the
Internet*

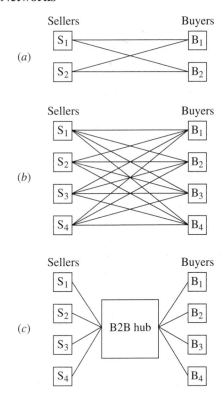

intermediary between steelmakers and users, and Chemdex which acts as the hub for suppliers to the life sciences industry. VerticalNet focuses on more than one industry. It provides hubs for many industries including electronics, process, telecommunications, and utilities. **Functional hubs** provide the same function for different industries, allowing them to build function-specific capabilities. An example is iMark.com which acts as an intermediary between sellers and buyers of used capital equipment in different industries. Whether vertical or functional, B2B hubs require detailed industry-specific or function-specific knowledge and capabilities.

Business-to-Consumer

In **business-to-consumer (B2C)** commerce, businesses sell to consumers. Two of the most famous examples are Dell Online and Amazon.com. The time moderator effect means that customers have access to e-shops 24 hours a day, everyday. The infinite virtual capacity property means that consumers face no lines anytime they go shopping. It also means that there is almost no limit to the number of goods that an online retailer can display on its virtual storefront or mall. Furthermore, it means that firms can collect rich data sets on customers and use them to personalize service for these customers. The distribution channel effect means that some goods (e.g., music and software) bought over the Internet can be received instantaneously. The low cost standard and universality effects mean that consumers can shop in the privacy of their own homes.

The exchange between business and consumer may or may not involve an intermediary. Where the cost of finding a seller is high, a consumer may prefer to go to an intermediary. For example, rather than worry about which of the thousands of book publishers produces a particular book, a consumer may prefer to go to Amazon.com to look for the book. On the other hand, a consumer who wants to buy a computer may purchase one directly from Dell or one of the other major PC makers. Laws can also dictate that intermediaries must be where they would not necessarily have to be. As of early 2000, for example, U.S. law did not permit consumers to buy automobiles directly from manufacturers. Consumers had to go through car dealers.

Consumer-to-Consumer

In **consumer-to-consumer (C2C)**, consumers sell to other consumers. Because there are millions of sellers with different items to sell and millions of buyers who want different items, the cost to sellers and buyers of finding each other can be exorbitant. The solution is to have an intermediary as shown in Figure 3.2(c). Auction houses such as eBay are such an intermediary. They mediate between consumers who want to buy or sell.

Consumer-to-Business

In early 2000, **consumer-to-business (C2B)** was not as developed as B2B, B2C, and C2C. In C2B, consumers state their price, and firms either take it or leave it. Under Priceline's model, for example, potential customers name their prices for a flight and leave them for the airline to accept or reject. This contrasts with B2C where a firm usually states its price for a product or service and customers take it or leave it. Again, an intermediary plays an important role. In our example, Priceline is the intermediary.

Intermediary Models

Where **intermediaries** play a role in commerce, different models are usually used in pricing the goods that are exchanged in transactions. These models include auction, reverse auction, fixed or menu pricing, bargaining, and barter. Again, one of the most popular models used by intermediaries in C2C is the auction model as practiced by eBay. We will explore these models in Chapter 4.

Community

Groups with like interests, or **community**, can congregate online through chat rooms or message boards. Electronic communities have many advantages over physical communities. The universality and low cost standard properties mean that anyone from anywhere can join the group if he or she meets the group's criteria. Distance is no longer a drawback to belonging to a community. The time moderator effect also suggests that groups do not have to meet at the same time.

Some of the most important communities for firms are user groups. Lead users, for example, are customers whose needs are similar to those of other users except that they have these needs long before most of the marketplace and stand to benefit significantly by satisfying those needs earlier.[14] A community of lead users that can discuss their needs as they use early versions of a design can be extremely valuable in helping each other discover their needs. More important, the developer of the product has access to this critical information. Customer user groups, in general, can be important resources for firms. For example, users of Cisco products learned so much from each other that they did not have to ask many questions of Cisco about how to use the products in their own system. This not only freed Cisco applications engineers to develop more products (instead of hand-holding customers), but also meant happier customers who wanted more Cisco products.

The network externality property suggests that the larger the community, the more valuable it is. This in turn suggests that once one belongs to a large network, the less easy it is to switch to a smaller network. One strategic implication is that firms might want to build such communities early.

37

CHAPTER 3
*Competitive
Landscape-
Changing
Properties of the
Internet*

Content

Content is the information, entertainment, and other products that are delivered over the Internet. Entertainment includes Disney online, MTV online, interactive video games, and sportscasting. A person can play games with friends and relatives located thousands of miles away. Information content includes current news, stock quotations, weather forecasts, and investment information. Both contents rest on the distribution channel, low cost standard, and mediating technology properties.

Communication

At the heart of the four Cs that we have just explored is the fifth: **communication**. Its uses go beyond coordination, commerce, community, and content. People use electronic mail (e-mail), Web phones, or real-time video to exchange messages for numerous bricks-and-mortar activities. Mediating and interactivity properties mean that people can exchange electronic messages real-time. The time moderator, low cost standard, and universality properties mean that one can send many messages at any time to many people. The infinite virtual capacity effect means that one can send many messages, each of which can have a high content. Every user also has the capability to broadcast messages. Broadcasting is no longer limited to the owners of radio and television stations.

Implications for Industries

Because the Internet has so great an impact on the 5-Cs (see Table 3.1), any firm whose activities involve coordination, commerce, community, content, and communication must take a good look at it as either a potential threat or opportunity. Consider again the automobile industry. In early 2000, it took 60 to 100 days from the forming of sheet metal to build a car to delivery of the finished vehicle to a customer.[15] Since it takes so long to build the cars, customers are unwilling to commit to buying one. Consequently, automakers have to build the cars and send them to dealers in hopes that they will sell. If the cars don't sell, they resort to rebates, advertising, and redistribution of cars that can account for as much as 30 percent of the price. Using the Internet to find out what customers want and then building to order could trim these costs. But building to order also means trimming the lead time from the previous 60 to 100 days. This means that the Internet must be used to coordinate information from customers and suppliers as well as for internal information. It also means using the Internet to collaborate with suppliers to meet these customer needs. All of this means that even the automobile industry is at risk with the Internet. We will say more about which firms and industries are at risk in Chapters 5 and 8.

LIMITATIONS TO TRANSACTIONS OVER THE INTERNET

The Internet is an information technology. The information sent over it must at some point be encoded into bits (ones and zeros) to be transmitted and received. Sooner or later, the information sent over the Internet must be handled by people. Therefore, the choice of transactions that can be performed over the Internet is a function of the nature of the knowledge on which the transactions rest and of the type of people who undertake the transactions. Thus, the nature of knowledge and people limit the extent to which the Internet can be used to conduct business.

Tacit Knowledge

Whatever is transmitted over the Internet usually has been knowledge at some point—knowledge that has resided in individuals or in organizational routines. E-mail messages sent by individuals derive from their stock of knowledge. The design of a car sent over the Internet is knowledge that has resided in individuals who work for the automaker or in its organizational routines and archival knowledge banks. For knowledge to be effectively transmitted over the Internet, it must be encoded in a form that can be transmitted; that is, knowledge transmitted over the Internet is **explicit knowledge**, not tacit. Knowledge is explicit if it is codified, spelled out in writing, and verbalized or coded in drawings, computer programs, or other products. It is also sometimes referred to as articulated or codified knowledge.[16] Knowledge is tacit if uncoded and nonverbalized. It may not even be possible to verbalize or articulate **tacit knowledge**. It can be acquired largely through personal experience by learning or by doing. Tacit knowledge is often embedded in the routines of organizations and the actions of an individual, and therefore is very difficult to copy. Thus, carrying out transactions over the Internet becomes a problem when the tacit knowledge on which the transactions rest cannot be encoded

TABLE 3.1 The 5-Cs and Key Internet Properties

Internet property	Coordination	Commerce	Community	Content	Communication
			5-Cs		
Mediating technology	X	X	X	X	X
Universality	X	X	X	X	X
Network externality		X	X		X
Distribution channel		X		X	
Time moderator	X	X	X	X	X
Information asymmetry shrinker	X	X			
Infinite virtual capacity		X	X	X	
Low cost standard	X	X	X	X	X
Creative destroyer		X		X	
Transaction-cost reducer	X	X			

into a form that can be put onto the Internet and transmitted. How can you transmit the smell and feel of a car over the Internet?

People

The other problem with transacting over the Internet is that human beings and their organizations, smart as they can be, are still limited cognitively. They have **bounded rationality**. According to Oliver Williamson:

> Bounded rationality involves neurophysiological limits on the one hand and language limits on the other. The physical limits take the form of rate and storage limits on the powers of individuals to receive, store, retrieve, and process information without error . . . Language limits refer to the inability of individuals to articulate their knowledge or feelings by use of words, numbers, or graphics in ways which permit them to be understood by others. Despite their best efforts, parties may find that language fails them (possibly because they do not possess the requisite vocabulary or the necessary vocabulary has not been devised) and they resort to other means of communications instead. Demonstrations, learning-by-doing, and the like may be the only means of achieving understanding when such language difficulties develop.[17]

Because individuals and organizations are cognitively limited, they may not be able to encode their knowledge into a form that can be transmitted over the Internet. Even if they could articulate this knowledge well, cognitively limited individuals at the receiving end might not understand. How does one describe the smell of a new car to other people and give them the sensation that they would get by themselves? Even if one could, would this other person get it?

Tacit knowledge and cognitive limitations of people make it difficult to perform some transactions over the Internet. Technological advances such as virtual reality may help to remove some of these limitations. In any case, as a firm develops its business models and strategies, it is important to understand some of the limitations of the Internet.

SUMMARY

The Internet has numerous properties that have the potential to transform the competitive landscape in many industries. Ten properties—mediating technology, universality, network externalities, distribution channel, time moderator, information asymmetry shrinker, infinite virtual capacity, low cost standard, creative destroyer, and transaction-cost reducer—have an impact on the way activities in a firm are carried out. In particular, they have a major impact on coordination, commerce, community, content, and communication—the 5-Cs. In coordination, the Internet reduces the cost of transactions, cuts lead times, and improves product-service features and quality. It takes commerce—business-to-business, business-to-consumer, consumer-to-consumer, or consumer-to-business—to a different level. The Internet redefines communities, making them virtual, larger, and much more valuable. More content is available to more people. Communication now has the potential to offer everyone not only large virtual capacity but also the ability to broadcast information. The Internet also has the potential to change the way the 5-Cs are carried out—thus having a large impact on the way business models are conceived and executed—and to have a huge impact on nearly every industry.

39

CHAPTER 3
Competitive
Landscape-
Changing
Properties of the
Internet

KEY TERMS

B2B exchanges   34
B2B hubs   34
bounded rationality   39
business-to-business (B2B)   34
business-to-consumer (B2C)   35
commerce   34
communication   37
community   36
consumer-to-business (C2B)   36
consumer-to-consumer (C2C)   36
content   37
coordination   32
creative destruction   31
distribution channel   29
explicit knowledge   38

extension effect   29
functional hubs   35
infinite virtual capacity   30
information asymmetry   30
intermediaries   36
mediating technology   27
Metcalfe's law   29
network externalities   28
replacement effect   29
tacit knowledge   38
time moderation   29
transaction costs   31
universality of the Internet   28
vertical hubs   34
5-Cs   32

DISCUSSION QUESTIONS

1. Where do you expect network externalities to have the most impact: intrafirm, business-to-business (B2B), business-to-consumer (B2C), consumer-to-consumer (C2C), or consumer-to-business (C2B) transactions? Start by estimating the network size in each case.

2. Of the 10 major properties of the Internet, which one do you consider the most powerful in terms of the impact on firm activities? (*Hint:* What is the impact of each property on each of the 5-Cs?) Does the type of industry in which these activities are performed matter?

3. Which of the 5-Cs stands to be most impacted by the Internet and why? Does the type of industry matter?

4. Which industries stand to benefit the most from the Internet?

5. Which activities are least likely to be impacted by the Internet?

REFERENCES

1. J. D. Thompson, *Organizations in Action* (New York: McGraw-Hill, 1967); C. B. Stabell and O. D. Fjeldstad, "Configuring Value for Competitive Advantage: On Chains, Shops, and Networks," *Strategic Management Journal* 19 (1998), pp. 413–37.

2. M. L. Katz and C. Shapiro, "Technology Adoption in the Presence of Network Externalities," *Journal of Political Economy* 94, no. (4) (1986), pp. 822–41.

3. B. Arthur, "Positive Feedbacks in the Economy," *Scientific American.* February 1990, pp. 80–85.

4. See, for example, L. Downes and C. Mui, *Unleashing the Killer App: Digital Strategies for Market Dominance* (Boston: Harvard Business School Press, 1998).

5. Kevin Kelly, *New Rules for the New Economy: 10 Radical Strategies for a Connected World* (New York: Penguin, 1999).

6. These examples are from N. Kumar, "Internet Distribution Strategies: Dilemmas for the Incumbent," *Financial Times,* March 15, 1999.

41

*CHAPTER 3
Competitive
Landscape-
Changing
Properties of the
Internet*

7. "The Net Imperative: Survey of Business and the Internet," *The Economist,* June 26, 1999.

8. J. A. Schumpeter, *Capitalism, Socialism and Democracy,* 3rd ed. (New York: Harper, 1950).

9. This example is from "Newspapers and the Internet: Caught in the Web," *The Economist,* July 17, 1999, pp. 17–19.

10. R. H. Coase, "The Nature of the Firm," *Econometrica* 4 (1937), pp. 386–405; O. Williamson, *Markets and Hierarchies* (New York: Free Press, 1975).

11. Downes and Mui, *Unleashing the Killer App,* pp. 35–39.

12. A. Marlatt, "Creating Vertical Marketplaces," *Internet World,* February 1999, pp. 85–92.

13. M. Sawhney and S. Kaplan, "Let's Get Vertical," *Business 2.0,* September 1999.

14. E. Von Hippel, "Lead Users: A Source of Novel Product Concepts," *Management Science* 32 (1986), pp. 791–805.

15. "Cars: Wheels and Wires," *The Economist,* January 8, 2000, pp. 58–60.

16. See, for example, M. Polanyi, *Personal Knowledge: Towards a Post Critical Philosophy* (London: Routledge, 1962); G. Hedlund, "A Model of Knowledge Management and the N-form Corporation," *Strategic Management Journal* 15 (1994), pp. 73–90.

17. Williamson, *Markets and Hierarchies,* p. 21; K. Conner and C. K. Prahalad, "A Resource-based Theory of the Firm: Knowledge versus Opportunism," *Organization Science* 7, no. 5 (1995), pp. 477–501.

Components, Linkages, Dynamics, and Evaluation of Business Models

CHAPTER 4

Components of a Business Model

In Chapter 3 we explored those properties of the Internet that could transform the competitive landscape in many industries. The question now is, How can a firm take advantage of these properties to gain and maintain a competitive advantage? That is, how can a firm use the Internet to be more profitable than its competitors over the long term? How a firm plans to make money long term using the Internet is detailed in its Internet business model. In this chapter, we explore the components of an Internet business model and the linkages between these components. We will begin with a definition of business models and a brief mention of the growing taxonomy of business models that seek to exploit the Internet. We will then examine the components of a business model and the linkages between them, paying particular attention to the role of the properties of the Internet that we explored in Chapter 3. The dynamics of business models and their appraisal will be discussed in Chapter 5.

INTERNET BUSINESS MODEL

Each firm that exploits the Internet should have an Internet **business model**—how it plans to make money long term using the Internet. This is a set of Internet- and non-Internet–related activities—planned or evolving—that allows a firm to make money using the Internet and to keep the money coming. If well formulated, a firm's business model gives it a competitive advantage in its industry, enabling the firm to earn greater profits than its competitors. Whether implicit or explicit in a firm's actions, a business model should include answers to a number of questions: What value to offer customers, which customers to provide the value to, how to price the value, who to charge for it, what strategies to undertake in providing the value, how to provide that value (see Figure 4.1), and how to sustain any advantage from providing the value. Answering these questions entails an understanding of the firm's industry and the key drivers of value in that industry, customers and what they value, the activities that undergird delivering value to these customers, the impact of the Internet on the industry and these activities, and the firm's distinctiveness and how best to exploit it. The firm can be a supplier to the Internet, a service provider within the Internet infrastructure, or a user.

FIGURE 4.1 Determinants of Firm Performance

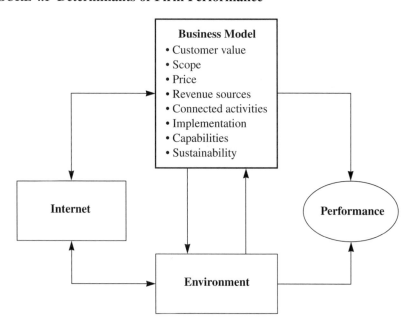

A Taxonomy of Business Models

Internet business models abound and vary not only from industry to industry but also from firm to firm within the same industry. Moreover, they are still evolving. Michael Rappa and Paul Timmers have identified several generic business models: brokerage, advertising, infomediary, merchant, manufacturer, affiliate, community, subscription, and utility.[1]

Brokerage

In the **brokerage model**, firms act as market makers who bring buyers and sellers together and charge a fee for the transactions that they enable. They can be business-to-business, business-to-consumer, or consumer-to-consumer brokers. Examples include travel agents, online brokerage firms, and online auction houses. Brokerage business models can be further broken down into different types: buy/sell fulfillment, market exchange, buyer aggregator, distributor, virtual mall, metamediary, auction broker, reverse auction, classifieds and search agent.[2]

Advertising

In the **advertising model**, the owner of a website provides some content and services that attract visitors. The website owner usually makes money by charging advertisers fees for banners, permanent buttons, and other ways of getting a client's messages to visitors.[3] Some of the most famous users of the advertising model are Yahoo, Excite@Home, and Altavista. Almost anyone with a website that attracts visitors has the potential to compete in this model. Advertising models can be further broken down into generalized portal, personalized portal, specialized portal, attention/incentive marketing, free model, and bargain discounter.

Infomediary

In the **infomediary model**, a firm collects valuable information on consumers and their buying habits and sells it to firms which in turn can mine it for important patterns and other useful information to help them better serve their customers. The infomediary firm usually offers consumers something in return, such as "free" content, cash, or PCs, for information about them. An infomediary can also collect information about firms and their websites and sell it to consumers. Infomediaries can be further broken into two types: recommender system and registration model.

Merchant

The **merchant model** is the "e-tailer" model in which wholesalers and retailers sell goods and services over the Internet. The goods can be sold by list prices or through auctions. These include virtual merchant, catalog merchant, surf-and-turf, and bit vendor.

Manufacturer

In the **manufacturing model**, manufacturers try to reach end users directly through the Internet instead of going through a wholesaler or retailer. By doing so, they can save on costs and better serve customers by finding out directly what they want. Channel conflicts present a challenge for such manufacturers. In the late 1990s computer maker Compaq decided to drop the computer dealers who had been its distributors and go directly to customers. The distributors fought the changes and Compaq had to reconsider its decisions.

Affiliate

In the **affiliate model**, a merchant has affiliates whose websites have **click-through** to the merchant. Each time a visitor to an affiliate's site clicks through to the merchant's site and buys something, the affiliate is paid a fee, usually a percentage of the revenues.

Community

The **community model** rests on community loyalty rather than traffic. Users have invested in developing relationships with members of their community and are likely to visit the website frequently. Members of such a community can be a very good market target. A good example is iVillage.

Subscription

Access to a website is not free. Members pay a subscription price and in return receive high-quality content. Some sites offer both subscription and nonsubscription content with differences in service to match. **Subscription models** have a *moral hazard* component to them: Once customers have paid the subscription fee, they sometimes use the service much more than they ordinarily would. America Online (AOL) found this out the hard way when it introduced flat-rate pricing. Some customers logged on and stayed logged on even when they were not using the service, thus tying up the telephone lines to local access.

Utility

In the **utility model**, firms pay as they go. Activities are metered and users pay for the services that they consume.

Rationale

While all these models are different and serve their owners well, they have one thing in common: They are designed to make money for their owners long term. Rather than try to enumerate the numerous and changing business models in different industries, we will explore those elements that are common to all business models and on which making money rests. For a firm to keep making money, it must keep offering customers something that they value and that competitors cannot offer.[4] **Customer value** can take the form of differentiated or lower-cost products. Such a firm must also target the right market segments with products or services that have the appropriate value mix since not all customer value is meant for all customers. That is, market and product *scope* are also important. Offering the right customers the right value is only part of the equation. The firm must *price* them properly. To offer value to customers, firms must perform the *activities* that underpin the value.[5] These activities must be carried out or *implemented* by people who have to be managed well. How well these individuals and firms perform the value-adding activities is a function of the superiority of their **capabilities**.[6] How much of a competitive advantage they have is a function of the distinctiveness of the capabilities. Often a firm has more than one *revenue source* and should take all sources into consideration as it decides what value to offer customers, how to price it, what activities to perform, and so on. A well-conceived business model with all these components can be profitable. Once a firm starts making money, however, competitors usually want a piece of the action. A firm with such an advantage must also worry about **sustainability** of profits. It must find ways to keep making money. It must find ways to retain its competitive advantage.

Table 4.1 summarizes some questions that a firm should ask itself at all times about its business model in general, and Internet business models in particular.

CUSTOMER VALUE

Customers would buy a product from a firm only if the product offers them something that competitors' products do not.[7] This something, or customer value, can take the form of differentiated or low cost products/services.

Differentiation

A product is differentiated if customers perceive it to have something of value that other products do not have. A firm can differentiate its products in eight different ways: product features, timing, location, service, product mix, linkage between functions, linkage with other firms, and reputation.[8]

Product Features

A firm can differentiate its products/services by offering features that competitors' products do not have. For example, a manufacturer of memory microchips might differentiate its products by emphasizing the speed of its chips. Distinctive

TABLE 4.1 Elements of a Business Model

Component of Business Model	Questions for All Business Models	Questions Specific to Internet Business Models
Customer value	Is the firm offering its customers something distinctive or at a lower cost than its competitors?	What is it about the Internet that allows your firm to offer its customers something distinctive? Can the Internet allow you to solve a new set of problems for customers?
Scope	To which customers (demographic and geographic) is the firm offering this value? What is the range of products/services offered that embody this value?	What is the scope of customers that the Internet enables your firm to reach? Does the Internet alter the product or service mix that embodies the firm's products?
Pricing	How does the firm price the value?	How does the Internet make pricing different?
Revenue source	Where do the dollars come from? Who pays for what value and when? What are the margins in each market and what drives them? What drives value in each source?	Are revenue sources different with the Internet? What is new?
Connected activities	What set of activities does the firm have to perform to offer this value and when? How connected (in cross section and time) are these activities?	How many new activities must be performed as a result of the Internet? How much better can the Internet help you to perform existing activities?
Implementation	What organizational structure, systems, people, and environment does the firm need to carry out these activities? What is the fit between them?	What does the Internet do to the strategy, structure, systems, people, and environment of your firm?
Capabilities	What are the firm's capabilities and capabilities gaps that need to be filled? How does a firm fill these capabilities gaps? Is there something distinctive about these capabilities that allows the firm to offer the value better than other firms and that makes them difficult to imitate? What are the sources of these capabilities?	What new capabilities do you need? What is the impact of the Internet on existing capabilities?
Sustainability	What is it about the firm that makes it difficult for other firms to imitate it? How does the firm keep making money? How does the firm sustain its competitive advantage?	Does the Internet make sustainability easier or more difficult? How can your firm take advantage of it?

features are probably the most familiar form of product differentiation, and better coordination of activities within and outside a firm using the Internet can result in better product features for customers. For example, the Internet offers the possibility of made-to-order cars, customized to individual taste. The Internet also offers 24-hour service, no lines, and access to a community of customers. It also can offer personalized service for everyone.

Timing

A firm can differentiate a product by being the first to introduce it. Since such a product is the only one on the market, it is, by default, differentiated because no other product has its features. Thus, two personal computers with identical physical attributes—speed, main memory capacity, disk capacity, operating system, and the number of applications running on it—are seen as highly differentiated if one was produced in 1999 and the other in 2000. For a time, Compaq differentiated its IBM-compatible personal computers by being the first to introduce computers that used the latest version of Intel microprocessors. The Internet allows product developers to reduce the lead times of their products. Improved coordination using the Internet allows a manufacturer to complete the design of a product faster and to bring the product to market earlier than it might otherwise have done. Again using our chip design example, if Intel can have engineers in Japan work on a design, turn it over to engineers in Israel who continue the work on it before handing it over to engineers in the United States, Intel can finish the product faster than it could if engineers in only one country worked on the design. The building construction case in Chapter 3 is another example of the importance of timing.

Location

Two products with identical features can still be differentiated by virtue of their location. One differentiating factor may be the ease of access to the products. For example, if an Internet service provider (ISP) in Ann Arbor, Michigan, offers identical service to that offered by another ISP in New York, the two services are differentiated because a customer in Ann Arbor does not have access to the services in New York. The universality property, however, suggests that the Internet may take away some of the advantages of location for many products and services. The most popular example is the bricks-and-mortar bookstore whose differentiating factor was its location. Now customers worldwide have the potential to buy books from anywhere in the world. With products that are bits of zeros and ones, such as music, videos, and books or services like insurance, banks, and brokerage firms, location is less of a differentiator.

Service

A firm's products may also be differentiated by how quickly they can be repaired if they break down. For example, an automaker in a developing country can differentiate itself by the amount of service that it offers. With the Internet, the role of user groups is larger than ever before. Users of most systems and complex products such as the automobile can exchange information on how to service their cars. The larger such groups are, the better the service will be since size increases the chances that someone in the group can solve a problem and then share the knowledge with other members of the group.

The mix of products that a firm sells can also be a source of product differentiation. Customers who prefer one-stop shopping or variety would find such product mixes valuable. Virtual stores offer a tremendous amount of choice. Bookseller Amazon.com, for example, offered 16 million items for sale on its storefront in May 1999,[9] differentiating it from other retailers. Furthermore, the firm can use data gathered on its customers to suggest personalized choices for them.

Linkages

Association with another firm can also be a source of differentiation. An Internet upstart or bricks-and-mortar firm associated with AOL gains some credibility in the eyes of the many customers who perceive AOL as reputable. The network externalities property suggests that the larger a Web community is, the more valuable its membership, which distinguishes the community from others.

Brand-Name Reputation

Finally, a firm's brand-name reputation can go a long way in making customers perceive that its products are different. The Internet offers one more channel to establish brand-name reputations. This time, however, the channel can be more worldwide than any time before since the Internet reaches many more people.

Low Cost

Low cost means just that—a firm's products or services cost customers less than those of its competitors. The idea is that it costs the firm less to offer customers the product/service, so the firm passes some of the cost savings on to customers. Reduction in information asymmetry means savings in transaction costs. The distribution channel effect means large savings and better ways of disposing of a firm's output. For example, a software developer or musician who sells her products by posting them on the Internet saves on distribution, packaging, and transportation costs. Better coordination of activities also means lower costs for producers. The savings can then be passed on to customers.

SCOPE

While customer value is about offering low cost and/or differentiated products, **scope** is about the market segments or geographic areas to which the value should be offered as well as how many types of products that embody versions of this value should be sold.[10] A firm can market either to businesses or households. Within the business markets are different industries and, within each of these industries, firms of different sizes and technical sophistication. Households also consist of many segments that are a function of demographics, lifestyles, and incomes. iVillage, for example, is targeted largely toward women. Then there is geography. Often a firm must decide where in the world it wants to market its products—North America, Europe, or Africa—and within each continent, which country to serve. The universality property of the Internet makes geographic expansion a great deal more feasible than in the bricks-and-mortar world. For example, a person in South Africa with an Internet connection can shop in Amazon.com's Seattle storefront.

A firm's task of making decisions on scope is not limited to the choice of market segment. A firm must also decide how much of the needs of the segment it can profitably serve.[11] For example, an Internet firm that targets teenagers must decide how many of their needs it wants to meet. It could provide them only with basic hookup services and chat rooms or provide content such as movies and math tutoring. It might also decide to provide the same type of service to all demographic groups.

PRICE

An important part of profiting from the value that firms offer customers is to price it properly. A bad **pricing strategy** can not only leave money on the table, but also kill a product or stifle its prosperity. Most products and services in the so-called knowledge economy are, well, knowledge-based.[12] **Knowledge-based products** are heavy on know-how and have very high up-front costs relative to the variable cost of producing and offering each unit to customers. For example, a software developer can spend millions of dollars to develop a software application while the cost of selling a copy to customers is almost zero because all the developer has to do is post the software on the Web for customers to download. It cost AOL hundreds of millions of dollars to build its software, hardware, brand, and subscriber base, but once the initial amount is spent, the monthly relative cost of maintaining each member is negligible. To illustrate some of the underpinnings of the pricing strategies for knowledge-based products and services, let's start with a simple but revealing example:

> Consider two firms, A and B, each of which has developed a proprietary software package. Each spends $500 million (M) a year on research and development (R&D), marketing, and promotion, with the bulk of that sum on R&D.[13] Since the software can be downloaded by customers, let's assume that it costs both A and B $5 to sell each copy (for credit card verification and management of the marketing website) at a unit price of $200. Suppose firm A, through the right strategic decisions and endowments, has a market share of 80 percent of the 10 million units in 1999 while B has the remaining 20 percent.

> Using the extremely simple but enlightening relation:

$$\text{Profits} = \Pi = (P - V_c)Q - F_c$$

> where P is the price per unit of the product,
> V_c is the per unit variable cost,
> Q is the total number of units sold, and
> F_c is the up-front or fixed costs,

> we find that in 1999:

> Firm A's profits = $(200-5) \times 8M - 500M = 1,560M - 500M = \$1,060M$
> Firm B's profits = $(200-5) \times 2M - 500M = 390M - 500M = -\$110M$

Thus, while firm A earned more than $1 billion in profits in 1999, firm B actually *lost* $110 million. What a difference market share makes for high fixed cost, low variable cost products! This very simple example brings out several underpinnings of pricing strategies for products with high fixed costs and low variable costs—

both characteristics of knowledge-based products. To illustrate the role of market share, margins, revenues, and growth, we have extended our simple calculation to include the years 1998 and 2000. The results are shown in Table 4.2.

Market Share and Margins Are Critical!

As we have noted, market share is critical to knowledge-based products. In our example, the firm with an 80 percent market share in 1999 earned more than $1 billion in profits while the one with 20 percent lost money. A firm's strategy early in the life of such products, then, is to strive for high market share. Strategies for attaining such a high market share include (1) giving away a product and charging for later versions, (2) giving away product X and charging for related product Y, and (3) pricing low to penetrate the market. Note that if firm A gives away its product in 1998 and 1999 to help it attain the 80 percent market share in 2000, it loses $1.044 billion in those two years but more than makes up for it with a $15.1 billion profit in 2000. Also note that firm A can cut its sales price by half and still make over $7 billion. One way of looking at this is that A's profit margins are higher because its fixed costs are spread over more units.

It's Growth! It's Revenues

Notice in Table 4.2 that although firm A's market share in 1998 was 80 percent, it actually lost $344 million even though its losses were less than those of firm B. However, firm A earned $1.06 billion in profits in 1999 and a whopping $15.1 billion in 2000 even though in both years its market share was still 80 percent. The difference is that it sold only 800,000 units in 1998, but 8 million units in 1999 and 80 million in 2000. Indeed, even firm B earned $3.4 billion in 2000. The most important strategy, then, is to develop the market. Sell more units! It is in the interest of both firms to increase the size of the market. It is not so much the fractional share as the revenue share that matters.

Lock-in

An important question is, Why can't firm B reduce its price low enough to grab some of the market share from firm A? One answer is that such pricing strategies work best for products that not only have a very high ratio of fixed to variable

TABLE 4.2 Market Share and Profitability for Knowledge-Based Products

	1998			*1999*			*2000*		
	Market Share (%)	Market Share (1,000 units)	Profits ($ millions)	Market Share (%)	Market Share (1,000 units)	Profits ($ millions)	Market Share (%)	Market Share (1,000 units)	Profits ($ millions)
Firm A	80	800	344	80	8,000	1,060	80	80,000	15,100
Firm B	20	200	−461	20	2,000	−110	20	20,000	3,400

costs, but also exhibit **lock-in**, which means that the products have certain characteristics that lock in customers. First, switching to a new product means users must
learn how to use the new one if both old and new products are not compatible.
Unless the benefits of the new product outweigh those of the old one, customers
may not be willing to switch. For example, a person who has learned how to use
Microsoft's Windows operating system and decides to switch to UNIX must now
learn how to use this new operating system. Many customers regard **switching
costs** as important. The required new learning may not be worth the cost savings,
if any. Second, the product may have complementary products that are not compatible with those of competing products. In this case switching could mean buying a new set of compatible products. In the Windows example, switching to UNIX
could mean having to abandon all the applications programs that the user has accumulated over the years. Third, these products sometimes exhibit **network externalities**—the more users who own them, the more valuable they are to users. If
many people already own an IBM-compatible PC, it makes sense to stay with that
type of computer when you need a new one or go with what most people have
when you buy your first computer. That way, you can share user tips and software
with other users. These lock-in properties allow firms that are already ahead of the
competition to increase the distance between themselves and competitors.

Types of Pricing and the Influence of the Internet (Dynamic Pricing)

There are actually five main types of pricing: menu, one-to-one bargaining, auction,[14] reverse auction, and barter.

Menu

In **menu pricing**, or fixed pricing, the seller sets a price and buyers can either
take it or leave it. This is the most common form of pricing, used by nearly every
retail store in the United States. Menu pricing has two shortcomings. First, given
the value they are getting from the product, customers may be willing to pay more
than the menu prices set by the seller. In such a case, the seller is leaving money
on the table. There is also the possibility that the menu price is too high, cutting off
many buyers who would have bought the product at a lower price. At the same
time, the seller is forgoing extra revenue. These prices are also sticky because, once
set, they are difficult to change. The stickiness is a result of two factors. First, it is
not easy to detect changes in consumer preferences quickly enough to effect price
changes since menu prices reveal little about customer preferences. Second, it is
difficult to implement price changes. It takes time and costs money to change the
labels on products. Just think of how much it would cost to keep changing all the
prices in your grocery store as a function of the day of the week or time of day.
This could also be extremely confusing to customers. With the Internet, however,
customer preferences can be detected more easily. Moreover, it costs a lot less to
change prices since they are all virtual.

One-to-One

In **one-to-one bargaining**, a seller negotiates with a buyer to determine at what
point the buyer considers the price appropriate for the value that he or she is getting.
This overcomes the disadvantage of menu pricing which lets some customers get

away with a price that is less than they would be willing to pay, and misses out on customers who would prefer to pay less. This type of pricing is very common on the streets of most developing countries. The first disadvantage of one-to-one bargaining is that it is impractical in most large bricks-and-mortar stores; imagine customers trying to negotiate prices on all the items in a supermarket. The second disadvantage is that the seller cannot be sure that the prospective buyer is willing to pay what he or she believes the product is worth, nor can the buyer be sure that the seller necessarily wants to sell for the least price. With the Internet, changing prices is as easy as clicking a mouse. Moreover, customer personalization helps better determine each customer's willingness to pay and prices can be adjusted accordingly.

Auction

In **auction pricing** the seller solicits bids from many buyers and sells to the buyer with the best bid. This removes the second disadvantage of one-to-one bargaining. One problem with auctions is that buyers can collude to hold down the price of an item or sellers can limit the number of items up for bid at any time. The other problem with auctions in the bricks-and-mortar world is the difficulty in bringing together many buyers and sellers. This difficulty still exposes auction participants to some of the risk of not getting the best buyers and sellers that one-to-one bargaining faces. The large communities of the Internet, however, bring together many sellers and buyers, greatly reducing this problem. Moreover, on the Web auctioneers like eBay have developed programs that allow buyers to rate each other, helping to establish a rating reputation for performance. This goes a long way in reducing the fear of collusion and opportunism.

Reverse Auction

In a **reverse auction**, sellers decide whether to fulfill the orders of potential buyers. A buyer proposes a price for a good or service. Sellers then decide whether to accept or reject the bid. Priceline.com was one of the pioneers of the reverse auction model. A user of Priceline proposes a price he or she is willing to pay for, say, air transportation, between points A and B on a certain day. Priceline then presents this information to the airlines to see whether any are interested. If an airline is willing to sell tickets at that price, the deal is consummated and Priceline gets a commission from the seller.[15] This system also allows price discrimination by sellers because buyers do not know how much other buyers are willing to pay. The reverse auction is not as good for sellers as an auction since an astute buyer can capture all of the seller's surplus.

Barter

Probably one of the oldest pricing models first employed by our ancestors, **barter** refers to the swapping of goods for goods, or goods for services, and the use of those goods or services by the parties involved. Although it works for young companies strapped for cash, in general, barter is a relatively weak pricing model that has little long-term potential.

REVENUE SOURCES

A critical part of a business model analysis is the determination of the sources of a firm's revenues *and* profits. In the bricks-and-mortar world, many firms receive their **revenue sources** directly from the products they sell. Others receive their revenues from selling products *and* servicing them, with a larger share of their profits coming from the service. For example, a jet engine maker or earth-moving equipment manufacturer may receive large amounts of revenue from selling its products but make much greater profits from spare parts and servicing of the equipment. An understanding of the sources of profits allows a firm to make better strategic decisions. For example, the jet engine maker may decide to sell the engines at give-away prices and depend on after-sales service to make money.

With the Internet, the need to determine the sources of revenues and profits is even more critical largely because of its properties of mediating and network externalities. Consider an online stockbrokerage firm, for example. It has three sources of revenues: (1) the commissions that it collects on the stock trades it executes for clients; (2) the interest that it charges clients who must borrow from the cash reserves of other clients (deposited with the broker) to pay for any securities they buy on margin; and (3) the spread between the bid and ask prices of stocks. Thus, an online stockbrokerage may decide to charge extremely low commissions to increase the number of its clients with large assets. More such clients mean more revenues and profits from interest charges and spreads.

The mediating property also suggests that the revenue model of radio, print, and television media in the United States and Canada provides useful information in determining the sources of revenues and profits for the Internet. In the media model, firms offer value to their audience but charge advertisers, not the audience, for it. A firm may therefore sell its products at a discount but make money from selling advertising to merchandisers who value the firm's audience. An online auto dealer may collect a fee for referring customers to automakers but make its money by selling insurance to visitors to its site. Some firms might lose money in selling to customers but collect information on these customers that they can sell to other vendors. In early 2000, there were two problems with this model. First, almost anyone with a website had an audience and therefore the potential to sell advertising or capture customer data. Second, exactly what advertisers should be paying for has not been very clear. Table 4.3 traces some of the evolution of online advertising metrics.

CONNECTED ACTIVITIES: WHAT ACTIVITIES AND WHEN

To deliver value to different customers, a firm must perform the activities that underpin the value. If Intel is going to offer very fast microprocessors to its customers and charge a premium price for them, it must be able to perform some of the **connected activities** that underpin the making of microprocessors: R&D, product design, wafer fabrication, testing, marketing and sales, and field support. A set of these connected activities is normally called a value chain because value is added to materials or knowledge as it moves up the chain.[16] We will say more about value chains in Chapter 6. To offer better value to the right customers, a firm must carefully chose *which* activities it performs and *when* it performs them.

Which Activities to Perform

Five criteria guide a firm's choice of which activities to perform (see Table 4.4). First, the activities should be consistent with the value that the firm is offering. If

TABLE 4.3 Evolution of Advertising Metrics for Portals

Metric	Definition	Comment
Number of hits	Count of each time data is requested from a server while a Web surfer is at a website. There may be more than one hit each time a user clicks a mouse.	Number of hits does not say much about the types of customers and what they were doing.
Page views	The number of individual HTML pages that a surfer pulls out while at a website.	Number of surfers who respond to an ad still not given.
Click-through	Percent of prospective customers who respond to an online advertisement.	No information on the customers themselves.
Unique visitors	Count of individuals using their internet protocol (IP) address.	
Reach	Percent of sampled users who visit a page on a specific website in a given month.	
Length of stay	How long the user has been on the website.	
Registered users	Measure of website users likely to come back.	
Repeat visitors	The number of visitors at a website for two or more times.	

Source: S. V. Haar, "Web Metrics: Go Figure." *Business 2.0* (June 1999), pp. 46–47.

a firm positions itself as a low cost or product differentiator, the activities that it performs should be consistent with that position. Dell Computer, for example, by going direct not only cut the cost of offering PCs to its customers (consistent with a low cost strategy), but also considerably cut down the time between the production of a computer and the time a customer receives it. If an e-tailer is going to offer 24-hour-a-day shopping, it must not only have the right software and customer service (easy-to-use website and Web reps) to match, but also should have the logistics to deliver the products on time.

Second, the activities should reinforce each other.[17] A well-constructed virtual storefront should be accompanied with appropriate promotions to help establish brand-name reputation. The performance of the storefront helps reinforce the effectiveness of the campaign while the campaign further boosts the perceived performance of the storefront. AOL may have all the portal services and content, but if the Last Mile to the house is very slow and its customers have to wait a long time for

TABLE 4.4 Which Activities to Perform and When

In choosing which activities to perform, management should ask itself if the activities:

- Are consistent with customer value and the scope of customers served?
- Reinforce each other?
- Take advantage of industry success drivers?
- Are consistent with any distinctive capabilities that the firm has or wants to build?
- Make the industry more attractive for the firm?

In choosing when to perform the activities, management should ask:

- What are the characteristics of the industry at this stage of the life cycle and what will they be down the line?
- What are existing competitors doing and what are potential ones likely to do?
- Are the activities consistent timewise?

responses to their inquiries, the value perceived by these customers will not be as high as if the Last Mile were faster.

Third, the activities should take advantage of industry success drivers—the factors that are likely to have the most impact on cost or differentiation. For example, Dell's excellent performance in the 1990s is often credited to the firm's decision to sell directly to business customers instead of going through distributors. The apparent success of the decision may rest on two key characteristics of the PC industry. The first is that the rate of technological change is very rapid, so PCs that sit on distributors' shelves can become obsolete if not sold quickly. By selling directly to customers, Dell was able to get the products to customers early enough for them to enjoy the latest that processors can offer, before new products rendered them obsolete. The second is that the prices of PCs drop very fast so the more the PCs wait at distributors, the less the manufacturer will get for the PCs when they are eventually sold. Moreover, by going direct Dell also avoids the large number of returns that PC makers often have to take from dealers.

The fourth criteria for choosing which activity to perform is that the activities should take advantage of any distinctive capabilities that a firm may have or that it can build. Wal-Mart claims that one of its core capabilities is logistics.[18] Thus, it would make sense for logistics to be one of the activities that it performs in e-tailing.

Finally, and probably most important, the activities should be geared toward making the industry more attractive to the firm. As we will see in Chapter 8, one benefit of performing an analysis of industry attractiveness is finding out why the industry is attractive or unattractive so that a firm can make the industry more attractive for itself; that is, through strategic action, a firm can increase its bargaining power over suppliers and customers, reduce rivalry, raise barriers to entry, and reduce the power of substitutes. Offering customers better value than competitors is a necessary condition for making profits, but it is not a sufficient condition. A good example illustrates this. Suppose an entrepreneurial firm uses its proprietary technology to develop a custom electronic fuel injector that uses microprocessors from Intel and is 30 percent more fuel efficient, but it works only with Ford cars. Clearly this is a highly differentiated product with enormous customer value, but it probably will not be very profitable for the entrepreneur. For one thing, Ford has bargaining power over the entrepreneur since it is the only automaker that can use the product. For another, Intel is the only firm that manufactures the microprocessor and, because sales to the entrepreneur are so small compared to the millions of microprocessors sold to PC makers, Intel also has bargaining power over the entrepreneur. Thus, the choice of activities should go beyond providing better value than competitors. The activities chosen should allow a firm to be in a better position to exploit the value that it offers customers—to make the industry more attractive for itself.

When to Perform Activities

When a firm decides to perform an activity is also critical. Industry characteristics evolve and so should the kinds of activities a firm performs to take advantage of industry profitability. The activities that firms perform in an industry are a function of where the technology is in that industry's life cycle. In the emerging phase, firms must decide how they are going to adopt the technology and what role they see that technology playing in their revenue streams. In the growth phase, firms must decide what the basis for their competitive technological advantage should be and invest accordingly.[19] For example, if an online stockbrokerage firm decides that its profits will come more from the interest that it earns from members who borrow on margin than from commissions, the firm may want to invest in acquiring clients with large accounts who are less likely to switch. A portal firm may want to invest in building its brand name to differentiate its website from those of numerous potential competitors. It is also important to take cues from the point at which customers are in their own technological evolution. For example, timing was one reason why going direct worked for Dell. The company implemented that strategy when its industry had evolved to a point where many businesses had management information systems (MIS) groups that could better determine their PC needs without the help of distributors.[20] Before then, most customers needed the hand-holding that dealers provided. The PC had also evolved to a point where some kind of a standard had emerged making it easier for firms to specify their needs in a PC.

Finally, when a firm chooses to perform some activities is also a function of what competitors are doing. If a firm's major competitors are acquiring cable companies to allow them to offer broadband service over the Last Mile to homes, the firm may want to do something about that. Finally, the sequence in which activities are performed is also important. If a firm advertises its financial services to lure customers, but then lacks the computer services to match, its reputation may be damaged.

IMPLEMENTATION

A firm's decision concerning what value to offer customers, which customers to offer this value to, how to price it, and what activities to perform is one thing. Actually carrying out the decision—its **implementation**—is another. We next discuss the role of implementation, highlighting the relationships between strategy, structure, systems, people, and environment.[21]

Structure

The structure of a firm tells us who is supposed to report to whom and who is responsible for what so that the activities a firm has chosen to perform are carried out. In searching for the right structure, three questions must be explored. First is the question of *coordination*. While performing their own activities, how do inbound logistics and operations, for example, manage to exchange information at the right times in order to offer customer value? How does the firm ensure that the right resources are available at the right cost when needed? Second is the problem of *differentiation* and *integration*. A firm's logistics and marketing groups are maintained as separate functions because each necessarily has to specialize in what it does in order to keep building the stock of knowledge that underpins its activities—each one has its own unique tasks and roles to play. This is differentiation. At the same time, offering customers value often entails cross-functional interaction; that is, the differentiated activities of the different functions must be integrated for optimal value.[22]

Organizational structures are some variation of two major types: *functional* and *project*. In the **functional organizational structure**, people are grouped and perform their tasks according to traditional functions such as inbound logistics, R&D, operations, marketing, and so on. Grouping people together with similar competencies and knowledge enables them to learn from each other and to increase the firm's stock of knowledge in the particular area. Communication is largely vertical, up and down the hierarchy of each function.

In the **project organizational structure**, employees are organized not by functional area but by the project they are working on. For example, if the project is to develop a minivan, employees from marketing, design, manufacturing, engines, and other relevant functions are assigned to the project and work for the project manager, not their functional managers. Communication is largely lateral, an advantage for innovation.

Organizational structures also can be characterized as *organic* or *mechanistic*.[23] First, in the **organic organizational structure**, communications are lateral, not vertical as with **mechanistic organizational structures**; that is, product designers talk directly to marketing employees rather than through their boss. This allows for a better exchange of ideas. Second, in the organic structure, employees with the most influence are those with technological skills or marketing knowledge and not those ranking high in the organizational hierarchy. This allows them to make the best-informed decisions. Third, job responsibilities are more loosely defined in the organic structure, giving employees more opportunities to be receptive to new ideas and more objective about how best to use these ideas. Finally, the organic structure emphasizes the exchange of information rather than a one-way flow of information from some central authority as in the mechanistic structure.

Systems

An organizational structure tells us who does what but very little about how to keep people motivated as they carry out their assigned tasks and responsibilities.[24] Management must be able to monitor performance and reward and punish individuals, functions, divisions, and organizations in some agreed upon and understood way. For employees of many start-ups, the payoff at the initial public offering (IPO) is a strong incentive. In these firms, systems must be in place whereby information will flow in the shortest possible time to the right targets for decision making. In addition to performance and reward systems, information flow systems are critical. These can be grouped into information and communication technologies and the physical layout of the building. The Internet makes it possible for the CEO of Microsoft, for example, to see new product ideas from an engineer deep down the organizational hierarchy via electronic mail or an intranet. If such information had to pass up the organizational ladder, it would take much longer and face a good chance of distortion. An area manager for a U.S. multinational corporation who is resident in France does not have to go through loops to obtain information on a new product being developed in the United States. All she needs to do is go to the company's website in the company's intranet to get undistorted, up-to-date information on the product. A German driver should be able to test-drive a car in a virtual reality site in Stuttgart knowing that the results will be fed instantly to designers in Detroit, Los Angeles, and Tokyo.

People

Establishing control and reward systems to motivate employees, and building information systems that provide them with the best information for decision making is one thing. Whether these people are motivated or not, or make the right decisions with the available information, is another. This is a function of many questions: To what extent do employees share common goals? Is the manager of the brake division of an automobile manufacturer interested in building a personal empire or doing the best he can to make sure that the company builds the best car possible in the shortest possible time with the best brake system that can be manufactured in the most efficient manner? Does the manufacturing group see R&D as a "bunch of ivory tower, money-spending snobs" or colleagues with whom they can work to build the best cars in the shortest possible time at the lowest cost? To what extent do employees have the knowledge that underpins the various activities of the firm's value chain? How much is such knowledge valued? What really is the core competence of the firm and where does it reside—in people or organizational routines and endowments of the firm? What does it take to motivate employees? Paychecks, job security, stock options, implementation of their ideas, earning respect, or being "seen" as a person? Does management see unions as the adversary or part of a team with shared goals that is there as part of the checks and balances necessary to keep on course toward the firm's goals? Are managers leaders or systematic planners?

Recognizing the Potential of Innovation

The literature in technology management suggests that five kinds of individuals have been identified to play key roles in recognizing the potential of an innovation: idea generators, gatekeepers, boundary spanners, champions, and sponsors.[25] The more effective each of these individuals is, the better the chance a firm has in recognizing the potential of an innovation. For example, **champions** are individuals who take an idea (theirs or that of an idea generator) for a new product/service and do all they can within their power to ensure its success. By actively promoting the idea and communicating and inspiring others with their vision of the innovation, champions can help their organization realize its potential. Thus, champions with charisma and an ability to articulate their vision of a product/service to others are more effective than those that do not.[26]

Having **gatekeepers** and **boundary spanners** is critical to collecting information. A gatekeeper is an individual within a firm who understands the idiosyncrasies of the firm and those of the outside. It acts as a transducer between the firm and the outside world during the exchange of information that often takes place during technological innovation. Without ties to any particular functional organization, project, or product in the firm, gatekeepers are more likely to be objective when collecting new ideas from the outside. The danger is that a gatekeeper may also develop the same information filters that successful functions have. Some human resource practices ensure that two promotional ladders are present in their firms: a technical ladder and the more traditional administrative one. The idea is to free inventors or gatekeepers from administrative tasks so they can spend their time doing what they do best and still get rewarded as much as the administrative stars who get promoted to management positions. Boundary spanners play the role of gatekeepers between a team and an organization.

Organizational Culture

How well people perform their roles in the firm is a function of a firm's culture. **Organizational culture** is a system of shared values (what is important) and beliefs (how things work) that interact with the organization's people, organizational structures, and systems to produce behavioral norms (the way we do things around here).[27] Whether a culture is good at recognizing the potential of an innovation is a function of the type of culture. An entrepreneurial culture that keeps employees on the lookout for new ideas and holds the employees in high esteem when they turn those ideas into new products can be an asset in recognizing the potential of an innovation. However, some cultures can lead to evils such as the Not Invented Here (NIH) syndrome.

Different firms use different strategies to avoid such evils. For example, Sony looks for people who are *neyaka*, that is, open-minded, optimistic, and wide-ranging in their interests. It also prefers generalists compared to specialists. Sony's founder, Masuru Ibuka, says "Specialists are inclined to argue why you can't do something, while our emphasis has always been to make something out of nothing."[28]

CAPABILITIES

Resources

To perform the activities that underpin customer value, firms need resources. These **resources** can be grouped into tangible, intangible, and human.[29] *Tangible resources* are both physical and financial, the types usually identified and accounted for under assets in financial statements. These include plants, equipment, and cash reserves. For some Internet start-ups, these are their computers, pipes over the Last Mile to homes, and the money raised through IPOs. *Intangible resources* are the nonphysical and nonfinancial assets that are usually not accounted for in financial statements.[30] These include patents, copyrights, reputation, brands, trade secrets, relationships with customers, relationships between employees, and knowledge embedded in different forms such as databases containing the vital statistics of customers and market research findings. For many portals, ISPs, and e-tailers, these are their software, databases of visitor or customer profiles, copyrights, brands, and client communities. *Human resources* are the skills and knowledge that employees carry with them. For

Internet firms, these are the knowledge and skills embedded in employees on every-thing from how to code software to how to design and implement business plans.

Competencies

Resources in and of themselves do not make customer value and profits. Customers would not scramble to a firm's doors because the firm has great plants, geniuses, or a war chest from an initial public offering. Resources must be converted into some-thing that customers want. The ability or capacity of a firm to turn its resources into customer value and profits is usually called a **capability or competence**.[31] This usually entails the use or integration of more than one resource. G. M. Hamel and C. K. Prahalad argued that a firm's capabilities or competencies are core when they meet three criteria: customer value, competitor differentiation, and extendibility.[32] The *customer value* criteria requires that a core competence must make an unusu-ally high contribution to the value that customers perceive. For example, in the late 1980s and early 1990s Apple Computer's expertise in developing graphical user interface (GUI) software made its computers among the most user-friendly. A com-petence is *competitor differentiating* if it is uniquely held or, if widely held, the firm's level of competence is higher than that of its competitors. Many companies have the ability to develop user-friendly interfaces, but Apple Computer's Macin-tosh GUI remains, arguably, the most user-friendly. A competence is *extendable* if it is used in more than one product area. For example, Honda's ability to design excellent engines has allowed it to offer engines not only for cars but also for portable electric generators, lawn mowers, and marine vehicles.

Competitive Advantage

A firm's core competencies allow it to have a **competitive advantage** because, by definition, they allow the firm to offer its customers better value than competitors. The extent to which this advantage is sustainable is a function of how inimitable and difficult to substitute the capabilities are. Three reasons have been offered for why it may be very difficult to replicate or acquire distinctive capabilities.[33] First, it may be difficult to replicate the historical context in which the capabilities were developed. Caterpillar's worldwide service network of people trained in servicing its earth-moving equipment has its foundation in World War II, when its machines were the machines of choice by Allied forces in Europe. After the war many ser-vicepeople who returned to the civilian workforce had the skills and knowledge to service Caterpillar equipment. A firm would find it very costly to build an identi-cal network. Second, it may take time to develop these capabilities, giving first movers an advantage that is difficult to overcome. Merck's ability to get its drugs through clinical testing and approval by the U.S. Food and Drug Administration is outstanding. It rests on the relationships that the firm has created over the years with different physicians, research centers, and hospitals. These relationships can-not be created overnight. Third, to begin with, it may be very difficult to identify the core competence and even more difficult to find out how to copy it. What really constitutes Honda's ability to offer outstanding engines? How does one copy that? Answering these questions is difficult, suggesting that replicating the capability is also very difficult.

If a firm's business model enables it to gain a competitive advantage, the chances are that its competitors would like to catch up or maybe even leapfrog it. What can a firm do to maintain its competitive advantage? To sustain a competitive advantage, a firm can—depending on its capabilities, environment, and technology in question—pursue some subset of three generic strategies: *block, run,* and *team-up.*[34]

In the **block strategy**, a firm tries to erect barriers around its business model to prevent others from imitating it. For example, Priceline.com took a patent on its reverse auction model to prevent imitators from easily copying that part of its business model. Copyrights, unique capabilities, patents, and the threat of retaliation all constitute instruments for blocking. The problem with blocking is that competitors can always find a way around it. Moreover, the usefulness of blockades lasts only until discontinuities such as deregulation/regulation, changing customer preferences and expectations, or radical technological change render them obsolete.

A **run strategy** admits that perfect protection is not always possible. Sitting behind barriers only gives competitors time to catch up. The innovator must run; that is, it must keep innovating its business model. Often, however, a firm cannot do it all alone. It must team up with others through some kind of alliance, joint venture, or acquisition.

In the **team-up strategy**, a firm can pool others' resources to strengthen its business model. For example, users who accessed AOL's service in the 1990s using slower technologies, such as twisted copper wires, often found that they had to wait longer than they would like. Since speed is part of the value that customers get from using portals, AOL wanted more for its customers. By teaming up with a firm that could provide fast access over the Last Mile to homes and businesses, AOL could greatly improve its service. That is why its teaming up with Time Warner in early 2000 made sense. We will further explore the roles of block, run, and team-up strategies in the dynamics of business models in Chapter 5.

SUMMARY

A firm's business model is critical to its ability to gain and maintain a competitive advantage—it is critical to the firm's profitability. The success of a firm's business model in the face of the Internet challenge is a function of the type of value that it offers customers, the type of customers to which it offers that value, the range of products or services that contain the value, how it prices that value, the types of revenue sources it pursues, the way the activities that undergird customer value creation work as a system, the implementation of the activities and value creation, the capabilities on which value-creating activities rest, and the strategies used to sustain the firm's competitive advantage. How much of a competitive advantage is also a function of the extent to which the firm, in designing and executing its business model, takes advantage of those factors that make its industry attractive or unattractive as a result of the impact of the Internet.

Again, using the deceptively simple relationship, Profits $= \Pi = (P - V_c)Q - F_c$, we can see how each of the components of a business model impacts profitability. If a firm can offer its customers something distinctive (i.e., competitors cannot imitate it), it can afford to charge premium prices, P, for it. This leads to higher profits. If its per unit costs, V_c, are low, Π is higher. The more people in a particular market segment that can buy the product, the higher the quantity Q will be. The more each of the customers in the segment is willing to pay for the product, the higher P becomes. Pricing ensures that a firm gets paid for the value that it offers customers and not leave money on the table. It can also be used to gain a large market share early and build switching costs at customers ensuring a higher Q. Different revenue sources mean a higher Q and the appropriate $P-V_c$. Well-connected activities and good implementation reinforce higher P, lower V_c, and higher Q. So does a good sustainability strategy.

KEY TERMS

advertising model   46
affiliate model   47
auction pricing   55
barter   55
block strategy   64
boundary spanners   61
brokerage model   46
business model   45
capabilities   48
champions   61
click-through   47
community model   47
competence   63
competitive advantage   63
connected activities   56
customer value   48
functional organizational
   structure   60
gatekeepers   61
implementation   59
infomediary model   47
knowledge-based products   52

lock-in   54
manufacturing model   47
mechanistic organizational structures   60
menu pricing   54
merchant model   47
network externalities   54
neyaka   62
one-to-one bargaining   54
organic organizational structure   60
organizational culture   62
pricing strategy   52
project organizational structure   60
resources   62
revenue sources   56
reverse auction   55
run strategy   64
scope   51
subscription models   47
sustainability   48
switching costs   54
team-up strategy   64
utility model   47

DISCUSSION QUESTIONS

1. What is the relationship between profitability, fixed costs, variable costs, margins, and market share for knowledge-based products? What is the significance of this relationship for strategy formulation?
2. Name three firms that are key players in e-business. What is the competitive advantage of each? Are these competitive advantages sustainable? If so, brainstorm possible events or circumstances which could reduce their sustainability.
3. Is the magnitude of the role played by each component of a business model a function of industry? If so, which components have the most impact in which industries?
4. Name an e-business company that has an innovative pricing model? How has the company benefited from this strategy? Is such a model sustainable?

5. Look for news on an e-business firm introducing a new product and/or service. Does this new activity fit the criteria listed in Table 4.4?

6. What is the relationship between core competencies and competitive advantage?

7. Search the news for the latest merger in the Internet business. Does this alliance make sense? Why or why not?

REFERENCES

1. Michael Rappa, "2000, Managing the Digital Enterprise: Business Models." http://ecommerce.ncsu.edu/topics/models/models.html; Paul Timmers, "Business Models for Electronic Markets," *Electronic Markets* 8, no. 2 (1998) pp. 3–8.

2. For details on this and other types of Internet business models, see Michael Rappa, "2000, Managing the Digital Enterprise."

3. "Advertising That Clicks," *The Economist,* October 9, 1999.

4. M. E. Porter, "Towards a Dynamic Theory of Strategy," *Strategic Management Journal* 12 (1991), pp. 95–117.

5. M. E. Porter, *Competitive Advantage: Creating and Sustaining Superior Performance* (New York: Free Press, 1985).

6. R. Amit and P. Schoemaker, "Strategic Assets and Organizational Rent," *Strategic Management Journal* 14 (1993), pp. 33–46; J. Mahoney and J. R. Pandian, "The Resource-Based View within the Conversation of Strategic Management," *Strategic Management Journal* 13 (1992), pp. 363–80; C. Helfat, "Know-how and Asset Complementarity and Dynamic Capability Accumulation: The Case of R&D," *Strategic Management Journal* 18 (1997), pp. 339–60; B. Wernerfelt, "A Resource-Based View of the Firm," *Strategic Management Journal* 5 (1984), pp. 171–80.

7. M. E. Porter, *Competitive Strategy: Techniques for Analyzing Industries and Competitors* (New York: Free Press, 1980).

8. M. E. Porter, *Competitive Strategy: Techniques for Analyzing Industries and Competitors* (New York: Free Press, 1980); J. B. Barney, *Gaining and Sustaining Competitive Advantage* (Reading, MA: Addison-Wesley, 1997).

9. R. D. Hof and L. Himelstein, "eBay vs Amazon.com." *Business Week,* May 31, 1999.

10. For a more detailed treatment of this very important marketing subject, see P. Kotler, *Marketing Management* (Englewood Cliffs, NJ: Prentice Hall, 1994).

11. M. E. Porter, "What Is Strategy?" *Harvard Business Review,* November–December 1996, pp. 61–78.

12. W. B. Arthur, "Increasing Returns and the New World of Business," *Harvard Business Review,* July–August 1996, pp, 100–09.

13. For a related example, see A. James, "Give It Away and Get Rich," *Fortune,* June 10, 1996, pp. 90–98.

14. "The Heyday of the Auction," *The Economist,* July 24, 1999.

15. See Amy Cortese, "E-Commerce: Good-Bye to Fixed Pricing?" *Business Week,* May 4, 1998, www.businessweek.com/1998/18/b3576023.

16. Porter, *Competitive Advantage.*

17. The first two criteria are from Porter, "What Is Strategy?" pp. 61–78.

18. According to Wal-Mart's CEO in 1999, the firm's core competencies are logistics and information technology.

19. R. M. Grant, *Contemporary Strategy Analysis: Concepts, Techniques, Applications* (Oxford: Blackwell, 1998).

20. D. B. Yoffie, J. Cohn, and D. Levy, "Apple Computer 1992," Harvard Business School case #9-792-081.

21. This section draws heavily on *Innovation Management: Strategies, Implementation and Profits,* Oxford University Press, 1998, pp. 99–106.

22. P. R. Lawrence and J. W. Lorsch, *Organization and Environments: Managing Differentiation and Integration* (Burr Ridge, IL: Richard D. Irwin, 1967).

23. See, for example, T. Burns and G. M. Stalker, *The Management of Innovation* (London: Tavistock, 1961) and S. P. Robbins, *Organizational Theory: Structure, Design and Applications* (Englewood Cliffs, NJ: Prentice Hall, 1987).

24. C. W. L. Hill and G. R. Jones, *Strategic Management: An Integrated Approach* (Boston: Houghton Mifflin, 1995), p. 352.

25. See, for example, *Innovation Management.*

26. J. M. Howell and C. A. Higgins, "Champions of Technological Innovation," *Administrative Sciences Quarterly* 35 (1990), pp. 317–41.

27. B. Uttal and J. Fierman, "The Corporate Culture Vultures," *Fortune,* October 17, 1983, pp. 66–73. For a detailed discussion on culture, see, for example, E. Schein, *Organizational Culture and Leadership* (San Francisco: Jossey-Bass, 1990).

28. B. Schlender and S. Solo, "How Sony Keeps the Magic Going," *Fortune,* February 24, 1992, pp. 76–83.

29. R. M. Grant, *Contemporary Strategy Analysis* (Malden, MA: Blackwell, 1995), p. 120.

30. Given the critical role that intangible resources play in market value, many firms are taking another look at their financial statement reporting. See, for example, T. A. Stewart, *Intellectual Capital: The New Wealth of Organizations* (New York: Currency/Doubleday, 1997).

31. There is a lot of outstanding research done in the so-called resource-based view of the firm. For the tip of the iceberg, see, for example, R. Amit and P. J. H. Schoemaker, "Strategic Assets and Organizational Rent," *Strategic Management Journal* 14, no. 1, (1993), pp. 33–46; J. B. Barney, "Firm Resources and Sustained Competitive Advantage," *Journal of Management* 17, no. 1 (1991), pp. 99–120; C. Helfat, "Know-how and Asset Complementarity and Dynamic Capability Accumulation: The Case of R&D," *Strategic Management Journal* 18 (1997), pp. 339–60. The terms *resources, endowments, assets, competencies,* and *capabilities* have been used to mean different things by different authors. The terminology we use here is the most common. See, for example, G. M. Hamel and C. K. Prahalad, "Letter," *Harvard Business Review,* May–June 1992, pp.164–65.

32. Hamel, G. M. and C. K. Prahalad, *Competing for the Future* (Boston: Harvard Business School Press, 1994).

33. J. B. Barney, "How a Firm's Capabilities Affect Boundary Decisions," *Sloan Management Review* 40, no. 3 (Spring 1999), pp. 137–45.

34. See *Innovation Management,* chap. 12.

CHAPTER 5

Dynamics and Appraisal of Business Models

In Chapter 4 we explored the components of a business model and the linkages between them. This exploration was largely static because we described a business model at a point in time and said nothing about what would happen to the model in the face of change. We said very little about the changes in the components and linkages of a firm's business model that take place over time, either in response to the environment or to events initiated by the firm. Nor did we say much—beyond the description of the components and their linkages—about what constitutes a good or bad business model. In this chapter we explore the dynamics of business models and offer a method for appraising them (see Figure 5.1). We begin with a brief discussion of three generic strategies that play a key role in building business models to attain and maintain a competitive advantage. We then explore when each strategy is appropriate. Next we discuss the implications of the Internet for start-ups and incumbent bricks-and-mortar businesses. We conclude with a discussion of how to appraise a business model.

FIGURE 5.1 Role of Business Model Dynamics in Firm Performance

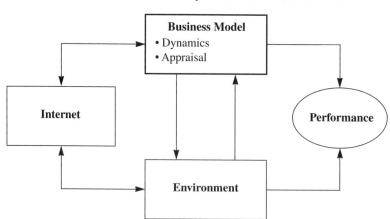

In the world of the Internet, nothing is static. Firms with a competitive advantage must find ways to defend it if they want to maintain it. Performance laggards want to improve their performance and possibly leapfrog those competitors with an advantage. There is also the constant threat of potential new entrants. On top of all that, the technology itself is evolving; what was the right move yesterday might not be today. Initiating or responding to change in an effort to sustain an advantage or gain one usually entails some combination of three generic strategies: block, run, or team-up.[1]

Block Strategy

In the **block strategy**, a firm erects barriers around its product market space. A firm can block in two ways. First, if its capabilities in any of the components of the business model are inimitable and distinctive enough to offer customers unique value, the firm can limit access to them and thereby keep out competitors. That would be the case, for example, when a firm has **intellectual property** (e.g., patents, copyrights, software applications, domain assets, service marks, trademarks, and trade secrets) that can be protected and sends signals to potential imitators that it means business in protecting the property. Amazon.com's 1999 lawsuit against barnesandnoble.com, charging the latter with copying its "1-Click" technology, is one such signal. Second, if all firms are equally capable of performing these activities, incumbents may still prevent entry by signaling that post-entry prices will be low. There are several ways a firm can achieve this.[2] For example, it can establish a reputation for retaliating against anyone who tries to imitate any component of its business model. It can also do so by making heavy, non-reversible investments in relevant assets. For example, if a firm spends billions of dollars installing fiber optics capability for all the households in a town, the chances are that it will lower prices if another firm wants to offer high-speed access to the same customers. In general, such signals can prevent profit-motivated potential competitors from entering.

Blocking works only as long as a company's capabilities are unique and inimitable or as long as barriers to entry last. But competitors can, for example, circumvent patents and copyrights or challenge them in court until they are overturned. Moreover, the usefulness of such capabilities lasts only until discontinuities such as deregulation/regulation, changing customer preferences and expectations, or radical technological change render them obsolete. The information asymmetry reduction property of the Internet also suggests that blocking is not going to be very effective. With the Internet, learning about competitors' products, the technologies that underpin them, and how to reverse-engineer these products is considerably easier. A software developer that once depended on the scarcity of distribution channels to keep out competitors, for example, can no longer do so since new entrants can now sell their products over the Internet. With the databases on patents available on the Internet, an imitator can quickly search through its own patents and those of its target competitors and be in a better position to challenge the patents or to determine what it needs to leapfrog the competitor. Special relations with customers that gave a firm an advantage may no longer do so because customers can solicit bids from many more suppliers over the Internet.

Run Strategy

The **run strategy** admits that blockades to entry, no matter how formidable they may appear, are often penetrable or eventually fall. Sitting behind these blockades only gives competitors time to catch up or leapfrog the innovator. An innovator often has to run. *Running* means changing some subset of components or linkages of business models or reinventing the whole business model to offer customers better value. In the 1990s Dell Computer often introduced new ways of selling its personal computers (PCs) before competitors copied its existing sales strategy. Running can give a firm many first-mover advantages, including the ability to control parts of its own environment. In an age of rapid technological change, the run strategy becomes extremely important because blocking is more difficult. Running sometimes means the **cannibalization**—introduction of new products that render existing ones less competitive, thereby eating into existing sales—of one's own products before competitors do. Intel Corporation offers a very good example. In the late 1980s and 1990s it usually introduced a new generation of microprocessors before unit sales of an existing one had peaked. If Intel had not done so, despite its microcode copyrights, other firms would have found a way to catch up.[3]

Team-up Strategy

Sometimes, a firm simply cannot do it all alone. It must pursue a **team-up strategy** with others through some kind of strategic alliance, joint venture, acquisition, or equity position. Teaming up allows a firm to share in resources that it does not possess and may not want to acquire or cannot acquire even if it wanted to. Shared resources also facilitate knowledge transfer. Teaming up has its disadvantages too. It is not easy for a firm to protect its technology or other aspects of its business model that it would like to keep proprietary. In teaming up, a firm also risks becoming too dependent on another firm's resources. Often, running also requires teaming up. For example, developing some chips on time may require more resources than one firm can afford, necessitating teaming up—witness the Toshiba, IBM, and Siemens alliance to develop the 256M memory chip.

Attaining and maintaining a competitive advantage often requires some combination of the three strategies. An important question is, When is each strategy or combination of strategies appropriate? Two factors influence the choice of strategy. First, the choice depends on what it takes for a firm to build a profitable business model. It depends on what determines profitability in the face of the technology in question. After all, a business model is about how to make money over the long term. Second, timing is of the essence. The strategy pursued is a function of the stage of evolution of the technology—the Internet in our case. It is also a function of when existing and potential competitors have pursued related strategies or plan to.

IT TAKES COMPLEMENTARY ASSETS TOO

In developing business models to exploit a technological change, it is important to remember that *it takes more than technology to profit from technology.*

Complementary Asset Framework

David Teece argued that two things determine the extent to which a firm can profit from its invention or technology: imitability and complementary assets (see Figure 5.2).[4] **Imitability** is the extent to which the technology can be copied, substituted, or leapfrogged by competitors. Low imitability may derive from the intellectual property protection of the technology or from the failure of potential imitators to have what it takes.[5] **Complementary assets** are all other capabilities—apart from those that underpin the technology or invention—that the firm needs to exploit the technology. These include brand name, manufacturing, marketing, distribution channels, service, reputation, installed base of products, relationships with clients or suppliers, and complementary technologies.

Figure 5.2 suggests when a firm is likely to profit from an innovation in this model. When imitability is high, it is difficult for an innovator to make money if complementary assets are easily available or unimportant (cell I in Figure 5.2). If, however, complementary assets are tightly held and important, the owner of such assets makes money (cell II). For example, CAT scanners were easy to imitate and EMI, the inventor, did not have complementary assets such as distribution channels and the relations with U.S. hospitals that are critical to selling such expensive medical equipment. General Electric had these assets and quickly captured the leadership position by imitating the innovation. Coca-Cola and Pepsi were able to profit from RC Cola's diet and caffeine-free cola inventions because they had the brand-name reputation and distribution channels that RC did not, and the innovations were easy to imitate.

When imitability is low, the innovator stands to profit from it if complementary assets are freely available or unimportant (cell IV). For example, the inventor of the Stradivarius violin profited enormously because no one could imitate it, and complementary assets for it were neither difficult to acquire nor important. When

FIGURE 5.2 Who Profits from Innovation

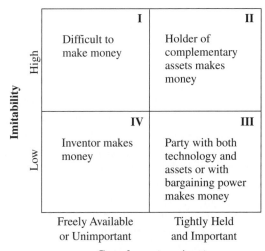

imitability is low as in cell III and complementary assets are important and difficult to acquire, whoever has both or the more important of the two wins. The better negotiator can also make money. Pixar's interaction with Disney is a good example. Imitability of some of its digital studio technology is somewhat low given the software copyrights it holds and the combination of technology and creativity it takes to deliver a compelling animation movie. But offering customers movies made with that technology requires distribution channels, brandname recognition, and financing which are tightly held by the likes of Disney and Sony Pictures. Before *Toy Story,* Disney had the bargaining power because it had all the complementary assets, and the technology had not been proven. After the success of *Toy Story,* when Pixar proved that it could combine technology and creativity—something that is more difficult to imitate than plain computer animation—there was a shift in bargaining power to Pixar which was able to renegotiate a better deal.[6]

Implications for Internet Business Models and Generic Strategies

Does this mean that a firm that finds itself in cell I should give up on making money? Of course not! It means that such a firm should take this important piece of information—that it is easy to imitate its technology and that complementary assets are either unimportant or easy to come by—into consideration as it develops and executes its business model. A firm in cell I can pursue a run strategy (see Figure 5.3); that is, since its technology can be easily imitated, the firm keeps innovating. By the time competitors catch up with yesterday's technology, the firm has moved on to tomorrow's technology. The more frequently encountered case is that of cell II: although complementary assets are tightly held and important, the technology is easy to imitate. The firm must develop the complementary assets internally or get them by teaming up with someone else. Either way, the key thing is timing. If the firm decides to build internally, it must do so before competitors with complementary assets have had a chance to copy the technology. If the firm is going to team up, it must do so while it still has something to bring to the table—while potential partners have not yet imitated the technology. As defined earlier, teaming up means forming some kind of partnership (e.g., joint venture, strategic alliance, or an acquisition) with a firm that has the important complementary assets (Figure 5.3). It can also mean offering the firm for acquisition by another firm that has the complementary assets.

In the early part of their life cycles, many Internet start-ups are positioned in either cell I or cell II, but they are chiefly in cell II since their exploitation of the technology is easy to imitate or substitute, and complementary assets are important. Through advertising, promotion, and performance, the start-up firms can build brand names, a large number of clients, customer databases, or communities before competitors have had time to imitate their technologies or build similar complementary assets. For this strategy of developing complementary assets to be successful, it is important that the firm builds in switching costs for its clients and customers. Given the network externalities feature of the Internet, switching costs can be network size. For example, the larger a community or number of clients, the more valuable it is to members and the more difficult it is for a member to switch to a lesser community. AOL, eBay, Amazon.com, and many others pursued these strategies early

FIGURE 5.3 Strategies for Building Business Models

	Freely Available or Unimportant	Tightly Held and Important
High	**I** Run	**II** Team-up • Joint venture • Strategic alliance • Acquisition Internal development
Low	**IV** Block	**III** Block Team-up • Joint venture • Strategic alliance • Acquisition

Imitability (vertical axis, High/Low)

Complementary Assets (horizontal axis)

in their life cycles. Amazon.com also continued to develop the software capabilities that allowed it to keep moving—first into books and music, then electronics, then auctions, then toys, then zShop, then home improvement, and so on.

In cell III, a firm can pursue one of two strategies: block or team-up. If it has both the technology and complementary assets, it can protect both. The danger is that sooner or later most technologies are imitated or become obsolete. Imitation or obsolescence moves the firm from cell III to cell II (in Figure 5.3) where it can use its complementary assets to team up with someone who has the new technology. In a world where technology is difficult to imitate but complementary assets are easy to come by (cell IV), a firm depends on protecting that technology if it is going to make money. Very few firms, especially those exploiting the Internet, can be found in cell IV.

At this point, an important decision for a firm that decides to team up, block, form a joint venture or strategic alliance is when to do so. The decision depends on timing.

TIMING

Everything has its time. So do good business models and strategies. A business model or strategy that is appropriate early in the evolution of a technology may no longer be so when the technology is mature. One that works when a firm is the first in a market may not work when the firm is a follower.

A Technology Life Cycle Model and the Internet

Technology life cycle models have been used as a framework for understanding the evolving competitive landscape following a technological change and the consequences for firm strategy (see Figure 5.4). According to these models, there is a great deal of product and market uncertainty in the emerging or **fluid phase** at the onset of an innovation.[7] Firms are not quite sure what should go into the product.

FIGURE 5.4 Internet Technology Life Cycle

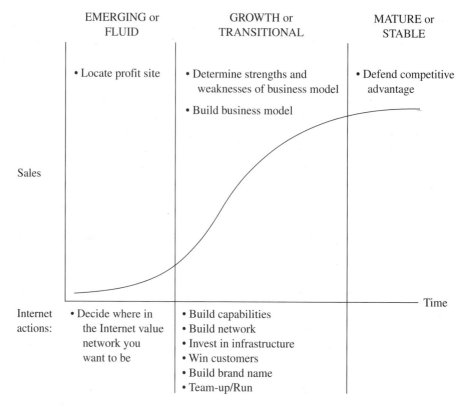

Customers too may not know what they want in the product. There is competition between the new and old technologies as well as between different designs using the new technology. Firms interact with their local environment of suppliers, customers, complementors, and competitors to resolve both technological and market uncertainties. Product quality is low, and cost and prices are high, as economies of scale and learning have yet to set in. Market penetration is low and customers are largely **lead users**—customers whose needs are similar to those of other users except that they have these needs months or years before most of the marketplace[8]—or high-income users. At this time, firms must place their strategic bets by choosing where in the value chain or network they want to exploit the technological change. By the year 2000, this stage had passed for many industries using the Internet. This was the stage when firms made their initial decisions about their location in the Internet value network: as an ISP, backbone supplier, content supplier or as a firm utilizing the Internet to transform some part of its existing value chain or value network, or some subset of these.

The technology enters the **growth phase** when some standardization of components, market needs, and product design features takes place, and a standard or common framework emerges signaling a substantial reduction in uncertainty, experimentation, and major changes. The customer base increases from lead and high-income users to mass market during the growth phase. At this time a firm should determine where it excels or wants to excel and try to reinforce or build upon that. In 2000 the

Internet was in the growth phase for many industries. The Web had emerged as a standard. Firms were building their networks (for externalities), establishing brands, winning customers, and modifying their initial bets as uncertainty unfolded. America Online (AOL), for example, spent a lot of money to increase the number of members in its network. It bought Netscape to increase its online membership and invested in Hughes Electronics to give its customers access to high-speed lines. AOL, Amazon.com, E*Trade, and Ameritrade advertised to increase brand-name recognition. AOL bought Mirabilis Ltd., for its Instant Communications and chat technology to boost the technical foundation for building a sense of community in its network. It also had struck contracts for developing content for its members.

In the **mature phase** (or specific phase), products built around the common framework or standard proliferate. Products are highly defined with differences fewer than similarities between competing products. Demand growth slows considerably with most output earmarked to satisfy replacement needs. Here a firm's strategies focus on defending its position and watching out for the next technological change that could start the life cycle over again. As of 2000, this next phase had yet to arrive for the Internet.

Implications for Generic Strategies

Before exploring the implications of the life cycle model for Internet firm strategies, it is important to note that different industries usually experience a technological change at different times.[9] Business-to-consumer (B2C) and consumer-to-consumer (C2C) were first, followed by business-to-business (B2B). Within each of these groups, different industries and firms within each industry adopted the technology at different times.

In the fluid phase, potential new entrants make their bets concerning where they want to locate in the value network that we discussed in Chapter 2. Choosing where to locate is not an exact science, but an entrepreneur can make a more informed decision with data on three factors: First, an entrepreneur should determine the problems that can be solved at each of the potential product market positions, what kind of value the firm can offer customers in solving the problem, and what it takes to get the other components of a business model in place. Second, an entrepreneur should perform an industry analysis to learn more about the attractiveness of the industry in question. (We will say more about industry analysis in Chapter 8.) Third, it should determine its capabilities and capabilities gaps in what it takes to craft and execute a winning business model for each product market position. Data from all three factors are critical in making a choice in what product market position to locate. Since a standard or dominant design/solution has not yet emerged in the fluid phase, it is important for the firm to learn as much as possible about the different design/solution options while establishing relationships with those who can tip the scales in the standards/dominant design race. In particular, teaming up with lead users can be critical because a firm can learn much from such customers about the emerging applications of the technology. It is also important to pay attention to lead products/service or so-called killer applications. Adult entertainment appears to be one of the early killer applications in the B2C and C2C businesses and can provide some valuable lessons.

During the growth phase, when a dominant solution or design has emerged, a firm should appraise its business model and determine its strengths and weaknesses.

From this appraisal, the firm can determine which elements to reinforce and which ones to build. In the case of the Internet, this means teaming up with firms that have complementary assets or technology. It also means teaming up to build a larger network of clients, customers, or community. Advertising (to build brand equity) and nonreversible investments all prepare for blocking later in the life cycle. Given how easy it is to imitate Internet business models, firms must keep introducing changes in the models or their components. Amazon.com's continuous extension of its capabilities illustrates how a firm keeps making incremental innovations to its business model.

INCUMBENTS: BRICKS-AND-MORTAR

While our discussion so far is applicable to start-ups and incumbents alike, incumbents carry some baggage along with advantages that deserve separate treatment. **Incumbents** are firms that were part of their industries prior to the industry's adoption of the Internet. Each of these firms had a business model, delivered some value to its customers, targeted particular segments of customers, focused on certain revenue sources, had pricing strategies, developed well-connected sets of activities, implemented the bricks-and-mortar strategy well, built certain capabilities, and may have sustained an advantage over some period. In the face of the Internet, some or all of the components of bricks-and-mortar models could be rendered obsolete. The question now is, How can these firms build profitable Internet business models, given their bricks-and-mortar models?

An incumbent's ability to conceive and execute a profitable Internet business model depends on the firm's incentives to invest in the new technology, and on the firm's bricks-and-mortar capabilities.

Incentive to Invest: Impact on Existing Products

A technological change usually results in products or services that render existing products and services noncompetitive, enhances them, or allows the old and new to coexist. If a change results in products or services that render existing products noncompetitive, it is said to be a **radical innovation** in the economic sense. In that case, incumbents in the industry with dominant market positions may be reluctant to invest in the new technology for fear of cannibalizing their existing products or services.[10] However, the realization that if they do not cannibalize their own products, someone else will, usually gives incumbents the incentive to invest in the new technology.

If the change results in enhancing existing products/services or allows them to remain competitive, it is said to be an **incremental innovation**. In that case, incumbents in the industry have an incentive to invest in the new technology.

Two things should be noted in these definitions of technological change. First, defining a technological innovation as radical or incremental in the economic sense is a matter of degree. In many radical innovations, some old products may still remain competitive. Also, most incremental innovations cannibalize existing products to some extent. Second, major technological changes usually create new markets. For example, new online stockbrokerage firms attracted investors such as day traders who ordinarily would have stayed away from the stock market.

Competence Enhancing or Destroying

It is not unusual that some firms with an incentive to invest in a technological change—and that did invest in it—still fail to exploit the technology.[11] This suggests that it takes more than an incentive to invest in a new technology in order to profit from it. Success is also a function of the extent to which the capabilities (knowledge, skills, assets, relationships) that underpin the new technology build on existing ones or are radically different. If the capabilities to exploit the new technology are very different from existing ones, the change is said to be radical, or **competence destroying**, in the organizational sense.[12] For example, the capabilities that were required to develop electronic point-of-sale (POS) registers were very different from those required to develop the old mechanical cash registers. Thus, electronic POS registers were a radical technological change in the cash register industry.

There are two reasons why incumbents in industries that face radical or competence destroying technological changes often have difficulty hanging onto any competitive advantage they held prior to the change. First, because their capabilities have been rendered obsolete, they do not have the ability to perform well with the new technology. Second and more important, the old capabilities are a handicap to the incumbent's pursuit of the new technology. As Compaq found out, for example, a firm's links with channels that were critical in the bricks-and-mortar world can stifle its attempts to take full advantage of the Internet. Listening too often to large customers who are not yet ready to move to the Internet can also delay a firm's efforts to exploit the technology. Also, learning new ways of doing things means discarding the old ways first.[13] Unlike incumbents, **new entrants** do not have old knowledge to unlearn. If those in power in an organization derive their power from the old technology, they will not let the old technology die since their power will die with it. One reason why IBM had problems with the PC was that most of its executives derived their power from the mainframes threatened by the PC.

The positive side of the capabilities story for incumbents is that despite the competence destroying technological changes, many of the firms' complementary assets such as distribution channels, relations with customers, and brand-name reputations are left intact.[14] New entrants do not have these capabilities and incumbents can use them to their advantage.

On the other hand, if an innovation is incremental because the capabilities required to exploit the new technology build on the firms' existing capabilities, the innovation is said to be **competence enhancing**. Most technological changes are incremental and incumbents usually reinforce their competitive advantages.

The Internet: A Disruptive Technology?

For many industries, the Internet is a **disruptive technology** that threatens the basis of bricks-and-mortar competitive advantage and presents new competitors with a chance to enter the industries. The basis for competitive advantage is being challenged because of one factor, or a combination of three. First, the value that the Internet allows firms to offer their customers is superior, or stands to be superior, to that offered by bricks-and-mortar incumbents. Take banking. With the Internet, banks are no longer limited to their local bricks and mortar; potentially, they have access to customers all over a country or the world. Service is available 24 hours a day and customers can examine their accounts at anytime. Such service requires an entirely different set of capabilities. Consider a less obvious but nevertheless important example of why the Internet is a disruptive technology. In the automobile industry, distribution can account for one-third of the sticker price of an automobile in the industry's bricks-and-mortar system.[15] The primary reason for the high distribution cost is the industry's supply-push system—especially in the United States—in which automakers build large numbers of cars without paying enough attention to customer needs, and then put pressure on dealers to sell the cars. Where supply outweighs demand, automakers offer huge discounts and marketing promotions. With the Internet, firms can better collect and analyze data on their customers and offer them the cars they want. This reduces unnecessary discounting, marketing promotion, and inventory holding costs.

Second, the way key activities in the industry's value chain used to be performed has been radically changed. For example, software and music used to be sold to customers through distributors. The Internet allows software and music developers to distribute their products over the Web. Auctions depend on getting people together and having them bid for items—the more people, the better. Thanks to its universality property, the Internet brings more people together than bricks-and-mortar auctions. Another less obvious but good example is Cisco. It was estimated that Cisco, which earned $1.4 billion in profits in 1999, saved about $500 million that year by using the Internet at various stages of its value chain.[16] Customers placed their orders on the company's website. Prior to the creation of the site, as many as 33 percent of customer orders were inaccurate. The website eliminated nearly all the errors. After-sales support groups also use the Web for help in configuring and integrating the network equipment bought from Cisco into their own systems, freeing Cisco engineers to tackle other tasks. Furthermore, Cisco's customers not only share information with each other on how to use Cisco's products in different systems, but also share information with Cisco so that the firm can develop better next-generation products. Closing the company's quarterly accounts, which used to take 10 days, was performed in only 2 days when Cisco started using the Web. Travel and expenses were also put on the Web and reimbursement time fell to two days. Procurement, employee benefits, and recruitment are also placed on the Web. Suppliers know which components to ship to what Cisco manufacturing site by accessing the company's custom software on its website. Most firms, like Cisco, not only save on costs but gain in accuracy of performing activities and in offering better customer value.

Third, the Internet has overturned the primary basis for industry success. For example, industries whose competitive advantage rested largely on information asymmetries face a serious threat from new entrants. These include real estate, travel, airline and concert ticketing, car dealerships, and stockbrokerages. Prior to the Internet, real estate agents had easy access to multiple housing listings, local chamber of commerce information, and knowledge of neighborhoods. Travel agents had access to airline schedules and pricing that travelers did not have. Car dealers had information on car features and prices that customers lacked. Stockbrokers had access to investment research and to timely stock quotes that most investors did not have. The Internet makes all that information available to customers.

Adopting the Internet: Separate Entity or a Unit Within?

One question faced by those incumbents for whom the Internet is a disruptive change is whether to develop the technology within the existing bricks-and-mortar organization or create a separate legal entity. There are many arguments for creating a separate legal entity. Doing so avoids the dominant managerial logic of the old bricks-and-mortar organization which can only hurt the new endeavor. It avoids the political haggling that can crush a fledgling group within the incumbent. The separate legal entity attracts more talent that would prefer to work in the entrepreneurial environment of a start-up and participate in the potential payoff of an initial public offering (IPO). If the group is within a larger corporation, the criteria of strategy, structure, system, people, and environment (S³PE) suggest that the firm now needs two very disparate compensation systems within the same organization, which can cause equity problems. The fear of the cannibalization of existing products/services takes attention away from the longer-term issues of the Internet. Finally, if the valuations of dot-com companies are high relative to their bricks-and-mortar competitors, a separate legal entity could raise a lot more and cheaper capital through an IPO. There are also good arguments for developing new technology within. Most incumbents have complementary assets that can be used. By developing the group within, the bricks-and-mortar personnel can learn from it. Moreover, the firm would not have to worry about the painful process of integrating the entity into the larger organization later. In any case, the option that is best for a firm depends on the firm, its business model, and industry.

APPRAISING BUSINESS MODELS

Given the central role that business models play in firm performance, it is important to be able to understand how one business model compares with another. Such an appraisal is important for several reasons. First, when making choices about components and linkages of a business model, a firm needs to be able to determine which business model alternatives are best. Second, a good analysis of competitors ought to include a comparison of business models; such a comparison needs some way of appraising business models. In this section we present the elements of such an appraisal.

When we explored the pricing component of a business model in Chapter 4, we encountered the following simple but useful equation:

$$\text{Profits} = \Pi = (P - V_c)Q - F_c$$

where

P is the price per unit of the product,

V_c is the per unit variable cost,

Q is the total number of units sold, and

F_c is the up-front or fixed costs.

From this relation, we said that profit margins, market share, and revenue growth were good predictors of profits. These in turn were driven by the components and linkages of a business model. This suggests that we can measure how good a business model is at three levels: measures of profitability, profitability prediction, and business model component attributes (see Table 5.1).

TABLE 5.1 Business Model Appraisal Levels

Level 1	Profitability measures • Earnings • Cash flow
Level 2	Profitability predictor measures • Margins • Market share • Revenue share growth rate
Level 3	Component attribute measures • Value • Scope • Price • Revenue • Activities • Implementation • Capabilities • Sustainability

Profitability Measures

The raison d'être of a business model is to make money, so what better way to measure how good a business model is than to compare its profitability to that of its competitors. Any one of many **profitability measures** can be used. Here we use *earnings* and *cash flows* because analysts use them most frequently in valuing businesses. If a firm's earnings or cash flows are better than those of competitors, we say that it has a competitive advantage. This suggests that the firm has a good business model. The problem with using profitability as a measure of the soundness of a business model is that many businesses with solid business models, especially start-ups, are not profitable even though down the line they might become very profitable. Moreover, a business that is profitable today may have a poor business model whose effects are still trickling down the profit chain. These two reasons suggest that we need to find a deeper measure.

Profitability Predictor Measures

As we saw in Chapter 4, profit margins, revenue market share, and revenue growth rate are good **profitability predictor measures** for knowledge-based products, and we can use them to appraise Internet business models. The procedure is to compare a firm's profit margins, revenue market share, and revenue growth rate with those of industry competitors. Again, a firm has a competitive advantage if it scores higher in these measures than industry competitors. Since these profitability predictor measures rest on the components of a business model and the linkages between them, there may be things about the model that have not trickled down the chain to profit margins, market share, and revenue growth rate. We next turn to the components of a business model.

Business Model Component Measures

While not as objective or as easily available as the measures of the first two levels of Table 5.1, **business model component measures** get to the source itself:

the business model. Table 5.2 provides some benchmark questions that can be used to appraise each component.

Customer Value

When customers buy a product, they do so because they value something in it. As we saw in Chapter 4, this value could be in product features such as location and the timing of the product's delivery. For a portal, value could be in the number of subscribers, repeat clients, unique visitors, or page views. For a manufacturer of cholesterol drugs, value could be in how much its drugs reduce high cholesterol levels. The first question (see Table 5.2) that a firm should be asking itself is: Is the firm's customer value distinct from that of competitors? If not, is the firm's level of value higher than that of competitors? If the answer is yes, an H for "high" can be placed in the "rank" column. If the answer is no, an L for "low" can be placed in the "rank" column. The next question—Is the firm's rate of increase high in customer value relative to that of competitors?—addresses the issue that while a firm's value may be higher

TABLE 5.2 Appraising a Business Model: Component Measures

Component of Business Model	Benchmark Questions	Rank
Customer value	Is customer value distinct from that of competitors? If not, is the firm's level of value higher than that of competitors?	H/L
	Is the firm's rate of increase in customer value high relative to that of competitors?	
Scope	Is the growth rate of market segments high?	H/L
	Is the firm's market share in each segment high relative to that of competitors'?	
	Is potential erosion of products high? If so, in what segments?	
Price	Is the quality-adjusted price low?	H/L
Revenue source	Are margins and market share in each revenue source high?	H/L
	Are margins and market share in each revenue source increasing?	
	Is the firm's value in each source of revenue distinctive? If not, is the level of value higher than that of competitors?	
Connected activities	What is the extent to which activities:	H/L
	Are consistent with customer value and scope?	
	Reinforce each other?	
	Take advantage of industry success drivers?	
	Are consistent with the firm's distinctive capabilities?	
	Make the industry more attractive for the firm?	
Implementation	Is the quality of the team high?	H/L
Capabilities	To what extent are the firm's capabilities:	H/L
	Distinctive?	
	Inimitable?	
	Extendable to other product markets?	
Sustainability	Has the firm been able to maintain or extend its lead in its industry?	H/L

or more distinct than that of the competition, the firm should be worried if competitors are closing the gap. Such a threat might come from a competitor's new strategies or a technological change that allows competitors to catch up or leapfrog a firm. A ranking of H means the firm is increasing its lead or competitors are not catching up.

Scope

Recall from Chapter 4 that *scope* refers to the market segments to which a firm offers customer value and the range of products that contain the value. Here we appraise a firm's strength in each market segment and in each product that embodies the value. The first question—Is the growth rate of market segments high?—tells us how the segment itself is doing. But we also want to know how well the firm itself is doing in each segment relative to its competitors. Hence the question: Is the firm's market share in each segment high relative to that of competitors? Finally, the firm may want to know how well each product is doing in each segment, particularly if the products are threatened by new products in competitors' pipelines. The answers to these questions tell us how much pressure is being exerted on the firm in each of its market segments. An overall ranking of H indicates that the products embodying value and the market segments served are doing well, suggesting that the firm's choices in the scope element of its business model are good.

Price

If a firm offers its customers something distinctive or a higher level of value, the question is, How much is the firm charging for it? What is the value for the customer's dollar? What is the bang for the buck? How much does a patient pay for a 1 percent drop in bad cholesterol? The less a firm charges per unit of value, the more difficult it is for other firms to take away its market share. A high value per dollar may also be an indication of customer bargaining power or pressure from potential new entrants, or rivals.

Revenue Sources

The questions to be asked in this component are (1) Are the market share and margins in each revenue source high? (2) More importantly, are the market shares and margins increasing at each revenue source? If the competitive forces in a market are high, the margins may be decreasing. This was the case in 1999, for example, with online brokerage firms where the margins for brokerage fees were dropping. (3) Is the firm's value in each revenue source distinctive? If not, is the level of it higher than that of competitors? The third question addresses the matter that high and even growing margins may be determined by a firm's bargaining power and may hide the actual decline in value of the firm's products/services. Again, if all the answers in the revenue sources category are yes, place an H in column three. This is an indication of the strength of the firm in each revenue source.

Answers to the remaining business model elements are more qualitative than quantitative but nonetheless very important.

Connected Activities

Recall from Chapter 4 the following questions for connected activities: Are the activities consistent with customer value and scope? Do they reinforce each other? Do they take advantage of industry success drivers? Are they consistent with a firm's distinctive capabilities? Do they make the industry more attractive for the firm? If the answers to these questions are yes, column three gets an H, indicating a sound strategy.

Implementation

Implementation is critical to the success of a business model. Unfortunately, much less research has been done on what constitutes good or bad implementation than on the other components of a business model. In any case, the idea is to get a feel for the extent to which a firm's strategy, structure, systems, people, and environment fit. One measure of the likelihood of good execution is the type of people on the team. The rationale is that people are central to everything, especially at a start-up firm. The right people can structure the organization well and set up the right systems to implement the business model. In deciding whether to invest in a venture, venture capital firms usually put a lot of emphasis on the quality of the team members who are going to carry out the business model. The quality of the team is measured not only by the quality of individuals within the team, but also by how much the skills of individuals complement each other. The quality of each individual is measured by his or her relevant knowledge and a number of intangibles such as enthusiasm.

Capabilities

If a firm's value to customers rests on its capabilities, then the extent to which competitors can replicate this value is determined by how easy it is to duplicate or substitute capabilities. The ease of doing this can be determined by answers to the questions: Are the capabilities distinctive? Inimitable? Prahalad and Hamel pointed out, another desirable characteristic of capabilities is **extendability**—the degree to which those capabilities can be used to offer other products.[17] Thus, another question is, Are capabilities extendable to other product markets? If the answer to these questions is yes, place an H in column three.

Sustainability

Appraising sustainability entails a determination of the extent to which a firm's block, run, or team-up strategies work. If the firm opts for a block strategy, then the appraisal process focuses on determining what is inherent in the firm and its competitors that will make *blocking* work. For example, does the firm have many patents, copyrights, and trade secrets that are difficult to imitate or substitute? If the run strategy is used, the firm must then ask whether it has what it takes to run. For example, does it have the personnel and financing to keep innovating? Can it afford to reinvent itself? If the firm relies on teaming up, the question becomes, What can it bring to the table in teaming up and how much complementarity do the partners have? What kinds of partners does it attract? If the ingredients exist for making the firm's strategy work, sustainability gets an H rank.

If column three of Table 5.2 has many highs, the business model is strong. If it has many lows, the model is weak. This is important information for the development of strategy and the business model.

Important!

Often the most important thing to take away from the appraisal of an Internet business model is not so much that the business model is strong or weak, *but to identify why it is strong or weak. In this way, the strong components and links in the model can be reinforced and the weak ones strengthened.* In competitor analysis, the important thing is not so much to find out whether competitors have a stronger or weaker business model, as to find out *where* and *why* they are stronger or weaker.

SUMMARY

Business models are not static. The technology on which they rest and the environments in which they operate continually change. The firms and competitors who design them initiate or react to change. In responding to or initiating change to sustain or attain a competitive advantage, a firm can use a combination of three generic strategies: *block* in which the firm prevents competitors from imitating its business model; *run* in which the firm keeps innovating or reinventing its business model; and *team-up* in which the firm enters into alliances, takes an equity share in a venture, acquires another firm, or is acquired. Which strategy is appropriate and when is a function of the type of technology and the importance and availability of complementary assets. It is also a function of the stage of evolution of the technology.

In designing Internet business models, incumbents have some unique disadvantages and advantages. The Internet is a disruptive technology to many bricks-and-mortar incumbents and as such their capabilities can be a handicap. At the same time, some of their complementary assets can be an advantage. They often have to make a choice between developing the Internet business within the firm or creating a separate legal entity. Each option has its merits and drawbacks; which one will be appropriate for a firm is a function of its capabilities and its industry.

Appraising a business model helps a firm to make choices. It tells a firm how good its business model is compared to that of competitors or how good alternative business models under different scenarios can be. More importantly, it enables a firm to understand which components and linkages of its business model are weak or strong compared to those of competitors. With this information, a firm can continue to build a better business model.

KEY TERMS

block strategy   69
business model component measures   80
cannibalization   70
competence destroying   77
competence enhancing   77
complementary assets   71
disruptive technology   77
extendability   83
fluid phase   73
growth phase   74
imitability   71
incremental innovation   76

incumbents   76
intellectual property   69
lead users   74
mature phase   75
new entrants   77
profitability measures   80
profitability predictor measures   80
radical innovation   76
run strategy   70
team-up strategy   70
technology life cycle   73

1. What is the significance of this statement from the text: "It takes more than technology to profit from a technology"?
2. Consider a bricks-and-mortar retailer that wants to enter the online retailing business. Is it better off (1) creating a separate legal firm, (2) establishing a separate unit within the firm, or (3) scattering employees with Internet skills in its bricks-and-mortar units? Would it be different for a bank or automaker? Does industry matter for each of the three possibilities?
3. What is the most important thing that one gets from appraising a business model?
4. It has been argued that one must "keep moving"—that is, pursue the run strategy—to be successful with the Internet. What are the constraints on a run strategy?
5. When would you advise a start-up Internet firm to offer itself for acquisition by another firm? Does the type of purchaser matter?
6. Why might an incumbent want to buy a start-up Internet firm?
7. Does the success of a run, block, or team-up strategy depend on the type of industry in which it is being carried out?
8. Name an e-business firm that has been successful at blocking. Why is it successful?

REFERENCES

1. See A. N. Afuah, *Innovation Management: Strategies, Implementation, and Profits* (New York: Oxford University Press, 1998), chap. 12, which illustrates these strategies with detailed examples about Intel and Sun Microsystems.
2. There is an immense literature on this topic with its roots in economics. See, for example, P. Ghemawat, *Commitment: The Dynamics of Strategy* (New York: Free Press, 1991); S. Oster, *Modern Competitive Analysis,* 3rd ed. (Oxford: Oxford University Press, 1999).
3. In 2000 Advanced Micro Devices had made considerable progress but was far from catching up with Intel in revenues and profits.
4. D. J. Teece, "Profiting from Technological Innovation: Implications for Integration, Collaboration, Licensing and Public Policy," *Research Policy* 15 (1986), pp. 285–306. see also Afuah, *Innovation Management.*
5. R. P. Rumelt, "Towards a Strategic Theory of the Firm," in *Competitive Strategic Management* ed. by R. B. Lamb (Englewood Cliffs, NJ: Prentice Hall, 1984).
6. Catherine Crane, Will Johnson, Kitty Neumark, and Christopher Perrigo, "PIXAR, 1996," University of Michigan Business School case, 1998.
7. J. M. Utterback, *Mastering the Dynamics of Innovation* (Cambridge: Harvard Business School Press, 1994); A. N. Afuah with J. M. Utterback, "Responding to Structural Industry Changes: A Technological Innovation Perspective," *Industrial and Corporate Change* 6, no. 1 (1997).
8. E. von Hippel, *The Sources of Innovation* (New York: Oxford University Press, 1998).
9. See Afuah, *Innovation Management,* chap. 6.
10. R. Henderson, "Underinvestment and Incompetence as Responses to Radical Innovation: Evidence from the Photolithographic Alignment Industry," *Rand Journal of Economics* 24, no. 2 (Summer 1993), pp. 248–69; also see Afuah, *Innovation Management,* chap. 12.
11. R. Henderson and K. B. Clark, "Architectural Innovation: The Reconfiguration of Existing Product Technologies and the Failure of Established Firms," *Administrative Sciences Quarterly* 35 (1990), pp. 9–30.

12. M. L. Tushman and P. Anderson, "Technological Discontinuities and Organizational Environments," *Administrative Science Quarterly* 31 (1986), pp. 439–65.

13. C. M. Christensen, *The Innovator's Dilemma* (Boston: Harvard Business School Press, 1997); R. A. Bettis and C. K. Prahalad, "The Dominant Logic: Retrospective and Extension," *Strategic Management Journal* 16 (1995), pp. 5–14.

14. W. Mitchell, "Whether and When? Probability and Timing of Incumbents' Entry into Emerging Industrial Sub Fields," *Administrative Sciences Quarterly* 34 (1989), pp. 208–30; M. Tripsas, "Unraveling the Process of Creative Destruction: Complementary Assets and Incumbent Survival in the Typesetter Industry," *Strategic Management Journal* 18 (1997), pp. 119–42.

15. This example is from "Breakdown," *The Economist,* May 22, 1999, pp. 69–70.

16. The Cisco case comes from "Cisco@Speed" in "Survey: Business and the Internet," *The Economist,* July 26, 1999, p. 12.

17. C. K. Prahalad and G. Hamel, "The Core Competences of the Corporation," *Harvard Business Review,* May–June 1990, pp. 79–91.

CHAPTER 6

Value Configurations
and the Internet

In Chapter 4 we introduced the idea of customer value as a prime component of analyzing a business model. We also discussed the importance of connected activities and how the execution of connected activities was a source of competitive advantage for firms. In this chapter we elaborate on the concept of customer value and how it relates to three proposed value creation logics based on Professor James Thompson's typology of long-linked, intensive, and mediating technologies.[1] These three value creation logics are related to three generic "value configurations": the value chain, value shop, and value network.[2] We discuss each value configuration in turn and demonstrate the primary "activities" associated with each. Finally, we show how the misapplication of a proposition oriented more toward manufacturing and products—the value chain framework—to Internet services and brokering can lead to the building of the wrong kinds of capabilities. The result of this misapplication could be an uncompetitive position in the market. Likewise, we show how firms building capabilities consistent with the correct value configuration can develop and maintain a competitive advantage. Thus, in this chapter we go well beyond value chain analysis to a new kind of value configuration analysis aligned more with the kinds of services that are proliferating in the new Digital Economy.

This chapter serves as a basis for analyzing the connected activities of two types of firms. For incumbents, it aids in understanding the impact of the Internet on the current value configuration (in any industry) and in choosing the most appropriate response in terms of connected activities. For new entrants, it aids in understanding the three value configurations so entrants can choose the most appropriate value configuration and the most appropriate set of connected activities.

VALUE CREATION AND ORGANIZATIONAL TECHNOLOGIES

Recall from Chapter 4 that companies are mainly concerned with creating value in terms of differentiated products or services, or in offering undifferentiated products at a lower price to customers. In which areas should companies focus if they want to build competencies that create the most value? At the heart of every business is a **value configuration**: The company is adding value in some way that makes customers willing to pay. One might imagine that there is a huge number of value configurations in the world. However, management researchers in Norway found that these value configurations can be grouped into only three fundamental "value creation configurations" in the economy.[3] These models are based on the notion of a value chain, value shop, and value network and are themselves derived from Thompson's three generic "organizational technologies."

In his landmark book, *Organizations in Action,* Thompson proposed a **typology of organizational technologies**.[4] He categorized technologies as long-linked, intensive, and mediating. In a **long-linked technology**, interdependencies are sequential and tasks are accomplished serially. Thompson cited the continuous process (e.g., continuous chemical processing) and assembly lines (e.g., automobile manufacturing) as the ultimate embodiment of long-linked technology. Other hallmarks of long-linked technologies are continuous output of standardized products, repetitive tasks, the conversion of raw materials into finished goods, clear-cut criteria for the selection of capital and labor, and continuous improvement in production.

An **intensive technology** is oriented toward solving highly specific problems. Thompson called this type of technology "intensive" to signify that the choice of techniques needed to solve a problem was based in an iterative fashion on the progress made toward solving the problem. There would likely be an intensive interaction between the problem solvers and the object of their attention. Professors Charles Stabell and Øystein Fjeldstad named the value configuration analogous to the value chain, but one based on intensive technologies, the **value shop**. The value shop is based on most types of service provision (with the exception of intermediaries, as discussed below). Thus, a hospital's primary business—healing—may be thought of as creating value as a value shop based on an intensive technology:

> At any moment an emergency admission may require some combination of dietary, X-ray, laboratory, and housekeeping or hotel services, together with the various medical specialties, pharmaceutical services, occupational therapies, social work services, and spiritual or religious services. Which of these, and when, can be determined only from evidence about the state of the patient.[5]

A **mediating technology** provides the service of a connection between two or more customers who wish to be interdependent, such as borrowers and lenders (depositors) or buyers and sellers. Thus, mediating technologies facilitate the role of the aptly named intermediary service, with the associated value configuration named the **value network**. Thompson stressed the importance of standardized criteria and decision making, as well as scale of operations. As an example of standardized criteria for taking on a customer (providing the intermediary service), decisions on creditworthiness of a potential borrower must be done in a standardized fashion to avoid bank solvency problems later on.

As mentioned in Chapter 4, a company can make money in only two ways: (1) to add value that customers are willing to pay for and (2) to have the lowest possible costs.[6] The model built on the value chain and reproduced in Figure 6.1 involves the production and sale of manufactured goods.[7] This does not necessarily involve selling to the general public (retailing), although it could.[8] Many businesses have a tangible product that is sold, so "adding value" involves the transformation of "raw materials" into that tangible product. For example, a manufacturer

FIGURE 6.1 A Typical Value Chain

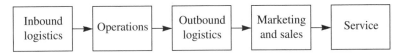

of chairs may take in materials such as wood stain and blocks of wood, and transform them into finished chairs. The value chain concept was popularized by Professor Michael Porter as a way to catalog the kinds of activities that add value. Using this model, we see that there are several areas in which a manufacturer such as the chair manufacturer can add value. One is inbound logistics: moving the raw materials into the plant in a more efficient way. The next is operations or transforming the raw materials into a more finished product. Next we have outbound logistics, marketing, sales, and service. These activities are called the **primary activities** of the value chain because they are most closely associated with transforming inputs into outputs and with the customer interface—the most important additions to value in the short term. The primary activities are backed up by the longer-term **secondary (support) activities** of firm infrastructure, human resource management, technology development, and procurement.

Stabell and Fjeldstad, however, proposed that the value chain does not apply to all industries and is not always a useful metaphor for managers searching for competitive advantage. For example, how does a hospital fit into the value chain analysis? Are the sick patients the "raw materials" and healthy patients the "product"?* They concluded that for most services, *value shop* was a more apt analogy.

Finally, Stabell and Fjeldstad proposed a third type of value configuration, the *value network,* which involves brokering and intermediating. Companies competing under the value network model facilitate transactions between diverse communities, for example, by bringing buyers and sellers together.

In the next three sections we explore these three value configurations and relate them to the segments of the Internet economy developed in Chapter 2 and the properties of the Internet described in Chapter 3. While most students will be familiar with the concept of the value chain, we briefly summarize the basic framework below. We then devote one section each to the value shop and value network.

THE VALUE CHAIN

To deliver low-cost or differentiated products, a firm must perform a series of activities. The different functions that perform each of these activities are called the firm's **value chain**. Most students should have had some exposure to the value chain from a course on introductory business strategy. In this section we briefly examine a value chain for manufacturing products.

*MBA students may also recognize the mismatched concept of being called the "customers" of an educational system, a fact that the faculty often heatedly dispute! Are they instead the "raw materials" of the educational system?

A Manufacturer's Value Chain

The typical assembler/manufacturer's value chain should at this point be fairly well understood. For review purposes, we use the example of a manufacturer of computer hardware, such as a personal computer. The *inbound logistics* stage involves raw materials handling, such as computer CPU chips, memory modules, disk drives, fans, and so forth. A manager would also have to worry about an inspection of the materials, selection of parts, and delivery issues. The *operations* involve the production of in-house components, assembly of the computer, testing and tuning, maintenance of equipment, and operation of the plant. The *outbound logistics* stage involves order processing and shipping. The *marketing and sales* stage is concerned with advertising, pricing, promotion, and management of the sales force. Finally, the *service* stage involves managing technical support and service representatives and replacement and repair of computers.

In performing the activities of its value chain, a firm must interact with suppliers, customers, and firms in related industries. The other firms also have value chains of their own. What we really have, then, is a system of value chains called the value chain system (see Figure 6.2).

If you think about it, the value chain is more about efficiency than about new product development. It is about process more than product. And it is about low cost more than differentiation. The value chain describes the necessary activities once a product and its features have been conceived, and it is not necessarily concerned with developing a continual stream of innovations. However, marketing does have two roles in the value chain. The first was implied above: to stimulate demand for the product. The second role, however, is to provide input into the product specifications themselves, along with estimates of expected volume. This allows for limited differentiation.

How Does the Internet Affect the Primary Activities of the Value Chain?

The seminal article on Internet business models by Paul Timmers is an important touchstone in understanding how the Internet affects the connected activities of the value chain.[9] Timmers made the first attempt to classify the different ways of doing business in the Internet era and provided some preliminary categories, such as "e-shop," "e-procurement," and "e-mall." In some sense, Timmers was concerned with a virtual value chain and how the Internet was affecting that chain.[10] Abstracting from Timmers' categories, we will demonstrate that several properties of the Internet developed in Chapter 3 influence the connected activities of the value chain.

FIGURE 6.2 The Value Chain System

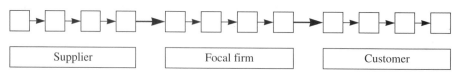

The connections enabled by the Internet might allow a firm to learn more about end users; that is, a denser social web may allow the marketing and sales functions to be in more direct contact with downstream (direct customers) and end users (final users). This will allow a two-way flow of information corresponding with the dual role of marketing: By becoming more familiar with end-user customers, marketing may be better able to assess market needs or facilitate user-developed or -induced innovations.[11] Likewise, by having more direct contact with end users, it may be easier to stimulate demand from the downstream end of the channel. This process has been used with some success in the software industry, where Netscape prereleased free beta versions and employed user input to improve and debug its browser releases.[12]

Universality, Time Moderation, and Distribution Channels

The geographic scope argument is perhaps the best known and understood story in electronic commerce. The Internet, by enabling a wider geographic scope, represents another medium in which to market and sell to customers. Local companies without a large national or international presence can now serve a larger audience outside their geographic area. The best-known story is Amazon.com's book business and its geographic reach which would have been viewed as impossible before the advent of the Internet. The marketing function thus sees the Internet as, at a minimum, an additional catalog venue. For example, L.L.Bean and most other retailers were early in putting catalogs on the Web. In addition, advertising on Internet portals and other Web pages has grown from nothing in 1995 to a projected $2 billion in 2000.[13] This, however, represents only 1 percent of total advertising spending. Other geographic effects of the Internet include the ability of existing sales and service representatives to expand their geographic reach by being in contact with a larger number of people without necessarily having to be in close physical proximity.

The ability to cover a larger geographic area and to shift in time also affects the earlier stages of the value chain; specifically, it may allow a wider choice of inputs, distributed manufacturing, and remote testing. These benefits are especially relevant to software production but may apply to other industries as well. Companies are experimenting with round-the-clock software production that can take place in the United States, Europe, and India with each team picking up where the last one left off.

Information, software, and content can also be delivered instantaneously, affecting the outbound logistics part of the chain. For example, firms such as Intuit now offer customers the ability to download their products rather than wait for a diskette or a CD to be shipped.[14] This saves the company in several ways: It eliminates the costs of the disks, the storage of information on the disks, and shipping costs. Some of those savings are passed on to the customer, who finds value in the timely delivery, the lower price, and in the product itself. Most of the major record labels, including Capitol Records and Sony, have begun experimenting with the delivery of music over the Internet,[15] perhaps in response to audio formats such as MP3 that promise reasonable audio quality over the Internet. The reasoning is that if the labels do not control the Internet distribution by means of antipiracy digital watermarks or the equivalent, the intellectual property of the labels lose any ability to generate rents. Thus, we see both the positives and negatives of instantaneous delivery.

The main and most celebrated effect of the Internet on the value chain is a company's ability to carry lower amounts of inventory by ordering directly from a manufacturer and shipping directly to a customer. This argument can be extended to all sorts of value chain bypassing.[16] The news and business press lately has often used the term **disintermediation** and foretold its inevitability in the Digital Economy. The concept behind disintermediation springs directly from the value chain system discussed above.

Here we draw a distinction between the downstream (direct) customer—henceforth called the *broker* or *distributor*—and the end-user (or final) consumer. Note that in many cases the direct downstream customer is not the same as the end-user consumer. Why would the upstream firm ever enter into business with the downstream customer (*not* the end-user customer) in the first place? It could be that the firm has a specific capability in manufacturing and does not know much about marketing the products. Further, the distributor might aggregate orders from other manufacturers and have large warehouses and distribution capabilities. Or the distributor might know a certain geographic area very well, but the firm is too far away to devote much time, attention, and money to that remote area.

The concept of disintermediation is that a firm upstream may **leapfrog** a downstream firm and sell directly to the distributor's customer. This is also referred to as "cutting out the middleman." Why would a firm want to do this? For one thing, the distributor might be in a more profitable line of business. For another, the distributor usually marks up the price of the firm's products through a commission or margin, thereby charging a higher price to the end user and thus dampening demand for the product.

Prior to the widespread use of the World Wide Web, the only story behind disintermediation was vertical integration: The firm could buy out the broker or try to match internally the distributor's capabilities—for example in marketing or distribution. However, since the diffusion of the World Wide Web, it occurred to many manufacturers that they might be able to sell directly to end users. This is the travel agency story that we referred to earlier. Before the Web, airlines could sell to the public over the telephone, but it was much easier to simply let travel agents sell to the public and pay the travel agents a commission to sell tickets. The travel agents had the specialized knowledge of schedules and fares, and people were willing to go to a travel agent close to home to find out the available fares and schedules. Following the advent of the Web, the airlines began selling tickets in large volume to the general public by making their schedules and fares available to anyone with an Internet connection. When direct sales rose to a sufficiently high level, the airlines cut commissions to travel agents from 20 percent to 10 percent and then to 8 percent with a $50 cap for domestic and $100 for international flights.[17] Travel agents responded by charging end users a $10 fee to book a ticket. This further reduced demand for travel agents.

The most famous example of disintermediation is no doubt Amazon.com.[18] Legend has it that Amazon cut out several middlemen in offering books for sale to the public directly from its website. Specifically, as a retailer the company could bypass both wholesalers and distributors and buy directly from the publishers. It could generate more volume from its website than a store that was wedded to a geographic area.

Dell Computer, with its famous "direct method" and the Internet version of that, Dell Online, followed a similar logic by cutting out distributors and retailers. The public can buy directly from Dell, which cuts out the reseller's markup and also keeps channel inventories low. This means that the computers in the channels are more up to date on average than those of Dell's competitors, thereby avoiding the problem of "fire sales" when new chips or other highly depreciating components hit the market.[19] In 1999 Apple began selling direct to the public, using the same method in its "Apple Store."

Scalability and Infinite Virtual Capacity

For many information-intensive businesses, advances in computer technology, combined with the larger customer base provided through the Internet, enable a much larger scale of operations than was previously possible. For example, the ability of online retailers such as barnesandnoble.com to serve millions of customers simultaneously sets them apart from bricks-and-mortar retailers, such as Barnes and Noble's retail outlets.

In sum, the Internet has had a profound impact on many if not all the primary activities of firms in information-based industries and of many retailers. For most other businesses, the Internet primarily interacts with the value chain's primary activities in the marketing and sales stage, which may in turn trigger substantial changes in the other stages of the value chain.

THE VALUE SHOP

Since Porter's work on the topic of value chains, much business analysis has focused squarely on improving the position of the firm relative to its competitors by **benchmarking** (comparing in a carefully controlled and objective way) its performance against the primary activities of the value chain. However, Stabell and Fjeldstad pointed out that benchmarking against the primary activities of the value chain was forcing the company into a business model centered around manufactured goods. Should an e-mail service, consulting company, travel agent, or other service provider really care about inbound logistics? Stabell and Fjeldstad argued that they should not, that **service provisioning** has a different **value creation logic**. Service providers tend to customize their service to the needs of their clients rather than mass-produce—or even mass-customize—as in the value chain model. This distinction is key: Service providers tend to work in real time to come up with new solutions, rather than fixing on one solution and reproducing it time and again.

Value Creation Logic and Service Provision

The basic example of this sort of value creation logic is the travel agent. When a client visits a high-end, service-oriented travel agent,[20] the agent must first determine what the customer wants. Compared to a manufacturer, who knows mainly what the customer wants, a travel agent has a much wider latitude of possible solutions. For example, there are various means of transportation (e.g., car, airplane, cruise ship, train), locations, dates, and potential services (e.g., hotel, car, plane). Some clients simply want to "go someplace warm" for a low price, while others want to travel by train to a specific location on a specific day. Therefore, the travel agent must ascertain exactly what the customer needs and then propose a method of filling that need. Then the agent must see if the proposed plan meets with customer approval and charge the customer the appropriate amount.

One can see that this is similar to the value chain logic described above, yet different from it. The logic of the value shop is not the logic of producing anything in particular, but honing in on what the customer actually wants and finding a way to fulfill it. One might argue that an automaker is in the same position, trying to figure out what kinds of cars the clients want and fulfilling those orders. However, that is not where the automaker adds the most value; it adds value by manufacturing and assembling cars, albeit with some design input from marketing. In any case, marketing's job is mainly to promote cars that have already been designed, not to design new ones, especially not in real time.

To give another example, consider the case of Yahoo![21] as a service provider. Yahoo started as a search engine, cataloging and categorizing sites on the World Wide Web. As that business became more commoditized, competitive, and more efficiently operated, Yahoo began searching for other services that would enable it to continue attracting visitors. First, they developed my.yahoo.com, one of the first personalized content pages. Then came the free e-mail followed by pager services. This is a type of value shop logic, although it is not targeted at a specific customer. There is a constant, real-time search for a service that will provide value to the customer, then a quick response developing that service. Time horizons are important in distinguishing value shops from value chains. With value chains, the time lag between searching for a solution and commercializing one may take years while it is only a matter of hours with the value shop.

Finally, the entire business does not have to be a service provider for a value shop logic to prevail. Service-oriented divisions or parts of larger companies can operate under the value shop logic. For example, many retailers such as L.L.Bean have customer service organizations. Even though the business itself operates under the logic of the value chain, the customer service area is more of a value shop. Likewise, internal service departments (e.g., software engineering organizations or even new product development teams) can also be thought of as value shops.

Primary Activities of the Value Shop

The hallmark of these examples is the primary concentration on **iterative problem solving** in real time; that is, a firm concentrates on discovering what the client wants, figuring out a way to deliver value, determining whether the customer's needs were fulfilled, and, if necessary, repeating the process all over again. Stabell and Fjeldstad proposed the following *primary activities* of the value shop as shown in Figure 6.3: (1) problem finding and acquisition, (2) problem solving, (3) choice, (4) execution, and (5) control and evaluation. We briefly discuss each of these.

FIGURE 6.3 Primary Activities of the Value Shop

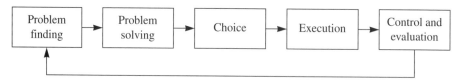

Problem Finding and Acquisition

Problem finding and acquisition involves working with the customer to determine the exact nature of the problem or need. It also involves deciding on the overall plan of approaching the problem. As mentioned above, this is highly related to the marketing function in the traditional value chain framework.

Problem Solving

Problem solving is the actual generation of ideas and action (or treatment) plans.

Choice

Choice represents the decision of choosing between alternatives. While the least important primary activity of the value shop in terms of time and effort, it is also the most important in terms of customer value. Indeed, one of the hallmarks of the value shop compared to other value configurations is the *information asymmetry* between the service provider and the customer. The service provider has information or expertise that the customer lacks. Thus, the choice activity represents real value to the customer.

Execution

Execution represents "communicating, organizing, and implementing" the decision, or performing the treatment.

Control and Evaluation

Control and evaluation activities involve monitoring and measurement of how well the solution solved the original problem or met the original need. This feeds back into our first activity, problem finding and acquisition, for two reasons. First, if the proposed solution is inadequate or did not work, it feeds back into learning why it was inadequate and begins the problem-solving phase anew. Second, if the problem solution was successful, the firm might enlarge the scope of the problem-solving process to solve a bigger problem related to or dependent upon the first problem being solved.

How Does the Internet Affect the Primary Activities of the Value Shop?

The activities of the value shop have been influenced in several important ways by the development of the Internet. The Internet affects these activities in four main ways:

1. It enables a larger scale of operations.
2. It widens the geographic scope of the area the firm represents.
3. It allows more information to be collected and processed by the service provider.
4. It enables a new delivery medium or mechanism.

Note that these influences are not unequivocally good for the service providers. Each has advantages and disadvantages, which we describe below.

Universality, Time Moderation, and Distribution Channel

The ability to deliver service in distant regions is another aspect of the value shop that has changed considerably. Certainly such services as haircuts remain distinctly local, but clearly others are now turning to a wider geographic base than ever before. These include bill payment, consulting (especially information technology consulting), travel agencies, real estate agencies, and possibly law services, architecture, engineering, and even medical services. This geographic expansion is both an opportunity and a threat to value shop–oriented companies. A wider geographic base allows companies to serve a larger population, but, as above, the threat of competition from distant locales is very real.

For the sheer number of resources to throw at solving a problem, the Internet opens up some exciting possibilities involving collaboration. Problem solving can be enhanced in two ways. The first is collaboration on group decisions. Several systems centered on collaborative groupware are currently in use, such as Lotus Notes. These systems allow input by means of the Internet from geographically dispersed participants, allowing the participation of many more people than could physically meet together and providing a higher level of brainstorming or input selection while exploring options.

The second way problem solving can be enhanced is for single-decision makers. A single-decision maker now has the option of researching information to aid in the decision-making process, not from other people, as above, but from information archives now available on Web servers worldwide. For example, an art appraiser could easily search the latest auction prices for a certain artist over the Web, an endeavor that formerly was very time and resource consuming.

The disadvantage of the sheer number of resources is **information overload**. Decision-making quality might actually drop if the decision makers are not careful. Further, the decision maker must have some confidence in the authenticity of the research sources available over the Web. A medical doctor, for example, may not necessarily believe everything he or she reads about a certain condition on every website. Likewise, in our example of the art appraiser, unless the appraiser goes to the websites of major auction houses, there is always the possibility that the prices quoted on a website are incorrect, or worse, that the work auctioned was not an authentic piece by the artist in question.

For some services, the Internet may be used as a delivery medium. Fax service from overseas is one example of using the Internet for service delivery. From a computer in France, one sends an e-mail message to a certain address in the United States. The computer at that address forwards the message to an address near the intended recipient, where the computer converts it into a fax that is sent to the recipient. The sender is charged only a nominal fee for the service, which enables customers overseas to send documents to people who do not have e-mail access and without having to pay for an international telephone call. Thus, the existence of high-speed connections may become a viable method for service providers to deliver services themselves—clearly in telecommunications as in the above two examples, but also potentially in any virtual, information-based service such as stock quotations and architectural design.

Information Asymmetries and Transaction Costs

Value shops are both made and unmade by information asymmetries. The entire value proposition of the value shop is its ability to solve problems that the client cannot. Thus, the Internet represents a fundamental hazard to the very core of the value shop: As an increasing amount of information is available online, the more competition the general knowledge base provides against the value shop firm. This does not mean that there will be no more consulting companies, architects, or professional service firms. Reputation, information from a trusted source, and personalization will always have value to many customers. However, the information-based value shop businesses will be expected to encounter competition from the general knowledge base available over the Internet. This will be especially true for information asymmetries based on explicit rather than tacit knowledge.

Scalability and Infinite Virtual Capacity

The advantage of the Internet is its ability to serve more customers at once, especially in information-intensive services. Previously a firm was limited by the number of people it could hire to perform customer service. Now the number of inputs can be greatly increased by allowing many more simultaneous connections. For example, many companies, such as L.L.Bean, are allowing live "chat" with customer service agents over the Web. This allows the same number of agents to serve more customers; in addition, it increases the total number of customers that L.L.Bean can serve at the same time.

Getting basic information back to customers *without* the intervention of customer service agents in a timely and cost-efficient fashion is also an advantage of the Internet. It is clear that value shops are the primary beneficiaries of the ability to store information on servers and pass them along to customers on demand. For example, airlines have moved to a system whereby not only the fares and schedules are available over the Web, but also flight status, airplane layouts, seat locations, and more. In 1999 Delta Airlines tried to charge more for customers who purchased a ticket over the telephone because of the higher cost structure. However, after a firestorm of criticism, Delta decided to drop this charge. We believe that the Web-based approach must be providing cost savings for Delta in addition to providing more information for customers.[22] Likewise, diverse organizations such as the Vanguard Group (mutual funds and financial services), and the Internal Revenue Service have put all of their customer service forms online. This allows many more customers to be served simultaneously, gets the information to the customer more quickly (see below), saves printing and postage costs, and reduces the need for staffing customer service telephone centers.

The disadvantage of these approaches, again, is that as the size and scale of service providers increase, surviving competitors will tend to grow bigger while the smaller, less aggressive firms will find themselves under more intense competitive pressure. This is a potential hazard to the smaller companies that have been playing comfortably in a niche market for many years.

In sum, the Internet touches most, if not all, of the primary activities of the value shop. Information-based value shops cannot expect that all of the changes will be positive.

THE VALUE NETWORK

Despite the story related above about travel agents, we believe that the inevitability of disintermediation has been greatly exaggerated. In fact, the third value configuration we will explore—the value network—is a direct outgrowth of *brokering*. The value network is the value configuration that exists when a firm is an intermediary, such as a broker (or market maker in the terminology of Chapter 2). The broker brings buyers and sellers together and makes money by doing so. While the above concerns about disintermediation are very real in the bricks-and-mortar world, one needs only to look at the list of top retailers to see that most of them are intermediaries! Indeed, most of the top consumer websites are either travel agents or brokerage houses. Let's look briefly at each of these.

Examples of Value Network Businesses

Online travel agents, such as Travelocity/Preview Travel and Expedia, provide convenient summaries of fares and schedules. They also allow the user to search for the lowest fare across several airlines and to search by schedule, type of ticket (restricted or unrestricted), number of connecting flights, and so forth. These agencies get the same commissions as bricks-and-mortar travel agencies, but they are able to sustain huge volumes owing to the scalability of their Internet services; that is, Internet travel agencies can handle thousands (even millions) of users simultaneously while a typical corner travel agency can handle only three or four. Thus, the fixed costs are spread over a great many more users and the marginal costs of servicing each additional user is much lower than it is in a bricks-and-mortar organization. The Internet travel agencies make money by taking a low commission on a large volume of purchasers while the bricks-and-mortar agencies make money by taking a higher commission on a low volume. Now that the services are virtually indistinguishable, however, the Internet agencies are putting competitive pressure on the bricks-and-mortar agencies because customers are unwilling to pay the higher commissions.[23]

Another growing area of electronic commerce is Internet brokerage houses such as E*Trade or Ameritrade. Once again, we have a similar brokering value configuration. The online brokerages bring buyers and sellers together and shave off a small commission, in some cases as low as $7, for each trade. The very high volumes of trading allowed by high-speed servers and the ability to service many people at the same time compensate for the lower per-trade commission.

To summarize, we can see that there is money to be made by an intermediary if both buyers and sellers perceive value from that intermediary. Customers must perceive that there is value in being part of the "network" that the intermediary controls or supports. In the case of the travel agencies, airlines want to sell more tickets. Customers, however, cannot trust the airlines to offer them the lowest possible fares. Therefore, customers are willing to use the online travel agency which acts as an information broker to find the lowest fares across all the airlines. The same logic applies to online brokerages. Any individual company could (subject to securities regulations) theoretically sell stock directly to the public; however, most would-be buyers could not be sure that they were getting a suitable price and therefore go through an online broker to get the best price. The more companies an online brokerage interacts with, the more valuable the service to the end-user customers.

Likewise, a bank (online or otherwise) performs a service, which is to bring together people with capital (savers) with those who need capital (borrowers). The value to each of these sets of customers depends on the bank's capabilities in building a network of savers and borrowers.

Generally speaking, a broker, distributor, or other intermediary must pursue several activities if it wants to remain or become competitive. Rather than focusing on logistics such as the importation and delivery of raw materials and how they are transformed into finished goods, the intermediary must focus on the following items:

1. Network promotion and contract management.
2. Service provisioning.
3. Infrastructure operations.

We discuss each of these in turn.

Network Promotion and Contract Management

This activity involves promoting and building the network, acquiring customers, and managing contracts for service provision. The management of contracts involves the initiation, maintenance, and termination of contracts to provide whatever service the intermediary proposes to furnish. This activity is distinguished from sales and marketing in the value chain by its active selection of customers to join the network. As the level of commitment rises, the complexity of the contracting process and of the contracts themselves rises.

Service Provisioning

Service provisioning involves linking people in the network and then collecting payment from them for making the connection. Specifically, it involves setting up contacts—directly, as in real-time chat telephone service, or indirectly, as in banking or electronic mail—seeing that the contacts are maintained for the appropriate amount of time, and ending the contact at the appropriate moment. Collecting payment is about tracking the usage (both *volume* and *time*) and billing for direct contact or, in the case of indirect contacts, collecting a commission for putting the two parties together. Upon receiving a service request, the intermediary needs to check the feasibility of making the connection as well as the eligibility of the requestor.

Infrastructure Operations

These activities allow the infrastructure to operate efficiently and remain in a state of readiness to provide service to the next customer. It can include both a physical and information infrastructure. Stabell and Fjeldstad provided examples of different types of infrastructure activities that vary with the type of network: For telecommunications providers, the main infrastructure is embedded in switches and distribution centers; for financial services companies, it is embedded in the branch offices, financial assets, or connections to trading floors.[24] Figure 6.4 provides an example of the value network activities of a financial services provider.

How Does the Internet Affect the Primary Activities of the Value Network?

Analogous to the case of the value shop, the Internet also influences the activities of the value network in three main ways:

1. It compounds network externalities.

FIGURE 6.4 Activities of the Value Network

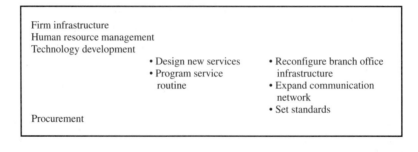

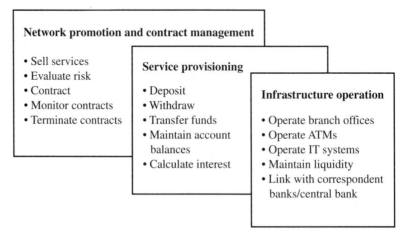

Source: Charles B. Stabell and Øystein D. Fjeldstad, "Configuring Value for Competitive Advantage: On Chains, Shops, and Networks," *Strategic Management Journal* 19 (1998), p. 430. Reproduced by permission of John Wiley & Sons Limited.

2. It widens the geographic scope of the network.
3. It enables a larger scale of the network.

Note that these influences are not unequivocally good for service providers. Each of them has advantages and disadvantages, which we describe below.

Mediating Technology and Network Externalities

The network externality effect is the most important property influencing the value network. Arguably, the network externality property enables the large number of Internet intermediaries. *The size of the network is the most important criterion of merit for users evaluating a value network oriented business.* A bank that has no lenders, only borrowers, will not be solvent for long. A used-car service with access to one dealer is of little use to potential buyers. Likewise, a music service that recommends CDs based on one you recently bought will not make very good recommendations if it has only three customers. As described in Chapter 3, this is a virtuous cycle (or vicious cycle, depending on where the firm starts and what competitors do) with a larger network attracting more users and complementors. For example, not only will car purchasers shun the "network" of one dealer, but other dealers will be reluctant to sign up with so few customers. In contrast, a large network of dealers and customers encourages more customers to want to use the service (more dealers) and more dealers to participate (more customers).

This can lead to a kind of "crowd mentality" behavior in value network oriented businesses. Initially, there may be several firms providing similar intermediary services. Eventually—because of the company's strategy, chance, or something else—one or a small number of the firms may enjoy a small lead in the size of their network. Once this happens, the crowd will rush to the doors of the larger networks, leaving the smaller rivals with no customers. Thus, as we discussed with lock-in in Chapter 4, it is extremely important for intermediaries to think about how they will develop the size of the network.[25]

Universality, Time Moderation, and Distribution Channel

The Internet, as in all previous examples, widens the geographic scope of the network. This is especially important for value networks, as the size of the network affects its usefulness to users. A larger geographic base of users allows the network to grow more quickly. Thus businesses that were once constrained to a small geographic area (and slow growth for their networks) are now free to expand more quickly. The downside, as always, is that once comfortable, slow-growth networks can now be won and lost in a matter of months or even weeks.

In terms of a distribution channel, Qwest Communications, among others, is experimenting with providing long-distance telephone service over the Internet. Long-distance service works in one of two ways: with or without special equipment. With special equipment, your phone is connected directly to the Internet, and the receiver must also have the same specialized phone. The voice traffic is broken into packets and reassembled at the other end. For people with standard phones, the voice data are connected through a circuit to the switch of the long-distance carrier, at which point it is broken into packets and transmitted to a remote switch where it is reassembled and sent through a circuit to the destination. In both cases, the current capacity of Internet bandwidth means that the packet connection is of low quality (e.g., missing packets are "dropped" due to the real-time requirement of voice communication). With expected advances, however, packet-switched voice communications may become a viable option in the next few years. Other examples include the development of electronic markets that use the Internet for trading, not simply for entering orders.

Scalability and Infinite Virtual Capacity

Again, infrastructure operation enables the network to have a larger scale, which is the primary way that a firm oriented to the value network adds value. Thus, in addition to a larger geographic reach, the increase in computing power has made it possible to serve many more customers. Businesses that were originally constrained by their capacity (and were also found in comfortable, slow-growth niches) now find themselves able to expand their networks rapidly, which in turn raises the value of their networks.

MAKING A FIRM'S VALUE CONFIGURATION CONSISTENT WITH ITS ACTIVITIES

One main conclusion that we might draw is that it is better to figure out the value configuration and then pursue the activities that are more appropriate for that particular value configuration. An interesting example is the progression of the state of real estate brokerages and the evolution in the way they make money. Real estate agencies at one point offered "exclusive" listings; that is, a seller who wanted to sell a house would go to one real estate office, which would "list" the house. If anyone else wanted to buy the house, that buyer would have to contact the listing agent directly. Therefore, the value of an agency was in the number of direct connections it had to sellers: a classic value network. Upon sale of the house, the seller paid the real estate agency a commission for listing and selling the house—a practice that has continued to the present.

At one point the Multiple Listing Service (MLS) came into being and agents could choose to adopt it. The concept behind the MLS should be familiar to anyone with an interest in e-commerce. If an agency chose to join the MLS, the agency would report all of its listings to the MLS, which would pass them along to all the other members. While the MLS is clearly a value network as we understand it, it should be noted that with the advent of the MLS, the uniqueness of a real estate agency began to diminish from the point of view of the value network. In an abstract way, the value of the agency was still the value of its connections, but because of its membership in the MLS, the agency's connections became in some sense a commodity. Real estate agencies began at this point to look more like value shops than value networks. We also began at this point to see the use of "buyers' brokers" whose role was to work for the buyer. Agencies made money on volume (more people could see their own listings) and competition drove down or held in check the commissions that agencies could charge.

The Internet has now enabled a new form of real estate firm: an online agency that again looks like a value network, possibly supplanting the MLS, and further driving the agency into the role of a pure service provider (a value shop) rather than a value network. In the latest phase, home owners can list their own homes on the websites of certain online brokerages for a low flat fee, or even for free. The MLS is also available on some websites such as Cyberhomes.com, bringing the listing information directly into the hands of potential buyers. Yahoo, for example, has grown the network quickly by integrating information from several diverse networks and allowing free listings and easy search facilities. In response, some bricks-and-mortar agencies began introducing fee-for-service plans, where an agent would work with a client on an hourly basis rather than on commission. It has begun to look as if the bricks-and-mortar agencies are in danger of being bypassed by online brokerages or becoming fee-for-service providers.

An oft-quoted example of disintermediation is Amazon.com which, when analyzed from a value-chain standpoint, seems to be eliminating book distributors from the value chain. If Amazon thought of itself as primarily a bookseller/retailer, then it should concentrate entirely on value-chain activities such as logistics (e.g., shipping, warehousing, distribution) and operations (e.g., order processing). From this point of view, Amazon's celebrated hiring of Wal-Mart's information technology/logistics experts seems like a brilliant move.

There is, however, another point of view on Amazon.com. It could also be thought of as a firm in the value network configuration. Its success would therefore spring not from efficiency of ordering and delivery of books, but from brokering information about book-buying behavior. By selling the largest number of books, Amazon collects information on what other customers with similar tastes do. For example, if a customer buys book A, Amazon can inform that person that customers who bought book A also bought book B. Further, descriptions of books are accompanied by reviews written by the publishers, authors, critics, and anyone who wants to contribute a review. Thus, the value of the information that Amazon has increases with the size of the network, which is represented by the number of book purchasers. In this light, Amazon's pursuit of warehouses and logistics personnel seems like optimizing on the wrong variable. Instead, if the firm considered itself a value network, it would focus its efforts on personalization, collaborative filtering, and information brokering.

SUMMARY

Eliminating geographic distance is the most important property of the Internet for all three value configurations, but the reduction in distance interacts with other properties uniquely for each configuration. Table 6.1 summarizes these important interactions. For the value chain, it is keeping costs low through more efficient procurement and logistics. For the value shop, it is the increasing amount of available exploitable information while simultaneously recognizing that value shops based on explicit rather than tacit knowledge will be rendered uncompetitive. For the value network, it is the ability to build the network quickly to take advantage of network externalities.

Value configurations, such as the value chain, are based on Thompson's three generic organizational technologies:

- Long-linked—sequential interdependencies, serial tasks, continuous output of standardized products, clear criteria for capital and labor selection.
- Intensive—for solving highly specific problems in an iterative fashion.
- Mediating—facilitate intermediary services; focus on standardized criteria and decision making and scale of operations.

The value chain is a value configuration (or value creation logic) that is applied most appropriately to manufacturing and product-oriented businesses. In light of the growing service and digital economies, other models are needed to explain value creation for competitive advantage.

The focus of the value chain (that is, firms oriented toward a value chain logic) is on efficiency, process, and lowering cost. Disintermediation is a possibility for both logistics and procurement. The focus of the value shop is on customizing service(s) to the need(s) of clients, new product development, and differentiation. The value shop is based on constant, iterative problem solving in real time (solving problems the client cannot solve). For value shop oriented firms, the Internet

TABLE 6.1 The Most Important Properties of Each Value Configuration

Value Configuration	Most Important Properties
Value chain	Universality
Value shop	Reduces information asymmetries
Value network	Compounds network externalities
Support activities	Reduces transaction costs

104

PART II
Components,
Linkages, Dynamics,
and Evaluation of
Business Models

allows for a larger scale of operations, a wider geographic scope, more information to be collected and processed, and a new delivery medium or mechanism. The focus of the value network is on brokering, building the network of users (buyers) and suppliers, contract management, service provisioning and infrastructure operations. For value network oriented firms, the Internet allows for a larger scale of the network, a wider geographic scope of the network, and a speedier compounding of network externalities.

KEY TERMS

benchmarking 93	secondary (support) activities 89
disintermediation 92	service provisioning 93
information overload 96	typology of organizational
intensive technology 88	technologies 88
iterative problem solving 94	value chain 89
leapfrog 92	value configuration 88
long-linked technology 88	value creation logic 93
mediating technology 88	value network 88
primary activities 89	value shop 88

DISCUSSION QUESTIONS

1. Why should a firm bother to choose the most appropriate value configuration?
2. List one firm for each value configuration. Why is the value configuration you assigned the most appropriate?
3. How do the three firms you listed in your answer to No. 2 make money? What are the core competencies of each firm? Which competence is the most extensible? Why?
4. In the value shop example, what is the problem that the firm is solving for clients/customers?
5. Give an example of:
 - a long-linked technology
 - an intensive technology
 - a mediating technology

Show how each fits into the value configurations mentioned above.
6. To what value configuration does America Online (AOL) most closely conform? Is this true of the many companies it has acquired (e.g., Netscape, Time Warner)?

REFERENCES

1. James D. Thompson, *Organizations in Action* (New York: McGraw-Hill, 1967).
2. See Charles B. Stabell and Øystein D. Fjeldstad, "Configuring Value for Competitive Advantage: On Chains, Shops, and Networks," *Strategic Management Journal* 19 (1998), pp. 413–37. The value chain configuration has been the dominant value creation logic in the economy for the last century. However, over the last 10 to 20 years, the "service economy" has equaled, and recently surpassed, the manufacturing economy. The Internet has played a role in speeding up this transition. Thus, management

researchers prior to the rise of the Internet and the service economy had little need to describe a different type of value creation logic.

3. Stabell and Fjeldstad, "Configuring Value for Competitive Advantage," pp. 414–15.

4. Thompson, *Organizations in Action,* pp. 15–18.

5. Thompson, *Organizations in Action,* p. 17.

6. These are not mutually exclusive: A company could have both differentiated products and a low cost structure.

7. Michael Porter, *Competitive Strategy* (New York: Free Press, 1985).

8. Some question the concept of the value chain as it relates to retailing. Retailers can also be thought of as intermediaries, bringing buyers and sellers together (although they do not facilitate a spot transaction, most hold inventory). This will be discussed further in the next section.

9. Paul Timmers, "Business Models for Electronic Markets," *Electronic Markets* 8, no. 2 (1998), pp. 3–8.

10. Timmers also introduced the categories of "e-auction" and "virtual communities" which were primarily value network configurations as described below.

11. Eric von Hippel, *The Sources of Innovation* (New York: Oxford University Press, 1988).

12. Raghu Garud, Sanjay Jain, and Corey Phelps, "From Vaporware to Betaware," *STERNBusiness* 4, no. 2 (1997), pp. 20–23.

13. Jupiter Communications, www.jupitercommunications.com/home.jsp

14. www.quickenstore.com.

15. Mihir Parikh, "The Music Industry in the Digital World: Waves of Change." Working paper, Institute for Technology and Enterprise, 1999; see also G. Raik-Allen, "Players Line Up for Battle over Online Music Industry," *Red Herring,* February 1999, www.redherring.com/insider/1999/0202/news-music.com; "Music over the Web," *Business Week,* March 2, 1998, p. 89; and "Diamond Multimedia and the Rio Player," NYU Stern School of Business, Case #991-071, 1999.

16. It should be noted that the disintermediation argument can be equally applied to the secondary or support activity of procurement. Procurement is a secondary activity that supports all three value configurations. See Timmers, "Business Models for Electronic Markets," p. 5 ("e-procurement").

17. Joel J. Smith, "Northwest Bypasses Agents," *Detroit News,* February 18, 1999, www.detnews.com/1999/technology/9902/19/02180177.htm.

18. See below why this might not really be the only story, or even the story at all.

19. "Selling PCs like Bananas," *The Economist,* October 5, 1996, p. 63.

20. Travel agents, especially those who only sell tickets to people who already know what they want, might be thought of as intermediaries. This will be discussed in the next section.

21. Henceforth we will eliminate the exclamation point from the name to minimize distraction.

22. It could also be that Delta's marginal costs are higher with the telephone while the fixed costs are higher with the Internet. Therefore, even though one might argue that the total cost is lower with the telephone, Delta is attempting to discourage its use to exploit lower marginal costs.

23. Expedia, owned by Microsoft, had not made a profit as of early 2000; Microsoft uses its deep pockets to fund the fixed costs of Expedia's capacity. However, the trend mentioned above—the replacement of bricks-and-mortar agencies by Internet agencies— is expected to continue.

24. Stabell and Fjeldstad, "Configuring Value for Competitive Advantage," p. 429.

25. For more information about the dynamics of the Internet's effect on value networks, see Larry Downes and Chunka Mui, *Unleashing the Killer App* (Boston: Harvard Business School Press, 1998); see also Carl Shapiro and Hal R. Varian, *Information Rules* (Boston: Harvard Business School Press, 1999).

Valuing and Financing an Internet Start-Up

As we noted in Chapter 1, most people go into business to make money. If the business has what it takes to be profitable, its founders often have to decide when to take out their share of the profits. They usually face at least two options: (1) They can collect the profits over the life of the business or (2) sell part or all of the business to investors who, for a price, get the right to collect some or all of the future cash flows from the business. To carry out the second option, it is important to determine how much the company is worth—it is important to value the business. In the first part of this chapter, we explore the cash flow, price earnings (P/E) ratio, price-earnings growth (PEG), and business model based methods for valuing technology start-ups. We also take a look at the role of intellectual capital in valuing companies. We begin with a brief discussion of the initial public offering (IPO) process.

In the second part of the chapter, we recognize that somewhere in the process of conceiving and executing a business model, a firm usually needs money; that is, before a firm can start making money, it needs money. Finding, obtaining, and allocating this money to the right components of the business model is called financing. We explore the different sources of financing for a start-up and suggest that although low-cost money is important, the complementary assets and intellectual capital that often come with some financing sources can be even more important for start-ups.

WHEN TO CASH OUT

Over a Firm's Life Cycle

Over each accounting period, a firm receives money from its revenue sources but must also spend money to cover the costs that it incurs in offering value to its customers. The cash that the company generates is normally called *cash inflows* while the cash that it consumes is called *cash outflows*. The excess of cash inflows over cash outflows is the amount of money available to the owners of the business to take out or plow back into the business.

Collecting Early

Rather than wait to collect profits over the life of a firm, an entrepreneur may decide to collect today by selling his or her right to collect future profits to someone else. Very early in the life of a start-up, this someone is usually a venture capital firm. The funds collected at this stage, however, usually go to meet the large cash outflows required to keep the fledgling start-up going, not for the owners to take out. In return for the funding, the venture capital firm usually gets a share of the company and the right to a piece of future cash flows. Founders can also sell part of their company to institutional investors such as retirement funds or to rich individuals often known as angel investors. A popular way, however, is to sell shares of the company to the public by means of an **initial public offering (IPO)**. In an IPO, anyone can buy shares of the company and, in return, is entitled to an appropriate share of the company's future free cash flows. Indeed, the primary motivation for venture capital firms and other early investors is the anticipation of cashing out at the time of the IPO or shortly thereafter. They usually do not invest in a start-up with the intention of waiting to share in future earnings from the firm.

THE IPO PROCESS

In the late 1990s wealth in the billions of dollars was created for many Americans through the IPO process. The process of issuing an IPO starts with building a viable business.[1] The firm then finds an underwriter, usually an **investment bank** such as Goldman Sachs, Solomon Smith Barney, or Morgan Stanley Dean Witter (see Figure 7.1). The investment bank determines how much the firm is worth, how many shares to issue to the public, when to issue the shares, and what to price the shares. According to the full disclosure requirement of the Securities Act of 1933, the investment bank must file a registration statement with the Securities and Exchange Commission (SEC) in which it provides a description of the business, financial statements, the purposes of the money raised from the stock issue, any legal proceedings involving the firm, biographical information on the officers of the firm, and the number of shares owned by officers of the company and any shareholder who owns more than 10 percent of the stock. Following the filing date is a **cooling off period** during which the SEC verifies that full disclosure has been made. When the SEC is satisfied, it gives its approval for the issue to be offered to the public. The date on which this approval comes is called the effective date since from that day on the firm can hold its IPO. While waiting for approval from the SEC, the investment bank usually tries to generate interest in the issue. The amount of interest from investors is an important factor in determining the price of the issue. Each of these investors, usually a select group (called Joe Privileged in Figure 7.1), makes a commitment to buy a certain number of shares at the **public offering price**.

If public interest in the issue is high on the IPO date, the price of the stock may rise quickly from the offering price, making Joe Privileged very rich. In 1999 most Internet-related issues closed higher than their public offering prices. Of course, if interest from the public is very low, then Joe Privileged may not be so lucky after all and the start-up firm that issued the stock gets a lower price than the public offering price.[2] The difference, also called the *spread,* is used to pay the underwriter. The

108

*PART II
Components,
Linkages, Dynamics,
and Evaluation of
Business Models*

FIGURE 7.1 The IPO Process

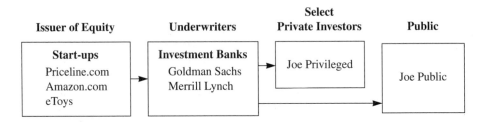

underwriter usually enters one of two types of agreements with the firm. In a firm commitment, the underwriter guarantees to sell a certain number of shares. If the public does not buy all the shares, the underwriter will buy the rest. In a "best efforts" agreement, the underwriter only commits to do the best that it can to sell the shares, leaving the issuing firm responsible for any unsold shares.

Impact of the Internet on the IPO Process

Technically, start-up firms could go straight to the public to sell their stocks. One main reason why such firms have traditionally hired investment banks is that these banks have information on how to value issues and drum up interest in an IPO through their established relations with clients—information that start-ups usually do not have. The backing of a stock issue by an investment bank lends credibility to the valuation and viability of the firm issuing the shares. Thus, investment banks act as intermediaries between issuing firms and investors. The Internet may make these benefits become less important. Now, an issue's prospectus can be posted on the Internet and instead of a select number of clients buying the shares at a guaranteed price before the rest of the public, the issues can be auctioned to the public through an Internet auction house such as eBay without passing through an investment bank. In any case, to determine the number of shares to be sold and at what price, the investment bank or the firm must value the business.

VALUATION OF A BUSINESS

We next explore several methods that have been used to value firms and businesses: Cash flow, price-earnings (P/E) ratio, price-earnings growth (PEG) ratio, and one based on the business model.

Cash Flows

In the Theory of Investment Value, *written over 50 years ago, John Burr Williams set forth the equation for value, which we condense here: The value of any stock, bond or business is determined by the cash inflows and outflows—discounted at the appropriate interest rate—that can be expected to occur during the remaining life of the asset.*

WARREN BUFFETT

The value of a business or firm, then, is the **present value** of its future free cash flows discounted at its cost of capital. Thus, the value of a firm V is given by:[3]

$$V = C_0 + \frac{C_1}{(1 + r_k)} + \frac{C_2}{(1 + r_k)^2} + \cdots + \frac{C_n}{(1 + r_k)^n}$$

$$= \sum_{t=0}^{t=n} \frac{C_t}{(1 + r_k)^t} \tag{1}$$

where

C_t is the free cash flow at time t, and

r_k is the firm's cost of capital.

This discounting reflects the higher value of money today than its value tomorrow.

If the value of a stock is determined by the present value of the cash inflows and outflows that can be expected to occur during the remaining life of the business, valuing a business boils down to determining what those cash inflows and outflows will be over the life of the business and the appropriate discount rate.

Free Cash Flow

Free cash flow is the cash from a business's operations that is available for distribution to its claim holders—equity investors and debtors—who provide capital. It is the difference between cash earnings and cash investments. A firm's free cash flow, C_t, in period t is given by:[4]

C_t = Cash earnings (from income statement) − Cash investments (from balance sheet)

= Operating income − Taxes on operating income + Depreciation + Noncash charges

− Increase in **working capital** (current assets − current liabilities) in period t

− Cash expenditures on investments in period t $\qquad$ (2)

Operating income, taxes on operating income, depreciation, and noncash charges are from the firm's income statement while increase in working capital and cash expenditures on investments are from the balance sheet.

Discount Rate

The **discount rate**, r_k, is the firm's opportunity cost of capital. It is the expected rate of return that could be earned from an investment of similar risk. It reflects the systematic risk that is specific to the firm and therefore undiversifiable. The discount rate can be estimated using a model such as the **capital asset pricing model (CAPM)**:

$$r_k = r_f + \beta_i (r_m - r_f) \tag{3}$$

That is, the discount rate is equal to r_f, the risk-free rate such as the interest rate on Treasury bills, plus a risk premium. This **risk premium** is equal to the **systematic risk** or beta coefficient, β_i, for the business or firms, and the excess return over the market return r_m.

One advantage that Internet companies have over their bricks-and-mortar competitors is that they can take advantage of the Internet's properties in crafting their business models to improve their cash flows. Consider again Amazon.com. Before it built its own warehouses, it carried no inventory. Whenever a customer placed an order for a book, the customer paid with his or her credit card and Amazon collected the cash almost immediately. Amazon then ordered the book from a wholesaler or publisher who delivered it directly to the customer right away but did not collect the cash for the book from Amazon until 30 to 45 days later. Effectively, Amazon kept the customer's money for 30 to 45 days before paying the book wholesaler or publisher. This meant that Amazon had negative working capital for that particular transaction and from expression (2) above, this means positive cash flow for Amazon. Even after building its own warehouses, Amazon kept inventory for an average of only two weeks. Additionally, whenever Amazon doubled its sales it did not have to double the number of physical stores—as would a bricks-and-mortar competitor like Borders—because it had none. That also saved on cash expenditures for investment, effectively increasing free cash flow.

Free cash flow gains do not come only from pure play Internet firms like Amazon.com. Bricks-and-mortar firms could also boost their free cash flows by adopting the Internet. Consider automakers. In 1998 alone, automakers had an estimated $100 billion in inventory, much of it because of their inability to forecast what customers want. By using the Internet to "go direct" to customers using a Dell-type model,[5] much of the inventory could be eliminated. Less inventory means less working capital and therefore more free cash flow.

The main problem with using equation (1) for determining the value of a firm is that it is very difficult to predict what the cash flows and cost of capital will be in the future. The situation is particularly challenging for start-up firms, most of which do not have positive cash flows. One way to circumvent this problem is to find a firm whose systematic risk or beta coefficient is similar to that of the start-ups and use that firm's cash flows with the necessary adjustments to estimate the cash flows of the start-up. This procedure is analogous to the more widely used price-earnings methods that we discuss next.

Price-Earnings (P/E) Ratio

In the **price-earnings (P/E) ratio** method of valuing firms, a P/E ratio for the firm is first determined. By multiplying this P/E ratio by the firm's earnings, the price per share can be obtained. Also called the capitalization factor, the P/E ratio reflects investors' expectations of future earnings. The question is, How does one determine the P/E ratio for the firm to begin with? One thing to do is to find firms with similar beta coefficients and use their P/E ratio as a base; that is, look for firms whose systematic risk is similar to that of the firm in question. The P/E ratio from the reference group is then adjusted for any differences between the firm and the reference firms. The ratio is further adjusted for general conditions. For example, the ratio is adjusted upward in a bull market and downward in a bear market.[6] After all the adjustments have been made to the ratio, it is multiplied by the firm's earnings to obtain its share price.

SIMPLE EXAMPLE. It is now 2001 and back in 1999 you had founded an online auction firm that earned $3 million in 2000. You are about to go public. With the help of the venture capital firm that financed many of your start-up activities, you have found an investment bank which suggests that you issue 5 million shares in an initial public offering. What should be the share price of your firm? The P/E ratio of other online auction firms is 80. The earnings per share of your company is $3M/5M = $0.60. Since the P/E ratio is 80,

$$\frac{P}{E} = \frac{p}{\$0.6} = 80 \Rightarrow p = \$48$$

Thus, the share price that you should expect is $48.

This method, although very popular, has several shortcomings. First, although earnings are highly correlated with cash flows, they are not free cash flows. A firm can be profitable but have negative free cash flows and vice versa. Second, there is more than one type of earnings, so deciding on which one to use is not easy. Third, there is always the question of whether historical earnings are a good predictor of future earnings.

Price-Earnings Growth (PEG) Ratio

The **price-earnings growth (PEG) ratio** method more explicitly incorporates the role of growth. Calculations are similar to those that use the P/E with adjustments made for growth. Consider our online auction example. Suppose the firm is growing at 90 percent annually. Since its P/E ratio is 80, we obtain the PEG ratio by dividing the P/E ratio by its annual growth rate:

$$\frac{80}{90} = .89$$

What is considered a good PEG ratio is a matter of debate. Traditionally, stocks with PEG ratios of less than 1.00 were considered good buys. Anything above that was thought to be overpriced. Such generalizations are no substitute for careful research that digests a firm's business model to understand why one can expect profits from the company down the line.

The PEG ratio suffers from the same types of problems as the P/E ratio. In addition, ratios lose some useful information when data are simplified for better absorption. Consider firms A and B, each with a PEG ratio of 1. However, firm A has a P/E ratio of 50 and a growth rate of 50 percent while B has a P/E ratio of 4 and a growth rate of 4 percent. These seem to be two very different firms in different industries; therefore, each stock is likely to attract a different type of investor. Firm B may be early in its life in a fast-growing industry where it has invested a large amount of up-front capital that should pay off soon, while A is in a mature industry with high variable costs and not much hope of growth. In any case, using both methods to value start-ups is particularly problematic because most start-ups have negative earnings, even those that are going to be profitable later.

VALUATION OF BUSINESSES THAT ARE NOT YET PROFITABLE

Most start-up companies lose money and have negative cash flows in their formative years. In the late 1990s many Internet firms that went public had not yet become profitable. How do you estimate the value of a firm that has negative earnings?

Nothing in our discussion of price-earnings and price-earning growth said anything about negative earnings. We explore two methods of accomplishing this task.

Firm and Industry Proxies

In the firm and industry proxy method, a firm's share price is estimated using the P/E ratios of analogs—firms and industries that the analyst deems representative of the subject firm. This method is best illustrated by Henry Blodget's 1998 estimates of Amazon.com's share price (see Illustration Capsule 7.1).

Business Models Approach: Earnings and Cash Flow Chain

Instead of finding proxy firms and industries, we could turn to a firm's business model for some indication of future earnings potential. When we explored the pricing component of a business model in Chapter 4, we showed how a firm—with high up-front costs and relatively low variable costs—could lose a great deal of money early in the life of a product or technology but become very profitable later. We argued that the primary indicators of whether such a firm would be profitable in the future were its profit margins, market share, and revenue share growth. If a start-up is not profitable, some of the measures upstream of its profit/cash flow chain (see Figure 7.2) could be used in estimating share prices.

Profitability Predictor Measures

Since profit margins, market share, and revenue share growth are good **profitability predictor measures** of future profits, we can use price-margins, price-share, and price-share growth, rather than price-earnings (P/E) or price-earnings

---

Illustration Capsule 7.1
Estimating Share Prices of Firms with Negative Earnings

He starts by looking at the size of Amazon's target market. Worldwide, the market for books, music, and videos is around $100 billion. So how big a slice of that can the company get? Blodget draws an analogy between Amazon, the leader in its category, and Wal-Mart, the leader in discount retailing, which has a 10 percent market share. Since Amazon is adding to its product mix, he thinks it's fair to estimate that it could hit a 10 percent share in the next five years, which would amount to $10 billion in revenues. Then, he asks, what could the company's profit margin be? Traditional retailers typically achieve net margins of 1 percent to 4 percent. But Blodget believes Amazon will be able to run leaner than land-based types by paying less rent, keeping less inventory, and hiring fewer employees. Its net margin, he assumes, could be more like Dell's—a fatter 7 percent. So, 7 percent of $10 billion is $700 million in net income. The last question is, what price/earnings multiple will the market assign Amazon at that point? P/Es normally range from 10 or so for a slow-growth company to about 75 for one that's growing quickly. That means that a slow-growing Amazon could have a $7 billion market cap, or $44 per share (post-split), while a fast-growing Amazon could be worth $53 billion, or $332 per share. Using these assumptions, Amazon's current $25 billion market cap and $160 share price start to seem plausible.

Source: Fortune, February 1, 1999, p. 148.

FIGURE 7.2 Profits/Cash Flow Chain of an ISP

113

CHAPTER 7
Valuing and
Financing an
Internet Start-Up

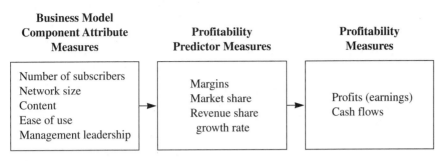

growth (PEG) ratios to determine a firm's share price. Their use is analogous to that of P/E and PEG. For example, if a new Internet service provider (ISP) is going public and we know of other ISPs that recently went public, we can estimate its value by comparing its margins, market share, or revenue share growth rate to that of the proxy firms.

Business Model Component Attribute Measures

Where margins, market share, and revenue share growth rates are not available, we could use measures of those business model component attribute measures that drive them (Figure 7.2). In valuing an ISP, for example, these measures are the number of subscribers, network size, amount and quality of content available, ease of use of system and management talent. For a biotechnology start-up, for example, the number of patents that the firm owns or the number of staff scientists with Ph.D.s would be a good metric.

INTELLECTUAL CAPITAL: VALUING THE PARTS

If a firm with three major product lines were to be broken up, one could value each product line because it is possible to estimate earnings and free cash flows from each. Now suppose a key individual threatened to leave a start-up company. What is his or her worth to the company? How much are a firm's client network, repeat customers, patents, and copyrights worth? Valuation of such "assets" can be problematic even for firms that have gone public and have stable cash flows and earnings. Valuing such intangibles is becoming increasingly important, especially in a knowledge economy, and has led to the term *intellectual capital* which we will define soon. For the moment, however, consider the simple but useful balance sheet equation:

$$\text{Assets} = \text{Liabilities} + \text{Shareholder equity}$$

Whence:

$$\text{Assets} - \text{Liabilities} = \text{Book value} = \text{Shareholder equity} \qquad \textbf{(4)}$$

One way to interpret this equation is if a firm were to close its doors to business, then what is left over to pay shareholders is the assets less liabilities—the **book value**. Prior to the decision to close its doors, however, what shareholders would get from the company if they were to sell their shares would be the **market value** of the firm (shares outstanding multiplied by share price). This suggests that

114

PART II
Components,
Linkages, Dynamics,
and Evaluation of
Business Models

market value ought to be close to book value. Table 7.1, however, indicates otherwise. Look at Microsoft. In 1994 its book value was $4.45 billion while its market value was $41.34 billion, or almost 10 times as much. In 1997 Microsoft's book value was $10.77 billion and its market value $199 billion, almost 20 times as much. Compare this to General Motors 1997 book value of $18 billion and market value of $54 billion. In 1999 Microsoft's market value was about 25 times its book value. While the differences in other firms' book and market values are not as astounding as Microsoft's, they are still very large.

The differences between book value and market value suggest that there is something else about each of these firms, other than the assets on their books, that makes investors believe that they will keep generating free cash flows or earnings. Why is it important to understand this difference? Because, managers would like to know how to manage it, given its enormous significance. This difference has been called **intellectual capital** and has been attributed to several factors: (1) underpriced physical assets or intangible assets such as patents, trade secrets, and trademarks; (2) human capital—the people who must turn assets, underpriced or otherwise, into products or services that customers want;[7] (3) the product market positions that firms chose in industries that are, by their nature, more profitable than others; (4) unique resources or capabilities that are difficult to imitate or substitute, the source of the enduring advantage that allows firms to keep earning profits; and (5) knowledge, whether embedded in employees, encoded in some physical form, or resident in organizational routines that firms use to offer better value to their customers than competitors.[8] Such knowledge gives a firm a sustainable competitive advantage so long as it is difficult to copy, replicate, or substitute.[9]

Components of Intellectual Capital

We can distinguish between three components of intellectual capital: intellectual property, human capital, and organizational capital.[10] All three are a function of where knowledge resides and of how it can be converted into customer value. Understanding these components and their contribution to the market value of a firm may enable us to determine the worth of, say, human capital and therefore the worth of key individuals within a firm.

TABLE 7.1 Sample Book and Market Values

Firm	March 15, 1994		March 15, 1997		March 15, 1999	
	Book Value ($ million)	Market Value ($ million)	Book Value ($ million)	Market Value ($ million)	Book Value ($ million)	Market Value ($ million)
Intel	$ 9,267	$35,172	$19,295	$125,741	$23,371	$196,616
Microsoft	4,450	41,339	10,777	199,046	16,627	418,579
General Motors	12,823	33,188	17,506	54,243	14,984	63,839
General Electric	26,387	92,321	34,438	260,147	38,880	360,251
Cisco			4,289	64,568	7,106	166,616
Dell			1,293	41,294	2,321	111,322

Intellectual Property

115

CHAPTER 7
Valuing and
Financing an
Internet Start-Up

The **intellectual property** component refers to codified knowledge in a form that enables a company to claim ownership, including patents, copyrights, trademarks, brand names, databases, microcodes, engineering drawings, contracts, trade secrets, documents, and semiconductor masks, as well as intangibles such as reputation, network size, installed base, client relationships, and special licenses.[11] These are the "havings" since they are things that a firm *has* opposed to the things that it *does*.[12] The extent to which intellectual properties are protectable, difficult to replicate, or substitute determines the extent to which firms can profit from any products or services that rest on them.

Human Capital

Intellectual property, in and of itself, will not give a firm a competitive advantage. It also takes employees with the skills, know-how, experience, and competencies to build intellectual property or use it to deliver value to customers.[13] It also takes **human capital** which is the specialist knowledge that is resident in employees. A top-notch scientist's knowledge of combinatorial chemistry is an example. Human capital is what Richard Hall calls the "doing" since it refers to the ability to perform value-adding activities—the ability to get things done.[14]

Organizational Capital

Intellectual property and human capital, in and of themselves, may not be sufficient to give their owners a competitive advantage. For example, a cache of patents and Nobel laureates alone are not likely to give a firm a competitive advantage. Factors internal and external to a firm allow firms to turn their intellectual property and human capital into customer value and to cultivate more intellectual property. For lack of a better name, we will call these factors **organizational capital**.[15] Internal to a firm, the factors of organizational capital are the firm's structure, systems, strategy, people, and culture that it uses to create, share, coordinate and integrate the knowledge and skills embodied in individual employees to make intellectual property and to convert the intellectual property into products that customers want.[16] A project structure, for example, is more conducive to tasks of short duration in environments that are not fast moving while, in some industries, projects with "heavyweight" project managers perform better than those without. Still, in other industries, the culture that firms have cultivated—the "system of shared values (what is important) and beliefs (how things work) that interact with the organization's people, organizational structures, and systems to produce behavioral norms (the way we do things around here)"—can be a source of competitive advantage.[17] Sometimes, factors external to the firm are also critical to the ability of firms to innovate. For example, firms in a region with a system that provides financial support and rewards for innovation, a culture that tolerates failure, the right suppliers, customers, complementors, competitors, universities and other research institutions, and supportive government policies are conducive to the creation of intellectual property and their conversion into new products.[18]

FINANCING A START-UP

A firm has several instruments for financing entrepreneurial activity: Internal assets in which the firm reallocates the resources it already has to the entrepreneurial

116

*PART II
Components,
Linkages, Dynamics,
and Evaluation of
Business Models*

activity; equity financing in which the firm issues equity to venture capital firms, private individuals, or the public in return for financing; debt in which the firm issues some form of debt; and complementary asset financing in which a firm reaches out for complementary assets through a strategic alliance or an acquisition.[19] The balance sheet relation in Figure 7.3 shows the relationships between the financing instruments.

Internal Sources: Assets and Activity

A firm has several internal sources to which it can turn for financing an entrepreneurial activity. First, a firm can use its retained earnings. As shown in Figure 7.3, retained earnings come from the profits that a firm makes, net of any dividends that the firm pays out to shareholders. Thus, a very profitable firm does not have to seek outside financing.[20] Second, a firm can use existing assets, originally earmarked for another project, for the innovation. Chrysler's need for outside financing of its blockbuster minivan was reduced because it already had a front-wheel-drive engine and

FIGURE 7.3 Sources of Financing: The Balance Sheet Context

Revenues − Expenses = Net Income

Beginning Balance of + Net Income − Dividends = Ending Balance of
Retained Earnings   Retained Earnings

Assets = Liabilities + Paid-in Capital + Retained Earnings

Assets	= Liabilities	+ Shareholders' Equity
Tangible assets	Accounts Payable	Common Stock
Cash	Notes Payable	Issued to venture capitalist
Marketable Securities	Interest Payable	Issued to the public
Accounts Receivable	Income Taxes Payable	Preferred Stock
Notes Receivable	Advances from Customers	Retained Earnings
Interest Receivable	Rent Received in Advance	Treasury Shares
Inventories	Mortgage Payable	
Prepaids	Bonds Payable	
Land	Capitalized Lease Obligations	
Buildings	Deferred Income Taxes	
Equipment		
Leasehold		
Intangible assets		
Client relations		
Distribution channels		
Brand-name reputation		
Patents		
Copyrights		
Trademarks		

Source: Reprinted from *Innovation Management: Strategies, Implementation, and Profits* (New York: Oxford University Press, 1998), p. 200.

transmission—critical components in the minivan—that it used in its Dodge Omni and Plymouth Horizon cars.[21] Entrepreneurs often use personal assets. Hewlett Packard and Apple began in garages in the Silicon Valley.

Equity

To finance its activities, a firm can issue equity; that is, through **equity financing**, a firm can sell shares of the company to investors in return for money that the firm needs. Figure 7.4 provides some elements of the equity market. Equity can be issued to the public through a stock exchange such as the NASDAQ (National Association of Securities Dealers Automated Quotations) or the London Stock Exchange. The issue can take the form of an initial public offering (IPO) in which, for the first time, a firm offers its shares to the public for purchase. For many Internet start-ups in the late 1990s, this was one of the most popular sources of financing.

For many start-ups whose products have not yet been proven, the most likely buyers of their equity are private equity firms. Private equity can be venture or nonventure. **Venture equity** is issued by start-ups in the early or later stages of their start-up cycle. In return for part ownership in the start-up, a venture capital firm or other financier will finance the start-up. Their primary motivation is to cash in during the IPO which will eventually come after the start-up has proven itself dynamic enough to go public. In addition to providing the much-needed money, venture capital firms can also offer management expertise which can be critical for a start-up. Some venture

FIGURE 7.4 Different Elements of Equity

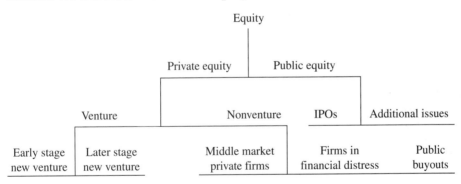

Major players
- Venture capital firms such as Kleiner, Perkins, Caufield, and Byers; and Asset Management
- SBICs

Source of funds for major players
- Own money
- "Angels"
- Partnerships

Major players
- Buyout groups such as Kohlberg, Kravis, Roberts

Source of funds for major players
- Partnerships

Source: Reprinted from *Innovation Management: Strategies, Implementation, and Profits* (New York: Oxford University Press, 1998), p. 202.

capital firms have networks of firms in which they have stakes, and such firms can become the start-up's first customer or supplier. Such intangibles are often critical in the life of a start-up. One major drawback to obtaining venture capital is that the start-up firm often loses control of a large part of the company to the venture capital firm. The money that venture capital firms use to finance ventures can be their own or that of limited partners. In the United States, venture capital can also come from small business investment companies (SBICs). These are private corporations that have been licensed by the Small Business Administration to provide financing to risky companies. To encourage them to undertake these risky loans, the federal government gives SBICs tax breaks and Small Business Administration (SBA) loans.

Debt

A firm can also borrow money from a money-lending institution such as a bank, or sell bonds or notes; that is, it can acquire debt. The problem with **debt financing** is that the financier usually wants some physical assets as collateral—something that most start-ups usually do not have. Their assets are often intangible, largely intellectual capital, which may not be enough collateral for some banks. The drawback in borrowing is that interest payments may drain off profits that could have been plugged back into the business or paid out as dividends to investors. If a start-up does issue debt, sometimes the debt is convertible to equity.

A smart form of debt financing for start-ups is the one undertaken by Amazon.com, which we described earlier in our discussion of cash flows. Recall that the firm collected from its customers right away but did not pay its vendors until 30 to 45 days later. During that time, it used the money that it owed its vendors to finance its activities. This is sometimes called **working capital financing**.

Complementary Assets

As we saw in Chapter 5, complementary assets are critical to profiting from an innovation. Unfortunately, most start-up firms lack these assets. We also said that some complementary assets are difficult to replicate or substitute. For example, it is very difficult for a fledgling Web advertising firm to replicate the kinds of relationships that bricks-and-mortar firms have had for decades with Fortune 500 clients. Money from a venture capital firm or bank may not be able to buy such relations right away. An alternative is to enter some form of strategic alliance with an owner of the complementary assets, buy that owner, or sell your firm to the owner.

SUMMARY

Firms are in business to make money. But to make money, they often need money up front to get going. Thus, a firm has two finance-related problems: How to find and use the money that it needs, and how to cash out. An entrepreneur can collect the money from the free cash flows of his or her business over the life of the business or sell the right to collect some of the future free cash flows to venture capitalists, angels, or to the public through an initial public offering (IPO). In either case, the business must be valued so that the financier can know the value of his or her investment. Many methods have been used to value firms: free cash flow, price-earnings (P/E) ratios, price-earnings growth (PEG) ratios, and the business model. Valuing Internet start-ups is particularly troublesome because most of them have neither positive free cash flows nor positive earnings. In such a case, proxies together with predictors of earnings and cash flows such as profit margins, market share, and revenue share growth rate can be used to value a firm. Beyond that, measurable business model component attributes can be used.

There are several sources of financing for a start-up: a firm's own assets, venture capital, debt, IPO, and some form of teaming up with a firm that has complementary assets. The most important thing about financing a start-up is that money purchased with the lowest interest rate is not always the best money because start-ups usually need important complementary assets that are difficult to acquire or substitute. And teaming up with another firm that has such assets or selling an equity share to a venture capital firm may be the best way to get access to such assets.

KEY TERMS

book value   113
capital asset pricing
   model (CAPM)   109
cooling off period   107
debt financing   118
discount rate   109
equity financing   117
free cash flow   109
human capital   115
initial public offering (IPO)   107
intellectual capital   114
intellectual property   115
investment bank   107

market value   113
organizational capital   115
present value   109
price-earnings growth (PEG) ratio   111
price-earnings (P/E) ratio   110
profitability predictor measures   112
public offering price   107
risk premium   109
systematic risk   109
venture equity   117
working capital   109
working capital financing   118

DISCUSSION QUESTIONS

1. What is the difference between earnings and cash flows? Can an unprofitable firm have positive free cash flows?
2. What are drawbacks of using P/E and PEG ratios to value firms?
3. Why is negative working capital a good thing?
4. Why might a firm that is still unprofitable have a very high market value? How would you value such a firm?
5. When might a start-up give up an interest-free loan from a bank and take venture capital money even though the owners of the start-up may lose the control of and equity in their firm?

REFERENCES

1. See, for example, S. C. Blowers, P. H. Griffith, and T. L. Milan, *The Ernst & Young Guide to the IPO Value Journey* (New York: John Wiley, 1999).
2. www.internetnews.com/stocks/ipodex/

120

PART II
Components,
Linkages, Dynamics,
and Evaluation of
Business Models

3. See, for example, R. A. Brealey and S. C. Myers, *Principles of Corporate Finance* (New York: McGraw-Hill, 1995).

4. See, for example, C. P. Stickney and R. L. Weil, *Financial Accounting,* 7th ed. (New York: Dryden, 1994); W. Petty, "Harvesting," in *The Portable MBA in Entrepreneurship,* ed. by W. D. Bygrave (New York: John Wiley, 1997), pp. 414–41.

5. In the United States, however, franchise laws do not permit direct sales of cars to customers.

6. M. J. Dollinger, *Entrepreneurship: Strategies and Resources* (Burr Ridge, IL: Richard D. Irwin, 1995).

7. D. Ulrich, "Intellectual Capital = Competence × Commitment," *Sloan Management Review* 39, no. 2 (1998), pp. 15–27.

8. L. Edvinsson and P. Sullivan, "Developing a Model for Managing Intellectual Capital," *European Management Journal* 14, no. 4 (August 1996), p. 356; I. Nonaka, "A Dynamic Theory of Organizational Knowledge Creation," *Organization Science* 5, no. 1 pp. 477–501; T. A. Stewart, *Intellectual Capital: The New Wealth of Organizations* (New York: Currency/Doubleday, 1997).

9. M. A. Peteraf, "The Cornerstones of Competitive Advantage: A Resource-based View," *Strategic Management Journal* 14 (1993), pp. 179–91.

10. Edvinsson and Sullivan, "Developing a Model for Managing Intellectual Capital," p. 356; H. Saint-Onge, "Tacit Knowledge: The Key to the Strategic Alignment of Intellectual Capital," *Strategy and Leadership* 2 (March–April 1996), p. 1014.

11. Edvinsson and Sullivan, "Developing a Model for Managing Intellectual Capital," p. 356.

12. R. Hall, "A Framework Linking Intangible Resources and Capabilities to Sustainable Competitive Advantage," *Strategic Management Journal,* 14 (1993), pp. 607–18.

13. C. K. Prahalad and G. Hamel, "The Core Competencies of the Corporation," *Harvard Business Review,* May–June 1990, pp. 79–91.

14. Hall, "A Framework," pp. 607–18.

15. In Edvinsson and Sullivan's (1996) and Saint-Onge's (1996) taxonomy, structural capital includes both organizational capital and human capital.

16. Saint-Onge, "Tacit Knowledge," p. 1014.

17. B. Uttal and J. Fierman, "The Corporate Culture Vultures," *Fortune,* October 17, 1983; J. Barney, "Organizational Culture: Can It Be a Source of Sustained Competitive Advantage?" *Academy of Management Review* 11 (1986), pp. 656–65.

18. This draws on A. N. Afuah, *Innovation Management, Strategies, Implementation, and Profits* (New York: Oxford University Press, 1998), chap. 12.

19. Ibid., chap. 10.

20. The type of financing that is best for a firm and how the firm should go about obtaining that financing are very important topics in corporate finance. See, for example, Brealey and Myers, *Principles of Corporate Finance.*

21. A. Taylor III, and J. E. Davis, "Iacocca's Minivan: How Chrysler Succeeded in Creating the Most Profitable Products of the Decade," *Fortune,* May 30, 1994, pp. 56–63.

PART III

The Role of Competitive and Macro Environments

CHAPTER 8

Competitive and
Macro Environments

So far in this book, we have focused on business models and the Internet, only sparingly referring to the environment in which firms and their business models must operate. But as we pointed out in Chapter 1, a firm's profitability rests as much on its business model as on its environment. In this chapter we explore the role of a firm's environment in determining its business model and profitability (see Figure 8.1). In particular, we explore the impact of the Internet on the competitive and macro environments of a firm and the resulting consequences for business models.

FIGURE 8.1 The Role of the Environment

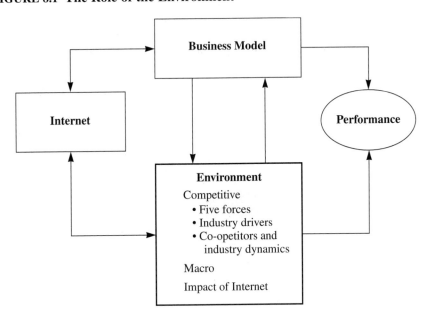

THE ENVIRONMENT AS DETERMINANT OF FIRM PERFORMANCE

As Figure 8.1 shows, a firm's environment is not only a determinant of its performance. It also influences the type of business model that the firm adopts as well as how the Internet evolves. The business model itself is influenced by the Internet and firms. Two types of environments can impact firm performance.[1] First is the **industry** or **competitive environment**: the suppliers, customers, complementors, rivals, substitutes, and potential new entrants with which a firm must interact or take into consideration in making its strategic decisions. Then there is the **macro environment**, the overarching environment of regional and national governments and institutions in which firms in an industry must operate.

The Competitive Environment

For an industry to be profitable, the firms in it must be able to provide products or services whose value to customers considerably exceeds the cost of providing them. But as Michael Porter pointed out, there are five forces—bargaining power of suppliers, bargaining power of buyers, threat of new entrants, rivalry among existing firms, and threat of substitute products—that can prevent firms in the industry from being profitable.[2] The impact of **Porter's five forces** on firm profitability can be understood by considering the simple relationship of equation (1), which states that the profits that firms make are equal to the revenues that they receive from customers in exchange for the products or services that they offer, less the costs of offering them.

$$\text{Profits} = \text{Revenues} - \text{Costs} = P(Q) \times Q(P) - C(Q) \qquad \textbf{(1)}$$

If suppliers have high enough bargaining power to extract higher prices from industry firms, the costs to the firms are higher and their profits reduced. If these powerful suppliers instead get away with offering firms lower-quality inputs, these firms will end up with inferior products for their customers. This in turn will reduce their ability to charge premium prices for the products or they may have to spend more to improve product quality. Either way, industry profits are reduced.

Powerful customers have an analogous effect on firm profitability. They can extract lower prices and higher-quality products from firms. Lower prices and higher quality mean less profitability. A high threat of new entrants forces firms to charge less for their products. They may also be forced to take costly measures to create barriers to entry or differentiate their products. Either way, firm profitability is reduced. Increased rivalry among existing firms can lead to price wars or costly attempts to differentiate products, both of which reduce profitability. Substitute products provide a powerful alternative to firms' products, thereby putting pressure not only on the prices that firms can charge, but also the quantities that they can sell. An industry in which suppliers and buyers have bargaining power, and rivalry, the threat of new entry, and the power of substitutes are high, is said to be **unattractive** because, on the average, the industry's profits are low.

Industry Characteristics and Critical Success Drivers

Every industry has its idiosyncrasies. These may be in the customers, customer value, distribution channels, activities performed to deliver the value, or in the technology that underpins the value and activities. These can lead to certain **industry success drivers** or factors that are critical to success. Firms must exploit these factors if they are going to gain and maintain a competitive advantage in the industry. Critical factors are those that have the most impact on a firm's cost or the distinctive value that it can offer customers. In consulting, for example, capacity utilization is critical. Few firms can afford to have MBAs, who cost over a quarter of a million dollars a year each, idling. Relations with clients are also critical if the consultants are going to win contracts and complete them successfully. So is the ability to create and share knowledge since, when all is said and done, consulting is a knowledge management business. In pharmaceuticals, two industry success drivers are R&D and the ability to perform clinical trials quickly and efficiently. Both determine the efficacy and safety of drugs.

In formulating Internet business models, it is important to identify these industry success drivers and go after them. In the automobile industry, for example, distribution accounts for 30 percent of the price of a car while an inability to forecast what customers want accounts for most of the cost. Well-conceived and well-executed Internet business models for automakers could trim many distribution costs by using the Internet to better forecast. In auctions, the size of the network is critical. Thus, a firm may want to build a loyal clientele early and quickly.

These idiosyncrasies on which industry success drivers rest often distinguish one business model from another. Auction models differ from manufacturing models, and within manufacturing models there are also industry differences.

THE INTERNET AND ENVIRONMENTAL DETERMINANTS OF PERFORMANCE

The question is, though, How do the properties of the Internet that we explored in Chapter 3 impact industry profitability and, in turn, a firm's ability to profit in this new frontier? To explore this question, we focus first on the industry environment and then on the macro environment.

Impact of the Internet on Industry Environment

One way to explore the impact of the Internet on industry profitability is to use Porter's five forces model.[3]

Suppliers

As we saw earlier, suppliers in an industry may be powerful enough to extract the industry's profits through high input prices or low-quality inputs. One source of this power is the information that suppliers may have on their products, prices, and costs that no one else has. The better informed that firms are about their suppliers and the products they are buying, the better their bargaining position. The World Wide Web equalizes this firm-supplier bargaining power somewhat because it reduces the information asymmetry that often exists between firms and their suppliers. Information on products, prices, and firms is more available to more people. For example, by accessing one of many websites, a potential car buyer can obtain detailed information on cars, their prices, and financing—information that was once the main source of power for car dealers. The result is that firms have more power over their suppliers, all else being equal. The distribution channel property means that more suppliers can reach industry firms than could do so before the Internet. For example, a software developer whose products were shunned by computer dealers (stores) can now post its products on the Web. This effectively increases the number of suppliers, giving more power to industry firms (their customers). The universality property has a dual effect. On the one hand, it means that firms in one region do not have to depend as much on local firms for supplies as they did before the Internet. Firms can solicit bids from suppliers worldwide. On the other hand, it also means that suppliers can sell their products to more firms worldwide.

Customers

For the same reasons why the Internet gives more power to firms over their suppliers, it also gives more bargaining power to customers over firms. Customers have more information on firms' products, prices, and costs; more firms compete for customers' attention; and distribution costs are lower, allowing more firms to reach customers. However, the mediating technology nature of the Internet suggests that the relationship between customers and firms is much more than analogous to that between suppliers and firms. Mediating technologies usually have more than one type of customer who is interdependent through the mediating firm. Consider a newspaper, for example. It has customers who buy the paper for the news, and customers who buy the advertising space to sell their products or services to those who read the newspaper. Effectively, the newspaper is a medium of exchange for the two groups of customers.[4] The larger a newspaper audience, the more power the newspaper has over advertisers. The network externality property also suggests that for certain applications, firms with large networks have some bargaining power since the larger the network, the less likely customers are to switch.

Rivalry

Recall that rivalry between existing firms may result in price wars that lower their prices, or advertising and promotion wars that increase their costs. Both result in lower profits for firms in the industry. For many products, the advent of the Internet means more rivalry. Why? Well, look at book retailing. A local bookseller used to face competition only from its bricks-and-mortar neighbors whose stores were located in the same or neighboring towns. With the Internet, the number of competitors increases rapidly because local customers can now buy from Web sellers, which greatly increases rivalry. The universality property also has two opposing effects. On the one hand, competitors can come from anywhere in the world. This increases rivalry. On the other hand, the market is also the whole world, which decreases rivalry since there is a larger pie to be shared.

Threat of New Entrants

Recall that the threat of new entrants forces incumbents to charge less for their products or take costly steps to keep them out. The result is that incumbent profits are lower. Such a threat is reduced if potential new entrants have little information available about incumbents, their products, costs, and prices. Potential new entrants would enter the new industry if they believe that they stand to make money in it. Making such a determination entails knowledge of incumbent costs and prices.

Again, where the Web makes such information available to potential new entrants, the threat of entry increases and potentially reduces profits for incumbents. The threat of new entry also increases where the Internet serves as a distribution channel for some products. Consider, for example, a software developer who, prior to the Internet, had no chance of getting shelf space at computer and software retailers. With the Internet, all the developer has to do is develop the software and post it on the Web for customers. This increases the number of firms that can enter the industry. The universality property also suggests that the threat of new entrants increases since a firm from Bali is as likely to sell software to customers in Tokyo as one from Tokyo itself or one from Boston.

Finally, since the Internet is a low cost standard, the threat of new entry looms large for nearly all industries whose barriers to entry rest on some form of mediating technology. These range from telephone long-distance service to newspapers to television, radio, and financial services.

Substitutes

Substitute products or services reduce demand by providing buyers with alternative products. The Internet increases this possibility because it offers more information on the prices and attributes of substitutes and the extent to which they can substitute for industry products, making it easier for customers to find and use these substitutes. For substitutes that can be distributed over the Internet, the threat to industry firms is even higher. The universality property also suggests that there are more of such substitutes because makers of substitutes from all over the world can participate.

Complementors

Complementors are firms that produce complementary goods and services for industry products. For example, gasoline makers are complementors to the automobile industry because gasoline is a complementary product essential to the operation of automobiles. Complementary products increase demand for firm products. Thus, the more software that is developed for a particular computer standard, the more valuable the computer. The Internet provides more information on complementary products, thus increasing rivalry (in offering complementary products) and the number of complementary products that are sold. This in turn increases the number of industry products that are sold, augmenting industry profits.

The Internet's Multiple Forces

One underlying assumption in Porter's five forces is that customers are the ones who pay firms for the customer value offered by these firms. When an automaker sells a car, the buyer pays for it. The more power the customer has, the less a firm can expect for the customer value it offers. The mediating and network externalities properties of the Internet, however, suggest that frequently the customer who gets value from a firm is not the one who pays for it. This has significant implications for the competitive forces that impact an industry. Take the newspaper industry, which we said has two interdependent types of customers: its audience and advertisers. A newspaper actually has two types of rivals: those in the news business and those who sell and buy the kinds of things advertised in newspapers. Thus, with the Internet, a newspaper's rivals are not only other newspapers (or online news services), but also the auctioneers like eBay who advertise *and* sell many of the same items that are—or used to be—advertised in newspapers. The threat of new entry also takes a different dimension since anyone with a website and the capability to offer any of the content that newspapers do (e.g., news, weather, advertising, sports scores, and stock prices) is a potential competitor for newspapers.

In the bricks-and-mortar world, a retail store in Bentonville, Arkansas, does not compete intensively with one that is 200 miles away. In the virtual world, it competes with one that is thousands of miles away. Also, any store can potentially compete with any other store. This takes rivalry to a different dimension.

For many industries, then, the Internet shifts the bargaining power from suppliers to firms and in turn from firms to customers. To determine how attractive an industry is, however, we still need to perform a five forces analysis for that particular industry. The Internet service provider (ISP) industry serves as our example.

A Five Forces Analysis of ISPs

Internet service providers (ISPs) in 1998 provided their customers with basic Internet access to information, e-commerce, entertainment, community, and communications.[5]

Threat of Entry

The threat of entry was high. There was plenty of communications capacity available from competing telephone, cable, and wireless providers. The computer hardware, such as servers and routers, and the basic software required to enter the industry were inexpensive and readily available. There was no clear product differentiation; strong brand loyalties were yet to be established. There was no fear of retaliation since this was a new industry with no incumbents.

Suppliers

Suppliers were the owners of communications infrastructure, makers of hardware and software, and the providers of content (e.g., entertainment, e-commerce, information and communications) such as Disney, Playboy, and news networks (see Chapter 2). Some of these suppliers had their own ISPs, demonstrating a credible threat of forward vertical integration into ISPs. They were also relatively less fragmented than the thousands of ISPs in business in 1998. Effectively, suppliers of content had bargaining power over ISPs while suppliers of equipment such as hardware and software did not.

Buyers

Buyers in 1998 were the businesses and individuals that used the Internet. Since the service ISPs provided was undifferentiated with little switching costs, customers had the bargaining power.

Rivalry

In 1998 the Internet service provider industry was highly fragmented, with over a thousand ISPs and no sign of a slowdown of entry (see Chapter 2). The service offerings were still largely undifferentiated with low switching costs. On the other hand, the industry was experiencing high growth. Competition also tended to be regional; for example, ISPs that served Ann Arbor might not serve Los Angeles. Overall, despite the high industry growth and regional competition, rivalry was high.

In 1998 customers used ISPs to communicate and access information, e-commerce, entertainment, and community. Many customers still had plenty of alternative ways to satisfy these needs at low cost. The telephone and traditional hardcopy mail still allowed customers to communicate inexpensively. Television and theaters still provided entertainment while bricks-and-mortar stores still supplied low-cost shopping alternatives.

An Important Point about Industry Analysis

Our analysis suggests that the ISP industry in 1998 was very unattractive. Does this mean that in 1998 no firms could make money in the industry and that firms such as America Online (AOL) should have pulled out of ISP activities? Of course not! Does it mean that an industry analysis is useless? Of course not! It provides us with critical information. It tells us that the industry is, on average, not very profitable at the time the cross-sectional analysis was performed (1998). More important, an industry attractiveness analysis tells us why the industry is unattractive or attractive and a firm can, through appropriate strategic actions, make the industry more attractive for itself by influencing the competitive forces in it. For example, this analysis suggests that the service offered by ISPs in 1998 was, on average, undifferentiated. Thus, firms could differentiate themselves, for example, by building strong brands. AOL has taken several strategic steps to differentiate its service, including building a brand name. Since a critical success driver in the ISP industry is network size, AOL has also taken strategic steps to build loyal subscribers in a larger network. Brand and membership loyalty can help AOL stand out in the ISP market. Thus, a five forces analysis allows a firm to ask itself the following questions:

What can we do to moderate rivalry in this industry?

What can we do to reduce the viability of substitutes?

How can we create and maintain barriers to entry?

What can we do to increase our power over buyers and suppliers?

In general, firms should be asking, If the Internet has caused power to shift from suppliers to firms and from firms to customers, what strategic steps must we undertake to prosper from these shifts? The answers to these questions should be incorporated in the firm's business model.

In any case, our five forces analysis of the industry so far has two major shortcomings. First, it sees suppliers and customers as competitors over whom firms fight to gain bargaining power. But we know that suppliers and customers are more than just competitors. Second, the analysis is static because it considers industry attractiveness at a particular point in the life cycle of the industry.

CO-OPETITORS AND INDUSTRY DYNAMICS

Co-opetitors

The sole focus on the competitive relationship between a firm and its **co-opetitors**—the rivals, suppliers, customers, complementors, and potential new entrants with which a firm must compete *and* cooperate—does not do justice to the critical role that these co-opetitors can play in helping firms exploit the Internet. First, the value that customers perceive is very difficult to break down into the contributions from firms, suppliers, customers, and complementors. Look at a tantalizing game played over the Internet. Is it fascinating because of the ISP's portal site, the speed with which signals are delivered over the Last Mile to the house, the backbone provider, or the way the game is designed? The point is that it takes all of these players to deliver the right value to customers. Thus, an industry analysis should also include an analysis of the industries of major suppliers, customers, and complementors. It should consider that customers are there not only to exercise any bargaining power they may have, but also that they may be interested in cooperating with firms. Much of the advantage that Japanese automobile companies had over their U.S. and European competitors in the 1980s came from cooperative relations with suppliers.[6]

Industry Dynamics and Evolution

In the five forces industry analysis, in which we predicted the likely outcome of the impact of the Internet on competition and profitability in industries, we assumed that these industries were static. However, following a major technological change such as the Internet, competition is a dynamic process in which firms fight for competitive advantage and survival. Industry structure and conduct change as the industry evolves.

Evolution of Technology

The rate at which firms enter or exit an industry parallels the evolution of the technology.[7] Early in the life of a technology, venture capitalists and other investors want to invest in it, entrepreneurs want to take advantage of the opportunities it offers, the product/service and its components are still ambiguous, and there are a large number of entries and few failures. In the late 1990s, for example, plenty of venture capitalists and many entrepreneurs took advantage of the Internet. The ISP industry alone attracted hundreds of new entrants. In the growth stage, firms fight for standards, establish relationships with customers, build brand-name loyalty, and struggle for market share. For most Internet start-ups, this has meant acquiring subscribers and clients, building large communities and infrastructures, winning "mindshare," and establishing brands. At the same time, customers are trying to "discover" their needs. Eventually, some product/service designs emerge as dominant designs. Some firms are forced to exit, others merge, and the number of surviving firms is greatly reduced as the evolution enters the stable state. As of 2000, the Internet had not yet reached the mature phase in any industry.

EXAMPLE. The automobile industry illustrates what may be in the future of the Internet and the many industries exploiting it. In the early and growth phases of the automobile industry from the 1890s to the 1930s, more than 2,000 companies entered the industry in the United States. Just as the catchword in 2000 is "dot-com," the catchword in the automobile industry was "motor." In 2000, there were only two major U.S. automobile companies (Chrysler is now considered a German company since it merged with Daimler Benz to form DaimlerChrysler). In the mature phase of the Internet, there is likely to be a lot fewer Internet-based firms than existed in 2000.

Firms, suppliers, customers, and complementors do not operate in a vacuum either; they are surrounded by the macro environment of government policies and laws, social structure, technological environment, demographic structure, and the natural environment which directly impact the industry environment. Regulation and deregulation can increase or decrease barriers to entry and therefore the profits that firms can make. By issuing a limited number of taxicab licenses, for example, a city is creating industry barriers to the taxicab market and how much cab owners can make. The increasing number of people who have grown up with the computer and see it as an integral part of their work and social lives means different customer expectations and preferences and different opportunities for creating new industries that depend on computers. National and international economic factors such as interest rates, exchange rates, employment, income, and productivity also impact an industry. Government plays a critical though indirect role in creating new industries. The Internet itself and the World Wide Web derived from government research and development.

Impact on Performance

A firm's macro environment indirectly impacts its performance by influencing the competitive environment and business models. As we indicated earlier, it does so by impacting the industry environment; that is, the properties of the Internet may suggest, for example, that the retail book industry is a good candidate for transformation and that anyone anywhere can start an online retail bookstore to sell to customers anywhere in the world. But it still takes a certain kind of environment to launch an Amazon.com. In other words, some environments are more conducive to innovation than others.[8] We consider four attributes of such environments: (1) a system that provides financial support and rewards for innovation; (2) a culture that tolerates failure; (3) the presence of related industries, universities, and other research institutions; and (4) government policies.[9]

Financial Support and Rewards: IPOs and Venture Capital

Money still talks, even on the Internet. It takes money to finance Internet activities. Many entrepreneurs or employees are attracted to the Internet by expected future earnings. Thus, an environment that provides both would be more conducive to Internet businesses than others. Let's start with the reward system, which differs from country to country. In the United States, for example, the rewards for innovation can be astronomical. These rewards come in several forms. First, as we described in Chapter 7, there is the initial public offering (IPO) in which firms sell their stock to the public for the first time. In one day, following one to five years' work, an entrepreneur can become a billionaire while many others see their personal wealth go up by millions of dollars. A firm can also push up its net worth by spinning off an entrepreneurial unit and offering its stock for purchase. Expectation of such rewards can be an excellent incentive to start new Internet businesses and work hard at them. Money raised in IPOs and subsequent stock valuations can be a valuable resource for pursuing a strategy. As James H. Clark, cofounder and former chairman of Netscape, explained, "Without IPOs, you would not have any start-ups. IPOs supply the fuel that makes these dreams go. Without it, you die."[10]

Internet firms, such as Amazon.com and many others, do not even have to be making a profit at the IPO date. Unfortunately, not all environments offer such rewards and sources of financing. In Japan, for example, firms must show several years of decent profits in order to be listed on that country's over-the-counter (OTC) market.[11] That can take as many as 10 years compared to 5 or less in the United States, and even less in 1998 and 1999 for Internet-based IPOs.

The availability of venture capital, partly a result of the expectations of financial rewards, also plays a critical role in Internet business formation. By making money available for projects that banks and other financing sources would normally consider too risky, venture capitalists allow firms to be more daring in their pursuit of new ideas. Some entrepreneurs use personal or family savings or loans from friends to finance their innovations, again in anticipation of the rewards. Anticipation of such rewards, coupled with readily available venture capital, allows more people to search for more innovative ideas. Many of those who succeed usually reinvest in other innovation-searching activities.

Culture That Tolerates Failure

Many start-up firms never get to the payoff at an IPO, or they fail right after it. For several reasons, such failures stop neither the entrepreneurs nor the venture capitalists who finance the innovations from founding other start-ups. First, those who fail learn in the process and that can improve their chances of doing well the next time around. They acquire competencies that can be used to tackle another innovation. Even if all they learn is what not to do next time, that can be useful too. Second, venture capital firms have seen many failures before and have found ways to reduce their risk, for example, by offering management expertise to ventures. Moreover, some of the venture capital comes from entrepreneurs who had succeeded only after having failed earlier. During their stints in Silicon Valley, the authors do not remember seeing anyone point a finger at a person and say, "That's an entrepreneur who failed." Whereas in Europe bankruptcy laws are harsh and entrepreneurs who fail are stigmatized, in the Silicon Valley, "bankruptcy is seen almost as a sign of prowess—a dueling scar."[12] In general, firms in the United States, be it in New York City's Silicon Alley or California's Silicon Valley, have these conditions in their favor.

Presence of Related Industries, Universities, and Other Research Institutions

The environment constitutes a very important source of innovations. Since tacit technological and market knowledge is transferred best by personal interaction, local environments that are good sources of innovation can make it easier for local firms to recognize the potential of an innovation. The presence of related industries is an example; being close to suppliers or complementary innovators increases a firm's chances of picking up useful ideas from them. Amazon.com's founder Jeff Bezos went west where he could find a large number of computer software developers and be located close to book distributors.

The proximity of universities or other research institutions helps innovation in two ways. First, these institutions train personnel who can go on to work for firms or found their own firms. From Yahoo! founded by graduate students at Stanford to Netscape started by students from the University of Illinois, examples abound. The knowledge that they acquire gives them the **absorptive capacity** to assimilate new ideas from competitors and related industries. Second, scientific publications from the basic research often act as a catalyst for investment by firms in applied research.

Government Policies

Finally, governments play a critical role—direct or indirect—in creating environments conducive to innovation.[13] The direct role may be in sponsoring research at the National Institutes of Health or the Defense Department. The Internet itself traces its roots to the Defense Department's DARPA project. More important, the U.S. government sponsored research in computer science and communication networks while training hundreds of thousands of people in electrical engineering and computer science who now fill Internet business jobs.

The government's indirect role is in regulation and taxation. Lower capital gains taxes or other regulations that allow firms to keep more of what they earn allow them to spend more on innovation. Taxing e-commerce can have a huge impact on the Internet. Other regulations also can be critical. In July 1999, for example, Internet signatures were not available; that is, people could not sign documents over the Internet. This meant that people still had to personally deliver documents or send them by "snail" mail to be signed. Making signatures delivered over the Web legal could increase the use of the Web. Government laws on intellectual property protection also influence the effectiveness of block strategies.

SUMMARY

A firm's performance is determined by three factors: its business model, its environment, and change such as the Internet. In this chapter we explored the environmental factors and the impact of the Internet on these factors and vice versa. Two environmental factors determine firm profitability: industry and macro environment. Some industries are, on average, more profitable than others. The profitability of these industries is determined by the extent to which suppliers, customers, rivals, potential new entrants, and substitutes exert competitive pressures on industry firms. These competitive pressures are themselves a function of the macro environment—the overarching political/legal, national/international, social, technological, and demographic forces.

Industry analysis provides information that firms can employ in formulating their business models and strategies. For example, a Porter's five forces analysis of an industry in the face of the Internet tells a firm how attractive that industry is, but more importantly, it tells the firm what this industry has that makes it attractive or unattractive. With this information, a firm can take the necessary strategic steps, in building its business model, to make the industry more attractive for itself. By developing more content, building a large network of subscribers, and establishing a brand name, AOL made an otherwise unattractive ISP industry more attractive for itself. An analysis of industry success drivers provides firms with key information that they can use in making decisions about business model components and linkages. In understanding how the macro environment can shape the extent to which an industry can profit from the Internet, firms in that industry can do something about the macro environment. For example, automakers are not allowed to sell cars directly to customers in the United States; they have to sell their products through dealers. But they might choose to lobby to scrap these laws so that they can better exploit the Internet. An industry analysis also has implications for policy makers: They can know better what kinds of macro environments they must create to make firms in their jurisdictions more innovative. For example, countries with low financial reward systems for Internet entrepreneurs and little or no venture capital may find it difficult to compete with the United States, which has a generous reward system and plenty of venture capital. Therefore, policy makers in other countries may want to find ways to change their environments.

KEY TERMS

absorptive capacity   133
co-opetitors   129
competitive environment   124
complementors   127
industry environment   124

industry success drivers   125
macro environment   124
Porter's five forces   124
unattractive industry   124

DISCUSSION QUESTIONS

1. Name an industry in which new entrants have an advantage over incumbents. What factors allow them to have this advantage?
2. How might the Internet be different if it had been developed commercially instead of by the government?
3. Which properties of the Internet increase industry rivalry?
4. Name an industry that was created as a result of the Internet? What "traditional" industries could be threatened by this emerging industry? Why? Be specific.
5. Give examples of co-opetitors. Why do they cooperate? How do they compete?
6. Why do e-business "hotbeds" such as Silicon Valley emerge? What contributes to their formation?
7. Give an example of when offering customer value is a necessary but insufficient condition for a firm's profitability.

REFERENCES

1. C. W. L. Hill and G. R. Jones, *Strategic Management: An Integrated Approach* (Boston: Houghton Mifflin, 1995).
2. M. E. Porter, *Competitive Strategy: Techniques for Analyzing Industries and Competitors* (New York: Free Press, 1980); A. M. McGahan and M. E. Porter, "How Much Does Industry Matter? Really?" *Strategic Management Journal* 18 (Summer special issue, 1997), pp. 15–30.
3. Porter, *Competitive Strategy*.
4. Newspapers are often referred to as a print medium because they are a medium through which news and information are delivered to readers, not because they are a medium through which advertisers and producers are brought together.
5. C. W. L. Hill, "America Online and the Internet," in C. W. L. Hill and G. R. Jones, *Strategic Management: An Integrated Approach,* (Boston: Houghton Mifflin, 1998), pp. C92–C106.

6. K. B. Clark and T. Fujimoto, *Product Development Performance: Strategy, Organization, and Management in the World Automobile Industry* (Boston: Harvard Business School Press, 1991).

7. J. M. Utterback, *Mastering the Dynamics of Innovation* (Boston: Harvard Business School Press, 1994).

8. M. E. Porter, *The Competitive Advantage of Nations* (New York: Free Press, 1990).

9. This section draws heavily on A. N. Afuah, *Innovation Management: Strategies, Implementation and Profits* (New York: Oxford University Press, 1998).

10. C. Farrell et al., "The Boon in IPOs," *Business Week,* December 18, 1995, p. 64.

11. "Japanese Venture Capital: In Need of Funds," *The Economist,* October 16, 1993, pp. 91–92.

12. "Please Dare to Fail," *The Economist,* September 28, 1996, pp. 21–22.

13. See Chapter 15 of Afuah, *Innovation Management.*

PART IV

Applying
the Concepts,
Models, and Tools

CHAPTER 9

The General Manager and the Internet

A general manager can be a chief executive officer (CEO), president, chief operating officer (COO), vice president, director, administrator, product line manager, profit center manager, or any other person who is responsible for the performance of an organization that has more than one functional area. This executive's primary responsibility is to guide his or her organization to meet its performance goals and mission or, better still, to attain and maintain a competitive advantage. In the face of the Internet, the general manager's responsibility includes using the new technology to reinforce an existing competitive advantage or to gain and maintain a new one. The extent to which he or she can meet this challenge is a function of three factors: (1) whether the firm is an incumbent or a pure-play Internet new entrant, (2) the formulation and execution of a good strategy, and (3) the characteristics of the general manager. We explore these three factors.

We begin by defining competitive advantage and explaining why it is an important performance goal of many firms. Then we explore the characteristics of incumbents or so-called legacy or bricks-and-mortar firms that must adopt the Internet, and those of new entrant or so-called pure-play Internet firms. In the face of the Internet, each exhibits some characteristics that make managing it a challenge. Next, we examine the process of formulating and implementing an Internet strategy that entails answering four important questions:[1] Where is the firm now as far as the Internet is concerned? Where does the firm go next? How does it get there? How does it implement the decisions to get there? Finally, we examine some traits that would serve a general manager well in the face of the Internet.

COMPETITIVE ADVANTAGE AND THE GENERAL MANAGER

An organization's **competitive advantage** lies in those characteristics that allow it to outperform its rivals in the same industry or market.[2] As we noted in Chapter 1, performance has many definitions but we will focus on profitability. Thus, we say that a firm has a competitive advantage over its rivals if it earns a higher rate of profits than those rivals or has the potential to do so.[3] Why is having a competitive advantage so important? First, investors are more likely to invest in firm A than in firm B if A is more profitable than B, even if both A and B are profitable. There are three types of investors here: the equity investors who prefer the better price-earnings (P/E) ratios, cash flows, profit margins, or business model attribute; suppliers who extend lines of credit, or debtors; and potential employees who would rather work for a winner. Second, during bad times for an industry, firms with a competitive advantage are more likely to survive than those with a disadvantage. During such times, the industry is less profitable, making it more likely that marginal firms that made money in good times will lose money. With fewer investors likely to invest in them, their chances of being forced out of business are higher. A general manager's primary responsibility, then, is to develop and sustain a competitive advantage for his or her organization. How successful the manager is in doing so is a function of the type of firm.

INCUMBENTS VERSUS NEW ENTRANTS

Managing Bricks-and-Mortar Incumbents

Incumbents are firms that were in existence prior to the adoption of the Internet by their industries. These are the so-called bricks-and-mortar or **legacy firms**. In early 2000 the vast majority of firms belonged to this category. Many of them were grappling with the question of what to do about the Internet. As incumbents in their industries, they had disadvantages and advantages that promised to have a large impact on their abilities to successfully adopt the Internet and the ability of their managers to guide them through the change.

Potential Disadvantages for Incumbents[4]

Certain characteristics of incumbents make them particularly vulnerable to new entrants in the face of the Internet. Many of the characteristics served these firms well prior to the Internet—in some cases they were the cornerstones of their competitive advantage—but are now useless or may have become handicaps. If an incumbent has a chance to defend or maintain its competitive advantage in the face of the Internet, it must pay particular attention to these advantages-turned-handicaps and find ways to overcome them.

DOMINANT MANAGERIAL LOGIC. Each manager brings to each decision a set of biases, beliefs, and assumptions about the market served by the firm, who to hire, who the firm's competitors are, what technology to use to remain competitive, and how to develop and execute a business model.[5] This set of biases, assumptions, and beliefs is a manager's **managerial logic**. It defines the frame within which a manager is likely to scan for information and approach problem solving. It is the mental model that a manager brings to each decision. Depending on a firm's strategies, systems, technology, organizational structure, culture, and record of success, there usually emerges a **dominant managerial logic**, a common way of viewing how best to do business as a manager in the firm. The longer a management team has been at the company and in the industry, and the more successful the firm has been, the more dominant and pervasive the managerial logic.

In relatively stable environments or in the face of competence-enhancing changes, dominant managerial logic can be a competitive weapon because it is business as usual, and management has the capabilities in place which, combined with its dominant logic, reinforce or extend the firm's competitive advantage. However, in the face of radical or disruptive change such as the Internet, dominant managerial logic can have disastrous consequences. It prevents managers from understanding the rationale behind the new technology—from "getting it." And when they eventually do get it, they still have difficulty in carrying out their new functions efficiently because managers imbued with the dominant logic tend to think and act as if it were business as usual, and they fight to maintain the status quo.[6]

COMPETENCY TRAP. Even if management overcomes its dominant logic handicap and sees the Internet for what it is—a disruptive change—and decides to exploit it, the same capabilities that may have given a competitive advantage to a firm can become a handicap.[7] Recall that a disruptive technology is one that overturns an existing business model. For example, an important part of Wal-Mart's bricks-and-mortar capabilities is in logistics—its ability to move goods into and out of its large distribution centers to the shelves in its retail stores. Online retailing requires a completely different logistics system—one that can efficiently sort out single item orders, package them, and deliver single packages to individual households on time with few errors. A **competency trap**—an inability to shed old successful ways of doing things and to embrace new ones—can occur because of several reasons. The firm's managers may not want to spend so much money building a new logistics system when they believe that the firm already has one. Their dominant bricks-and-mortar logic may prevent them from seeing the differences in the requirements of the two types of retailing. Also, they cannot ditch the old logistics system because they still need it for bricks-and-mortar activities. Moreover, it takes more than the decision alone to build a new logistics system that will be successful. It also requires building and developing the capabilities to integrate it into the firm's retail system and running it. But doing this requires skills, knowledge, and routines which the firm must learn. Learning in the face of a disruptive change, however, usually requires *un*learning the old ways of doing things first.[8] Anyone who has had to break longtime personal habits or routines knows how difficult it is to unlearn old ways of doing things. Thus, in the face of the Internet, old capabilities are sometimes not only rendered obsolete, but also become a handicap.

FEAR OF CANNIBALIZATION AND LOSS OF REVENUE. The Internet often renders many of a firm's existing products/services noncompetitive. The new product/service often offers better customer value than the old one. Offering these new products means the **cannibalization** of existing ones since fewer customers would buy the older product. The fear of cannibalizing existing products often makes firms reluctant to adopt technologies such as the Internet that render existing products/services noncompetitive. An increasing number of managers are, however, beginning to realize that if their firms do not perform cannibalization themselves, someone else will do it for them and they will miss out on both the old and new revenues.

CHANNEL CONFLICT. The Internet renders some existing distribution channels and some sales skills obsolete. In that case, **channel conflict** often occurs because existing sales forces and the distributors fight hard against the new channel rather than see their revenues go to the new channel. Consider the popular example of Compaq's attempts to emphasize selling its PCs directly to customers over the Internet, rather than depending largely on dealers. The PC dealers fought hard against Compaq's decision to go direct as Dell Computer had done. Prior to the World Wide Web and the use of the Internet as a distribution channel, Compaq's relationship with dealers had been a key factor in its rise to the top of the personal computer manufacturing industry. The Internet not only radically reduced the importance of these relationships, but also turned them into a handicap. When Merrill Lynch decided to offer online brokerage, its own sales force fought hard to keep it out.

POLITICAL POWER. Throughout most of this book, we have treated a firm as if it were a homogeneous entity with congruent goals and employees whose primary interest is to pursue these goals. Often, however, top management does not share a common purpose and the interest of the firm may not be the primary consideration in every manager's decision. As such, firms can be thought of as comprised of political coalitions formed to protect and enhance their vested interests.[9] The extent to which each of these coalitions can influence the decisions a firm makes is a measure of how much power it has. **Political power** is defined here as the ability to have one's preferences or inclinations reflected in any actions taken in the firm or organization.[10] A coalition whose interests are often reflected in a firm's decisions is said to be a **dominant coalition**. Each of these coalitions acts in its own interests. One can expect incumbents to be more likely to adopt the Internet if it enhances the power of its dominant coalition. If it appears that the Internet will destroy the power of the firm's elite, the elite may work hard to impede its adoption.[11]

CO-OPETITOR POWER. The customers, suppliers, and complementors with whom a firm has to compete and cooperate also play a role in how successful a firm can be in adopting the Internet. If a firm's customers do not want the new technology, it risks not adopting it early. If such customers possess **co-opetitor power**—that is, they are powerful and are the primary source of revenues for a firm—the firm will tend to listen to the customers in an effort to satisfy their needs. However, listening too much to powerful customers can be detrimental to a firm's adoption of the new technology.[12] One can imagine a case where a firm that leans too much on a supplier who dominates the supplier-firm relationship and also has no incentive to invest in the Internet will also be detrimental to the firm's ability to adopt a new technology. Complementors who have power may not want to change either, further slowing down a firm's efforts.

EMOTIONAL ATTACHMENT. Many general managers were promoted to their top position or brought in because of the valuable contributions they had made to the invention and commercialization of an existing technology or to existing business models. In some cases a firm's competitive advantage also rests on such a technology. In either case, these managers may—in the face of a disruptive Internet that potentially might replace the technology that made them what they are—have such strong **emotional attachments** to the existing technology that they will delay adoption of the Internet. For example, some of Intel's managers were reluctant to get out of the DRAM (Dynamic Random Access Memory) business and

concentrate on microprocessors.[13] They were emotionally attached to DRAMs
which Intel had invented and from which it had, for a while, earned a lot of money.

Incumbent Advantages

COMPLEMENTARY ASSETS. Incumbents also have some advantages. Recall from
Chapter 5 that it takes more than technology to profit from technology. It also takes
complementary assets such as brand name, distribution channels, client relations,
important clients, marketing, manufacturing, shelf space, supplier relations, and so
on. Many incumbents have these complementary assets and while the Internet may
render some of them obsolete or turn them into handicaps, it leaves many intact for
use with the new technology. Those complementary assets that can be used to profit
from the Internet are a primary asset for the general manager of an incumbent firm.
Where such assets are difficult to acquire and new entrants have difficulty obtaining them, the general manager can use them to improve the firm's chances of catching up or overtaking new entrants who moved first. Merrill Lynch was late entering
the online brokerage business, but its reputation, strong relationships with clients,
large clients, and monetary assets gave it a chance to catch up and overtake Internet firms like Ameritrade. Earlier, IBM was late in entering the PC market, but the
IBM name helped it gain a huge market share as soon as it entered the PC market.
In making acquisitions or entering strategic alliances, useful complementary assets
are an important part of what the general manager of an incumbent firm brings to
the table in any negotiating process.

TECHNOLOGY IS EASY TO IMITATE. Another thing that incumbents have going
for them is that parts or the whole of an Internet business model are usually easy
to imitate or outdo. Although Merrill Lynch was late to adopt the Internet, it still
was able to develop and execute a good business model. The complementary assets
model presented in Chapter 5 suggests that if technology is easy to imitate and
complementary assets are important and difficult to get, owners of complementary
assets are usually the firms that make money from the technology. Thus, incumbents have an advantage in industries where incumbents have the important complementary assets and the Internet technology is easy to imitate.

Overcoming the Disadvantages

For the general manager, the most important question is a simple one: How
can he or she overcome these disadvantages while exploiting the advantages?

GENETIC MIX. C. K. Prahalad and Gary Hamel wrote that firms need some kind
of **genetic mix** in their management if they are to overcome the dominant logic
problem and exploit new opportunities.[14] A firm whose management is made up
entirely of electrical engineers is more likely to miss out on disruptive marketing
changes than one that has a mix of engineers and marketers, all else being equal.
The goal is to find people with complementary skills who share the overall objectives and mission of the firm.

S³PE. A genetic mix of people in a company is only one of the elements of the
strategy, structure, systems, people, and environment **(S³PE) system**. Many of the
disadvantages that incumbents face can be mitigated by the right S³PE system. At

3M, for example, at least 25 percent of a division's sales in any given year must be from products introduced within the last five years.[15] Resources are then allocated to back the expectations: Employees are expected to spend 15 percent of their workweek on anything they want, so long as it is product related. Employees who come up with a viable product are given grants to pursue the idea. An environment as vibrant as the Silicon Valley is likely to keep a firm on its toes and reduce its chance of lapsing into complacency. Employees are constantly reminded of why paying attention to change is good.

SEPARATE ENTITY. One way to avoid the problems of dominant managerial logic, emotional attachment, political power, co-opetitor power, and the competency trap is to form a separate unit that is organizationally and physically separated from the incumbent but is still a unit within the firm. Another is to go even further and create a separate start-up company. As you read in Chapter 5, a separate company attracts more talent who prefer to work in the entrepreneurial environment of a start-up and earn the rights to the potential payoff at the IPO. Moreover, given the valuations of dot-com companies relative to their bricks-and-mortar competitors in the late 1990s and 2000, a separate legal entity could raise much more and cheaper capital through an IPO. A key decision for the general manager is whether to keep the Internet unit within the firm or spin it off as a separate unit. Charles Schwab created a separate unit and later reabsorbed it. General Electric decided to have its own units cannibalize themselves. The company did not see why there should be different Internet units within GE with different compensation systems from those of its bricks-and-mortar units. Some firms form **joint ventures** with venture capital firms who provide not only financing, but also some of the nurturing that start-ups need. Procter and Gamble formed a joint venture with a venture capital firm to launch Reflect.com to offer beauty products directly to customers.

Managing New Entrants

There are two kinds of **new entrants** or so-called pure-play firms: Those that enter markets that rest on the Internet and were nonexistent prior to the Internet, and those that use the Internet to enter existing markets.

New Entrant Advantages

LESS INERTIA. New entrants do not have many of the handicaps of incumbents: no dominant managerial logic, no competency traps, no channel conflicts, no fear of cannibalization, no emotional attachment to an older technology, no co-opetitor power, and less internal politics. New entrants do not have any legacy systems to handicap them. Thus, they are more nimble and can adopt the new technology more easily.

EQUITY CAPITAL. In the late 1990s and early 2000, the market valuations of many pure-play Internet companies were high relative to those of the bricks-and-mortar firms that they were attacking. Whether they were worth those high valuations was the topic of debate. But their high valuations constituted a source of **equity capital** for new entrants that their bricks-and-mortar competitors did not have. Such relative differences in valuations are consistent with Schumpeter's notion of creative destruction[16] where, in the face of a technological change such as the Internet, waves of new firms are created at the expense of older established ones, many of which die off.

ATTRACTION FOR TALENT. Partly attracted by stock options and the potential payoff at the IPO, young, educated talent would rather work for a pure-play start-up than for an established bricks-and-mortar firm. In the late 1990s and early 2000, young talent found Amazon.com more attractive to work for than Borders. The belief that they can learn more from an Akamai Technologies, Vertical Net, or Commerce One than from a Ford or General Motors also attracts college graduates to the start-ups. Many college graduates seem to prefer the start-ups, which have a more entrepreneurial environment and provide more options to learn.

New Entrant Disadvantages

New entrants frequently lack the requisite complementary assets and must develop them from scratch. Some complementary assets such as brand names can be expensive and elusive. In 1999, for example, many dot-coms spent as much as 70 percent of the money raised from venture capital on marketing. Another disadvantage is that the technology could be easy to imitate; therefore, any lead that new entrants have over incumbents may be difficult to protect. This suggests that new entrants may want to develop complementary assets that are more difficult to imitate, rather than depend on their early lead in technology.

Overcoming the Disadvantages

TAKING ADVANTAGE OF THE INTERNET'S PROPERTIES. Although adoption of the Internet is easy to imitate by competitors, some of its properties give new entrants a better chance at first mover advantages. The network externalities effect, for example, suggests that if a firm is able to enter a market first, it can build a large network before competitors come in. Since the larger the network, the more valuable it is, followers who enter later have less of a chance because first movers have the opportunity to capture a large network. Moreover, first movers can advertise and build brand loyalty before incumbents can recover from dominant logic and other incumbent problems.

RUN AND EXTENDABILITY. Since most business models or parts of them are easy to imitate, a firm may want to emphasize a run strategy. It may want to innovate parts of it or reinvent the whole model before competitors catch up or leapfrog it. Since distinctive capabilities are at the heart of business models, a firm may want to build capabilities that can be extended so that different or better value is offered to the same or different customers in order to generate greater revenues and profits. Amazon.com is a good example of a firm extending its capabilities, although it had not made a profit by early 2000. With capabilities in selling books, music, and videos, Amazon's marginal cost of adding toys was lower than the cost to a new entrant of entering the toy retail market with the same scale as Amazon.

Incumbent/New Entrant Race

Where new entrants are attacking markets, they are in a race of sorts with incumbents: New entrants have the technology and are racing to develop the complementary assets while incumbents have many of the complementary assets and must develop the technology. A new entrant's general manager's responsibility is to decide when and how to go after the complementary assets. If a new entrant wants to develop its own complementary assets rather than team up with another firm that has them, it may want to start early, especially with complementary assets such as network size and brand-name reputation where first mover advantages are important. If a new entrant wants to team up with an incumbent that has the assets, the timing has to be right. If it moves too early, the incumbent's dominant logic may still be too much of a problem for it to understand the value of the new technology. If it waits too long, incumbents might have developed their own technologies and no longer need those of the new entrant.

FORMULATING AND IMPLEMENTING A STRATEGY

Change and the Strategic Management Process

Change is one thing that we can be sure about in a technology that is in its early growth phase. The technology is changing, firms are changing their business models, and the environment is changing. To take advantage of change or avoid competitors taking advantage of them, firms may frequently want to undergo a **strategic management process**; that is, to answer the four strategy formulation and implementation questions: Where is the firm now concerning the Internet? Where does the firm go next? How does it get there? How does it implement the decisions to get there?

Where Is the Firm Now?

This is an analysis of how well the firm is performing, what determines that performance, and how the forces of change may or may not impact that performance (see Figure 9.1). Understanding where a firm is now entails an analysis of the firm's performance, its business model, its competitive (industry) environment, its macro environment, and the change that it is likely to experience. The analysis explores the firm's strengths and weaknesses as well as the threats and opportunities that it faces.

Performance Evaluation

PROFITABILITY MEASURES. The analysis of where a firm is now starts with an evaluation of the firm's performance. It explores such basic questions as, How profitable is the firm? What are its cash flows? What are the firm's profit margins, market share, and revenue share growth rate? (Recall that profit margins, market share, and revenue share growth can be predictors of future profitability for knowledge-based products.) For bricks-and-mortar firms facing attack from new entrants, the question might be: How much market share is being captured by the attackers? The bottom line is whether the firm has a competitive advantage and, if so, whether it is sustainable.

INTELLECTUAL CAPITAL. Rather than assess a firm's performance using profitability measures, a general manager may also want to pay attention to its market valuations. Table 9.1 shows the differences between the book values and market

FIGURE 9.1 Where Is the Firm Now?

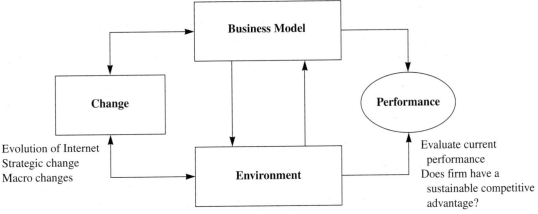

Appraisal of firm's business model
What are the firm's strengths and weaknesses?
What are the sources of competitive advantage?
Are the sources sustainable?

Evolution of Internet
Strategic change
Macro changes

Evaluate current
performance
Does firm have a
sustainable competitive
advantage?

Competitive analysis
  Appraisal of competitors' business models
  Porter's five forces
  Likely actions and reactions of competitors

Industry value drivers
  What are the major drivers of cost
    and differentiation?
  How has the Internet impacted them?

Macro environment
  Economic, social, demographic,
    and political forces

Opportunities and threats

TABLE 9.1 Market Valuations and Intellectual Capital

	1998 Revenues ($ millions)	1998 Profits ($ millions)	*March 15, 1999*		
			Market Value (MV) ($ millions)	Book Value (BV) ($ millions)	Intellectual Capital MV − BV ($ millions)
General Motors	$161,315	$2,956	$63,839	$14,984	$48,855
Ford	144,416	22,071	70,881	23,409	47,472
Cisco	8,458	1,350	166,615	7,106	159,209
Amazon.com	610	−125	22,383	139	22,244
Barnes & Noble	3,006	92	2,045	679	1,366

Source: Company Financial Statements, *Fortune,* April 26, 1999.

values of a sample of leading firms. Two things stand out. First, the differences between book value and market value are very large. Second, the differences vary considerably from firm to firm. In any case, what each difference says is that there is something about each firm—about its competitive and macro environments and, above all, *something* about its business model—that makes investors believe that its future free cash flows and profits will be higher than its book value. The differences say that there is something about each firm, other than the assets on its books, that makes investors believe that it will be profitable enough or generate enough free cash flows to be worth that much. This something, as we suggested in Chapter 7, has been called *intellectual capital*, intangible assets, human capital, or knowledge. Thus, Cisco's intellectual capital in March 1999 was $159 billion while that of General Motors, a company with about 20 times Cisco's revenues, was only $49 billion. Amazon.com's intellectual capital is more than 20 times that of its bricks-and-mortar foe Barnes & Noble. Rather than dismiss other firms' valuations as ridiculously high or a market bubble, the responsibility of general managers is to understand why the intellectual capital in their industry is lower than that in other industries, why their firms' intellectual capital is higher or lower than that of rivals, and, above all, what the relationship between intellectual capital and the Internet is.

Business Model Appraisal

A primary determinant of a firm's performance is its business model. Thus, determining where a firm is now entails an appraisal of the firm's *Internet* business model. This is the appraisal that we explored in Chapter 5, in particular, the questions in Table 5.2. The result is a determination of the firm's strengths and weaknesses in the components and linkages of the business model. For a bricks-and-mortar firm under attack, the appraisal should include a comparison and "what if" analysis for both its bricks-and-mortar business model and potential Internet business models.

Environmental Analysis

The other key determinant of a firm's performance is its environment—both the competitive (industry) and macro environments.

COMPETITIVE ENVIRONMENT. The first thing in a competitor analysis is to appraise the Internet business models of key competitors. This appraisal reveals to the general manager the strengths and weaknesses of competitors. With this information, the manager can better know where his or her firm may be attacked, which competitors would make for good team-up partners, and what the actions and reactions of competitors are likely to be. The second important analysis is one of industry attractiveness. This consists of the now-familiar Porter's five forces to identify what makes an industry attractive or unattractive. The focus is on the potential impact of the Internet on industry attractiveness. Recall that because of the Internet's information asymmetry property, there is a shift in bargaining power from suppliers and firms to customers. The exact nature of this shift should be analyzed.

INDUSTRY VALUE DRIVERS. The analysis here focuses on those things that drive cost or differentiation in a firm's industry—more importantly, the extent to which the Internet has or can impact them. The analysis entails a value chain, value shop, or value network detailed analysis that determines the firm's cost and differentiation structures. This is then followed by an analysis of how the Internet is likely to impact the structure. Recall the automobile example in Chapter 8 in which the cost structure is heavily skewed toward the back end of the value chain where 30 percent of the price of a car covers the cost of distribution attributed largely to the inability to forecast, which in turn leads to unnecessary advertising, promotion, discounting, and transportation costs. Information movement inefficiencies are also partly to blame for the length of time (60–100 days) it takes from the bending of metal to the customer receiving the car. These are examples of opportunities in the value chain of an industry that a manager can target so that the firm can take advantage of the Internet.

MACRO ENVIRONMENT. Recall that an environment with a good financial support and reward system for entrepreneurs, a culture that tolerates failure, the right co-opetitors, and innovation-friendly government policies is more conducive to innovation than an environment that is void of these elements. An analysis of the macro environment should include an examination of the strength of the environment in each of these factors. Government policies and rulings on patents and other intellectual property issues related to the Internet should be carefully analyzed. This has an impact on whether a firm pursues a block strategy or not. Demographic, sociological, political, and legal trends should also be surveyed. Particular attention should be given to legislation that affects the Internet. Increasingly, the natural environment also plays a critical role and its potential impact on the Internet should be examined too.

Change

There are three external sources of change: the Internet, competitors, and the macro environment.

THE EVOLVING INTERNET. Recall that technology usually evolves from an early phase through a growth phase to a stable phase, and each phase requires different capabilities and strategies. In many industries the Internet is in the early or the growth phase. Also recall that over the life cycle of the automobile industry, more than 2,000 companies were started in the United States. The catchword that had to be in each company's name was "motor" just as in the growth phase of the Internet the catchword is "dot-com."[17] In 2000 there were just two major automobile companies left in the United States. Along the way, all the horse-driven cart companies that the automobile firms replaced also disappeared. The point is that eventually most of the existing dot-com companies will exit their industries or merge with others. General managers must take this into consideration as they explore the threats and opportunities that face their firms.

In focusing on the Internet, it is easy to forget about other technologies that might complement a firm's Internet strategy. Technologies such as wireless communications can offer alternative or complementary infrastructures for data communications.

COMPETITIVE ENVIRONMENTAL CHANGE. Rivals are constantly changing their strategies and such changes, especially new game strategies, have to be watched very carefully. A firm is said to pursue a **new game strategy** if by performing value chain, value shop, or value configuration activities that differ from what the dominant logic of the industry dictates, or by performing the same activities differently than the logic dictates, the firm is able to offer superior customer value. Wal-Mart's early strategies were new game strategies. It decided to move into small towns, saturate adjoining towns with stores, build distribution centers, and improve logistics, with an empowering culture and information technology to match. This allowed Wal-Mart to achieve high economies of scale and bargaining power over its suppliers. This in turn allowed the firm to offer its customers lower prices than its competitors. Kmart's management did not pay attention to this new game strategy, which resulted in the firm being overtaken by Wal-Mart. Kmart has never recovered.

CHANGES FROM MACRO ENVIRONMENT. Many changes from the macro environment have the potential to cripple even the best of strategies and must therefore be watched. Managers should note any changes in the environmental factors cited above as conducive to innovation. Potential changes in exchange rates, especially unanticipated large ones, central bank policies that raise interest rates, and taxation laws, along with demographic and sociopolitical changes, all have the potential to impact firm strategies. Managers should examine them carefully for potential threats and opportunities. In particular, they should examine the potential impact of changes in tax policies concerning the Internet.

This analysis of a firm's current performance, appraisal of its business model, appraisal of its competitors' business models, analysis of industry attractiveness, assessment of its macro environment, projection of the evolution of the Internet, and a forecast of its environmental changes is sometimes called a strengths and weaknesses, opportunities, and threats (**SWOT**) analysis.[18]

Where Does the Firm Go Next?

From the exploration of where a firm is now, a manager has many strategic alternatives from which to choose. After such an analysis, for example, AOL might discover that to maintain its subscription pricing model successfully, it needs more content. It may then decide to add more content. A manager may find out that its fledgling Internet start-up does not have the complementary assets that it needs to offer competitive customer value and must get them if the start-up is to gain a sustainable advantage. An Amazon.com may find out that, in selling books, it has developed capabilities that can be extended to sell music, videos, electronics, home improvement, toys, and even to create online malls. So it decides to move into these areas.

After an analysis of where the firm is now, a manager may also decide not to pursue profits as previously planned but to hone the firm's capabilities to fit another firm's portfolio of capabilities so that it can be acquired by the other firm. On the other hand, a firm whose exit strategy had been to be acquired, with no intention of ever making profits, may decide that it now wants to become profitable after all.

In all these cases, a firm has decided to move into new areas. It is now intent on doing certain things that it had not done before. If moving into these new areas requires entirely new capabilities, the objective to do so is sometimes referred to as a firm's **strategic intent**.[19]

How Does the Firm Get There?

Take the example of the fledgling start-up that needs complementary assets to offer the right customer value. The question now becomes, How does the start-up get the complementary assets? It has the option of developing the assets internally or teaming up with a firm that already has them. In teaming up, the firm may decide to be acquired rather than form a strategic alliance. AOL, for example, could develop the content alone or team up with a Disney to do so. It might also buy a Time Warner company that has the content. By and large, getting there usually requires new capabilities. When a firm wants to get somewhere but lacks the capabilities to do so, it is said to have a **capabilities gap**. To fill this gap, a firm usually must decide whether to develop the capabilities internally or obtain them from outside. E. B. Roberts and C. A. Berry developed a model that can be used to guide managers in their choice of how to get the capabilities that they need.

Roberts and Berry Model

Offering new value to customers or assuming a new product market position usually requires both technological and marketing capabilities. The more unfamiliar firms are with the technology or market, the higher their risk of failure since they will have a difficult time building the capabilities from scratch. Since these capabilities take time to build, a firm may be better off teaming up with another firm that has them. The **Roberts and Berry model**[20] of Figure 9.2 depicts this. In other words, the mechanism that a firm uses to build the capabilities that it needs

FIGURE 9.2 Roberts and Berry Model on Acquiring Capabilities

Market	Existing	New but familiar	New and unfamiliar
New and unfamiliar	Joint venture	Venture capital Educational acquisition	Venture capital Educational acquisition
New but familiar	Internet market capabilities development Acquisition	Internal ventures Acquisitions Licensing	Venture capital Educational acquisition
Existing	Internal development (or acquisition)	Internal technological capabilities development Acquisitions Licensing	Strategic alliance

Technology

Source: Adapted from: E. B. Roberts and C. A. Berry, "Entering New Businesses: Selecting Strategies for Success," *Sloan Management Review* 26, no. 3 (1985), pp. 3–17.

is a function of the extent to which it is familiar with the technology and market. Roberts and Berry explored seven such mechanisms for acquiring new capabilities: internal development, acquisitions, licensing, internal ventures, joint ventures, venture capital, and educational acquisitions.[21]

If the technology and market are familiar, the firm may be better off developing the innovation internally because it has the capabilities to do so. If the market is new but familiar while the technology exists in the firm, the firm can also pursue internal development since the required marketing capabilities build on existing ones and the firm already has the technological capabilities. Amazon. com's move from books, music, and videos to toys, auctions, and electronics is a good example. A similar strategy applies when the technology is new but familiar, and the market is an existing one; that is, a firm can also develop the technology internally since the required capabilities build on existing ones. In both cases, the firm can also buy the technology or license it from someone because it has the absorptive capacity to assimilate it.

When the technology is familiar but the market is new and unfamiliar, a joint venture becomes a very attractive mechanism. Why? Because, in a joint venture, two or more firms set up a separate and legal entity that they own, and pool their capabilities to achieve a common goal. Thus, a firm that is familiar with the technology but not with the market can form a joint venture with others that are familiar with the market. With their complementary capabilities, they can offer customer value to the market earlier while learning from each other and building capabilities in the areas they lack.

When both the market and technology are new but familiar, a firm can use other mechanisms such as internal ventures, acquisitions, and licensing. In an internal venture, a firm sets up a separate entity within itself to develop a new product, usually employing those entrepreneurial individuals who would otherwise move out on their own to found a competing firm. A firm can also buy another firm that has the capabilities that it needs. This gives it immediate access to the necessary capabilities and it can start learning right away. Rather than buy, a firm can also license the product from another firm.

When both the technology and market are new and unfamiliar to a firm, the required capabilities are different from its existing capabilities. Roberts and Berry suggested using venture capital and educational acquisitions. In venture capital, a firm makes a minority investment in a young firm that has the capabilities (usually technological). In either case, by taking interest in the start-up, the investing firm obtains a window on technology and markets, and can learn. **Educational acquisition** is the purchase of a firm by another one for the sole purpose of learning from it, not to keep it as a subsidiary. It is the reverse engineering of an organization— buy, open up, and learn from.

Implementation

Deciding where a firm should go and how to get there is one thing. Implementing the decision is another. If AOL has decided to add more content and wants to develop it internally, the questions now include: How should the organization that will develop the content be structured? Who will report to whom? How will performance be measured and rewarded? Who should be hired? The strategy, structure, systems, people, and environment (S^{3}PE) framework that we described when exploring the implementation component of a business model applies here. If AOL decides to team up with someone, who should that be, who will stay where, and what type of employees will each contribute to the team? Of particular interest for a manager facing the Internet are two key points: the need to use information technology to better manage people and its limitations.

Employee Needs and S^{3}PE Fit

The Internet is about information and knowledge which means that the individuals who have this knowledge are extremely important. In designing organizational strategies, structures, and systems for a good S^{3}PE fit, a firm needs to know more about what makes each individual tick. Sure enough, on average, employees may want stock options in their firm. But there may be software engineers who would rather have their names in some part of the software so that their friends and relatives can access it and see that they actually played a major part in developing the software. Moreover, what happens when everyone offers stock options to their employees? The point is that managers need to know more about each employee in order to better decide to whom they should report, how their performance is measured, how that performance is rewarded, and during what times of the day they are most productive.

Physical Colocation

Many of the properties of the Internet indicate that distance is less of a constraint than it used to be for many activities. As general managers structure their organizations, however, it is important for them to remember that certain transactions may still require in-person physical interaction. Some kinds of tacit knowledge are difficult to unstick and encode in a form that can be transmitted and received over the Internet. In pharmaceuticals, for example, doctors can post data from the clinical testing of a new drug on a website for sharing with other doctors, thus increasing the efficiency and speed of testing. This can lead to faster approval of drugs for marketing by the Food and Drug Administration and an increase in a firm's profits over the life of the drug's patent. However, the Internet is no substitute for the informal exchange of ideas that takes place over the water cooler, in the parking lot, in the cafeteria, and in the hallways that is critical during pharmaceutical drug discovery. Physical colocation is still critical for such R&D activities.[22] To the extent that people have emotions, it may also be a good idea to visit customers even if there is a website that people use for transactions.[23]

PERSONAL ROLE OF THE GENERAL MANAGER

General managers have been described as thinkers, controllers, leaders, champions, sponsors, and doers.[24] While some of these characteristics are desirable in general managers, we will concentrate on two that would serve managers well in the face of the Internet: champion and sponsor. The importance of these characteristics rests in part on the tendency for leadership and power in firms whose products are knowledge-based to reside with those individuals who have the knowledge— and these individuals are not necessarily the managers. Thus, a manager is more a facilitator of knowledge exchange than the controller of resources. Facilitating means the ability to articulate a vision of what the firm and its business model are all about. Champions and sponsors do this best.

Champions

Champions are individuals—sometimes called advocates or evangelists or entrepreneurs—who take an idea (theirs or that of an idea generator) and do all they can within their power to ensure its success.[25] In the process, they risk their position, reputation, and prestige. They actively promote the idea or business model, inspiring others with their vision of its potential. Jeff Bezos, of Amazon.com, was a champion for his firm in the late 1990s and early 2000. Champions must be able to relate to the whole value configuration and therefore require T-skills.[26] (T-skills are deep expertise in one discipline combined with a sufficiently broad knowledge in others to see the linkages between them.) Despite frequent opposition, especially in the face of disruptive technologies like the Internet, champions persist in their articulation and promotion of their vision of the technology. They usually emerge from the ranks of the organization and cannot be hired and groomed for the purpose of being champions. By evangelically communicating the vision of the potential of an innovation, a champion can go a long way in helping an organization better understand the rationale behind the innovation and its potential. General managers could benefit from having this characteristic. The other characteristic is being a sponsor.

Sponsors

Also called a coach or mentor, a **sponsor** is a senior-level manager who provides behind-the-scenes support, access to resources, and protection from political foes. Such support and protection serves two purposes.[27] First, in the case of a bricks-and-mortar firm adopting the Internet, for example, a sponsor's support sends a signal to political foes of the Internet that they are messing with a senior manager and sponsor. Second, it reassures the champion and other key individuals that they have the support of a senior manager. Lee Iaoccoca, former CEO of Chrysler, was the sponsor of the company's minivan. Edward Hagenlocker, Ford's vice president for truck operations, backed and boosted funds for a radical new approach to designing new cars that was instrumental to the success of Ford's trucks such as the F-150.[28]

SUMMARY

In the face of the Internet the primary responsibility of general managers is to guide their firm to gain or reinforce a sustainable competitive advantage. The extent to which they can meet this challenge is a function of three factors: whether their firm is an incumbent or a pure-play Internet new entrant, how they can guide the firm through the formulation and execution of a good strategy, and the characteristics of the general manager. General managers should understand some important differences between incumbents—the bricks-and-mortar or legacy firms that were in their industries before the Internet was adopted by those industries—and new entrants, the pure-play firms that entered using the Internet. Incumbents have to deal with the legacy problems of dominant managerial logic, competency traps, channel conflicts, internal political power, co-opetitor power, and emotional attachment to older technologies and capabilities. On the other hand, they may have complementary assets that they can use. Moreover, portions or all of many Internet business models can be imitated, giving incumbents a chance to catch up. New entrants do not have the legacy handicaps of incumbents, and attract more equity capital and knowledge employees. However, they do not have complementary assets and must build them from scratch.

Whether a firm is an incumbent or new entrant, it must formulate and execute an Internet strategy if it is going to have a sustainable competitive advantage. This entails answering four important questions: (1) *Where is the firm now?*—that is, how well is it doing? What is the basis of its performance? What are its strengths and weaknesses? Are there any threats and opportunities that it faces? (2) *Where does the firm go next?* Given the firm's performance, its positioning relative to its rivals and competitive and macro environments, it may want to pursue different goals. (3) *How does the firm get there?* Pursuing new goals usually means finding different ways to achieve them. (4) *How does the firm implement the decisions to get there?* Deciding where to go to next and how to get there is one thing. Executing the strategy is another. Guiding a firm through this strategy requires a general manager to have certain characteristics, among them being a champion and sponsor.

KEY TERMS

cannibalization   141
capabilities gap   151
champions   154
channel conflict   141
competency trap   141
competitive advantage   139
complementary assets   143
co-opetitor power   142
dominant coalition   142
dominant managerial logic   140
educational acquisition   152
emotional attachments   142
equity capital   144
genetic mix   143

incumbents   140
joint ventures   144
legacy firms   140
managerial logic   140
new entrants   144
new game strategy 149
political power   142
Roberts and Berry model   151
S³PE system   143
sponsor   154
strategic intent   150
strategic management process   146
SWOT   150

DISCUSSION QUESTIONS

1. Why do incumbents have such a difficult time adopting radical technological changes?
2. When is an incumbent more likely to win an Internet race against new entrants?
3. In the face of the Internet, what type of firm would you rather manage: an incumbent or an attacker? Provide detailed evidence backing your choice.
4. It has been said that the best way to beat change is to change first. Does this statement apply in the face of the Internet? Any industries in particular?
5. What areas of government regulation do you think would have the most influence on the Internet: taxation of e-commerce, intellectual property laws, or privacy laws?
6. In a firm's Internet strategic management process, which of the four major steps do you believe require the most attention from a general manager: Where is the firm now as far

as the Internet is concerned? Where does the firm go next? How does it get there? How does it implement the decisions to get there? Explain.

7. Apart from being sponsor and champion, what type of person do you believe the general manager of a firm should be? Does the type of industry in which the person manages make a difference?

8. It has been said that with the Internet, geography no longer matters. Do you agree or not? Explain.

REFERENCES

1. For the first three questions in a "bigger" picture, see C. A. de Kluyver, *Strategic Thinking: An Executive Perspective* (New York: Prentice Hall, 2000).

2. S. Oster, *Modern Competitive Analysis,* 3rd ed. (Oxford: Oxford University Press, 1999), pp. 128–140.

3. R. M. Grant, *Contemporary Strategy Analysis* (Malden, MA: Blackwell, 1995), p. 151.

4. This section draws on A. N. Afuah, *Innovation Management: Strategies, Implementation, and Profits* (New York: Oxford University Press, 1998), pp. 217–222.

5. G. M. Hamel and C. K. Prahalad, *Competing for the Future* (Boston: Harvard Business School Press, 1994), pp. 49–71; R. A. Bettis and C. K. Prahalad, "The Dominant Logic: Retrospective and Extension," *Strategic Management Journal* 16 (1995), pp. 5–14.

6. D. C. Hambrick, M. A. Geletkanycz, and J. W. Fredrickson, "Top Executive Commitment to the Status Quo: Some Tests of Its Determinants," *Strategic Management Journal* 14 (1993), pp. 401–18.

7. D. Leonard-Barton, *Wellsprings of Knowledge* (Boston: Harvard Business School Press, 1995).

8. Bettis and Prahalad, "The Dominant Logic," pp. 5–14.

9. J. Pfeffer, *Managing with Power: Politics and Influence in Organizations* (Boston: Harvard Business School Press, 1992).

10. ———, *Power in Organizations* (Mansfield, MA: Pitman, 1981).

11. C. H. Ferguson, and C. R. Morris, *Computer Wars: How the West Can Win in the Post-IBM World* (New York: Time Books, 1993).

12. C. M. Christensen and J. L. Bower, "Customer Power, Strategic Investment and Failure of Leading Firms," *Strategic Management Journal* 17 (1996), pp. 197–218.

13. R .A. Burgelman, "Fading Memories: The Process Theory of Strategic Business Exit in Dynamic Environments," *Administrative Science Quarterly* 38 (1994), pp. 24–56.

14. Hamel and Prahalad, *Competing for the Future,* pp. 49–71.

15. The General Mills, Hewlett-Packard, and 3M examples are based on a homecoming speech given by General Mill's CEO Steve Sanger at the University of Michigan Business School on October 26, 1995; S. Hickman, "General Mills Delivers Success Story," *The Monroe Street Journal,* October 30, 1995; K. Labich, "The Innovators," *Fortune,* June 6, 1988, p. 49; R. Mitchell, "Masters of Innovation," *Business Week,* April 10, 1989, p. 58; K. Kelly, "3M Run Scared? Forget about It," *Business Week,* September 16, 1991, pp. 59–62; M. Loeb and T. J. Martin, "Ten Commandments for Managing Creative People," *Fortune,* January 16, 1995.

16. J. A. Schumpeter, *Capitalism, Socialism and Democracy,* 3rd ed. (New York: Harper, 1950).

17. For a fascinating account of the dynamics of technological change in the automobile and other industries, see J. M. Utterback, *Mastering the Dynamics of Innovation* (Cambridge: Harvard Business School Press, 1994).

18. A. A. Thompson and A. J. Strickland, *Strategic Management: Concepts and Cases* (Homewood, IL: Richard D. Irwin, 1990).

19. Hamel and Prahalad, *Competing for the Future,* pp. 129–290.

20. S. C. Johnson and C. Jones. "How to Organize for New Products," *Harvard Business Review*, May–June 1957, pp. 49–62; E. B. Roberts and C. A. Berry, "Entering New Businesses: Selecting Strategies for Success," *Sloan Management Review* 26, no. 3 (1985), pp. 3–17.

21. Roberts and Berry, "Entering New Businesses," pp. 3–17; see also M. H. Meyer and E. B. Roberts, "New Product Strategy in Small Technology-Based Firms: A Pilot Study," *Management Science* 32, no. 7 (1986), pp. 806–21.

22. T. Allen, *Managing the Flow of Technology* (Cambridge: MIT Press, 1984).

23. T. Peters, *Liberation Management* (New York: Alfred A. Knopf, 1992).

24. H. Mintzberg and J. B. Quinn, *The Strategy Process: Concepts, Contexts and Cases* (New York: Prentice Hall, 1996).

25. The concept of champions was first developed by D. A. Schön in his seminal article, "Champions for Radical New Inventions," *Harvard Business Review* 41 (1963), pp. 77-86; see also J. M. Howell and C. A. Higgins, "Champions of Technological Innovation, *Administrative Sciences Quarterly* 35 (1990), pp. 317–41; E. B. Roberts and A. R. Fusfeld, "Staffing the Innovative Technology-Based Organization," *Sloan Management Review* (Spring 1981), pp. 19–34.

26. M. Iansiti, "Real-World R&D: Jumping the Product Generation Gap," *Harvard Business Review,* May–June 1993, pp. 138–47.

27. Roberts and Fusfeld, "Staffing the Innovative Technology-Based Organization," pp. 19–34; M. A. Maidique, "Entrepreneurs, Champions, and Technological Innovation," *Sloan Management Review* (Winter 1980), pp. 59–76.

28. K. Naughton, "How Ford's F-150 Lapped the Competition," *Business Week,* July 29, 1996, pp. 74–75.

Sample Analysis of an Internet Business Model Case[1]

In this section we apply several of the theories and frameworks discussed in prior chapters to a classic question, Should a company diversify into a new business model? We use the case of Amazon.com's decision in 1999 to inaugurate the zShops as an example of analyzing and appraising a business model.[2]

AMAZON.COM: zSHOPS*

On May 15, 1997, Amazon.com completed one of the most successful initial public offerings (IPOs) in history. Its success ushered in a new era in the Internet, the era of e-commerce (electronic commerce). As the market price continued to rise, many at Amazon became overnight millionaires, and Jeff Bezos, its founder, a billionaire.

By October 1999, with Amazon's market capitalization at $28 billion—substantially more than Sears, Roebuck & Co. and Kmart Corp. combined—Bezos needed to look at new products to maintain Amazon's growth rate. The company had added no new product categories that year until July, when it opened toy and electronics shopping, and annual quarter-to-quarter growth had slowed, to 7 percent from 33 percent the previous year. That growth rate did not justify its market value (see Table 10.1).

Seeking to generate more growth, Amazon introduced the *zShops*. The zShops are a bazaar of online stores that make up an online mall. The zShops concept allows other companies to open online stores under the Amazon.com brand, and customers to benefit from a larger selection of products. As Bezos sat in his office, he wondered whether he had made the right decision to move Amazon away from e-tailing history and refocus the company as an e-commerce mall.

*New York University Stern School of Business MBA Candidates Youngseok Kim, Myriam E. Lopez, Suzanne Schiavelli, Heshy Shayovitz, and Steve Yoon developed this case under the supervision of Professor Christopher L. Tucci for the purpose of class discussion rather than to illustrate either effective or ineffective handling of an administrative situation.

TABLE 10.1 Amazon Timeline

July 1995	Amazon begins selling books online.
May 15, 1997	Amazon goes public.
March 1998	Amazon.com Kids books available on the Web.
June 11, 1998	Amazon diversifies to include CDs.
August 4, 1998	Amazon purchases Junglee Corp. and PlanetAll
November 16, 1998	Amazon introduces video and gift stores.
March 29, 1999	Amazon releases its auction site to counter eBay.
July 1999	Amazon opens toys and electronics stores.
September 29, 1999	Amazon announces zShops.

Source: Seattle Times; Amazon.com press releases.

Amazon.com

After graduating summa cum laude from Princeton in 1986, Jeff Bezos joined FITEL, a high-tech start-up company in New York. Two years later Bezos moved to the Bankers Trust Company where he led the development of computer systems that helped manage more than $250 billion in assets. He became the bank's youngest vice president in February 1990. From 1990 to 1994, Bezos helped build one of the most technically sophisticated and successful quantitative hedge funds on Wall Street for D. E. Shaw & Co., becoming their youngest senior vice president in 1992. Bezos said that he had a quarter of the company reporting to him at the time he came up with the idea for Amazon. He considered the consequences of pursuing the idea:

> I projected out to being 80 years old and put myself in a regret-minimization framework. Would I ever ask myself, "Boy, what would my 1994 Wall Street bonus have been?" Not likely! But I could sincerely regret not doing this . . . [3]

With that, he quit his job and drove west with his wife. At the time, he didn't even know where to ship his furniture. As his wife drove, he tapped out Amazon.com's business plan on a laptop computer and lined up financing on his cell phone. Eventually, he settled on Seattle, mainly because of its proximity to the Roseburg, Oregon, warehouse of Ingram, the giant book distributor. Before the truckload of his belongings arrived, Bezos and four software designers had set up shop in his garage to create the foundations of their company's website. His team spent a year developing database programs and creating the website. Amazon.com opened its virtual doors for business in July 1995.[4]

Amazon.com's greatest strength may be that it was the first online bookseller armed with substantial capital from its IPO, impressive service (including innovations like "1-Click" shopping), and a gigantic selection of titles (the company claimed to have a virtual inventory of 3.5 million books by 1996). Its strategy marked a clear challenge to established book chains like Barnes & Noble, whose superstores generally stock only 175,000 titles (see Table 10.2). In 1996 Amazon earned revenues of $15.8 million (see Table 10.3 and Figure 10.1).

Amazon's Diversification Strategy

The company's success did not go unnoticed. Both Barnes & Noble and Borders bookstores entered the market. The former represented a particularly strong challenge.

TABLE 10.2 Amazon versus Barnes & Noble: Some Statistics

	Amazon	Barnes & Noble
Number of stores	1 website	1,011
Titles per superstore	3.1 million	175,000
Book returns	2%	30%
Sales growth*	306%	10%
Sales per employee (annual)	$375,000	$100,000
Inventory turnovers per year	24	3
Long-term capital requirements	Low	High
Cash flow	High	Low

*Third quarter, 1998.

Source: Business Week, December 14, 1998, www.businessweek.com/1998/50/b3608006.htm.

TABLE 10.3 Amazon Financials

AMAZON.COM INC
Annual Income Statement
(in millions except EPS data)
Fiscal Year End for AMAZON.COM INC (AMZN) falls in the month of December.

	12/31/98	12/31/97	12/31/96	12/31/95
Sales	609.99	147.76	15.75	0.51
Cost of goods	476.11	118.94	12.29	0.41
Gross profit	**133.88**	**28.81**	**3.46**	**0.10**
Selling and administrative, and depreciation and amortization expenses	195.62	58.02	9.44	0.41
Income after depreciation and amortization	**(61.74)**	**(29.21)**	**(5.98)**	**(0.30)**
Nonoperating income	(36.15)	1.90	0.20	0.00
Interest expense	26.63	0.28	0.00	0.00
Pretax income	**(124.54)**	**(27.59)**	**(5.78)**	**(0.30)**
Income taxes	0.00	0.00	0.00	0.00
Minority interest	0.00	0.00	0.00	0.00
Investment gains/losses	0.00	0.00	0.00	0.00
Other income/charges	0.00	0.00	0.00	0.00
Income from continuing operations	N/A	N/A	N/A	N/A
Extras and discontinued operations	0.00	0.00	0.00	0.00
Net income	**(124.54)**	**(27.59)**	**(5.78)**	**(0.30)**
Depreciation Footnote:				
Income before depreciation and amortization	(49.67)	(24.47)	(5.69)	(0.29)
Depreciation and amortization (cash flow)	12.07	4.74	0.29	0.02
Income after depreciation and amortization	**(61.74)**	**(29.21)**	**(5.98)**	**(0.30)**
Earnings Per Share Data (EPS):				
Average no. of shares	**296.34**	**260.68**	**271.86**	**227.20**
Diluted EPS before nonrecurring items	(0.25)	(0.10)	(0.02)	(0.00)
Diluted net EPS	**(0.42)**	**(0.10)**	**(0.02)**	**(0.00)**

Source: Zacks Investment Research.

FIGURE 10.1 Amazon's Annual Sales

161

CHAPTER 10
Sample Analysis of
an Internet Business
Model Case

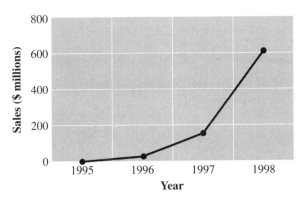

Source: Zacks Investment Research.

Amazon responded by securing a contract to sell books to America Online's 8 million subscribers.[5]

Amazon meanwhile extended its existing online stores to appeal to more customers. In March 1998, for example, it opened Amazon.com Kids, which it dubbed "the most comprehensive resource for children's and young adult books on the Web." With its success in the book market firmly established, Amazon was poised to proceed with the next phase of its plan. Its scalable architecture (the ability of its information infrastructure design to handle growth) allowed it to sell additional items other than books. "The real benefit is for our customers," said Amazon.com spokesman Bill Curry. "We want to be the leading destination for e-commerce"[6] (see Table 10.4).

On June 11, 1988, Amazon extended its product line by introducing compact disks (CDs), with the ability to select among more than 125,000 music CD titles—10 times the CD selection of the typical music store. At the time Roy Satterthwaite, Gartner Group's electronic commerce analyst, thought that Amazon.com might be making a mistake. Satterthwaite said that in most e-commerce markets, companies need to concentrate on their specific categories, for example, Amazon.com and books. Because those companies specialize, they can concentrate on consumers "who limit their choices to the top three in each category."[7]

It took just four months to roll over the leading online music retailer, CDnow, to post music sales of $33.1 million during the fourth quarter of 1998 compared to $20.9 million for CDnow. Seeing their formula was successful, Bezos and company leveraged the brand to expand into more markets. In November 1998, just before the start of the holiday shopping season, Amazon introduced a video and gift section on its website. The video part of Amazon.com opened with 60,000 video titles and 2,000 digital videodisk (DVD) offerings, providing direct competition for online stores like Reel.com. In addition, several hundred gift items were added, ranging from Barbie dolls to Nintendo video games. Most of the gift items were chosen because they related either to what Amazon.com offered in books, music, or videos or "because they would appeal to [their] regular customers."[8]

Countering eBay's success in the online auction market (see the eBay case in Part V of this book), Amazon introduced its own person-to-person auction site in

TABLE 10.4 Amazon Properties

INTERNET DOMAINS

amazon-electronics.com	zshop.com
amazon500.com	prizewinners.com
book-ology.com	amazontelevision.com
bookmatcher.com	amazon-electronic.com
amazontube.com	acimages.com
zpays.com	bookology.com
zdvds.com	zshoppe.org
amazonvideo.com	zsearchs.com
amazonelectronic.com	z-shoppe.net
friend-click.com	filmlovers.com

LISTING OF ALL NEW TRADEMARKS FILED IN THE LAST 6 MONTHS

Trademark No.	Description
75-775431	Book-ology
75-770523	zShops
75-765373	Quickclick
75-765372	Powerclick
75-765371	First Bidder Discount
75-765370	Crosslinks
75-765369	Charitylinks
75-765367	2-Click
75-765366	0-Click
75-760190	Crosslinks
75-755296	Selling circles
75-755295	Buying circles
75-755294	Bidding circles
75-755292	Auction circles
75-755291	Purchase circles
75-775431	Book-ology
75-770523	zShops
75-765373	Quickclick
75-765372	Powerclick
75-765371	First Bidder Discount

Patent No.	Description
5,963,949	Method for data gathering around forms and search barriers

Source: www.companysleuth.com/askjeeves/index.cfm?INFO=AMZN.

March 1999. The auction included many trust-building features that made eBay such a success. In addition, the company reimbursed customers up to $250 if they could prove they were victims of fraud or did not receive paid-for auction items. In July Amazon introduced another store to sell electronics.

Adding another piece to the company's strategy, Amazon built a massive, $300 million, 5 million square foot warehouse in Fernley, Nevada, the first of seven it was to open by the end of 2000. It then hired Wal-Mart's logistics chief, Jimmy Wright, as vice president and chief logistics officer. This hire suggests that Bezos took seriously the challenges of establishing a powerful, rapid supply and distribution network.

Amazon's dream was to become a place where people can find not only books, but everything. Amazon has defined e-commerce as we know it: 1-Click shopping, customer reviews, online gift-wrapping—Amazon has invented them all. Amazon now offers 19 million items. Despite the huge number of items it sold, Amazon realized that it could not sell everything. Thus, the idea for the zShops emerged.

zShops

The zShops concept is a bazaar of online retailers who want to set up shop under the Amazon umbrella. Amazon opened its website to these merchants for a minimal fee. In return, the selling powerhouse will gather huge amounts of information on consumer buying habits. Amazon expects to help these companies and to expand well beyond its base of books, CDs, and so forth.

The biggest benefit for Amazon is a steady cash flow without the costs associated with a warehouse of products. Each online store pays a $9.99 monthly fee, which is less than the average for such a service, and commissions of 1 percent to 5 percent in return for access to Amazon's 12 million customers (see Table 10.5). If the zShop chooses to have Amazon process its billing, the shop will pay an additional 4.75 percent of the total sale. This arrangement will also give Amazon valuable information for its database on consumer preferences and habits and provide target-marketing capabilities.

This new business model has two strategic implications. On the one hand, its move to become an unlimited shopping mall is an attempt to compete with Internet portals like America Online and Yahoo, which offer links with millions of websites and have substantially more monthly traffic. On the other hand, it provides an opportunity to take away some of the small-business revenue flooding into auction sites like eBay, Microsoft, Excite@Home, and Lycos, which agreed to share their auction listings.

Amazon's zShops will be organized essentially by product and product category, not by stores. After a customer has picked an item from a list, he or she is sent to a merchant-controlled page that would include a picture and description of the item. Amazon temporarily offered for free (until Christmas 1999) several of the marketing tools it had refined, and let any merchant offer 1-Click shopping in return for a percentage of the sale.

TABLE 10.5 Price Range for Selected Companies

MSN:	1.5% and 5%, based on the purchase price.
eBay:	Sliding listings fee based on the opening bid; then receives a final fee of between 1.25% and 5% of the selling price.
Amazon:	5% for $0–$25, 2.5% for $25–$999, and 1.25% for $1,000 and over.

Source: Compiled from each company's website, www.msn.com, www.ebay.com, and www.amazon.com.

According to Forrester Research, consumer sales over the Internet will increase to $184.0 billion by 2004 from $3.9 billion in 1998,* and most major merchants are trying to develop a business strategy that will ensure a dominant position in this emerging marketplace. Two years ago Amazon had cyberspace largely to itself. Now the Internet is teeming with e-tailers. Buy.com, for example, is programmed to scan Amazon.com's prices and automatically undercut them.

Competitors

Online malls provide convenience, helping shoppers find an array of items in a single place. Portals, including Yahoo!, America Online, Excite@Home, MSN, and Lycos, are competing in this market with large customer bases and different services, such as online wallets and shopping carts that let buyers pick and choose from multiple stores with minimal hassle. The performance of online malls has been mixed. Big merchants, from Eddie Bauer to FAO Schwarz, continue to buy space, but Amazon is trying to put an end to marketing tie-ins with Internet portal sites. America Online is among the most successful online shopping destinations so far, luring more than 1 million first-time shoppers in December 1998 alone and generating sales of $1.2 billion over the holiday season. Yahoo's online mall rivals Amazon's, with 7,000 stores and over 4 million items, including books, clothes, music, and toys. In July, Excite@Home bought iMall, a Santa Monica, California, company that provided Web hosting and design services for the 2,000 small and midsize merchants listed in its online mall.

Smaller sites are consolidating their listings and their users, seeking "critical mass" to build competencies against much larger players. Where the small players would otherwise wither away in an unknown corner of cyberspace on the Web, alliances offer customers many points of entry to a central location and may well be a threat to Amazon's zShops.

Threats

In reality, Amazon is having trouble with every one of its new categories. It is getting clobbered in auctions by competitors: eBay has 3 million listings; Yahoo!, nearly 4 million; Amazon, at last count, only 140,000. The electronics store launched in July 1999 is off to a bad start: Pioneer and Sony, two of the biggest manufacturers, say they will not allow Amazon to sell their products and they will take action against third-party dealers that try to sell their products through Amazon's consumer electronics site. Amazon's toy shop has similar problems. Some manufacturers are either refusing to supply Amazon or are in a "test mode" with the company. The lack of confidence in Amazon's distribution capability seems to be the issue. Thus, the biggest challenge for zShops will be to attract top-tier, best-of-breed, name brands. Unless it can promise a full range of merchandise, the appeal of the zShops will be limited and could potentially hurt Amazon's credibility.

*Seema Williams, David M. Cooperstein, David E. Weisman, and Thalika Oum, "Post-Web Retail," *The Forrester Report*, September 1999, p. 1.

With zShops, Amazon risks losing control over its famed customer relationship management. Seventy percent of Amazon's revenues come from repeat business because the company is famous for its customer service. But now a retailer—known only by its online ID—is responsible for sending the product ordered from Amazon.com. If there is any problem with the delivery, Amazon's reputation will surely suffer. The company says it is trying to solve those problems, many of which are the growing pains of a new business. It currently offers customer reviews of each zShop merchant. Amazon has said it will guarantee merchandise up to $1,000 if it handles the credit card payment and up to $250 if it does not. The risk to Amazon could be well worth it if the company becomes the preeminent vault of information for Internet shopping habits.

Proponents say that just because Amazon can sell books online, doesn't mean it can sell everything else. Amazon has yet to turn a profit. For now, Amazon can afford to make mistakes. In late 1999, it had $1 billion in cash from its bond offering. So, even if the stock market continues to head south, Amazon would still be able to carry out its plans.

The zShops Dilemma

Bezos insists zShops are a winner. He figures customers of zShops will wind up buying more from Amazon, especially as it moves into new areas such as travel. "The number of items that Wal-Mart can offer online will certainly pale next to what Amazon with other merchants can sell," says Ken Cassar of Jupiter Communications.[9]

But the jury is still out on the e-mall concept. Yahoo and Excite have been running online malls for some time, but the customers are not flocking in. Online specialty foods purveyor Greatfood.com is part of zShops, but CEO Ben Nourse concedes, "I wonder if the mall strategy is the right one."[10]

"Brand names are more important online than they are in the physical world," Bezos once said.[11] As Bezos sat looking at the plans for the warehouses being built, he wondered if Amazon was risking too much. Amazon's brand, positioning, and reputation may all be affected by how it implements its diversification strategy. Should the company cut its losses and pursue other expansion ideas, stick to the zShops concept, or try to focus on the categories in which it is already established? A decision would need to be made soon if Amazon were to exit this latest market.

WHAT IS THE zSHOPS NEW PRODUCT CONCEPT AND HOW DO THEY ADD VALUE TO STAKEHOLDERS?

The first questions that we must address with any new product are, What is the concept? How does this concept add value? These questions help us appraise the first component of the business model.

In 1995 Amazon established an unbeatable online bookseller brand name. Since then, Amazon has diversified its product offerings while remaining within the pure retailer model. Its new product line includes CDs, videotapes, gifts, toys, auctions, and electronics. Amazon's auction site is the only product that steps out of the boundaries of the pure retail model and extends the company into the world of the market maker (intermediary).

In September 1999 Amazon added another new category, the zShops, which offers an unlimited number of independent shops and products. This action made it clear that Amazon had the intention of not only diversifying its retail business, but also of solidifying its position as a market maker by diversifying into zShops and the e-mall concept.

Unlike retail, where Amazon sells and controls the service to the customer, Amazon acts as an intermediary in zShops, offering a cyber shop space where zShops can sell their products to customers. (Figure 10.2 shows zShops purchasing procedure.) Amazon charges a monthly flat fee and a commission on the transaction. (See Table 10.6 for the revenue structure of zShops.)

zShops have a common attribute with Amazon's auction site because, at that site, Amazon also acts as an intermediary. However, these two models have different customer expectations and product availability. While auction customers expect sporadic product availability and do not have an identified performance level for the auctioneers, zShops customers are likely to expect a higher product selection and high-quality service.

Finally, zShops allow Amazon to offer a very large number of products and to become the premier shopping destination for online shoppers by exploiting Amazon's brand recognition and large and growing customer base.

How the zShops Add Value to Customers

- *Convenience of one-stop shopping.* With zShops, customers enjoy a dramatically increased product selection from one site, Amazon, instead of spending

FIGURE 10.2 Purchasing Procedure

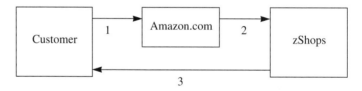

1. Customer places order in Amazon's zShops website.
2. Amazon processes order and notifies zShops stores.
3. zShops stores deliver the product directly to customer.

TABLE 10.6 Revenue Structure of zShops

A. Hosting fee	$9.99 per month (for up to 3,000 products)
B. Transaction commission	
Order size:	Commission (%):
• Less than $25	5.0%
• $25 to $1,000	2.5
• Over $1,000	1.25
C. 1-Click service fee	4.75% of price and $0.60 per each transaction

Source: www.amazon.com/.

time "surfing" on the Web for every product they want to buy. In addition, customers avoid having to type their shipping address and credit card information every time they complete a transaction.

- *Reliability and credibility.* Customers are using a more reliable and credible service provider when they buy a product through Amazon than through an unknown individual online retailer. When customers order the product and give their credit card information, they feel comfortable because of Amazon's reliability and credibility.
- *Guarantee by Amazon.* Amazon's A-to-Z guarantee gives protection to its customers by providing a $250 guarantee for "regular" purchases and a $1,000 guarantee for purchases made through its 1-Click ordering capability.

How the zShops Add Value to Shop Merchants

- *Brand recognition.* By operating under Amazon's umbrella, zShops benefit from the brand recognition Amazon has been able to build, thus attracting customers who value Amazon's reliability and credibility. An individual store would be unable to build a strong brand name and customer recognition level in such a short period of time.
- *Access to a large customer base.* By being affiliated with Amazon, zShops obtain a large distribution network that gives them access to the large number of customers who visit Amazon. It would cost the individual zShops too much in advertising and marketing expenses to obtain even a fraction of Amazon's large customer base.
- *E-commerce package from Amazon.* It is too costly for a small retailer to open an independent online store that has the e-commerce capabilities Amazon currently has. By joining zShops, they can avoid this information technology expenditure and enjoy Amazon's information technology infrastructure.
- *Guarantee and credibility.* The individual stores in zShops obtain credibility by being under Amazon's umbrella. In addition, Amazon's guarantee to customers of up to $1,000 for each purchase gives the zShops site an aura of quality.
- *Access to Amazon's client database.* zShops can potentially share the information on customers accumulated and analyzed by Amazon. Thus, they can have a better understanding of customers' needs and carry out a more focused business.

How the zShops Add Value to Amazon

- *Additional stable source of revenue to increase profitability by means of the subscription model.* In 1999 Amazon observed only a 4 percent sales growth in the U.S. market, compared to the 40 percent it experienced in 1998. (See Figure 10.3 for sales growth data.) zShops bring an additional and stable source of revenue to Amazon through the monthly fees paid by the stores. Since Amazon has a strong brand name and a growing customer base, it should be relatively easy for it to attract retailers and have them join the zShops network. Thus, we see a diversification from what we described in Chapter 4 as a merchant model to a merchant plus brokerage plus subscription model.

FIGURE 10.3 Amazon's U.S. Book Sales and Growth Rate

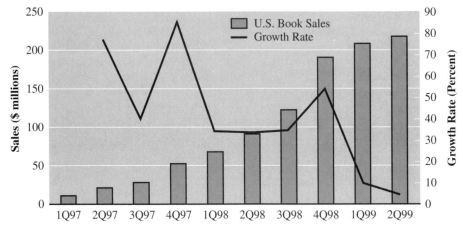

Source: Mark J. Rowan, "Amazon.com Inc.," Prudential Securities Research Report, September 23, 1999, p.12.

- *Customer information.* In the bookselling business, Amazon has been extremely successful in turning their first-time customers into repeat customers (see Figure 10.4). Amazon has been able to achieve this customer loyalty by offering not only competitive prices, but also community features such as book reviews from various sources and recommendations for other books. These community features have been made possible by processing and analyzing the data that has been obtained over a long period of time on the purchasing behavior of customers. As an intermediary of every single transaction in the zShops network, Amazon will be able to accumulate and analyze customer behavior data in the much broader product range offered by the zShops. The ability to provide better and more tailored information to the customer is likely to result in attracting and retaining an increased number of customers. For example, when a new PC camera is on sale in Amazon's zShops or in its proprietary electronics shop, Amazon could e-mail

FIGURE 10.4 Revenues from New and Repeat Customers

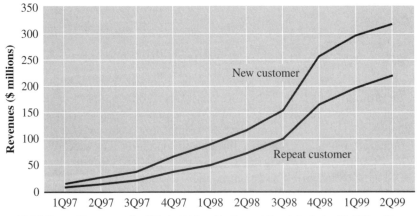

Source: Mark J. Rowan, "Amazon.com Inc.," Prudential Securities Research Report, September 23, 1999, p. 11.

customers who they believe might be interested in buying this product based on the customer's purchasing history, thus fostering additional revenues for Amazon.

WHAT VALUE CONFIGURATION ACTIVITIES SHOULD AMAZON BE UNDERTAKING?

Value Network Components

Amazon has the capabilities to support the components of the value network. As we discussed in Chapter 6, firms should focus on one value configuration and pursue the connected activities that are most appropriate for that configuration, rather than simply pursuing the connected activities of the value chain. We also mentioned in Chapter 6 that Amazon.com is an example of a company that appears unfocused in its value configuration, simultaneously pursuing both a value chain and a value network approach, with the emphasis on value chain activities despite its apparent customer value as an intermediary. If Amazon were to pursue activities related to the value network rather than to the value chain, the components of the value network shown in Table 10.7 would be natural places to start.

DOES AMAZON HAVE CONTROL OVER KEY ASSETS?

Complementary Asset Framework

Please refer to the imitability and complementary asset framework (see Figure 10.5) that we developed in Chapter 5.

- *Imitability.* Amazon.com possesses tight control over the intellectual property associated with the most important aspects of its product development, implying

TABLE 10.7 Value Network Components for Amazon as an Intermediary

Network promotion and contract management
- Brand name and awareness
- Customer acquisition
- Merchant acquisition
- Merchant monitoring and evaluation

Service provisioning
- Providing recommendations based on interests or previous purchases
- Wide range of products
- Convenience
- Reliability
- Guarantee

Infrastructure operation
- Consumer interface
- Knowledge database
- Technological infrastructure
- Logistics expertise (although this would not be the primary source of value)

FIGURE 10.5 Viability of the zShops Strategy for Amazon

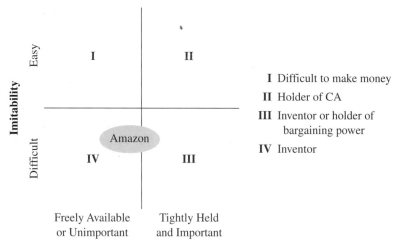

I Difficult to make money

II Holder of CA

III Inventor or holder of bargaining power

IV Inventor

Complementary Assets: zShops merchants

that it is difficult for competitors to imitate or replicate. Amazon's brand awareness, customer interface, knowledge database, and technological infrastructure are all necessary attributes that are difficult to replicate and provide Amazon with an advantage. Not all of these attributes are pure intellectual properties, but the company has protected those that are with trademarks, patents, or trade secrets.

- *Complementary assets.* The complementary assets necessary to create a viable online mall are freely available. Thousands of potential zShops participants would benefit from a relationship with Amazon. These participants are powerless to demand more from the relationship than Amazon is willing to provide because there are so many potential substitutes. It could be argued, however, that Amazon should selectively seek relationships with websites that already have some brand recognition, quality products, or other attributes, which would enhance the power of zShops participants.

- *Summary.* Low imitability combined with freely available complementary assets place Amazon's zShops model in quadrant IV bordering quadrant III in Figure 10.5. Existence in quadrant IV implies that the inventor will be the extractor of revenue from the invention. Therefore, Amazon is in a good position to make money from the zShops concept. If we consider Amazon's existence in quadrant III, the company is still in a good position to extract revenue from the zShops concept because it is both the inventor and the holder of superior bargaining power.

ARE THE zSHOPS A VIABLE GROWTH STRATEGY FOR AMAZON?

The zShops may be a viable growth strategy for Amazon.com. Amazon has been seeking to grow through diversification of its product lines within the boundaries of the retailer model. zShops provides an opportunity to diversify Amazon's product offerings at a much faster rate than would be possible as a stand-alone retailer. Amazon has the capabilities necessary to make zShops a successful online shopping destination. They include the following:

- *Large and growing customer base.* Among e-commerce companies, Amazon has the number one presence in terms of customer reach (percentage of a given population that is a customer). As of May 1999, it had a 17.5 percent customer reach, whereas barnesandnoble.com, which was in third place, had only 7 percent. This large number of customers, many of whom were repeat customers, demonstrates Amazon's strong presence in the e-commerce business.
- *Technological infrastructure.* Amazon has the technological infrastructure in place to offer customers superior service in their shopping experience. Product recommendation services and a secure transaction system are two of them. For zShops, this infrastructure can be easily adapted and utilized without significant cost.

Finally, the presence of other online market makers implies that this business model can work. eBay, for example, has succeeded in bringing a large number of buyers and sellers to its unique community. Today it is regarded as a differentiated Internet-based company. From a financial point of view, eBay also has been successful, with revenues growing eightfold and net income growing by 275 percent between 1997 and 1998.[12] Projections show high growth rates for 1999 as well. As of late 1999 Amazon had not recorded positive earnings.

Analysis of Business Model Components

Amazon's move from a pure retailer to a retailer + market maker is not an unequivocal win—although it may have some merit—according to our analysis of business model components (Table 10.8).

- *Customer value.* This was discussed above in the section on the zShops product concept. As a pure retailer, Amazon has knowledge of its customer preferences and uses that knowledge to recommend new products to the customer. As a market maker, it may not use this knowledge in such a proactive manner. Thus, customers may not consider Amazon to provide value at the same level as a pure retailer. On the other hand, customers may appreciate having a larger selection

TABLE 10.8 Appraising the Move to Retailer + Intermediary Models for Amazon

Component	Pure Retailer	Retailer + Market Maker
Customer value	High	High
Scope	High	Medium
Revenue source	Low	Medium
Pricing	Low	Medium
Connected activities	Low	Low, or worse
Capabilities	High	High
Sustainability	Low	Medium
Implementation	High	High

of items to choose from, much as they do in the bricks-and-mortar world. In addition, the avoidance of retyping (and redistributing) credit card information might be potentially valuable. It is difficult to reconcile these conflicting predictions, but it is most likely that customer value would remain at a high level.

- *Scope.* The primary identification of populations served is and remains B2C (business to consumer). As a pure retailer, Amazon had economies of scope in its prior diversification moves (e.g., from books to CDs). As a market maker, it is only taking advantage of the economies of scope with its brand name, customer interface, and technological infrastructure, not of its knowledge database, warehouse infrastructure, or expertise in logistics. Therefore, Amazon's scope value would move from high to medium in its move to the zShops model.

- *Revenue sources.* As a pure retailer, Amazon's revenue was generated by end-user consumers. They were squarely in the "merchant" revenue model we discussed in Chapter 4.[13] As an intermediary, Amazon is also receiving revenues from the stores that form the network of zShops. The zShops merchants also pay a fixed fee to be affiliated with Amazon. Therefore, Amazon will expand into two new revenue models: *commission* (transaction fee from consummating each zShops purchase) and *subscription* (the flat fee paid monthly by each affiliated merchant). Thus, it is moving from a low to a medium outlook in terms of revenue sources.

- *Pricing.* As a pure retailer, Amazon's revenue stream was variable and dependent on the number of transactions. As a market maker, Amazon has both a variable and fixed revenue stream, the latter due to the flat fee it charges retailers when they become affiliated with the zShops. From past behavior it seems that Amazon had little control over pricing in the retail market. The addition of the zShops may bring an improvement in its pricing power. Thus, it could be argued that Amazon is moving from low to medium control over pricing.

- *Connected activities.* As discussed above in the section on value configuration activities and in Chapter 6, Amazon has always pursued a somewhat schizophrenic approach to its connected activities. While its main value-added has been personalization, book reviews, and product suggestions—suggesting the value network approach—in practice its connected activities have been centered around the value chain. For example, it has focused on logistics, buying warehouses, shipping, and distribution. If Amazon continues in its current activities and simultaneously becomes more of an intermediary through the zShops, its connected activities will become even more of a mismatch, moving from an outlook of low value to something worse than low. However, if Amazon focuses more on the appropriate value configuration activities, as discussed above, it may be possible to move from an outlook of low value to something much better than that. Assuming that the company continues down its current path, we assign Amazon a low value for both the pure retailer and the retailer + market-maker models.

- *Capabilities.* As discussed in the section on the viability of zShops as part of Amazon's growth strategy, in both business models the company is providing a customer value that is higher than that of its competition. That is difficult to imitate because of several factors, including expertise in product development, customers and customer needs, interfacing with personalization software, data collection and mining, protection of intellectual property in terms of trade-marks and patents (e.g., software and algorithms, including 1-Click), brand name, and logistics. Thus, we expect Amazon's capabilities to remain at a high level with or without the zShops.

- *Sustainability.* As a pure retailer, Amazon has been able to sustain its growth rate by "running:" diversifying its product line, providing higher customer value by means of its knowledge database and investment in its brand equity. As a retailer, Amazon has sustained its leading position through several extensions, although it remains to be seen whether its current business model is truly sustainable in financial terms. Will Amazon become the next AOL (which lost money for years acquiring customers but eventually became profitable and dominated its market) or will it simply lose money until investors run for the exits? Comparing the sustainability of Amazon's retailer model with that of the retailer + market maker, it seems as if this new business model is certainly no less sustainable than the old one. As discussed in the section on the viability of Amazon's growth strategy, it appears that relative to the zShop merchants, Amazon has reasonable control over the key assets. Further, it appears to have the upper hand with respect to other alliance partners. Therefore, we conclude that Amazon's sustainability could actually improve from low to perhaps medium or better.
- *Implementation.* As a pure retailer, Amazon has appeared to execute its chosen strategies well, regardless of whether one thinks those strategies are valid. The case does not give enough information to recognize whether Amazon's systems, structure, people, and environment fit well with that strategy. It seems plausible that Amazon's ability to execute and implement its strategies would be largely unaffected by the move to the market-maker model. Thus, we conclude that the outlook for Amazon's implementation is rather high in both the retailer and the retailer + market-maker model.

In summary, Amazon's move from a pure retailer to a retailer + market maker results in a business model with some promise but not without pitfalls. Of the eight components listed in Table 10.8, three improve when moving to the intermediary model. On the other hand, two get worse. Therefore, this might be a reasonable move, especially if Amazon reconfigures its connected activities to reflect the increasing importance of the value network configuration in its new business model.

RECOMMENDATIONS: IS AMAZON RISKING TOO MUCH FROM THE STANDPOINT OF BRAND NAME AND REPUTATION?

One of Amazon's most important assets is its brand and reputation. Amazon has been able to build a strong brand name synonymous with quality products and reliable service. This success has come despite the hesitancy of a large proportion of shoppers to shop on the Internet because of their concern about reliability, privacy, and security. Amazon cannot afford to dilute its brand or harm its reputation. If it does, it risks losing its large installed customer base and growing percent of repeat users as well as the potential to attract new customers. The customers' experience with the various zShops will reflect directly on Amazon, even though the shops are independent entities. Amazon ties its own reputation to that of zShops participants by acting as an intermediary. If a customer has a bad experience utilizing the services of one of the zShops, it is likely to reflect badly on the other zShops and Amazon itself. Once customers become alienated, it is very difficult to convince them that the issues have been ironed out. It is often said that it is seven times more difficult to win back a lost customer than to gain a new customer.

Amazon also needs to be aware that externalities that were not part of the pure retailer model are important aspects of the market-maker model. In the market-maker model, both network size and quality as well as the size of the customer base matter. A small zShops network will not attract customers, which will lead to a small customer base, which in turn will influence potential zShops participants' decision to participate (see Figure 10.6).

Amazon has faced several situations where strong brands, such as Sony, have threatened to withhold products from distributors if they participate in Amazon's zShops. The negative press could affect consumers' perception of the quality of the zShops as a destination. Other brands state that their relationship with zShops is experimental, which lacks the permanency necessary to establish zShops as a viable alternative mall.

Amazon must try to mitigate these issues through some proactive steps.

- Develop a large, high-quality zShops network:
  → Obtain the best players in the categories.
  → Establish relationships with branded product manufacturers.
- Protect its brand name and reputation:
  → Liberally live up to its guarantee.
  → Exercise due diligence in the selection of participants.
  → Remove negligent zShops merchants from the network.

Amazon needs to walk a fine line between building a large network and protecting the quality of the consumer experience. The large network is probably the most important factor at this stage of the game, although Amazon should not neglect protecting the consumer experience.

FIGURE 10.6 Vicious Circle of Customer and zShops Participation

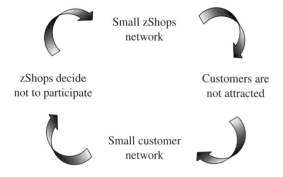

Small zShops network

zShops decide not to participate

Customers are not attracted

Small customer network

REFERENCES

175

CHAPTER 10
Sample Analysis of
an Internet Business
Model Case

1. Case adapted from Youngseok Kim, Myriam E. Lopez, Suzanne Schiavelli, Heshy Shayovitz, and Steve Yoon, "Amazon.com: zShops," New York University Stern School of Business, Case #991-121, December 1999. © 1999 Christopher L. Tucci, reprinted with permission; sample analysis is adapted from Youngseok Kim, Myriam E. Lopez, Suzanne Schiavelli, Heshy Shayovitz, and Steve Yoon, "Amazon.com: zShops Analysis," New York University Stern School of Business, Note #991-125, December 1999.
2. We realize that Amazon.com is one of the most overstudied companies in the world. Still, this case illustrates many of the concepts from this book and provides a familiar backdrop for students.
3. www.edventure.com/pcforum/pc97/agenda/panel4.html#bezos
4. www.redherring.com/mag/issue44/bezos.html
5. www.redherring.com/mag/digital/amazon.html
6. www.cnnfn.com/digitaljam/newsbytes/113186.html
7. www.cnnfn.com/digitaljam/newsbytes/113186.html
8. www.sjmercury.com/business/center/amazon111798.htm
9. www.businessweek.com/1999/99_41/b3650116.htm
10. www.businessweek.com/1999/99_41/b3650116.htm
11. inc.com/articles/details/0,6378,ART1314_CNT53,00.html
12. eBay 10-K filed on March 29, 1999.
13. Do not confuse the "merchant" model (e-tailer) with the transition to an intermediary between Amazon and so-called zShop "merchants."

Internet Protocols, More Details, and Further Reading

In this brief appendix, we provide a few more technical details as a reference for those interested in learning more about the technology of the Internet.[1] We describe the basic idea behind the main protocols and discuss domain names, the client-server model, and a few other technical details.

How Does the Internet Work?

Internet Protocol

The most important feature of the Internet is the Internet Protocol, which was developed years ago under the auspices of the Advanced Research Project Agency (ARPA), which was part of the United States Department of Defense. Indeed, the Internet was originally called the ARPAnet. The Internet Protocol (or IP for short) is a specification for how to share information across a network. It was called "Internet" in its inception because it was designed to connect disparate networks across the country and even the world.

IP was designed to break large amounts of information into small *packets* which were to be identified with a source and destination. The source was called the "sender's IP address" and the destination the "receiver's IP address." When a computer received a packet, it looked at the destination and decided where to send the packet next. It therefore routed the packet to the next stop-off point on the way from the source to the destination. The specialized computers that performed this task, for obvious reasons, became known as *packet switches* or *routers*.

---

1. The basics of this technology have not changed very much in the last 20 years, although some details do occasionally change: Technology advances every day and the physical infrastructure of the Internet along with it. Businesses merge, rename themselves, sell off business units, or go bankrupt. Companies launch new products and whole new segments are created seemingly overnight. While the basic ideas do not change very frequently, we have prepared as a service to our readers an up-to-date synopsis of developments; feel free to point your browser to <http://www.internetbusinessmodelsandstrategies.com> for some late-breaking news in both the technology and the business of the Internet.

Where do the addresses come from? Any organization or person can register for an IP address through a company (formerly, an agency) that administers the addresses. The organization can request any name that has not already been registered. Most companies would like to get a name that is identical to their actual name. For example, ABCD Corp. would most likely prefer abcd.com ("com" stands for "commercial," "edu" stands for "educational" institution, "gov" stands for "government," "mil" for "military," "net" for "network" (ISP), and "org" stands for nonprofit "organization," to name the most popular *domains*). If no one has reserved abcd.com, then ABCD Corp. will get the name and have a main IP address (and possibly a range of IP addresses) affiliated with that name.

Now, when a computer would like a document served up from across the network, there needs to be some way of mapping the Universal Resource Locators, or URLs, to numbers. In the early days, all computers stored all the IP addresses for all the other computers in a huge table. This, however, was not very efficient as the mapping of names to numbers occasionally changed, which meant the tables had to be reconstructed. The domain name system (DNS) was designed to manage this mapping of names to numbers. Assume you would like the document <http://www.abcd.com/corporate.html>. You need to know which IP address to put in the destination field of your packets. So your computer puts in a request at a local domain name server (also called a DNS) to see if it knows the IP address. If you are within the abcd.com intranet domain, the DNS will have this number available. However, if you are anywhere else, your request will be forwarded on to an appropriate DNS. It could go to a certain "master" name server called the InterNIC name server, which could give a primary and secondary DNS to contact. One of these servers should have the correct IP address for the host you are searching and will send that address back to you so you can make contact.

Client-Server Model

Many if not all of the interactions described here take advantage of an abstraction called a *client-server model*. The *client* runs on the end user's computer. It requests information or requests that a task be performed remotely by a *server.* For example, your electronic mail client executes on your computer. When you "check your e-mail," your client program will most likely send a message to a post office server where your e-mail is being held. It requests that all messages delivered since the last time you checked be delivered to your computer. The server sends the messages to the client and you can then read your e-mail on your own computer.[2]

Another example is a file server. On many systems that involve multiple users, such as those in an office, there are so-called *shared drives*. These shared drives are actually file servers and a client program runs on the office computers that treats the shared drives as local drives in a manner transparent to the employee. An example is the Netware product by Novell. When you start your computer, the client program asks you to log in. If this were your own personal computer with its own hard drive, there would be no need to log in. However, the client program asks you to log in so it can "mount the shared drive." When you look in the shared drive,

---

2. Unfortunately, the word "server" refers to both the hardware (especially if dedicated) and the software that executes on that hardware to perform the server functions.

the client program on your computer sends a request to the file server for the directory information. When you open a file on the shared drive, the client requests the contents of the file from the server. The server complies with these requests as long as you are an authorized user. Thus, the log-in procedure.

The client-server model therefore decouples the *processing* of information from the *storage* of information and accomplishes both in the most efficient way. File servers are highly specialized computers that are optimized to hold and deliver large amounts of data, while your computer is a more general purpose tool that is, in general, useful but lacks both storage space and speed. The development of the client-server model thus led to a more distributed computing environment, making the rise of the Internet possible.

Other Major Protocols

IP is not the only protocol currently in use. The other main protocols are (in order of level of abstraction) TCP, FTP, and HTTP. TCP (Transmission Control Protocol) keeps track of large amounts of information, breaking it into packets at the sender's computer and reassembling the packets into the original data stream at the recipient's computer. The reason you see IP/TCP written together is that they are almost always used in tandem. TCP breaks up the packets, numbers them, and sends them off with the correct IP headers so that the remote version of TCP can put them back together again. Since the information is broken up into packets and is not sent as a data "stream," it is highly likely that a later packet may arrive before an earlier one. Or a packet may get lost on the way and never arrive at all because of a failure in the computer hardware or a bug in the software. TCP keeps track of all of these things and makes various requests (by sending messages to the source's computer) to reassemble the original information stream in the correct and complete order. Most of the time, this happens so quickly that the average user does not notice it.

FTP is the file transfer protocol, which uses both IP and TCP to send a complete file across a network from an FTP server to an FTP client. HTTP is the hyptertext transfer protocol, which is the specification for sending and receiving a World Wide Web page from a Web server to a Web client which is also called a *browser.*

Universal Resource Locator (URL)

After HTTP was developed, a general way of specifying a specific Internet address using *any* of the protocols came into use. This came to be known as the Universal Resource Locator (URL). The URL comprises three parts: the protocol, the separator (://), and the path to a specific file resident on a specific computer.[3] By 2000, URLS have become almost synonymous with HTTP, but theoretically, they can be used with other protocols, such as FTP or Telnet. For example, a typical URL is:

http://www.best.edu/students/list.html

3. There are other usages of the URL. One is simply to connect using the Telnet protocol to a specific computer, thereby eliminating the need for a file name. Another use is to instruct the remote server to run a program, such as a CGI script, rather than serving a document (file) using http. This second usage is ideal for tailor-made situations where the served document must be created on the fly. For example, when you request a quote for a stock price, the price is constantly changing; therefore the quote provider cannot leave a static file to serve. When you request the quote, the price is checked and a new document is created with the most recent price in it.

which means, "connect to the host called www.best.edu using the hypertext transfer protocol, look in a subdirectory called 'students' and deliver the file in there called 'list.html' so I [the client/browser] can display it."[4] A non-HTTP example is:

ftp://ftp.mycompany.com/employees/list.doc

which instructs the computer to connect to the host ftp.mycompany.com using the file transfer protocol, look in a subdirectory called "employees," and deliver the file called "list.doc."[5]

Companies Supporting the Protocols

What sort of companies support these protocols? Internet service providers (ISPs) are basically in the business of renting IP addresses. Since the average consumer does not actually own a personal dedicated IP address, the ISP provides a telephone service (usually called PPP or SLIP) or other relatively low bandwidth network connection that lets the consumer borrow an IP address for the duration of the session. The user's own computer must support IP and TCP although the ISPs may sometimes provide the software that supports these protocols. The ISP also provides a connection to the Internet by connecting the user by means of the telephone network to its servers (such as e-mail servers or file servers) and packet switches. In addition, Last Mile providers (those companies providing the physical connection to the home as discussed in Chapter 2) introduced in 1999 a Digital Subscriber Line (DSL) service that involves a dedicated IP address and an "always on" connection over normal twisted-pair copper telephone wires. Large, industrial-grade ISPs do the same thing for companies except the service is often provided on high-capacity lines rather than individual telephone lines and may involve dedicated IP addresses for employees' computers.

Other software companies make applications that run on personal computers or workstations that support one or another of the Internet protocols. For example, some companies make electronic mail packages that support POP3 (one of the protocols for delivering e-mail to users) and SMTP (the protocol for sending e-mail from a user) clients and that organize e-mail into "inboxes" and allow the user to send replies to incoming messages. Other companies make Web browsers (supporting HTTP) that allow a user to view hypertext documents across the Internet. Still others provide packages that support FTP which allows the user to store documents on and retrieve documents from remote computers. Some software companies provide the server software to support these clients. For example, companies make software that stores e-mail until users request it, or software that organizes users' files so that e-mail is delivered to them on demand. Many companies provide both

---

4. When no file name is given, the default file name is "index.html" or "home.html." Thus, when you see a URL such as "www.mycompany.com," this actually refers to the file "index.html" in the uppermost directory of the computer www.mycompany.com.

5. Astute readers may wonder whether there is unnecessary redundancy in this system as computers beginning with the name www always seem to be http servers, while computers beginning with the name ftp always seem to be ftp servers. While this naming convention usually holds, it is not necessarily the case, as the same computer can theoretically support multiple protocols. Thus, it is possible that you could ftp from a site whose name begins with www, or Telnet to a site whose name begins with ftp, and so on.

client and server software, although some companies specialize in one or the other. Electronic commerce is another example of an application that runs over the Internet, involving both client and server software. Examples might include payment processing systems that support customers typing in credit card numbers.

Some companies provide the *content* that resides on the servers, especially the Web (HTTP) servers. These companies could be "portals," sources of information that users turn to first when they get on the Internet. Most of the so-called content providers, content creators, or aggregators are pure providers of information compared to most other companies, which sell products or services using the Internet as one possible medium.

Further Reading

This appendix has attempted to give a brief glimpse into some of the details behind the technology of the Internet. We have not provided details on all the different formats or types of multimedia information available, nor have we given other details on related technologies. Examples of these missing topics include details on routers, ISDN, network computers, satellite protocols, Usenet newsgroups, Internet Relay Chat and Instant Messaging, World Wide Web form interfaces, Java, Javascript, CGI scripts, audio and video formats, encryption, firewalls, proxy servers—and the list goes on. On our website, we have collected more information on many of these topics. However, as mentioned earlier in this appendix the basics of how the system works has remained relatively constant for over 20 years!

For more information, the reader should consult the many computer science, information technology, and electronic commerce texts. The best book at an intermediate level of technical detail is the millennium edition of Preston Gralla's *How the Internet Works,* published by QUE Press 2000. The classic computer science books in this area are Paul E. Green, Jr. (Editor), *Computer Network Architectures and Protocols,* Plenum 1982; and Andrew S. Tannenbaum, *Computer Networks,* 3rd Edition, Prentice Hall, 1996. For more information on the client-server model consult Robert Orfali, Dan Harkey, Jeri Edwards, *Client/Server Survival Guide,* 3rd Edition, John Wiley & Sons, 1999. For a good overview of electronic commerce issues with an emphasis on Internet security, see Marilyn Greenstein and Todd Feinman, *Electronic Commerce: Security, Risk, Management, and Control,* McGraw-Hill, 2000. For a managerial perspective on electronic commerce, consult Ravi Kalakota and Andrew B. Whinston, *Electronic Commerce,* published by Addison Wesley, 1997. Finally, for a history of the Internet based on primary interviews with its architects, refer to Stephen Segaller's *Nerds[2.0.1]*, published by TV Books, 1999.

PART V

Cases

BROADCAST.COM

Mark Cuban and Todd Wagner carefully contemplated their options. The past two days had been a whirlwind of activity as their Dallas-based firm, Broadcast.com, had been approached by Yahoo! During the Big Picture media conference, sponsored by Variety in New York City, Yahoo! CEO Tim Koogle made a tender offer to acquire Broadcast.com. Two days earlier, the news hit "the street" as a *Business Week* online story speculated about the potential merger. Shares of Broadcast.com surged 37 percent in one day of trading amid the rumors.[1] During the media conference, Tim Koogle declined comment on the rumor, but fueled the flames by announcing that Yahoo! was indeed seeking strategic acquisitions.

Broadcast.com was the current leader in audio and video broadcasting over the Internet. Since its inception, Cuban and Wagner had built superior Internet audio and video capabilities, and locked in predominantly exclusive contracts with over 300 radio stations, 40 television stations, 400 sports teams, and 600 business customers. However, its 4.6 million monthly viewers paled in comparison to the 30 million viewers of Yahoo![2] Additionally, Broadcast.com reported an operating loss of almost $15 million for the year ended 1998.

At the time, Yahoo! was the leading Internet portal with over 30 million visitors a month, but it was locked in a fierce battle with Microsoft and America Online (AOL) to retain its title. Despite its success, Yahoo! was mainly a text-based site that lacked "rich media" content. "Rich media" was the new phrase used to describe the mix of text, graphics, audio, video, animation, and interactivity. Koogle believed that users, advertisers, and online consumers all wanted TV-like content and services. A recent survey by Home Network found that users recalled seeing multimedia ads 34 percent more often than traditional banner ads.[3] The acquisition of Broadcast.com could place Yahoo! in position for a rapid shift to high-speed multimedia Internet services.

As the night fell on Gotham City, Cuban and Wagner mulled over the future of Broadcast.com.

New York University Stern School of Business MBA Candidates Sandy Chen, Arial Friedman, Darren Landy, Mark Stencik, and Joey Shammah prepared this case under the supervision of Professor Christopher L. Tucci for the purpose of class discussion rather than to illustrate either effective or ineffective handling of an administrative situation. Copyright © 2001 by McGraw-Hill/Irwin. All rights reserved.

Mark Cuban and Todd Wagner were both Indiana University alumni living in Dallas, Texas. During the winter, they missed attending Hoosiers basketball games and wished that there was some way that they could at least listen to the games. During the summer of 1995, Wagner wondered if the two would someday be able to listen to the games over the Internet.

With this idea and $5,000, Broadcast.com commenced in a spare bedroom in Cuban's house. Cuban bought a Packard Bell 486 PC for $2,995, $1,000 worth of network equipment, and spent $60 a month for a high-speed connection. The two then approached a local Dallas radio station, KLIF. They explained that in the near future, technology would lend itself to create a radio superstation on the Internet, and they wanted to work with KLIF to make this a reality now. Although KLIF agreed to give it a try, existing technology enabled Cuban and Wagner to simply tape the broadcast, digitize the recordings, and post it on their website. However, in September 1995 the two aspiring media moguls figured out how to broadcast live radio over the Internet. Their idea was primitive, but it worked. They hooked up a $15 radio tuner to the sound card of Cuban's computer and began to broadcast live.

Their initial marketing strategy was not much more sophisticated than the $15 tuner. Cuban, over the Internet, began delivering his sales pitch to the local Dallas market. He invited anyone interested in Dallas area sports to come visit his website. The response was incredible and soon Cuban and Wagner had a feeling that they were on to something big. The e-mails continued pouring in from Dallas natives living elsewhere as well as from office workers in the Dallas area.

Backed by the confidence from the overwhelming response to their website, Cuban and Wagner decided to launch their own company, AudioNet.com. The name was later changed to Broadcast.com to reflect the diversity of their programming and services. They felt that the success of their company was tied to their ability to attract content providers, such as radio stations and sports teams, nationwide. Wagner knew that it would take a little more to assure long-term success. He recognized the need to block out potential competitors and control as much content as possible. Wagner set out to sign up as many content providers as possible, usually with multiyear, exclusive agreements. Wagner and Cuban got their big break by giving up 5 percent of the company's equity to Host Communication, which owned the radio broadcasting rights for 12 NCAA basketball teams and the NCAA tournament. Because they were the first movers in live "Internet" broadcasting, they were able to build a large portfolio of content providers.[4]

At the time, Internet broadcasting rights were simply unheard of. However, in November 1995 Congress enacted the Digital Performance Right in Sound Recordings Act, which gave owners of sound recordings certain exclusive rights to retain fees for broadcasting. The Act, however, had not been sufficiently interpreted, and Cuban and Wagner believed that Broadcast.com was exempt from inclusion under this law.[5]

THE BUSINESS MODEL

Broadcast.com was different from other Web-based companies in that Cuban and Wagner were quite focused on actually generating profits from the start. Their business model was based on the premise that all content providers would want to expand their listener basis by using the Internet, thereby increasing their bargaining position with advertisers. Consequently, content providers would be willing to pay to "webcast" their programs.

Broadcast.com had three distinct sources of revenues: (1) Content providers paid to broadcast over the Internet, or bartered to provide free commercial airtime during programming. Broadcast.com used this airtime to promote its own site or resold the time to a third party. (2) The Business Service Group was established to provide cost-effective Internet and intranet broadcasting business services, such as earnings conference calls, investor conferences, press conferences, trade shows, stockholder meetings, training sessions, and even distant college courses. (3) Advertising space was sold on the site, including gateway ads that were broadcast prior to requested user programs with guaranteed click-thrus, channel and special event sponsorships, and multimedia and traditional banner ads.

Cuban and Wagner continued to build brand awareness through their exclusive agreements with most major colleges and universities and the NFL, including live coverage of the Super Bowl. However, by late 1995 they had spent close to $1 million, most of which was personally funded by Cuban. Feeling financial pressure and needing the infusion of a bit of cash, Cuban and Wagner turned to their friends who were eager to invest. Cuban and Wagner sold shares in $30,000 increments to their friends and local Dallas investors. However, since this new infusion of capital was only a short-term solution, Cuban and Wagner approached the services of investment bank Alex. Brown to handle their first private placement in 1996.

INTERNET BROADCASTING

The infusion of capital enabled Broadcast.com to expand its own private network. Broadcast.com received analog audio and video signals from its 22 satellites at its home office in Dallas. The company relied on streaming technology to convert the analog feeds into compressed digital information to feed directly through the Internet in real time. Its network consisted of over 550 multimedia-streaming servers that streamed the feeds and pumped them out to major net backbone providers through direct lines of 45 and 155 Mbps. Cuban and Wagner negotiated deals with the four largest backbone providers, GTEI, MCI, Sprint, and UUNET, which connected over 80 percent of the downstream Internet service providers (ISPs). The direct connections to the backbone providers allowed users to avoid congestion and delays normally caused by going through the downstream ISPs themselves.

Broadcast.com also relied on Unicasting technology which sends a single stream of digital video, audio, or data to each requesting user over the Internet. However, end users needed to download free software from Microsoft or RealNetworks in order to hear or view the audio or video broadcast. In September 1997 Broadcast.com started using the latest technology, multicasting, whereby a single stream of content was sent to multiple destinations without flooding all network connections. Cuban and Wagner signed a deal with UUNET to develop the first multicasting network to allow over 500 simultaneous live events, and provide content to 100,000 simultaneous users over a single connection.

Broadcast.com also leveraged its reliance on third-party technology through strategic relationships with key Internet companies. Cuban signed an agreement with RealNetworks to allow users to download RealPlayer in exchange for a link on RealNetworks' home site. Then, early in 1998, Cuban signed a distribution deal with Yahoo!, allowing this leading portal site to take a minority stake in Broadcast.com.

Armed with the latest technology, Broadcast.com aired a live webcast of NBC's top-rated television show *ER*. Later, it broadcast live, on-demand coverage of ABC's 1998 Academy Awards. In February 1999 Broadcast.com set the record for simultaneous viewers, when more than 1.5 million people logged on to see the live broadcast of a Victoria's Secret fashion show, which was later dubbed "the quintessential net event."[6] However, the ISPs could not handle the enormous demand of viewers, and thousands of additional viewers could not log on to view the show.

COMPETITION

The rapid shift toward streaming technology and attention generated by live webcasts caught the eye of other firms. The increased competition began to mount on several fronts: streaming media sites, videoconferencing, and traditional media firms.

Streaming Media Websites

The emergence of similar websites that provided streaming media content increased rapidly. Most sites specialized in one medium such as Netradio, which allowed users to create their own radio stations over the Internet, or CBS Sportsline, which aired certain sporting events each week. In August 1997, however, RealNetworks and MCI formed a strategic alliance to create a service called Real Broadcast Network to provide a wide array of streaming media content. But, unlike Broadcast.com, RealNetworks only provided a link to news and entertainment content providers, such as ABCNews.com and CNN.com.

Videoconferencing

Broadcast.com also competed with videoconferencing and teleconferencing companies, as well as with other companies that provided Internet broadcasting services to businesses. By 1997 the Business Services Group accounted for 30 percent of the total revenues of Broadcast.com (see Exhibits 1.1 and 1.2). The competition in this arena also increased rapidly as new sites such as Vcall.com and BestCalls.com provided free audio versions of conference calls and other business meetings. Additionally, as the cost for this technology continued to decrease and the quality of transmission improved, industry experts expected more companies to perform these services in-house. This meant greater competition for fewer available revenues.

EXHIBIT 1.1 Total Revenues for Year Ended December 31, 1997

	Year Ending December 31, 1997
Business services	$2,820,449
Web advertising	2,955,259
Traditional media advertising	942,090
Other	138,235
	$6,856,033

Source: Broadcast.com Prospectus, July 17, 1999.

Web advertising 43%

Business services 41%

Traditional media advertising 14%

Other 2%

Traditional Media

Broadcast.com competed with traditional media including radio, television, and print for a slice of the advertiser's budget. Some traditional services, such as CNN and the *New York Times,* established a viable presence on the Internet and had the benefit of existing relationships with advertisers and advertising agencies. Additionally, Broadcast.com competed with traditional media companies to sell its inventory of radio and television ad spots, which it obtained from content providers in exchange for the content provider's Internet broadcasting rights.

GOING PUBLIC

On July 17, 1998, Broadcast.com went public with the stated goal of becoming the top broadcasting portal on the Internet. After one day of trading, Broadcast.com set another high-water mark as the stock appreciated over 249 percent.[7] Cuban and Wagner were now millionaires. However, unlike many Web-based entrepreneurs, they never viewed their IPO as an exit strategy. Instead, the IPO process enabled them to build the company's brand name, and the infusion of capital allowed them to continue to build upon its strategic position. (See Exhibits 1.3 and 1.4 for financial information.)

CURRENT SITUATION

Following the success of its IPO, Broadcast.com continued to expand the volume of its content agreements and business services. In December 1998 Cuban and Wagner formed an alliance with NASDAQ for live streaming coverage of corporate quarterly earnings for the NASDAQ 100 Index companies. They then acquired Net Roadshow, which was the first company to receive permission from the Securities Exchange Commission (SEC) to provide IPO Roadshows over the Internet. Net Roadshow was also the leading provider of Internet Roadshows and had contracts with nearly every major investment bank. Finally, Broadcast.com set its sights on the global market when it established a joint venture with Soft Bank to launch Broadcast.com Japan with audio and video content in Japanese.[8]

When the Media Metrix rankings came out in March 1999, Broadcast.com was ranked 6th in news/info/entertainment and was classified as the 14th largest website

EXHIBIT 1.3 Broadcast.com Balance Sheets

	Year Ending December 31,		Quarter Ending March 31,
	1996	**1997**	**1998**
Assets			
Current assets:			
Cash and cash equivalents	$ 4,580,286	$21,337,116	$21,337,116
Accounts receivable	406,802	1,976,765	1,976,765
Prepaid expenses	65,760	1,032,198	1,032,198
Other	17,912	11,311	11,311
Total current assets	5,070,760	24,357,390	24,357,390
Property and equipment	1,186,182	2,812,971	2,812,971
Prepaid expenses	1,715,000	935,720	935,720
Intangible assets	182,414	126,733	126,733
Total assets	8,154,356	28,232,814	28,232,814
Liabilities and Stockholders' Equity			
Current liabilities:			
Accounts payable	91,545	362,214	362,214
Accrued liabilities	454,926	677,662	677,662
Total current liabilities	546,471	1,039,876	1,039,876
Stockholders' Equity			
Common stock	57,341	85,763	85,763
Additional paid-in capital	10,807,309	36,838,152	36,838,152
Accumulated deficit	(3,256,765)	(9,730,977)	(9,730,977)
Total stockholders' equity	7,607,885	27,192,938	27,192,938
Total Liabilities and Stockholders' Equity	$ 8,154,356	$28,232,814	$28,232,814

Source: Broadcast.com Prospectus, July 17, 1998.

overall. The company had clearly established itself as the leading Web portal for Internet broadcasting. Cuban and Wagner had developed an impressive network of content providers. They secured contracts with 385 radio stations, 40 television stations, and 420 sports teams. Among its more than 600 business clients were leading U.S. blue-chips firms such as AT&T and General Motors.[9]

In 1999, Broadcast embarked on a new medium: film. It accomplished this by signing a deal with Trimark Holdings, Inc., to license the rights to broadcast Trimark's entire film library over the Internet. However, given the nature of the Internet, Broadcast.com still lost $14.1 million for the year ended 1998.[10] In addition, the company prospectus came with the conspicuous caveat to potential investors that "the Company expects to continue to incur significant losses on a quarterly and annual basis for the foreseeable future."

THE OFFER

In April Yahoo! approached Wagner and Cuban with an offer to acquire Broadcast.com in a pooling of interest deal valued at $5.7 billion or $130 per share. At the end of March, shares in Broadcast.com traded in the $30 range. Yahoo! initially considered

	Year Ending December 31,		Quarter Ending March 31,
	1996	**1997**	**1998**
Revenues:			
Business services	$ 535,201	$ 2,820,449	$ 1,126,515
Web advertising	1,090,629	2,955,259	1,322,911
Traditional media advertising	0	942,090	516,707
Other	130,270	138,235	209,811
Total revenues	1,756,100	6,856,033	3,175,944
Operating Expenses:			
Production costs	1,301,253	2,949,641	1,224,957
Operating and development	1,506,449	4,659,249	2,247,141
Sales and marketing	717,547	3,389,069	1,670,727
General and administrative	751,785	1,416,276	588,179
Depreciation and amortization	544,003	1,129,120	442,456
Total operating expenses	4,821,037	13,543,355	6,173,460
Net operating loss	(3,064,937)	(6,687,322)	(2,997,516)
Interest and other income	76,090	213,110	275,066
Net Loss:	$(2,988,847)	$(6,474,212)	$(2,722,450)

Source: Broadcast.com Prospectus, July 17, 1998.

offering $110 to $120 per share, but feared a bidding war from rivals Microsoft and AOL.[11] As Wagner and Cuban considered the lucrative offer, they wondered about the benefits and risks of giving up their independence. Broadcast.com had built an impressive collection of licensing agreements and contracts with content providers and business clients, as well as a state-of-the-art network to "webcast" the content received. The $5.7 billion stock offer represented a hefty premium above the company's market value. However, the two moguls could not help but wonder if partnering with Yahoo! was the best strategic option for both parties to maximize synergies in the future.

REFERENCES

1. Kara Swisher and Evan Ramstad, "Yahoo! Holds Talks on Acquiring Broadcast.com, Boosting Shares," *The Wall Street Journal,* March 23, 1999, p. A3.
2. Don Jeffrey, "Yahoo! Eyeing Broadcast.com?" *Billboard,* April 3, 1999.
3. Linda Himelstein and Andy Reinhardt, "Putting More TV on the PC," *Business Week,* April 5, 1999, at www.businessweek.com/1999/99_14/b3623079.htm.
4. Richard Murphy, "Making a Killing on the Internet," *Success,* May 1999, pp. 54–59.
5. Broadcast.com Prospectus, July 1998.
6. Bob Trott, "Victoria's Secret for Webcasts Is IP Multicasting," *InfoWorld,* August 16, 1999.
7. Richard Murphy, "Making a Killing on the Internet," *Success,* May 1999, pp. 54–59.
8. Morgan Stanley Dean Witter Investment Research, April 30, 1999.
9. Broadcast.com Prospectus, July 1998.
10. Morgan Stanley Dean Witter Investment Research, April 30, 1999.
11. "Yahoo! to Acquire Broadcast.com as the Internet Leans toward Audio and Video Streaming," *Weekly Corporate Growth Report,* April 12, 1999.

WEBVAN: REINVENTING THE MILKMAN

"Webvan will go down in history either as the next Federal Express or as one of the biggest failed infrastructure bets in history."[1]

On November 5, 1999, Webvan completed its much-anticipated initial public offering (IPO) and made headlines across the business world. Despite tiny sales and big losses to date, shares of the two-year-old company, which combines Internet grocery shopping with home delivery, shot to an 80 percent premium on its first day of trading. As the trading day ended, Webvan had a total market value of more than $8 billion, nearly half the capitalization of grocery industry leaders such as Safeway, Inc., and Kroger Co.[2]

Webvan Chairman Louis Borders, founder of Borders Books, felt at once exhilarated and terrified. Naturally he was extremely proud of the company's achievements. While Webvan had operated for a mere five months in the San Francisco area, more than 10,000 people had signed up for the service—not bad considering that it has taken rival Peapod, Inc., 10 years to amass a customer base of 100,000 households. Borders was confident that Webvan could prevail over its existing online competitors by expanding aggressively. In the Internet economy, Borders argued that first-to-scale, not first-to-market, counted.

On the other hand, the lofty valuation caused concern. For one, Webvan's 1999 sales were expected to amount to $11.9 million—less than large grocery chains make in one day—while losses would amount to $35 million (see Exhibit 2.1).[3] Borders found himself already thinking of how he could ensure the sustainability of his company. Could Webvan deliver on its huge promise and potential now that expectations had catapulted? Moreover, he suspected, Webvan's IPO had been a huge wake-up call for traditional grocers. How would they—and perhaps other online competitors—react? Finally, Borders pondered possible new revenue streams. What additional, if any, delivery markets and products could Webvan pursue in the long term?

This case was prepared by University of Michigan Business School MBA candidates Denise Banks, Otto Driessen, Thomas Oh, German Scipioni, and Rachel Zimmerman under the supervision of Professor Allan Afuah as a basis for class discussion. © Copyright 2001 by McGraw-Hill/Irwin. All Rights Reserved.

Webvan Group, Inc.
Consolidated Statement of Operations
(in Thousands, Except Per Share Data)

	Year Ending December 31,	
	1997	**1998**
Net sales	0	0
Cost of goods sold	0	0
Gross profit	0	0
Operating expenses:		
Software development	$ 244	$ 3,010
General and administrative	2,612	8,825
Amortization of deferred stock	0	1,060
Total operating expenses	$ 2,856	$ 12,895
Interest income	85	923
Interest expense	69	32
Net interest income	16	891
Net loss	$(2,840)	$(12,004)
Basic and diluted net loss per share	$ (0.08)	$ (0.18)

Source: Webvan prospectus, SEC filing.

BORDERS BOOKS: REVOLUTIONIZING THE BOOK INDUSTRY

Back in 1971 Louis Borders and his brother Tom opened a "serious" bookshop in the heart of Ann Arbor, Michigan. Customers could expect friendly, well-informed store staff to help them locate their selections or let them browse solo for hours. With an unrivaled selection of topics, the first Borders store became known as one of the finest bookstores in the world.

Drawing upon Louis's study of mathematics, leading to a degree from the University of Michigan, and his graduate work at the Massachusetts Institute of Technology, Borders Books pioneered technologies and strategies that revolutionized the bookselling industry.

Inventory Management

Through its nationwide expansion, Borders Books devised and developed the most sophisticated computer inventory system in the book retailing business to date. As each store's purchases were recorded, the system used artificial intelligence technology to constantly adjust the store's inventory, thereby adding more books on topics that were selling and eliminating books on topics that were not. This technology allowed most Borders Books stores to stock over 200,000 book, music, and video titles, a selection unmatched by any other book or music store.

Customer Service

Not only did Borders Books cater to its customers through unparalleled selection, it also offered exceptional service. From the day the first store opened, Borders focused on hiring well-educated book lovers. Special efforts were made to hire people who were passionate about books and music. In addition, all potential employees were required to pass a book or music quiz. This process ensured that well-informed and trained staff provided personal in-store attention and expertise to customers who requested it.

Borders Books selection and service competencies converged when attending to special customer orders. If a certain book or CD was not available in the store, the computer system searched for the item across all Borders stores in the country. If the item was not in inventory within the Borders Books chain, a salesperson would query publishers, wholesalers, suppliers, and smaller bookstores. Wherever it was available, the Borders Books staff would secure the item and ship it to the location that was most convenient to the customer.

Through their inventory management innovations and customer focus, Louis and Tom Borders were widely recognized as single-handedly revolutionizing and increasing sales in the over $10 billion bookselling industry. In 1999 the Borders Group, Inc., was the second largest book and music retailing chain in the United States and an independent, publicly owned corporation with its shares traded on the New York Stock Exchange.

A NEW CHALLENGE: THE GROCERY INDUSTRY

Energized by the staggering success of his initial venture, the 48-year-old Louis Borders sought a new challenge. He discovered it one day in 1997 as he opened a catalog order that had arrived at his Silicon Valley home by Federal Express. At that moment, Borders recognized that retailing through the Internet, a phenomenon that had exploded throughout the 1990s, would never become really big unless someone could discover a more efficient and cheaper way to deliver products to people's doorsteps. This untapped business proposition intrigued Borders. By transferring the inventory management and customer focus learning he established in the bookselling business, Borders was confident that he could reinvent the colossal $453 billion traditional off-line grocery market. With this goal in mind, Borders founded Webvan, an online grocer that was "arguably the most ambitious e-commerce initiative to date."[4]

HISTORY OF THE ONLINE GROCERY INDUSTRY

Although the traditional off-line grocery market was huge, the online grocery market emerged slowly. The online grocery industry originated in the late 1980s, when small local companies began taking orders by phone and fax and hired "professional shoppers" who would purchase the groceries from existing grocery stores. Orders were then delivered by the local companies or held in the store for pickup. In 1990 Peapod emerged as a front-runner in this industry, and many smaller players followed suit. However, since these smaller players relied on partnerships with traditional grocery stores, they were not able to sell goods cheaper than the actual store. The grocery delivery industry stayed afloat by charging delivery fees.

The rapid growth of Internet usage by consumers in the 1990s facilitated the transformation of the grocery delivery business into an online version. With more consumers using the Internet for informational and e-commerce purposes, online grocers tried to benefit from the efficiencies associated with Internet technology. New competitors, such as Webvan and eGrocer, sprang up in the marketplace, while more seasoned competitors, such as Peapod and Streamline.com, attempted to stay competitive. The original phone-and-fax players who were already in the marketplace were anxious to take advantage of the Internet channel and soon developed websites with product offerings that included not only groceries, but other items such as videos, flowers, music, and toys.

The latest trend in online grocery delivery was a distribution-centric prototype system. Its primary aim was to achieve a sizable customer base, respectable levels of customer service, satisfaction, and repeat usage. New entrants to the grocery delivery businesses planned aggressive national expansion programs by rapidly rolling out high-capacity customer distribution centers in most major metropolitan areas. Their goal was to steal market share from the enormous off-line grocery market and also to create new market opportunities by providing combinations of delivery services that did not yet exist in the bricks-and-mortar world.

MARKET POTENTIAL

Opportunities

The primary benefit the online grocery channel provided to consumers was convenience. The average "stock up" grocery store trip took 47 minutes[5] so online grocery shopping returned this valuable time to busy consumers. Moreover, after a 45-minute initial setup, subsequent orders could be processed extremely fast and efficiently. In addition, since many online grocers achieved less overhead by using centralized warehouses and employed fewer people than traditional stores, cost savings could potentially be transferred to the end consumer. Lastly, eliminating the costly real estate and other expenses related to bricks-and-mortar companies made for exciting business propositions and growth.

Research indicated that the online grocery channel was making inroads. The vast majority (89 percent) of people who tried purchasing groceries online visited the grocery store less often.[6] This indicated that online shopping could become habit-forming, potentially providing a constant stream of revenue for online grocers.

Challenges

Despite the hype of Internet companies and e-commerce as the "wave of the future," analysts and grocery industry experts were unsure about the actual growth potential of the online grocery market. Industry analysts estimated online grocery sales of $156 million in 1998, less than 1 percent of the entire grocery market. Market projections for the year 2003 ranged from $4.5 billion (Andersen Consulting) to $10.8 billion (Forrester Research). With such vastly different market projections, it appeared difficult to predict which online companies would do well, if any. Additionally, of the 53.5 million people who were online in the United States, only 435,000 ever purchased food online. This number represented less than 1 percent of the 14.5 million users who had made purchases online.[7]

The biggest challenge in the development of the online grocery industry was to attract and retain enough customers to use this alternative method of purchasing groceries. While online grocery shopping was deemed incapable of replacing the desire to "touch and feel" items such as fresh produce, the most common type of groceries purchased online were perishables.[8] Other common customer criticisms of online grocery shopping included lack of selection, the amount of time it took to set up an order, and the high cost of delivery relative to the service's perceived value. In addition, the demographic population that was most likely to use the online service was also the segment that was least willing to sit around and wait for deliveries.

Margin structures were razor thin in the highly competitive grocery industry, causing some competitors to diversify beyond mere grocery delivery. The savings associated with online ordering were partially offset by expensive home delivery and servicing requirements and, like all e-commerce ventures, could vanish when faced with the costs incurred by building brand recognition.

WEBVAN'S VISION

"We are building the Last Mile to the consumer. It's a huge logistical problem."

—Louis Borders

Even in an industry rife with razor-thin margins, Louis Borders believed that by eliminating store costs, he could reap sizable profits. Instead of stock clerks and multiple warehouses, Borders envisioned giant distribution centers that would service major metropolitan warehouses around the globe.

Using Borders' analytical expertise, Webvan created a more efficient way to assemble customer orders, store them while in transit, and deliver them to homes within a 30-minute window. Borders estimated that Webvan could achieve 12 percent operating margins compared to the industry's traditionally low margins of 4 percent. To replicate this system nationwide, Webvan in 1999 signed a $1 billion agreement with Bechtel Group, an engineering and construction firm, to build distribution centers and delivery infrastructure in 26 new markets over the next two years. In addition, Borders foresaw a safe, secure online customer experience that offered nearly double the selection of products of a typical grocery store and at comparable prices.

With his compelling idea and vision in place, Borders set out to convince the business community that he had the retailing management expertise to crack the online grocery code. To build his business model, he duplicated the best operating practices from a myriad of cyber- and real-world businesses. Webvan looked to Federal Express as the blueprint for its hub-and-spoke delivery system, to traditional grocers as the model for maintaining food quality in transit, and to Wal-Mart as an example of breadth of product selection. Webvan's website emulated Yahoo! for speed and Amazon.com for the shopping experience. More than a few people were impressed as Webvan secured more than $120 million from hallmark investors such as CBS, Yahoo!, LVMH, Softbank, and respected venture capital firms Sequoia Capital and Benchmark Capital. In addition, Webvan was able to successfully recruit top, experienced management talent to join its mission. In a major coup, just prior to its IPO, Louis Borders convinced George Shaheen, CEO and 32-year veteran of Andersen Consulting, to forgo his imminent hefty retirement package and become Webvan's CEO.

THE WEBVAN MODEL

Building upon Borders' experience and expertise, Webvan differentiated itself within the online grocery market in two distinct areas: operations and customer service.

Operations

Webvan's 80 software programmers created proprietary systems that automated, linked, and tracked every part of the grocery ordering and delivery process. A new 330,000-square-foot distribution center in Oakland, California, utilized these proprietary systems to service customers within a 40-square-mile radius around the San Francisco Bay Area. The $25 million distribution center, a prototype for the 26 other centers Webvan intended to build, included 4.5 miles of conveyor belts, temperature-sensitive rooms for specialty items, and the ability to serve as many customers as 20 normal supermarkets.[9] The Webvan model could do all of this with half the labor and double the selection of products of regular supermarkets. Because of these innovative efficiencies, Borders believed that each of these facilities would make money within nine months of launch.

Once orders were placed on the Web, they were automatically routed to the warehouse. "Pickers" were stationed throughout the distribution center to assemble the orders in plastic boxes or totes, which were color-coded depending if the items were refrigerated, frozen, or dry. The pickers traveled no more than 19.5 feet in any direction to reach 8,000 bins of goods that were brought to the picker on rotating carousels.

A conveyor belt transported the totes throughout the facility until they were loaded onto refrigerated trucks. These trucks took the orders to one of 12 docking stations throughout the Bay Area where they were loaded onto one of more than 60 vans so that drivers could take the orders directly to people's homes. None of these vans traveled more than 10 miles in any direction and the route was mapped out by a system that optimized travel time. At peak performance, Webvan expected that each facility would handle more than 8,000 orders a day, totaling 225,000 items, and generate annual revenues of $300 million. In comparison, a conventional stand-alone supermarket brought in $12 million a year.

Customer Service

Webvan customers could order a shopping list of items and receive the groceries the next day within any specified 30-minute time period. Deliveries could be attended or unattended, meaning that the customer could either be home to receive the order, or the Webvan associate could drop off the order while the customer was away from home. Webvan couriers were not allowed to accept tips from customers, and were thoroughly screened and trained before starting their professional lives as Webvan "ambassadors." As of December 1999, delivery was free for orders over $50; delivery fees were $4.95 for orders under $50.

Additionally, Webvan aimed to provide its customers with 50,000 products from which to choose compared to a normal grocery store that carried 30,000 items.[10] Personalized shopping lists, which appeared after a customer's initial order, were also designed to provide faster and easier shopping services for the time-strapped customer. Webvan's market position as the quality-driven gourmet online grocer with everyday grocery prices was an attempt to differentiate itself from competitors. Webvan even employed its own culinary director, who was responsible for creating chef-prepared meals that catered to the lifestyle and tastes of Webvan customers. In addition, Webvan partnered with some highly regarded Bay Area suppliers to offer high-quality produce, meats, fish, and baked goods.

With high operational costs and low initial grocery sales, Webvan's 1999 losses were fore-casted to be $35 million. Total sales for 1999 were expected to be only $11.9 million.[11] Forecasts called for Webvan to have sales of $518 million by 2001, with an overall loss of $302 million for the year. Sales of $518 million would be less than 1 percent of the entire grocery market (including bricks-and-mortar sales). Factors affecting these sales targets included on-time development of distribution centers and an increase in demand for online grocery services.

Gross sales were important to the company, but average order size and repeat customer business were also key drivers in overall profitability. Webvan's average grocery order, as of September 1999, was $71. This was significantly below the average order size of approximately $101 that was needed to generate annual targeted revenues per distribution center of $300 million.[12] However, Webvan's services had only been operational for a few months, so management believed that the average order size would increase over time.

Webvan received revenue solely from sales of grocery products and delivery fees. The company did not intend to sell its customer data to third-party database firms, nor did it receive online advertising fees, since it wanted to remain neutral among the different product brands that it sold online.

COMPETITION

Although the online grocery industry was relatively new, a number of companies competed with Webvan in trying to capitalize on its vast potential.

Peapod.com

Peapod was the oldest and largest online grocery player. Founded in 1989, its pioneering customers—400 households in the greater Chicago area—had to download proprietary software to use the service. "Personal shoppers" would then fill customer orders in local supermarkets. In 1998 Peapod claimed an estimated 44 percent of the Internet grocery market.[13] By 1999 Peapod had its software online and operations in Austin, Texas; Boston; Chicago; Columbus, Ohio; Dallas/Ft. Worth; Houston; Long Island, New York; and San Francisco/San Jose.

To keep up with demand—approximately 100,000 customers in 1999—Peapod switched from the personal shopper model to a warehouse model for filling orders, though its warehouses were significantly smaller than Webvan's. As of 1999, Peapod's personal shoppers picked their products inside Peapod warehouses and prepared them for delivery in temperature-controlled delivery bins. In November 1999 Peapod started shipping non-perishable packages across the country by UPS. Moreover, the company also established strategic membership alliances with Walgreen's for delivery of health and beauty aids, and was considering delivery of nongrocery items such as books, dry cleaning, and flowers.

Membership at Peapod actually decreased over 1999.[14] While analysts felt that Peapod's stock was underrated, it seemed that Peapod might have lost focus. In any case, it missed out on the investor mania that impacted so many Internet stocks. In November 1999 Peapod released disconcerting information, claiming that its funds would run out in the third quarter of 2000.[15]

Streamline.com; Shoplink.com

Originating in Boston, both of these companies positioned themselves as a "complete lifestyle solution, simplifying the lives of busy suburban families." For a monthly fee, Streamline and Shoplink delivered a wide variety of products and services at one's doorstep once a week. Unlike conventional home-delivery grocery services such as Peapod and HomeGrocer, Streamline and Shoplink delivered using either a portable cooling container or a leased, pre-installed refrigeration/shelving unit located in the customer's garage that was accessible only to authorized delivery workers. Products and services included groceries, prepared meals, pet food and supplies, postage stamps, dry cleaning, video and video game rentals, film processing, bottled water, as well as package pickup and delivery.[16]

While their delivery model allowed for more delivery flexibility, these companies also had to overcome additional customer reservations about privacy, theft, and safety. Furthermore, apartment dwellers were not eligible for these services. According to some, the high fixed and variable costs of this model appeared unattractive, yet deeper customer retention might prove a long-term advantage.

Netgrocer.com

Founded in 1997 Netgrocer was the first online grocer to employ the warehousing delivery strategy. From its northern New Jersey warehouse, Netgrocer shipped groceries anywhere in the 48 contiguous states, using Federal Express three-day delivery. Thus, Netgrocer was the only online delivery service that charged by weight rather than by order.

Netgrocer could be thought of as an "automatic pantry restocker." The company delivered only nonperishable goods, and its selection was far from comprehensive. As observed, "the best way you use it is to compile shopping lists of the things you know you buy every month and then just hit one button to have the same order delivered on a recurring basis. Paper towels, toothpaste, diapers, pasta, cat food, cans of soup, that sort of thing."[17] Thus, Netgrocer was betting on consumers' preferences to separate recurring nonperishables from more instinctive or short-term fresh produce purchases.

Hannaford Brothers; eGrocer.com

Hannaford and eGrocer employed a "collection center" strategy, whereby collection centers could be located in convenience stores, office buildings, drive-through facilities, gas stations, or in existing grocery stores, as in the case of eGrocer.

Hannaford, a Boston-area grocery store chain, began offering HomeRuns Online Worksite Delivery toward the end of 1999. This service utilized the corporate parking lot as its outlet, as grocery and prepared meal orders taken online were delivered there at the end of the working day.

At eGrocer, a Palo Alto, California, association of existing grocery stores, customers selected the products they wanted to buy online. These data were transmitted to a local, affiliated supermarket which fulfilled the order. The customers then picked up their groceries at their local supermarket in a designated area during a predetermined time window. This approach not only saved the customer time in the store and at checkout lines, but also offered the customer the opportunity to select certain items themselves. Thus, the customer got the convenience and the ability to "squeeze the tomatoes." While the online grocer avoided the cost of a distribution infrastructure, it had to share its margin with the supermarkets.

Niche Players

Niche players such as Pink Dot and EthnicGrocer.com competed on speed and tailored selection, respectively. Pink Dot created a "Domino's Pizza meets 7-Eleven Stores"[18] model for delivery of groceries, sandwiches, salads, and beverages. It sought to counterbalance higher prices by offering delivery in 30 minutes or less. However, this remained a strategy focused on the fulfillment of "emergency" or "last-minute" needs. Accordingly, order sizes were smaller, while the delivery time proved a sizable task in Pink Dot's city of origin, Los Angeles.

Players like EthnicGrocer focused on nonperishable and high-margin "hard-to-find" products. Similar to Pink Dot's "speed" strategy, the economics of this business model looked more dubious because it was likely to encounter difficulties in achieving economies of scale independently.

REACTION OF INCUMBENT SUPERMARKETS

The reaction of the bricks-and-mortar supermarket chains to the impending online grocery invasion would undoubtedly alter the online grocery landscape. Wall Street analysts had not encouraged bricks-and-mortar grocery chains to make big bets on the Internet. Bricks-and-mortar chains needed to determine if they should dismiss the online grocery phenomenon as a passing fad, or if—and when—they should invest heavily to remain competitive in a completely new marketplace. Many incumbents were looking for appropriate ways to acquire the competence necessary to compete online.

In a reaction to emerging online grocery stores, the biggest grocery chains such as Kroger and Safeway planned to launch experimental online delivery in selected areas. While these were only trials for companies that served much larger markets, incumbents were struggling to determine to what degree they should react to the new competition. Despite its growth, the online grocery delivery segment was forecasted to capture only an insignificant part of the total grocery market between 1999 and 2002. This was poised to change, however, with more ambitious projections calling for 20 percent of all grocery orders to be placed online five years later.[19]

Once incumbents did make the leap into the online segment, they would be formidable competitors. Incumbents already had an existing logistics and distribution model in place, which in most cases would require modest investments compared to the investments Webvan was taking on. Some grocery chains in the United Kingdom had begun to make the transition. For example, Safeway UK gave away free PalmPilots with a dedicated shopping application to its best customers. Tesco, the self-announced "biggest Internet grocer,"[20] with an estimated 240,000 customers, was selling a bar-code scanner that allowed customers to scan products while cruising the aisles. These data would then be downloaded directly to the store's back-end facilities so that the items selected were prepared for home delivery at a convenient time.[21]

LOOKING TO THE FUTURE

Now that Webvan had become a public company, the pressure of investor sentiment would be a major factor in Webvan's future strategic choices. Every decision made would directly affect the company's stock price and standing among Wall Street analysts and individual investors. To meet the high expectations and become the dominant player in the industry, Webvan faced some important strategic choices for the immediate future.

Should Webvan use its large market capitalization to buy regional grocery chains in markets it was interested in pursuing? These regional chains already possessed supplier networks as well as their own distribution centers. Webvan could possibly leverage some equipment from these distribution centers while attempting to replicate its existing distribution centers. This option would also eliminate a few competitors in these regions. On the other hand, should Webvan ever consider a takeover offer from a large grocery chain? Although Webvan's lofty valuation provided some protection against takeover, this certainly did not provide a permanent guarantee.

Furthermore, should Webvan continue to push forward with additional product lines? As of December 1999, sales demand was modest, and the Oakland, California, distribution center operated at only 20 percent of capacity. Would Webvan remain an online grocery company or would it become the "Last Mile" pioneer for all consumer products and services?

With all of this weighing on his mind, Borders decided to leave the office early in celebration of a successful IPO, but also to think about these strategic options for Webvan.

REFERENCES

1. Mohanbir Sawhney, "The Longest Mile," *Business 2.0,* December 1999, p. 238.
2. George Anders, "Webvan's Splashy Stock Debut May Shake Up Staid Grocery Industry," *The Wall Street Journal,* November 8, 1999.
3. Ibid.
4. Linda Himelstein, "Can You Sell Groceries Like Books?" *Business Week,* July 26, 1999, pp. EB44–EB47.
5. "Market Spotlight: Grocery Shopping Online," *The Standard,* September 7, 1998.
6. Ibid.
7. Forrester Research, *Online Grocery Exposed,* December 3, 1998.
8. "Market Spotlight: Grocery Shopping Online," *The Standard,* September 7, 1998.
9. Linda Himelstein, "Innovators: Louis H. Borders," *Business Week,* September 27, 1999, p. 28.
10. Ibid.
11. Anders, "Webvan's Splashy Stock Debut . . . ," p. B1.
12. Webvan, SEC Prospectus Filing, Form 424B1, November 4, 1999.
13. Andrew Edgecliffe-Johnson, "Online Grocer's Funds Eaten Away," *Financial Times,* November 9, 1999.
14. Rick Aristotle Munarriz, "The Online Grocer Invasion," www.fool.com/specials/1999/sp991201groceries.htm, December 1, 1999.
15. Edgecliffe-Johnson, "Online Grocer's Funds Eaten Away."
16. Sawhney, "The Longest Mile," p. 238.
17. Don Wilmott, "So Long, Supermarket!" http://www.zdnet.com, December 5, 1997.
18. Sawhney, "The Longest Mile," p. 238.
19. Munarriz, "The Online Grocer Invasion."
20. Susanna Voyle, "Tesco Biggest Internet Grocer," *Financial Times,* December 1, 1999.
21. Penelope Ody, "Online Delights for the Adventurous," *Financial Times Information Technology Survey,* December 1, 1999.

NETSCAPE COMMUNICATIONS AND THE BROWSER (A)

It was late April in 1997, and Netscape's browser market share was hemorrhaging to dangerous lows. Jim Barksdale took a deep breath before uttering his stunning announcement. Barksdale, Netscape's CEO, would forgo his 1997 salary as a symbolic Band-Aid.

Just over a year prior to this somber day, Netscape's rival, Microsoft, made its own significant announcement; it would embrace the Internet, accept that standards would need to be met and created, and sacrifice some proprietary product profits in order to define this strategy. December 7, 1995, became a day of great consequence at Netscape. It was the day that Microsoft awoke. The stock market responded almost instantly; in five days Netscape had lost 28 percent of its value. While the valuation represented a paper loss, the market share plummet that followed was real. With the decline in market share, Netscape lost the de facto "monopoly" that they had developed in browser software. While the browser is based on open standards, Netscape had built in quasi-proprietary technology. Microsoft had introduced its own technology with Internet Explorer and was rapidly becoming fierce competition to Netscape's Navigator.

Barksdale was ready to confront the giant. He knew that there were profits to be made from Netscape's server software and other products. He pondered whether it was a mistake to reject a partnership with America Online (AOL) to become the default browser for AOL's software. Did he misstep when charging corporate clients for the use of Netscape Navigator? Surely the browser was key—the pivotal element in Netscape's rise to success, its subsequent loss to Microsoft, and perhaps its rise again.

HISTORY OF NETSCAPE AND ITS BROWSER

Netscape was born when Jim Clark, founder of Silicon Graphics, had an itch to leave his job. Clark was interested in high-volume consumer technology, specifically, inter-

New York University Stern School of Business MBA candidates Alyson Becker, Ulrich Blessing, Nicholas Danzis, Jack Enders, and Dave Ramaley prepared this case under the supervision of Professor Christopher L. Tucci for the purpose of class discussion rather than to illustrate either effective or ineffective handling of an administrative situation. Copyright © 2001 McGraw-Hill/Irwin. All rights reserved.

active television. Silicon Graphics, which created workstations for special effects, no longer fit with his technical strategy. In addition to Clark's interest in interactive television, he was intrigued by Mosaic, the popular Web browser developed at the University of Illinois at Urbana-Champaign. Clark took a chance and contacted Marc Andreessen, one of Mosaic's creators. Clark thought the browser concept might work in conjunction with his vision of interactive television. The unlikely pair, 49-year-old Clark and 22-year-old Andreessen, set out to create a proprietary browser for their new company (Mosaic Communications) and sketch out some applications for the browser.

What Is a Browser?

A browser is a graphical interface to the Internet. Browsers offer point-and-click network navigation across computers that run on different operating environments (e.g., Windows, Macintosh, or UNIX).

Vision for a New Browser

Andreessen and Clark agreed on a vision for the networked world of the future and the role that the browser would play in that world. The browser might eventually replace the operating system as the primary user interface. Eventually, this user interface would permit the network to grow and encompass all computer-driven devices.

Some Early Bumps in the Road

Mosaic Communications changed its name to Netscape in November 1994, just seven months after its founding. The name change came as a response to pressures from the University of Illinois at Urbana-Champaign. The National Center for Supercomputing Applications (NCSA) at the University claimed that it controlled the rights to the Mosaic name under a 1992 copyright, and while Mosaic Communications was working on a variation of the browser technology created under Mosaic, it was unacceptable to use the name. Just that August, the University announced an agreement to license the technological and commercial rights to Spyglass, Inc. This move would later come back to haunt Netscape when Microsoft purchased this license from Spyglass. Netscape settled with the University later that year, changed its name, and continued to market its modified browser products. After the name controversy was solved, Netscape introduced its first edition of the Navigator in December 1994. Shortly thereafter, Netscape took off, reaching software deals with MCI, DEC, and other major clients. In early 1995, Jim Barksdale entered the picture as president and CEO (Exhibit 3A.1).

NETSCAPE'S PLAN: "FREE, BUT NOT FREE"[1]

Netscape's original business plan/model, which was never written down, was based on three simple points:[2]

- Build a client (the browser) and give it away free of charge.
- Build servers and sell them for a fee.
- Build a secure transaction system that ties the client to the server, enabling secure communications via the Internet.

EXHIBIT 3A.1 Netscape's Chronology

1994

April 4	Jim Clark and Marc Andreessen found Mosaic Communications Corp.
August 24	The University of Illinois at Urbana-Champaign announces a master license agreement assigning all future commercial licensing rights for NCSA Mosaic to Spyglass, Inc.
October 13	Beta release of Navigator 1.0.
November 14	Mosaic changes name to Netscape Communications Corp.
November 21	MCI chooses Netscape client and server software as the basis of its new InternetMCI service.
November 29	Digital Equipment Corp. becomes the first reseller of Netscape server products.
December 15	Netscape ships Navigator 1.0.
December 21	Netscape reaches a settlement with the University of Illinois at Urbana-Champaign, leaving it free to market its products without a license.

1995

January 11	Jim Barksdale becomes Netscape's president and CEO.
March 6	Beta release of Navigator 1.1.
May 23	Netscape licenses Java from Sun Microsystems, Inc.
June 20	Beta release of Navigator 1.2.
August 9	Netscape's initial public offering values company at $2.2 billion.
August 24	Microsoft ships Windows 95, Microsoft Network, and Internet Explorer 1.0.
October 10	Beta release of Navigator 2.0.
December 6	Netscape's share price reaches an all-time high of $174.
December 7	Microsoft unveils its Internet strategy.

1996

February 5	Netscape ships Navigator 2.0.
February 20	Microsoft creates the Internet Platform and Tools Division.
March 12	America Online makes Internet Explorer its default browser.
April 29	Beta release of Navigator 3.0.
April 30	Microsoft ships Internet Explorer 2.0 for Windows 3.1.
May 28	Beta release of Internet Explorer 3.0.
August 12	Netscape sends letters to the U.S. Department of Justice, charging Microsoft with anticompetitive practices.
August 12	Microsoft ships Internet Explorer 3.0.
August 19	Netscape ships Navigator 3.0.
September 20	The Department of Justice renews its probe into Microsoft's business practices.
October 30	Netscape files for secondary offering of 5 million shares.

1997

April 8	Beta release of Internet Explorer 4.0.
April 29	Barksdale announces that he will forgo his salary in 1997.

Source: Abridged chronology from M.A. Cusumano and D.B. Yoffie, *Competing on Internet Time: Lessons from Netscape and Its Battle with Microsoft* (New York: Free Press, 1998), pp. 329–334. Copyright © 1998 by M.A. Cusumano and D.B. Yoffie. Abridged with permission of the Free Press, a division of Simon and Schuster.

The Browser Debate

Originally, Netscape planned to offer the browser for $99. A series of heated debates followed, and the innovative marketing concept of "free but not free" emerged as the winning strategy. Marc Andreessen led the charge to pursue this strategy, and explained his rationale in an interview:

> [Jim Clark] thought I was a little bit crazy. But we would give it away under specific terms, and to educational institutions for evaluation use. A lot of companies who are going to use it are going to pay for it because, among other things, they want to pay for it. Free software is usually more expensive in the long run for companies to use. It's not a major thing if you have a useful piece of software. It is not too dramatic to make it available to people who are going to pay for it anyway. In addition, we knew that we were going to be doing developments in a number of areas and have a range of products. The Web browser was going to be one of these, so in a sense we gave away one so that people could see the others.[3]

The implications of the "free but not free" strategy were broad. The company had to examine its approach and make certain that a business model was clear and viable. Todd Rulon Miller, head of sales, recalled the development of the sales plan:

> Andreessen was arguing hard for free everywhere, only pay if they want to pay. And I was going, "Marc, nobody's going to want to pay. You have to have some teeth in your license to pay after 90 days or whatever." [Presenting the alternatives to the sales force] we had a real donnybrook because Andreessen was a big believer in download it off the website for free and it'll all be made up in market share or something. And I kept saying, "Look, I'm a revenue hound. We have to have a good way to make money." That meeting . . . gave all the feedback to Jim [Barksdale]. And Jim said, "OK, we're going to have a tight license. Yep, it looks free optically, but it is not. Corporations have to pay for it. Maintenance has to be paid." We sales guys wrote it all down, and I said, "I got that. I can sell that." [4]

Netscape had a significant competitive advantage over its rivals. One element of this advantage is that the business model did not rely on significant revenues from browser sales; Netscape's other product, server software, could be sold to complement the browser. A second element is that Netscape had clear cost benefits. Its distribution model (over the Internet) helped Netscape eliminate costs associated with packaging and shipping software. In addition, Netscape wrote its own proprietary code, and was not subject to the same licensing fees that dogged competitors. At the time, most of Netscape's competition operated with a standard pack-and-ship model, and were subject to a $5 per copy licensing fee to NCSA or Spyglass. This competitive advantage drove Netscape's policy to offer a free download to students and educational institutions. It offered a free 90-day trial followed by a $39 fee (which was later raised to $49) to all others.

The decision to give away the browser technology to some and provide a 90-day trial to others proved controversial, but ultimately propelled Netscape's early success. Critics charged that a company with any hope of financial viability could not give away its flagship product. "People knew then that I was certifiably nuts starting this company, hiring a bunch of students, and now giving the software away," Clark chuckled.[5]

But Clark and Andreessen understood that the business dynamics of the software industry uniquely complemented the new economics of the Internet. In other words, the network becomes a primary medium for software distribution. Because the Internet had always operated loosely on the principles of a "gift economy," where software could be downloaded without charge from host servers directly to a user's desktop, costs associated with packaged-software distribution were virtually eliminated. Furthermore, the Internet provided an opportunity to capture an installed base of users in a relatively short period of time. This was essential: "Anybody who knows [the software industry] realizes that developing an installed base of users is worth its weight in gold," said Clark.[6]

The decision to "give away" the browser client was already based in part on the competitive threat that Microsoft might some day decide to play in the Internet market. The Internet standard, on which Netscape's software is based, evolved over several years and belonged to nobody. Unlike the PC of the early eighties, the Internet is not attached to one company's technology, and its users want it to stay this way. "Proprietary technologies don't work on the Net," said Andreessen.[7]

Strategy: Innovation

Netscape planned to stay ahead by out-innovating competitors, not by locking users into proprietary standards. Netscape got its cross-platform Navigator to market first, in December 1994, and had set a quasi-standard for openness, creating versions able to run on any desktop operating system—Windows, Macintosh, and UNIX—compared to Microsoft's Explorer 1.0 that ran only on Windows 95. To stay ahead, Netscape introduced three major updates of the browser within two years (see Exhibit 3A.2). As a result, Netscape was riding a wave of momentum created by capturing market share—estimated as high as 85 percent—as well as "mindshare" in the highly competitive browser market. That momentum was central to the success of Netscape. "If everyone thinks you're going to be the winner, everyone wants to join—there's a psychology associated with it," said Clark.[8]

Netscape's marketing strategy proved to be ahead of its time. It was this strategy that sparked the notion that software—like everything else on the Internet—should be "free." This notion failed to fit traditional developers' and marketers' business models.

EXHIBIT 3A.2 Timeline of Browser Releases

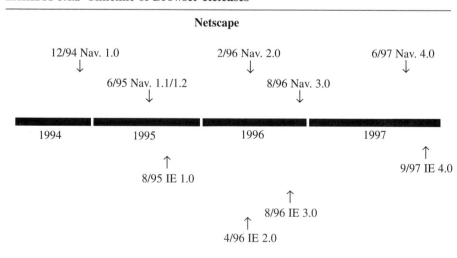

Source: Raghu Garud, Sanjay Jain, and Corey Phelps, 1998, www.stern.nyu.edu/~rgarud/browserchat/strat.html; M.A. Cusumano and D.B. Yoffie, *Competing on Internet Time* (New York: Free Press, 1998), pp. 233; 329–34.

However, some competitors recognized and copied Netscape's strategy. None of them were able to fully realize the benefits of this strategy, though, as the free option would completely "cannibalize" their other sales. Thus there was no incentive for competitors to promote their products and services as "free."

Netscape's visionary concept proved to succeed on two levels. First, it completely crippled competition, but more importantly, it set Netscape up for greater revenues than they ever would have realized had they charged up-front for the browser software. Even the most accomplished publicist couldn't have generated the attention showered on Netscape by the industry and the general public. Mike Homer, head of marketing, recalls the deluge following the release of Navigator 1.0: "The phones are ringing off the hook, and people are paying money."[9]

Netscape relied on the fact that most anybody will try something if it is free, and seems useful. The fact is, that if Netscape eventually wanted its customers to pay for the product, it had to be worthwhile. In this case, most of the corporate trial customers were hooked on the product, and completely unfazed by its post-trial cost. The "free but not free" strategy worked beautifully with corporate clients, but it became clear early on that Netscape would have difficulty reaching revenue targets if it focused on selling browsers to individual consumers. Netscape needed to establish a new strategy whereby they could slip into the corporate market and gain a strong hold without disturbing and inciting established players like Microsoft. "It did worry me," laughed Clark, "because we were burning through money real fast."[10]

The Server Software

At this point in time, Barksdale's objection to giving the browser away for free belied what many say was Netscape's most canny move: leveraging a free-for-the-taking piece of client software as a means of selling a server product. The second phase of the original business plan involved what Clark calls "servers on steroids" back-office functionality, integrated databases, authoring tools, and the ability to conduct full-fledged secure electronic commerce.[11] Netscape created three systems: the merchant system, enabling transactions and billing; the publishing system, including user registration and tracking; and the community system, incorporating real-time chat, bulletin boards, conferences, and hosted sessions. The core was the e-commerce-enabling merchant server. The company charged $1,500 for the communications server and $5,000 for the premium commerce server.

MCI Communications Corp. became the first big customer, essentially funding the development of the commerce system and smoothing the transition to the third phase, when Netscape began shipping server software. The company turned cash-flow positive in January of 1995—not yet profitable but generating a backlog of contracts, enabling Clark to project future revenues (see Exhibits 3A.3, 3A.4, and 3A.5). More importantly, the company discovered in the first quarter that corporations were the customers most ready for server products.

> Here's a product that was developed for the Internet—which you think of as a worldwide free-for-all, and [corporations] were interested in bringing Internet technology inside.[12]

The platform-independent architecture of TCP/IP server technology gives the corporate enterprise a means for internal communication and electronic publishing, as well as a way to connect to the outside world of the Internet. "Practically every company is taking this approach—I can't imagine any company that isn't throwing out its proprietary network technology," said Clark. [13]

EXHIBIT 3A.3 Netscape Communications Consolidated Statement of Operations

	10 Months Ending October 31, 1998	1997	1996	1995	1994	1993
	(in $000s)					
Revenues:						
Product revenues	$261,457	$383,950	$291,183	$77,489	$ 3,337	$ 1,006
Service revenues	186,352	149,901	55,111	7,898	801	100
Total revenues	447,809	533,851	346,294	85,387	4,138	1,106
Cost of Revenues:						
Cost of product revenues	29,896	36,579	25,552	9,177	186	28
Cost of service revenues	90,717	77,118	43,776	2,530	247	43
Total cost of revenues	120,613	113,697	69,328	11,707	433	71
Gross profit	327,196	420,154	276,966	73,680	3,705	1,035
Operating Expenses:						
Research and development	123,238	132,808	86,023	26,841	4,146	871
Sales and marketing	213,004	237,321	133,124	43,679	7,750	1,498
General and administrative	42,715	50,357	31,231	11,336	3,389	513
Property rights agreement	0	0	0	500	2,487	0
Purchased in-process R&D	0	23,250	0	0	0	0
Merger-related charges	0	5,848	6,100	2,033	0	0
Restructuring charges	12,000	23,000	0	0	0	0
Goodwill amortization	11,175	3,300	0	0	0	0
Total operating expenses	402,132	475,884	256,478	84,389	17,722	2,882
Operating income (loss)	(74,936)	(55,730)	20,488	(10,709)	(14,067)	(1,847)
Interest income	6,873	9,062	8,720	4,898	251	53
Interest expense	0	0	0	(304)	(14)	(18)
Other income	7,976	1,860	0	0	0	0
Equity in net losses of JVs	0	(5,939)	(1,928)	0	0	0
Other income, net	14,849	4,983	6,792	4,594	237	35
Income (loss) before taxes	(60,087)	(50,747)	27,280	(6,115)	(13,830)	(1,812)
Provision for income taxes		(11,788)	7,763	498	0	0
Net income (loss)	$(60,087)	$ (38,959)	$ 19,517	$(6,613)	$(13,830)	$ (1,812)
Shares outstanding	95,993	86,058	90,841	75,735	67,180	61,904
Earnings per share	$ (0.63)	$ (0.45)	$ 0.21	$ (0.09)	$ (0.21)	$ (0.03)

Source: Company SEC filings.

EXHIBIT 3A.4 Netscape Communications Revenue and Operating Income by Product Segment

	10 Months Ending October 31 Annualized	10 Months Ending October 31, 1998	1997	1996	1995
		(in $000s)			
Revenues					
Enterprise					
Product revenues	$313,789	$261,457	$383,951	$291,183	
Service revenues	79,136	65,947	54,552	31,831	
Total enterprise	392,885	327,404	438,503	323,014	
Netcenter					
Product revenues	0	0	0	0	
Service revenues	144,486	120,405	95,348	23,280	
Total Netcenter	144,486	120,405	95,348	23,280	
Total revenues					
Product revenues	313,748	261,457	383,951	291,183	
Service revenues	223,622	186,352	149,900	55,111	
Grand total	**$537,371**	**$447,809**	**$533,851**	**$346,294**	
Operating Income (Loss)					
Enterprise		(41,011)	11,051	61,729	
Netcenter		(10,750)	(11,382)	(34,891)	
All other		(23,175)	(55,399)	(6,350)	
Total		**$ (74,936)**	**$ (55,730)**	**$ 20,488**	
Segment Revenue*					
Enterprise (software and services)			333,204	142,102	6,097
Website (Netcenter)			95,117	23,039	1,801
Client (stand-alone)			105,530	181,153	77,489
Total revenues			**$533,851**	**346,294**	**$85,387**

* The company began giving away the browser for free in 1998 and changed its segment reporting to reflect the loss of client software revenue.
Source: Company SEC filings.

EXHIBIT 3A.5 Netscape Communications Balance Sheet

	10 Months Ending October 31, 1998	1997	1996	1995	1994
			Year Ending December 31, (in $000s)		
Assets					
Cash	$ 85,885	$ 55,172	$ 88,233	$ 55,276	$ 8,151
Mrktable securities	91,598	129,426	115,015	96,841	0
Receivables	164,892	153,191	110,821	27,099	1,061
Other current assets	64,305	57,297	37,275	6,405	163
Total current assets	406,680	395,086	351,344	185,621	9,375
Property, plant, and equipment	144,886	131,093	86,812	20,872	2,783
Long-term investments	89,169	76,698	90,504	21,684	0
Deposits and other assets	26,099	29,943	12,655	2,977	767
Total assets	666,834	632,820	541,325	231,154	12,925
Liabilities					
Accounts payable	50,214	40,081	27,752	8,533	1,005
Current long-term debt	0	535	733	1,326	725
Accrued expenses	62,957	54,055	29,963	12,658	1,413
Income taxes	0	2,709	7,731	20	0
Other current liabilities	148,582	106,170	80,308	30,032	3,713
Total current liabilities	261,753	203,550	146,487	52,569	6,856
Long-term debt	420	215	616	1,198	725
Total liabilities	262,173	203,765	147,103	53,767	7,581
Preferred stock	0	0	0	0	1
Common stock	10	10	9	8	1
Additional paid-in capital	579,842	549,186	404,063	207,188	18,215
Accumulated deficit	(103,104)	(119,201)	(3,705)	(22,716)	(12,873)
Deferred compensation	[1,306]	[940]	(6,145)	(7,093)	0
Total stockholders equity	404,661	429,055	394,222	177,387	5,344
Total liabilities and stockholders equity	$666,834	$632,820	$541,325	$231,154	$12,925

Source: Company SEC filings.

Netscape's corporate customer list at the end of 1995 was impressive: Lockheed-Martin, Hewlett-Packard, Eli Lilly, AT&T, McDonnell-Douglas, SGI, Wells Fargo Bank, National Semiconductor, EDS, CNN, and Dow-Jones.

The success of Netscape's strategy was verified on August 8, 1995, when the company went public. Its share price jumped from $28 to $75 before closing the day at $58. By December 5, 1995, Netscape's stock had reached $171 (presplit) per share, and the company was dominating the browser market with over 80 percent market share (see Exhibit 3A.6).

THE SLEEPING GIANT AWAKES

On December 7, 1995, Microsoft staged an Internet conference in front of 300 analysts, customers, and reporters to announce its Internet strategy. In an unprecedented move, Microsoft announced its plans to "embrace and extend" all the popular Internet protocols. The sea change in Microsoft's strategy was based on the belief that the Windows operating system might lose its dominance as the World Wide Web opened networking applications. In 1995 the "software world was abuzz about Java and the possibility of creating open, network-based, cross platform applications that would make complex operating systems—the foundation of Microsoft's power—a thing of the past."[14] The fear of new Internet software knocking Microsoft from its dominant position was

EXHIBIT 3A.6 Browser Market Share (Percent)

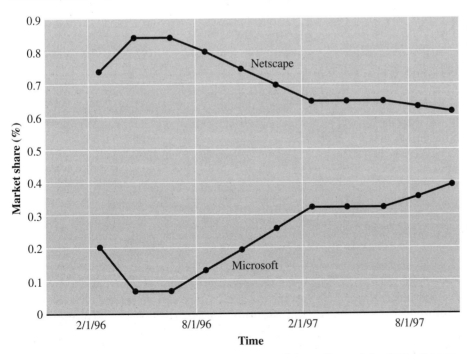

Source: Raghu Garud, Sanjay Jain, and Corey Phelps at www.stern.nyu.edu/~rgarud/browserchat/market.htm; Dataquest, Zona Research.

enough to cause the company to reverse its course from one of retaining proprietary systems toward one of embracing the Internet.

Microsoft's Dilemma and Response

By mid-1995, Microsoft seemed to ignore the Internet hype that was surrounding other software companies. Microsoft's management was focused on its bread-and-butter product, Windows 95. The first sign that Microsoft understood the importance of the Internet and the need to become a player in the online arena appeared in a memo drafted in May 1995 by Chairman Bill Gates titled "The Internet Tidal Wave." In the memo, Gates projected that improvements in computer power over the next 20 years would be far outpaced by improvements in communications networks over the same period. Gates now understood that the Internet was at the forefront of these communications networks, and assigned the Internet the *highest* level of strategic importance going forward. Gates went on to write: "The Internet is the most important single development to come along since the IBM PC was introduced in 1981 . . . the Internet is a tidal wave. It changes the rules. It is an incredible opportunity, as well as an incredible challenge."[15] While the outside world saw few signs that Microsoft was serious about the Internet, the company's senior management was beginning to get the message.

Microsoft awoke in 1995 to a marketplace where browsers, servers, and cross-platform programming techniques threatened to make Microsoft's dominance in PC operating systems obsolete. As computer users downloaded Java-written applications from the Internet, they would no longer be reliant on Microsoft's operating system. The decline in customer need would result in the loss of applications developers and computer manufacturers.[16] Netscape was leading the move toward this new, open Internet standard and leaving Microsoft behind.

Explorer's Beginnings

In December 1994 Microsoft had made a half-hearted gesture toward the Internet in a licensing agreement with Spyglass to use the Mosaic browser. While Microsoft usually believed in building its own software, in this instance it realized that the company needed to speed up the development process, and thus signed the deal. Based on the Mosaic browser, Microsoft eventually designed its own browser called Internet Explorer. In August 1995 Microsoft shipped Windows 95, which bundled software for the Microsoft Network (MSN) and the Internet Explorer browser. MSN was originally designed to be a proprietary platform that would support independent content providers. The basic idea was for MSN to compete with AOL and CompuServe as alternatives to the Internet. Microsoft gained a tremendous advantage by shipping Internet Explorer bundled with Windows 95 to over 90 percent of all computer purchasers. By offering the Internet Explorer free with new computers and over the Internet, Microsoft gained market share.

The announcement on December 7, 1995, that Microsoft would "embrace and extend" the Internet, integrate the Internet directly into Windows, and had become "very hardcore" about the Internet sounded a potential death knell for Netscape. Microsoft entered the market with the firm strategic intent to gain a 30 percent market share. Gates wanted 30 percent because that would give Microsoft credibility and prevent Netscape from gaining further critical mass as Web content providers pondered which browser would eventually become the standard. Upon the announcement of

Microsoft's strategic Internet direction, Netscape's stock valuation fell by 28 percent over the next five trading days (see Exhibit 3A.7).

Signs of Microsoft's Strength

Microsoft's first major victory in the browser wars occurred on March 12, 1996, when it signed a licensing agreement with AOL to become AOL's default browser. AOL had signed a licensing agreement with Netscape for Navigator and intended to use it as the service's default browser. However, the following day Microsoft came to AOL with an offer AOL couldn't refuse. The deal hinged on Microsoft offering to put AOL's icon on the Windows 95 desktop. This arrangement would give AOL access to new computer buyers and offered Microsoft legitimacy in the browser arena. After Internet Explorer 3.0 shipped in August 1996, Microsoft became a major player on the Internet. It is estimated that Netscape lost one percentage point of market share each month after Microsoft released Internet Explorer 3.0.

Netscape's Response

On August 12, 1996, Netscape sent a letter to the U.S. Department of Justice (DOJ) charging Microsoft with anticompetitive practices. The letter was prompted by the difficulties the company faced in attempting to distribute and sell its browsers. Netscape was experiencing "pushbacks" from distributors that it had not seen before, and the distributors cited their contracts with Microsoft as the reason they would no longer accept Netscape's products. Netscape believed that Microsoft was using predatory pricing

EXHIBIT 3A.7 Netscape's Stock Performance, August 1995–April 1997

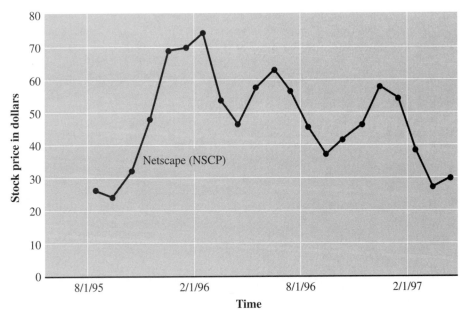

Note: Prices smoothed between monthly dates.
Source: Bloomberg.

(offering its browser for free) and its dominant position in operating systems (90 percent market share) to force it out of business. Netscape made its letter to the DOJ public to draw attention to the situation.

NEXT STEP?

By late April 1997 Netscape was faced with a strategic dilemma. Microsoft had proven that it was "hard core" about the Internet. By bundling its Internet Explorer with Windows 95 and offering the browser for free, Microsoft had substantially eaten away at Netscape's market dominance. Even Netscape's server revenue growth was slowing. How could Netscape compete with Microsoft? Should Netscape give the client software away? Was browser market share critical for server software sales? Did it need a strategic partner?

REFERENCES

1. This section draws heavily upon Michael A. Cusumano and David B. Yoffie, *Competing on Internet Time: Lessons from Netscape and its Battle with Microsoft* (New York: Free Press, 1998), pp. 89–155.
2. David Bottoms, "Jim Clark: The Shooting Star @ Netscape," *Industry Week,* December 18, 1995, p. 13.
3. Cusumano and Yoffie, *Competing on Internet Time*, p. 98.
4. Ibid, pp. 98–99.
5. Bottoms, "Jim Clark: The Shooting Star @ Netscape," p. 13.
6. Ibid.
7. "A New Electronic Messiah," *The Economist,* August 5, 1995.
8. Bottoms, "Jim Clark: The Shooting Star @ Netscape," p. 13.
9. Cusumano and Yoffie, *Competing on Internet Time,* p. 100.
10. Bottoms, "Jim Clark: The Shooting Star @ Netscape," p. 13.
11. Ibid.
12. Ibid.
13. Ibid.
14. Cusumano and Yoffie, *Competing on Internet Time,* p. 107.
15. Bill Gates, "The Internet Tidal Wave," Internal Microsoft memo, May 1995.
16. Cusumano and Yoffie, *Competing on Internet Time,* p. 108.

NETSCAPE COMMUNICATIONS AND THE BROWSER (B)

In late January 1998, Netscape CEO James Barksdale was sitting atop what appeared to be a sinking ship. Following a shocking $88 million fourth-quarter loss, Netscape's stock had plummeted to $21.35 a share, a mere one-quarter of its peak value. In light of these financial woes and the continued pressure of Microsoft's onslaught, the company was forced to lay off 11 percent of its workforce. Although revenue for the quarter had increased 9 percent to $125.3 million, sales from software products had dropped 11 percent to $85.7 million.

Considering the weakening financial picture and negative market sentiment, the decision had been made to follow Microsoft's lead and ship the browser for free. While many people within the industry viewed this as a personal blow to Barksdale and Andreessen, the browser war had left Netscape Communications Corporation with some very real hurdles. Without any future cash inflow from browser sales, Netscape would need to determine where it could realign its strategic focus and create viable future revenue streams. It seemed to some people that Netscape had simply lost out—Barksdale and Co. had their 15 minutes of fame and now they would either be swallowed or fade into a software company. Although Netscape's commitment to Internet standards and multiple platforms made it an important player, many IT executives were extremely concerned about the long-term viability of the company.

The Netscape browser was certainly a key driver in the commercial emergence of the Internet and the explosion of Web traffic. As the ultimate "Internet Play," the company's basic vision was to put browsers everywhere and the revenue would follow. Accordingly, Netscape rode that strategy to rapid growth and IPO success by cleverly pursuing the dollars pouring into the Internet frenzy. However, as the dust began to

New York University Stern School of Business MBA candidates Alyson Becker, Ulrich Blessing, Nicholas Danzis, Jack Enders, and Dave Ramaley prepared this case under the supervision of Professor Christopher L. Tucci for the purpose of class discussion rather than to illustrate either effective or ineffective handling of an administrative situation.

settle from the battle with Microsoft, the company appeared to be limited in its options for growth:

- *The low-hanging fruit had been picked.* Microsoft's assault on the browser market had eroded Netscape's potential revenues and stock price[1] (see Exhibits 3B.1 and 3B.2).
- *Microsoft continued to focus on excluding Netscape from core markets.* Gates's Goliath showed no signs of slowing down its attack and not only continued its browser and messaging offensive but also extended its "elimination" strategy to Web servers and application middleware.[2]

EXHIBIT 3B.1 Netscape's Stock Performance, November 1997–February 1998

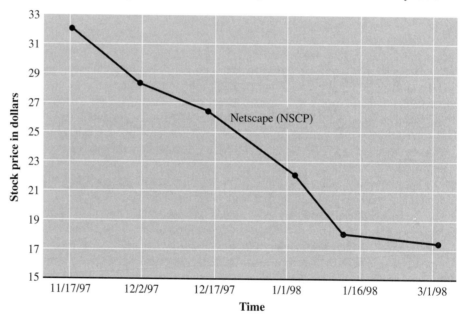

Note: Prices smoothed between semimonthly dates.
Source: Bloomberg.

EXHIBIT 3B.2 Netscape's Browser Revenue

	1997	1996	1995
Segment revenue			
Enterprise (software and services)	$333,204	$142,102	$ 6,097
Website (Netcenter)	95,117	23,039	1,801
Client (stand-alone)	105,530	181,153	77,489
Total revenues	**$533,851**	**$346,294**	**$85,387**

Source: Company SEC filings.

Down but not out, Barksdale and Co. made a dramatic decision not to simply give away the browser but to freely distribute the source code for future generations of Navigator and Communicator. Allowing anyone with the requisite skills to customize, extend, or enhance the browser, the move signified Netscape's commitment to an open source strategy. By putting its products on the Web and trading free software for customer testing, Netscape gave birth to the concept of "community release." The download-and-go strategy let Netscape build revenue before even funding a sales force. Indeed, the decision to embrace community development through the browser code giveaway had rejuvenated the company's creativity.

Having aggressively launched its open source strategy, the company created an internal organization to coordinate the efforts of thousands of developers who were interested in modifying and redistributing Netscape's client source. Dubbed "mozilla.org," the group was a dedicated team within Netscape that was tied to an associated website which promoted, fostered, and guided open dialog and expansion of the code.[3] The company also planned on incorporating the best modifications into a certified and supported release of the product. Marc Andreessen noted:

> By making our source code available to the Internet community, Netscape can expand its client software leadership by integrating the best enhancements from a broad array of developers. This Netscape team will be dedicated to assisting developers in the development of the source code, building a community that addresses markets and needs we can't address on our own, and allowing our customers to reap the benefits through access to superior products.[4]

The response to the open source/mozilla strategy was phenomenal. Within minutes of Netscape's announcement, computer science students at Berkeley began exchanging e-mail about the features they wanted to add to the browser. Although both Netscape and Microsoft had long used such students as unpaid beta testers, Netscape had essentially transformed this group into unpaid programmers. But it wasn't simply "the hackers" who were able to take advantage of Netscape's move. Indeed, any company with an intranet was able to build a browser fine-tuned to its own needs.[5] Linus Torvalds, the creator of Linux, commented on Netscape's move:

> The popularity and success of Apache, the Linux operating system, the BSD version of UNIX, and many other software applications prove the value and impact of open source development. By introducing mozilla.org, Netscape has created an environment that will bring the best of the Internet to a common locale, encouraging developers to create quality products for end-use needs—allowing, for example, direct communication with its existing, pre-Internet systems.[6]

NETSCAPE'S NETCENTER

Despite the many battle scars that the company suffered as a result of the conflict with Microsoft, Netscape's free distribution had stabilized its browser market share by March 1998 at 55.6 percent. Capitalizing on its diminished yet still formidable presence, Netscape chose to tightly link its browser to the Netcenter website. In a manner reminiscent of Microsoft's use of the Windows OS, Netscape began to leverage its large browser share to benefit its media property. Employing features like direct access to personal Web pages from the Communicator toolbar and "Smart Browsing" (a feature that ties the "go to" box into an intelligent Netcenter search), integrating the browser and the portal was the paramount order of the day.

pages from the Communicator toolbar and "Smart Browsing" (a feature that ties the "go to" box into an intelligent Netcenter search), integrating the browser and the portal was the paramount order of the day.

Throughout the early part of 1998, Netscape continued its aggressive efforts to build out the Netcenter website. In an effort championed by executive vice president and general manager Mike Homer, Netscape launched PROJECT 60—a 60-day plan to propel the company to a position of leadership in the Internet portal race. Banking on Homer's belief that individuals act as consumers whether they are at home or at the office, Netcenter focused on both consumer-targeted and business-targeted services. An example of these services included e-commerce solutions, such as providing software for corporate intranets.[7] In its commitment to this Web initiative, Netscape doubled the number of Netcenter employees to 500.

The Excite Alliance

Having reenergized itself through its strategic focus on the Netcenter portal, the company was able to enter into some significant partnerships. Realizing that many midlevel portals like Infoseek and Lycos were having difficulty building brand loyalty, Barksdale and Co. were well positioned to offer these players something that was crucial to achieving dominance in the evolving portal landscape: the millions of loyal eyeballs directly associated with Netscape's strong brand equity. Quite simply, Netscape had the traffic needed to attract strategic partners—Excite proved this to be true.[8] Following a heated bidding war, Netscape signed a two-year deal with Excite in May 1998. While the overall goal of the alliance was the continued upgrade of the Netcenter portal, the deal provided some very specific strategic insight:

- As an enterprise software company, Netscape lacked the crucial media skills like content programming, business development, and ad sales that were needed to be a successful portal. Excite filled this gap as its technology, content, and ad sales allowed for expansion of Netcenter channels—auctions, games, real estate, shopping, and classifieds were programmed by Excite and branded with Netscape.[9]
- Through past deals with Netscape, Yahoo!, Excite, Lycos, and Infoseek had received page views when users clicked on the Navigator "search" button. However, these portals were gradually becoming less dependent on Netscape's traffic, and therefore were unwilling to continue to pay high fees to the browser maker.
- For Netscape, the Excite deal preserved the search engine cash. Specifically, the agreement called for shared advertising revenue with Excite paying a $70 million up-front fee against future ad revenues, as well as warrants for 2 percent of Excite's stock. In addition, Excite would sell ads on cobranded pages and share that revenue with Netscape.

The CNET Deal

Continuing to focus on Netcenter, the company announced an agreement on May 28, 1998, with CNET, Inc., to establish computing content and services for a new channel on the Netcenter website. With the goal of leveraging CNET's award-winning editorial content and services, the new computing and Internet channel aimed to provide Netcenter users with technology news, information, software, and reviews. Robin Wolaner, executive vice president of CNET Online, commented on the deal:

As a leading resource for millions of computer users, Netscape Netcenter is a perfect outlet for CNET's broad range of information and services. We believe we can deliver tremendous value to Netcenter's audience of business and home computer users with our best-of-breed editorial content.[10]

The Netcenter Division's Mike Homer added:

CNET is a recognized leader in delivering timely technology news and computer information on the Internet, and now they have the opportunity to do the same for millions of Netcenter members. Our goal in creating a leading edge Computing and Internet channel is to help Netcenter members leverage the full power of the Internet. The channel is designed to provide the content and services users need to keep their systems up-to-date, to compare and evaluate product that might enhance or improve their time online, and to plan ahead for net technologies or products reaching the market in the months or years ahead. This announcement marks another step in our aggressive plans to turn Netcenter into a major online destination for business users and consumers.[11]

THE ROAD AHEAD

Surviving the Microsoft onslaught had proved to be a drain on all fronts. Emerging with a weaker yet still significant brand, Netscape had made the clear strategic commitment to allow open source community development of the browser, bolstering Netcenter, and forming alliances. Despite these endeavors, however, the company still faced some looming questions.

Netscape's open source initiative had some potentially very important strategic implications. With Communicator in the hands of thousands of programmers, the application was something that could be transformed extremely rapidly. Considering the volatile nature of the Internet environment, an ability to offer an application that changes quickly could create a significant competitive advantage over any program that changes only when its manufacturer issues a new release. Nonetheless, did Netscape's plan entail any strategic danger?

While Microsoft had used its cash coffers to destroy the dominance of the Netscape browser, its Internet Explorer still trailed on the technological/functionality curve. As users of the Unix operating system learned all too well, fragmentation and incompatibility are often problems in dealing with open source development. Would the community release strategy allow Communicator to maintain its technological prowess and its market share? Or would the browser's continued innovation founder under the confusion of open source coordination and the possible incompatibilities that might result? Would Netscape's focus on integrating the browser with the Netcenter portal cause Communicator to fall behind Internet Explorer's functionality? Netcenter's success was highly correlated to the continued market share of Communicator, but only time would tell whether the bold moves undertaken by Netscape would prove successful.

REFERENCES

1. Ted Schadler, Stan Dolberg, Elizabeth W. Boehm, and Joshua Walker, "Reinventing Netscape," *The Forrester Report,* February 1998, p. 3.
2. Ibid.

3. "Netscape Announces Mozilla.org, a Dedicated Team and Web Site," *M2 Presswire,* February 24, 1998.

4. Ibid.

5. Carl Shapiro and Hal R. Varian, "A Judo Blow against Microsoft," *The Wall Street Journal,* February 2, 1998, p. A22.

6. "Netscape announces Mozilla.org."

7. Steve Hamm, "No, Netscape Isn't Throwing in the Towel," *Business Week,* February 23, 1998, p. 37.

8. Chris Charron, "Netscape Fires Up Netcenter," *The Forrester Brief,* June 8, 1998.

9. Chris Charron, "Portal Shakeout Round One: Netscape-Excite," *The Forrester Brief,* May 8, 1998.

10. "Netscape and CNET Sign Agreement . . . ," *M2 Presswire,* May 28, 1998.

11. Ibid.

VERTICALNET: THE NEW FACE OF B2B

After showing the last reporter to the door, Mark Walsh finally had a chance to return to his office and reflect on the incredible events of the past 48 hours. Only the day before, on February 11, 1999, his company had staged a spectacular initial public offering (IPO). Shares of VerticalNet, Inc. (NASDAQ symbol VERT), had opened at $16 and skyrocketed 184 percent to $45 before the closing bell. This made Walsh the CEO of a company with a market capitalization of $738 million—and that company was less than four years old.[1]

Walsh was thrilled by the IPO results, but he also recognized that with the limelight came extensive public scrutiny and an intense pressure to perform. The business model he had developed for VerticalNet was solid enough not only to increase the growth of the company to its current IPO-ready size, but also to firmly establish VerticalNet as a leader in the business-to-business (B2B) electronic commerce arena. This market had evolved slowly over 15 years, but the pace of change had quickened considerably in the last 18 months. New players were rapidly entering the B2B marketplace and competition was increasing. With analysts' projections that B2B e-commerce would grow to a $1.3 trillion industry by the year 2002,[2] Walsh knew the stakes were extremely high: If he didn't continue to innovate and reinvent his firm, VerticalNet could be quickly overtaken by the competition.

EVOLUTION OF BUSINESS-TO-BUSINESS e-COMMERCE

Beginning in the early 1980s, businesses transferred information electronically using a system known as electronic data interchange (EDI). This system utilized a synchronous connection between two host computers to share various types of information, such as parts catalogs, delivery schedules, purchase orders, and payment verifications. EDI

University of Michigan Business School MBA Candidates Angie Bohr, Quitanne Delano, Paul Hofley, Paul Linton, Brad Stewart prepared this case under the supervision of Professor Allan Afuah as the basis for class discussion rather than to illustrate either effective or ineffective handling of an administrative situation.

provided a more efficient way for businesses to transmit information compared with traditional mail or fax machines, but operated on a proprietary network, which limited its ability to support multiple users. In addition, the proprietary nature of EDI systems made enterprisewide expansion difficult.[3]

B2B e-commerce overcame some of the shortfalls of EDI through Web-based Internet applications. Businesses initially used the Internet to connect to and communicate with other businesses through the use of electronic mail (e-mail). Eventually, as Web browsers evolved and Internet access grew more commonplace, businesses developed a practical method for transferring business-related information through the Internet. The development of extensible markup language (XML) used in conjunction with hypertext markup language (HTML), among other languages, provided the backbone upon which B2B exchanges were built.

Businesses originally used the Internet much in the same way as EDI: The Internet acted as the conduit between businesses but offered greater flexibility among users. Unlike EDI, the Internet did not require a single, dedicated computer line but connected users instead through a system network which allowed multiple users to access information from individual workstations. Some of the first companies to embrace the Internet for business transactions were large technology companies, such as Cisco Systems, an Internet networking company, and computer companies such as IBM and Dell, who turned to the Internet as a means to complete supplier purchases and business sales. Other businesses quickly followed suit as companies recognized the Internet's ability to fundamentally change business communications and reduce transaction times and costs.

A few key traits distinguished a successful B2B exchange: high availability, transaction support, XML, security, and timeliness. High availability translated into anytime, anywhere access for both buyers and sellers using the exchange. Transaction support involved standardizing quantity and quality information so that a fair price could be agreed upon. XML tags provided a common set of data fields so that information transfer could be streamlined and formatted properly. Security remained a vital issue for all Internet transactions. Advanced B2B exchanges used "digital certificates" to confirm the identification of users. Finally, timeliness was representative of network capacity, with bandwidth and processing power needed to support the requests of the users.[4]

Digital marketplaces evolved into three different business models: e-Communities, e-Distributors, and e-Exchanges. These business models demonstrated the current trends in the business-to-business electronic commerce arena, and each model had a different approach to revenue generation. Accordingly, value recognized by the marketplace was hard to determine.

e-Communities

Comprised of buyers and sellers exchanging information concerning a single vertical[5] market, e-Communities are digital publications that follow industry trends and news. Websites develop a user base through traditional advertising intended to draw traffic to the site. Revenue is generated primarily through advertising, sponsorships, and transaction fees. The viability of this revenue-generation model is unclear, which motivated companies to migrate to the distributor and exchange models.

e-Distributors

E-Distributors establish a single source for goods and services within a single vertical industry. Typically, goods and services from multiple vendors are aggregated to one comprehensive location, which helps to streamline the purchase process. In turn, the intermediary collects a transaction fee related to the services it provides. Traditional companies are adopting the e-Distributor model in addition to their existing bricks-and-mortar operation to provide customers with an alternative channel for purchasing goods and services.

e-Exchanges

This model brings together buyers and sellers within the setting of a vertical industry marketplace. Exchanges use an auction-pricing model to provide buyers with a competitive environment and lower costs, which makes the intermediary attractive to large purchasing organizations. The marketplace offers both commodity and custom-made products. Custom-made products require more information about design, functionality, and quality in order to be considered by buyers. B2Bs that use this model typically collect a transaction fee as a means of generating revenue.

As each of the e-business models evolve, industry experts expect online marketplaces to incorporate elements of each model and envision successful digital marketplaces to include varying levels of community, content, and commerce.

HISTORY OF VERTICALNET

In 1995 Mike McNulty began selling advertising space for a wastewater industry trade publication. His clients often complained about their inability to track the number of leads generated by the ads they placed in the publication.[6] As a result, many customers were unsure whether they were getting a sufficient return on investment in their ads. McNulty was convinced that he could develop a more efficient and effective method that would not only bring buyers and suppliers together, but also provide businesses with lead tracking and qualification. The Internet, he thought, could be the answer.

From the beginning, McNulty envisioned a website that contained up-to-date industry news, trends, and information, as well as a list of suppliers who offered related products and services. His hope was that users would come to the site to locate current industry information and highlights while buyers would use the site as a convenient and reliable place to source goods and services.[7] McNulty first pitched his revolutionary idea to his boss, but got nowhere. Undeterred, he called Mike Hagan, a long-time friend and vice president at Merrill Lynch Asset Management. Upon hearing McNulty's idea, Hagan immediately saw the great potential for this venture.

Enthusiastic about the new business idea and cognizant of the importance of gaining "first mover" advantage on the Internet, the two quit their jobs and established VerticalNet in Horsham, Pennsylvania, in August 1995. VerticalNet's first "online vertical trade community,"[8] WaterOnline, was introduced shortly thereafter, and McNulty heavily leveraged his wide-ranging industry contacts to drum up business. Initial revenues were derived from selling online advertising spaces, dubbed "storefronts," to various wastewater industry suppliers. Buyers could browse the storefronts free of charge and, with the click of a button, send an e-mail request for product information or quotes. Search engine functionality was soon added to facilitate this process, followed quickly by a tool that let buyers post specific requests for proposals/quotes (RFPs and RFQs) that suppliers could then browse and respond to as appropriate. Additionally, McNulty and Hagan hired editors to develop and monitor news, job postings, and informational content posted on the site.[9]

Initially, McNulty and Hagan funded their young company through credit cards and personal savings, together contributing $75,000 to get through the first year. Hagan's contacts on Wall Street helped them to secure much-needed venture capital in 1996, which they received in the form of a $1 million equity investment from Internet Capital Group (ICG). The two founders knew, however, that the initial funding would not be enough to make the company a major player in the emerging B2B market. Both McNulty and Hagan recognized that to raise the necessary level of funding—potentially millions of dollars—VerticalNet would need an experienced and well-respected leader to bring credibility, confidence, and business knowledge to the company in order to attract investors.

In August 1997 the company found the leadership it was seeking when Mark L. Walsh signed on as CEO. Walsh's background included several years as a general manager at CUC International, an early pioneer in online interactive services, as well as extensive experience with other online ventures, including the management of General Electric's online services and a position as senior vice president for America Online's B2B division. When Walsh was first approached for the VerticalNet position, he was immediately smitten with the idea. "This is sweet," Walsh recalls saying at the time. "This is a total pure play for what I believe is the future of the Internet."[10]

By the time Walsh joined VerticalNet, it had expanded into five verticals with a staff of less than 50. With Walsh's help, in late 1997 and again in 1998 the company secured additional equity-based funding from ICG, ultimately giving the investment group a 49 percent stake in the company.[11] VerticalNet moved quickly to take advantage of the new funding by developing several new verticals (including PollutionOnline, SolidWasteOnline, ChemicalOnline, and SemiconductorOnline), and by nearly doubling the number of its employees. As a result, the company booked revenues of almost $800,000 during the 1997 calendar year and headed into 1998 with highly aggressive growth plans (see Exhibit 4.1).[12]

In May 1998, VerticalNet won the coveted Tenagra Award for "Successful Internet Business Model" in recognition of VerticalNet's profitability and success with online publishing and "community building" across multiple industries.[13] VerticalNet's oldest and most profitable site, WaterOnline, was receiving approximately 80,000 unique visitors per month and generating more than $500,000 in revenue annually. Walsh expected most of the other sites to follow suit. Throughout the year the company added 14 more verticals, bringing the total to 29. The rapid growth was essential to lock in first-mover advantages, but expansion came at a high price as expenses outpaced revenues. As the year drew to a close, VerticalNet had accumulated an operating deficit of over $14 million and would soon run out of venture capital.[14]

Rather than go back for another round of financing, Walsh decided it was time to capitalize on the recent positive press coverage and to take advantage of an IPO-hungry market by taking VerticalNet public. On February 11, 1999, the IPO date, VerticalNet offered 29 communities and employed 190 people. The 29 sites together drew more than 650,000 unique visitors a month, resulting in the generation of over 40,000 sales leads.[15] Despite the company's expectation that it would not be profitable until 2000 or 2001, the optimistic public markets traded over 4 million shares during the IPO and drove up the price some 184 percent. Clearly, investors believed that VerticalNet's business model positioned the company to capture a significant portion of the B2B e-commerce space.

BUSINESS MODEL

VerticalNet created a scalable platform that made it the industry leader in the development and launch of verticals. These industry-centric portals served the business-to-business sector of the Internet. As the number of verticals was projected to grow from 29 to 150 by 2005, VerticalNet expected to benefit from its ability to launch new sites efficiently, spreading costs across the sites. Each vertical was an independent profit center. Users

EXHIBIT 4.1 VerticalNet Selected Financial Data

The following table sets forth selected financial data for the periods indicated:

	July 28–December 31, 1995	Year Ending December 31, 1996	1997	1998
		In $000, except share, per share data		
Statement of operations data:				
Revenues	$ 16	$ 285	$ 792	$ 3,135
Expenses, editorial and operational	24	214	1,056	3,238
Product development	22	214	711	1,405
Sales and marketing	147	268	2,301	7,895
General and administrative	33	292	1,388	3,823
Amortization of goodwill	—	—	—	283
Operating loss	(210)	(703)	(4,664)	(13,509)
Interest, net	(1)	(6)	(115)	(85)
Net loss	$ (211)	$ (709)	$ (4,779)	$ (13,594)
Basic and diluted net loss per share	$ (0.19)	$ (0.27)	$ (1.89)	$ (5.29)
Shares outstanding used in basic and diluted net loss per share calculation [1]	1,096,679	2,583,648	2,526,865	2,570,550
Pro forma basic and diluted net loss per share	$ (0.19)	$ (0.21)	$ (0.77)	$ (1.28)
Shares outstanding used in pro forma basic and diluted net loss per common share calculation [1]	1,096,679	3,326,284	6,184,326	10,635,489

(1) As described in Note 1 of the consolidated financial statements. The unaudited pro forma balance sheet as of December 31, 1998, reflects (a) our capitalization subsequent to the initial public offering closing, including the sale of 4,025,000 shares of common stock on February 17, 1999, resulting in approximately $58,322,000 of net proceeds; (b) all of the then-outstanding shares of our convertible preferred stock automatically converted into 9,734,845 shares of common stock on the basis that the Series A preferred stock converted to shares of common stock on a ratio of 4.7619:1 and the Series B, C, and D preferred stock converted on a ratio of 1:1; (c) the $5.0 million of convertible notes from Internet Capital Group and certain holders of the Series D preferred stock converted at the $16 offering price into 312,500 shares of common stock; (d) the repayment of the $2.0 million bank note.

	Year Ending December 31, 1996	1997	1998	Pro forma
		(In $000s)		
Balance sheet data:				
Cash and cash equivalents	$329	$ 755	$5,663	$61,985
Working capital (deficit)	150	(2,536)	938	59,260
Total assets	637	2,104	12,343	68,665
Short-term borrowings	—	2,651	2,288	288
Deferred revenues	216	710	2,177	2,177
Long-term debt, less current portion	167	400	5,352	352
Total shareholders' equity (deficit)	105	(2,424)	(276)	63,046

accessed verticals to view content developed by VerticalNet's editorial staff, while advertisers paid for banner ads or sponsored newsletters that were e-mailed to registered users. Technical, sales and marketing, and administrative personnel worked across multiple verticals to achieve economies of scale.[16]

Why Visit a Vertical?

Content

Each vertical served as a comprehensive resource for new product information and had a dedicated editor who managed the mix of news and commentary and ensured that the content was current and relevant. While the editors added original content, such as objective analysis of new products, the sites also provided recent press releases and news stories pertinent to the industry. Additionally, industry professionals could access product case studies or industry "white papers" to stay informed of recent innovations, and could utilize an archived information service for research. Finally, e-mail newsletters containing news updates, highlights, and special features were sent weekly to help generate repeat visits. [17]

Community

Verticals leveraged the power of the Internet to bring together industry professionals who could communicate efficiently and share information about upcoming trade shows and other industry events. VerticalNet planned eventually to offer its registered users free e-mail accounts as a way to both increase potential site usage and form a common community "identity." The proposed addresses would indicate the user's "community" by including the industry vertical name (e.g. "fredrick@poweronline.com"). Another community-building endeavor was the anticipated addition of a career center to provide employment services such as resume distribution and employment listings. Reports on companies would be available to assist the user in researching prospective employers and preparing for interviews.

Commerce

To ensure efficient and effective marketing, the sites provided products and services targeted at a narrow audience of users. The VerticalNet marketplace invited users to purchase a predetermined selection of books, videos, and software, and provided a library of demo-software and software sales service. Some verticals offered selections for continuing education and training services while third-party providers offered online courses with focused content and research to VerticalNet users. These services were of particular interest to those individuals looking either to acquire industry-specific licenses or to maintain specific industry certifications by regularly upgrading skills.[18]

Developing a Vertical

VerticalNet had a refined process for developing a new vertical through a series of steps. First, the company used various criteria to identify an industry sector that might benefit from a vertical portal (see Exhibit 4.2). Usually, industries with a substantial number of highly fragmented buyers and suppliers were prime targets. Next, VerticalNet recruited well-respected industry editorial talent who acted both as a content producer and a credibility builder for the site. A common site template provided the foundation for each new site, which would be formatted specifically to the site's industry. Finally, the company hired sales professionals to develop an industry buyer guide and a potential list of advertisers.

Communities	Website Address
Environment and Utility	
Water Online	wateronline.com
Pollution Online	pollutiononline.com
Solid Waste Online	solidwaste.com
Pulp and Paper Online	pulpandpaperonline.com
Power Online	poweronline.com
Public Works Online	publicworks.com
Process Industries	
Chemical Online	chemicalonline.com
Pharmaceutical Online	pharmaceuticalonline.com
Semiconductor Online	semiconductoronline.com
Hydrocarbon Online	hydrocarbononline.com
Paint and Coatings Online	paintandcoatings.com
Food Online	foodonline.com
Adhesives and Sealants Online	adhesivesandsealants.com
Electronics	
Computer OEM Online	computeroem.com
Medical Design Online	medicaldesignonline.com
Test and Measurement Online	testandmeasurement.com
Life Sciences	
Bioresearch Online	bioresearchonline.com
Laboratory Network Online	laboratorynetwork.com
Services	
Property and Casualty Online	propertyandcasualty.com
Food and Packaging	
Food Ingredients Online	foodingredientsonline.com
Packaging Network	packagingnetwork.com
Beverage Online	beverageonline.com
Bakery Online	bakeryonline.com
Dairy Network	dairynetwork.com
Meat and Poultry Online	meatandpoultryonline.com
Telecommunications	
RF GlobalNet	rfglobalnet.com
Wireless Design Online	wirelessdesignonline.com
Photonics Online	photonicsonline.com
Fiber Optics Online	fiberopticsonline.com

Source: www.verticalnet.com/communities.html.

The resources required for each vertical included an editor, an industry manager, and a sales manager. The editor worked full-time to write original content and identify relevant news, and usually worked from home. The industry manager was responsible for establishing relationships with key industry players and trade association representatives and for attending trade shows. Trade shows provided a prime venue for the industry manager to make new contacts and sell advertising. The sales manager targeted organizations whose products and services were typically purchased by vertical visitors. The sales staff usually had a background in trade publication advertising and sales.

VerticalNet Revenue Sources

Advertising was expected to account for roughly 97 percent and limited e-commerce for the remaining 3 percent of revenues in the first quarter of 1999. The primary sources of advertising revenue were storefronts, banners, and sponsorships. Historically, the company renewed 90 percent of all advertising contracts and expected to maintain this rate going forward. VerticalNet hoped to grow its e-commerce revenues as a means of diversifying its revenue streams.

Storefronts

The storefront product provided a simple means for advertisers to display company information and product overviews. Users were directed to storefronts from banner ads on a vertical's front page or through links from a keyword search. Storefront visitors interested in a particular product could request additional information, which the vendor then delivered by e-mail. These inquiries often materialized into high-quality leads. As lead tracking was an important part of VerticalNet's value to its advertisers, the company installed a lead-generation system similar to lead "scorecards," which traditionally were used by trade magazines.[19] Instead of a paper postcard, VerticalNet offered a service, called VirtualOffice, to its advertisers whereby all user inquiries were tracked on the vertical but monitored by the advertiser itself. This allowed each advertiser to respond quickly to inquiries and to evaluate the effectiveness of individual banners.

Storefronts accounted for 85 percent of revenues in 1998, but were expected to fall to 50 percent of revenues as other products (e.g., banner sales and sponsorships) became more popular. The number of storefronts grew from 67 in 1996 to 1,300 in 1998 and nearly 1,600 by the time of the IPO. Meanwhile, the average number of storefronts per vertical had risen from 22 in 1996 to 48 in the last quarter of 1998. Typically, an advertiser paid $6,500 annually for a storefront. VerticalNet was exploring ways to generate additional storefront revenues, including options that would allow vendors to add e-commerce functionality to their storefronts.

Banners and Sponsorships

Banner and sponsorship-related revenue was expected to reach 47 percent of revenues in the first quarter of 1999, up from just 5 percent in the same period in 1998. Banner ads were available in two formats: large banner ads, which usually appeared near the top of a page, and smaller banners, similar to buttons, which appeared throughout the website. Advertisers purchased two types of banners: general and vertical-specific. They paid a monthly fee for banners as opposed to the more common "cost-per-million" (CPM) pricing used by many consumer portals. Advertisers chose from two types of sponsorships: (1) sponsorship of a specific area, or channel, of a vertical or (2) sponsorship of a vertical's newsletter. Sponsorship of a specific area gave the advertiser prominent placement of a banner ad within a vertical. If a vendor sponsored the newsletter, the vendor's name and a link to its storefront was included in the newsletter. Vendors were charged $0.10 if the user clicked on the storefront link and $0.20 if the user clicked through to the vendor's external, company-run homepage.

e-Commerce

E-Commerce revenue was generated from the sale of an industry vertical's products and services, such as books and software, and accounted for roughly 3 percent of total revenue at the time of the IPO. VerticalNet also received a commission from the sale of books, computers, software, gifts, apparel, accessories, and entertainment purchased from external websites that were accessed through a VerticalNet vertical.

VerticalNet Expenses

Personnel Expenses

The primary expenses related to operating a vertical were salaries and marketing costs. Editors, sales staff, and engineers received salaries while compensation for industry and sales managers was commission-based. Each vertical had one dedicated editor and shared a pool of nine technical writers who provided editorial support. A total of 44 direct sales and support personnel were employed at the end of 1998. The telesales group, made up of 15 individuals, performed customer prospecting, lead generation, and lead follow-up activities. A staff of 43 engineers supported the day-to-day operation of the websites. As of the IPO, the company expected to add approximately 10 engineers annually. In-house product development was carried out by a staff of programmers that was expected to grow at the rate of two per quarter. Approximately $1.2 million was spent to develop proprietary technology in 1998.

Advertising Expenses

Marketing expenses were divided into two major categories: off-line advertising and online advertising. Off-line advertising for the verticals was placed in trade magazines and exhibited at trade shows. Because some companies produced multiple magazines or shows, VerticalNet negotiated up-front, multiple ad placements for several verticals at a time. However, future advertising in trade magazines could be limited because of VerticalNet's position as a direct competitor of traditional industry publications.

For online advertising, VerticalNet negotiated agreements with two major Internet portals: Excite and AltaVista. A three-year sponsorship agreement with Excite allowed VerticalNet to build and operate up to 30 industrial channels. The channels provided a preview of a vertical's front page, content, and features. Excite guaranteed minimum performance—exposures or impressions—in return for annual fees of $1.3 million in 1999, $2.3 million in 2000, and $2.0 million in 2001. VerticalNet also has a renewable one-year agreement with AltaVista. VerticalNet and AltaVista agreed to 31 "cobranded" or reciprocal-hyperlinked websites, while AltaVista guaranteed a negotiated number of site visits for an annual fee of $1 million. In addition, AltaVista and VerticalNet agreed to exchange $300,000 in advertising over the term of the agreement. Both the Excite and AltaVista agreements allowed VerticalNet to share advertising revenue generated from the cobranded websites.

COMPETITION IN THE ONLINE MARKETPLACE

Online B2B Intermediaries

FreeMarkets

FreeMarkets, Inc., manages and hosts business-to-business auctions for buyers of industrial parts, raw materials, and commodities. In 1998 online auctions covering approximately $1 billion worth of purchase orders were completed, with an estimated 30 buyers and 1,800 suppliers having participated in auctions through the end of 1998.[20] General Motors and United Technologies Corporation accounted for 77 percent of FreeMarkets' 1998 revenue of $7.7 million (see Exhibit 4.3). FreeMarkets' primary customers are large companies that purchase custom solutions. Buyers exchange confidential specifications with suppliers and FreeMarkets designs an auction customized to the buyer's purchasing processes.

The custom market requires four to eight weeks of preliminary work. FreeMarkets helps potential clients identify products that would benefit from online auctions. These are usually products that are custom made to buyer specification and that are available

EXHIBIT 4.3 Selected Competitor Income Statements

	FreeMarkets, Inc.		PurchasePro.com	
	1997	1998	1997	1998
	($000s except per share amounts)			
Revenues	$ 1,783	$7,801	$ 675	$ 1,670
Cost of revenues	1,149	4,258	214	446
Gross (loss) profit	634	3,543	462	1,225
Operating costs:				
Research and development	292	842	802	971
Sales and marketing	586	656	1,179	3,841
General and administrative	837	2,026	1,345	2,896
Total operating expenses	1,715	3,524	3,326	7.708
Operating (loss) income	(1,081)	19	(2,865)	(6,483)
Other income	20	215	(120)	(117)
Net (loss) income	$(1,061)	$ 234	$(2,985)	$(6,600)
Earnings (loss) per share:				
Basic	$ (0.10)	$ 0.02	$ (0.39)	$ (0.83)
Diluted	$ (0.10)	$ 0.01	$ (0.36)	$ (0.78)

	Penton Media, Inc.	
	1997	1998
	($000s except per share amounts)	
Revenues	$233,118	$204,931
Operating expenses:		
Editorial, production and circulation	94,560	101,793
Selling, general and administrative	78,523	93,886
Depreciation and amortization	6,551	10,720
Total operating expenses	179,634	206,399
Operating income	25,297	26,719
Other income	209	(6,586)
Income before income taxes	25,506	20,133
Net income	$ 14,874	$ 10,890
Earnings per share:		
Basic and diluted	$ 0.70	$ 0.50

Source: Respective Company SEC filings.

from many suppliers. The buyer prepares a request for quote (RFQ) that is sent to selected suppliers who in turn prepare bids. Suppliers are selected from both the FreeMarkets database and the company's vendor list and must be approved by the buyer. Once the vendors are trained to use FreeMarket's proprietary Internet-based BidWare software, the auction is held. The client can see the identity and current bid of each supplier, but the suppliers can see only competing bids. FreeMarkets staff monitor each auction and provide real-time assistance in over 20 languages.

Revenue is generated through service agreements with clients or may come in the form of fixed monthly fees or incentive payments based on volume or savings. Some supplier agreements allow FreeMarkets to earn a sales commission as well. Primary costs include staffing and general overhead. Sales and marketing expenses and general and administrative costs were 8.4 percent and 26 percent of sales in 1998, respectively.

PurchasePro

PurchasePro.com, Inc. (NASDAQ: PPRO), is a leading provider of Internet B2B e-commerce services. The company offers proprietary software that enables businesses to buy and sell products over the Internet. The Las Vegas–based company got its start by signing up Mirage Resorts, Inc., which in turn recommended the software to its vendors. Originally designed as a bidding tool for large hospitality companies to communicate with suppliers, the company has since expanded into a range of other industries such as the food and beverage, furniture, fixtures, and equipment industries where productivity of purchasing departments is a constant challenge. In two years PurchasePro.com has grown from about 20 employees in its Las Vegas office to more than 100 employees with new offices in Phoenix, Arizona, and Lexington, Kentucky.[21]

The PurchasePro.com e-commerce solution is comprised of public and private communities called "e-marketplaces" where businesses can buy and sell a wide variety of products and services over the Internet in an efficient, competitive, and cost-effective manner. CEO and founder of PurchasePro.com, Charles "Junior" Johnson, commented, "The buzzword is vertical marketing. We wanted to be the first electronic procurement application to cross every vertical line. Every other e-commerce (system) has pieces of what we do, but nobody has an aggregate of what we do."[22] PurchasePro.com equalizes the playing field by providing each business, from "mom-and-pop" shops to megastores, with the same software. PurchasePro.com makes its money by charging each of its businesses a nominal subscription fee of about $100 per month. Subscribers boast of making up the monthly fee with one purchasing order as lower prices are available in the e-marketplaces due to efficiency in purchasing and orders.

Industry-Specific Online Sites

Chemdex

Chemdex Corporation (NASDAQ: CMDX) is a provider of e-commerce solutions for the life sciences industry. Chemdex is part of a new breed of groundbreaking B2B e-commerce companies who leverage the Internet to unite buyers and sellers in a single, efficient virtual marketplace. Chemdex offers more than 240,000 products from some 100 suppliers—more than five times as many products as the industry's most comprehensive catalog.[23]

In December 1998 Genentech (NYSE: GNE), one of the world's leading biotechnology firms, fully implemented the Chemdex enterprise solution. With Chemdex,

Genentech will be able to access hundreds of thousands of products from suppliers by means of the Genentech intranet which links employees to a customized Chemdex site. The Chemdex system also allows suppliers to publish an unlimited amount of product and technical information, providing Genentech and other researchers with the resources they need to make purchasing decisions.[24]

E-Steel

In the past, manufacturing technology companies have focused on production in an attempt to squeeze time and cost out of the process and then rely on a network of distributors, brokers, and representatives to sell their goods, resulting in an inefficient imbalance between supply and demand. E-Steel, an ambitious online steel industry marketplace was launched in March 1999 and plans to combat those inefficiencies by leveraging the Internet.[25]

E-Steel will use one-to-one profiling software to deliver customized content to registered steel buyers. This software will also put suppliers' fears to rest as strategic information will not be available to competitors, and no general price lists will be posted. It is e-Steel's goal to allow buyers and sellers to mirror their existing relationships on the Web, while enjoying increased efficiency over the Internet. The company also hopes its marketplace will not only offer convenience to its patrons, but also an opportunity to reach more people through the Internet than through conventional means. E-Steel will earn its keep primarily through charging its sellers a transaction fee of less than 1 percent on all purchases initiated on its site and, secondly, by selling advertising.[26]

Traditional Trade Magazines and Publications

Penton Media

Penton provides its customers with a portfolio of advertising options including trade magazines, trade shows, and websites. Penton's 50 trade magazines had a 1998 circulation of 3.2 million.[27] Two of its publications, *Electronic Design* and *Machine Design*, rank among the top 10 trade magazines by advertising revenue.[28] Advertising revenue for business magazines was an estimated $8.9 billion in 1998.[29] To justify higher advertising rates than consumer magazines, Penton uses annual questionnaires to verify the job responsibility and purchasing authority of its subscribers. Dedicated editorial and sales staffs ensure that the needs of readers and advertisers are met.

Penton is also one of the largest trade show managers in the United States and, along with other top operators, is expected to produce an estimated 16 percent of the 3,900 trade shows in the United States and Canada.[30] Penton has increased the number of worldwide trade shows it produces to 118 since it started in 1990, and has developed relationships with more than 7,000 exhibitors, many of which also advertise in their magazines. Internet World, one of Penton's fastest-growing trade shows, is currently produced in 23 countries.

Penton targets its websites to professionals in many of the industries it serves through magazines and trade shows. Its network of 42 online communities benefits from proprietary content created for its magazines; however, online content is updated in real time to maintain and increase a loyal reader base. Advertisers generate sales leads and track customer purchase behavior to aid in their marketing decisions. Penton generates revenue through banner advertising, sponsorship of sites, user fees, and transaction fees based on users who click through to e-commerce sites. In 1998 electronic media accounted for less than 1 percent of its $207 million in revenues.

Cahners Business Information has a rich history of business-to-business publishing dating back to 1855 when *Iron Age*, the company's first magazine, premiered. The magazine's essence is incorporated into Cahners' modern-day publication *New Steel*.[31] Through the years Cahners' portfolio of publications grew into a variety of markets including *Hotel & Travel Index*, a staple guide for travel agents worldwide, and *Modern Materials Handling*, an operations publication.

Cahners has emerged as a major B2B publishing and trade show management company. The company was particularly busy during the 1980s with an aggressive acquisition program. Cahners also boasts a well-respected research information service in Cahners Advertising Research Reports (CARR). The service is designed to help customers better understand B2B publications and advertising (print and online), by providing benchmark research and strategic advice to advertisers about the bottom-line effectiveness of communications programs.

Distributors

W.W. Grainger

E-Distributors that consolidate goods and services offered by multiple vendors stand as competition to the VerticalNet business model. These sites offer a simple search process for a buyer to select a specific product. In addition, traditional bricks-and-mortar distributors such as Grainger Industrial Supply have moved to the Internet as an alternative channel for its customers. Grainger built its business through catalog sales, but now offers the full range of its products through its website, www.grainger.com. Grainger expects that online sales will exceed $160 million, making it one of the largest-volume sites for Web sales.[32]

NEXT STEPS

Walsh thought about his options as he gathered his things and prepared to leave. Now that VerticalNet was public, where should he take the company from here? How could he capitalize on the tremendous opportunity that lay before him? For starters, he wondered whether the company should continue to add new industry segments as aggressively as it had in the past, or if VerticalNet should slow down and entrench more deeply into the 29 communities it had already entered?

Furthermore, Walsh wondered about the company's revenue model. Thanks to the successful IPO, VerticalNet now had almost $57 million in the bank, but Walsh knew that the company would burn through that in just a few years unless it could find ways to become more profitable. Should the company stick with its current storefront model and focus on signing up more vendors as well as perhaps raising the price? Or should it expand into new offerings and services? And if so, what should those be? Finally, was it time to start looking for new partnerships and/or acquisitions? What types of companies would make the most sense?

Walsh left for home far more wealthy than he was just two days ago, very excited about the challenges ahead and yet cognizant that choosing the wrong strategy at this critical juncture could mean the end of VerticalNet.

1. Andrew Cassell, "VerticalNet Embraces Capitalism," *Philadelphia Inquirer,* February 15, 1999.
2. Andrew Marlatt, "Creating Vertical Marketplaces," *Internet World,* February 8, 1999.
3. Mary Addonizio, "Chrysler Corporation: JIT and EDI (A)," *Harvard Business School Case,* February 11, 1992.
4. Alan Zeichick, "B2B Exchanges Explained," *Red Herring,* November 1999, pp. 188–90.
5. A "vertical" is short for "vertical industry," "vertical market," or "vertical trade community" and refers to all buyers and suppliers (essentially the whole supply chain) within a given industry.
6. Martin Donsky, "VerticalNet Gets the Paper out of Publishing," *TECH Capital,* November 6, 1998.
7. Peter Kay, "VerticalNet Seeks to Raise $30M," *Philadelphia Business Journal,* December 14, 1998.
8. www.VerticalNet.com.
9. Bob Brooke, "Trade Pubs Moving Up and Online," *Philadelphia Business Journal,* January 19, 1998.
10. "Interview with Mark Walsh," *eMarketer,* August 17, 1998.
11. Kay, "VerticalNet Seeks to Raise $30M," p. 1.
12. Brooke, "Trade Pubs Moving Up and Online," p. 1.
13. "The 1998 Tenagra Awards," awards.tenagra.com/cat1vertical.html, May 1998.
14. "VerticalNet Shows Business Acumen," *Techweb,* December 23, 1998.
15. Darren Chervitz, "IPO First Words," *CBS Marketwatch,* March 18, 1999.
16. VerticalNet SEC filing, 1999.
17. Thomas Isakowitz, "VerticalNet Basic Report," *Janney Montgomery Scott,* June 22, 1999.
18. Ibid.
19. "Scorecards" are postcards that list vendor names and are placed in trade magazines. Interested subscribers check off a vendor of interest and send the card to the magazine, which in turn records the "lead" and then notifies the vendor.
20. Company information taken from FreeMarkets preliminary prospectus, September 8, 1999.
21. www.PurchasePro.com.
22. "Purchasing Pipeline," *Hoovers,* company press release, November 8, 1998.
23. Chemdex company press release, *Hoovers,* December 14, 1998.
24. Ibid.
25. C. Wilder, "E-commerce—Old Line Moves Online," *Information Week,* January 11, 1999.
26. Ibid.
27. Lauren Rich Fine, "Penton Media, Inc. In-depth Report," Merrill Lynch & Co., June 9, 1999.
28. *1999 Tradeshow Week Data Book,* Tradeshow Week, Inc.
29. *1998 Communications Industry Forecast,* Veronis, Suhler & Associates. The business magazine market is estimated at $10.8 billion and projected to grow at a compound rate of 8 percent through 2002.
30. *1999 Tradeshow Week Data Book,* Tradeshow Week, Inc. and Veronis, Suhler & Associates.
31. www.cahners.com.
32. Douglas Blackmon, "Selling Motors to Mops, Unglamorous Grainger Is a Web-Sales Star," *The Wall Street Journal,* December 13, 1999, p. B1.

RED HAT SOFTWARE AND LINUX OPERATING SYSTEM: WHERE DO YOU WANT TO GO TOMORROW?

It's the open source model that's actually the real value . . . The technologies that break through are the ones that deliver a unique value to the market place . . . For the first time the user has real control over the technology he is using. And that stems directly from it being free . . . Then we really aren't in the software business . . . We are in the brand management business. We like to use the ketchup analogy. When you think about it, all that's in a bottle of ketchup are things that you can make in your kitchen sink. So how does Heinz sell so much ketchup . . . ? They do that by building a valuable brand so that when you and I go to the grocery store it's simply easier to buy a Heinz bottle because we know it and we trust it.

— Bob Young, CEO, Red Hat Software, Inc.[1]

In April 1999 Bob Young, Red Hat's CEO, was riding the surging wave of public press and private investments in his young company. Started in 1994, the company markets a CD-ROM set and installation service for the renegade Linux operating system. An emerging alternative to proprietary operating systems, Linux penetrated the "techie" segment of the market by offering a stable operating system. Developed by a community of programmers working in an "open source" mode, whereby the programming code is available for modification by its users, Linux could be considered the crown jewel of the open source movement for its availability and flexibility. In 1998 *InfoWorld* magazine named Red Hat Linux 5.2 Product of the Year, for the third year in a row.

In recent weeks, a flood of leading companies in the high-tech industry began throwing their weight behind Linux and, specifically, Red Hat. Red Hat was viewed as the premier distributor of Linux. Intel, Netscape, and many others have invested in the company, providing a critical financial and symbolic boost to the company (see

New York University Stern School of Business MBA Candidates Anand Balakrishna, Maria K. D'Albert, Andrew B. Heifetz, and George Lu prepared this case under the supervision of Professor Christopher Tucci, for the purpose of class discussion rather than to illustrate either effective or ineffective handling of an administrative situation.

EXHIBIT 5.1 Red Hat Equity Investors

Benchmark Capital
Compaq
Greylock
IBM
Intel
Netscape
Novell
Oracle
SAP

Note: The terms of the investments have not been disclosed.

Exhibit 5.1). In the spring of 1999, Dell and Compaq began to offer Red Hat Linux pre-installed on many of their servers. IBM, Informix, Oracle, and Sybase all have either shipped or announced plans to deliver versions of their databases for Linux. Mass media picked up on the existence of Linux, calling it, among other things, "a dark horse challenger to Microsoft."[2] Under the scrutiny of a U.S. Department of Justice lawsuit, Microsoft appeared to be unable or unwilling to take an aggressive stance against Linux.

But underneath the largely positive spin on Linux and Red Hat lay many pressing concerns. Bob Young was betting that this "business model" of branding a free product would be profitable. But would he be able to leverage this branding beyond distribution of the product to creating ongoing revenues through delivery of value-added maintenance and service contracts in the commercial market? Did Red Hat have the resources and capabilities required?

Also, in an attempt to build brand image, Young welcomed the partnerships and financing of industry heavy hitters, such as IBM. But he knew that these companies were building an option through Red Hat. They had their own objectives. How could he use these resources to build sustainable competitive advantage? Was that even a realistic goal? How could he manage these relationships to ensure that these partners did not use Red Hat as a learning tool and then swallow up the lucrative service component of the business?

Finally, there was the question of Microsoft and other Operating System (OS) standards in the server market. How much longer could he expect the proprietary and open-system standards to peacefully coexist?

HISTORY OF LINUX

Linux is a freely distributed variant of the UNIX operating system originated by a Finnish programmer, Linus Torvalds, approximately a decade ago, utilizing the open source software approach. It competes with proprietary systems such as Hewlett-Packard's and Sun's versions of Microsoft Windows NT, and Linux is widely recognized for its stable configuration.

The Linux phenomenon began at the University of Helsinki in 1991, when Linus Torvalds—at the time in his early twenties—wrote his own operating system because he thought the prices of commercial operating systems were too high. He used his version of UNIX as the basis for this new system. Once the base operating system was developed, the Internet helped distribute the source code. Top-class programmers from around the world enhanced the base code in an effort to write the most reliable code. This ongoing process has created a community of support and intellectual resources for Linux.

Open Source Software (OSS) is a development process that promotes rapid creation and deployment of additional features and bug fixes for existing code. Programmers essentially donate their time toward creating this freely available operating system. The software license remains in the public domain; hence, everyone is free to use and modify the source code. Programmers can scrutinize the code, customize it, and catch security loopholes. This is in sharp contrast to the existing proprietary operating systems that are actually purchased and cannot be modified or replicated. The Linux OS not only has a very stable configuration, but also requires less computing power. Certain experts in the field believe that the quality of Linux rivals, or even surpasses, its more established commercial rivals.

The OSS movement would never have been possible were it not for proliferation of the Internet. The Internet has allowed thousands of developers worldwide to collaborate on Linux. Further, the deep-rooted Microsoft resentment among software professionals has created the desire to develop a viable alternative to Microsoft's operating systems.

A testament to Linux's growing popularity (see Exhibit 5.2) is the increase in its market share to 17 percent by the beginning of 1999. This trend can be attributed to Linux's affordability (it's free!), the ability to access and customize source code, and its increased reliability.

A market segmentation of OS users includes (see Exhibit 5.3):

- *Engineering and creative professionals.* These professionals demand high-performance workstations with advanced graphics capabilities for individual use. Notably, Digital Domain used Linux in creating special effects in the film *Titanic.*[3]

EXHIBIT 5.2 The Growth of Linux in the Marketplace

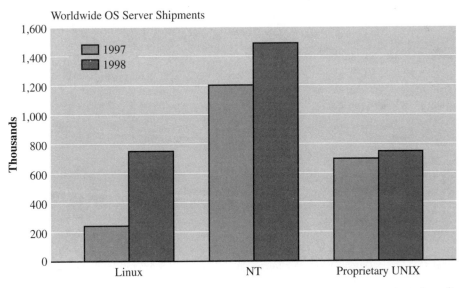

(continued)

EXHIBIT 5.2 The Growth of Linux in the Markeplace *(continued)*

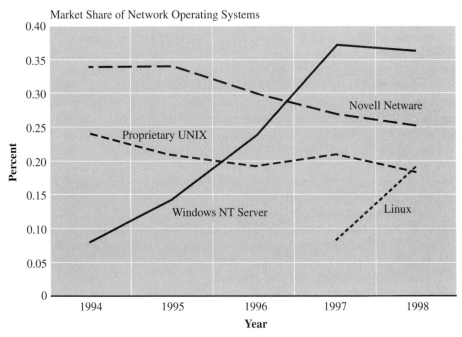

Market Share of Network Operating Systems

Source: Business Week, February 22, 1999, at businessweek.com/1999/99_08/63617024.htm; International Data Corp.

EXHIBIT 5.3 Market Segmentation and Commonly Used Products

	Chips (CPU)	Computer Hardware	Operating System	Application Software	Service
Engineering/creative	MIPS, Sparc	SGI, Sun	SGI (*IRIX*), Sun (*Solaris*), Microsoft (*NT*)		
Back office	Intel, Sparc, Alpha	Dell, Compaq, Sun, IBM	Sun (*Solaris*), Microsoft (*NT*), IBM (*AIX*), Hewlett-Packard (*HP-UNIX*) Linux	Microsoft, IBM, Oracle	IBM, Oracle
ISPs	Intel, Sparc	Dell, Compaq, Sun, IBM	Sun (*Solaris*), Linux, Microsoft (*NT*)	Free Ware, Microsoft, Netscape	
Power users	Intel	Dell, Compaq	Linux, Microsoft (*NT*)		
General users	Intel	Gateway, Compaq	Microsoft (*Windows 98*)	Microsoft	

- *Back office.* Corporate IT users need servers with high performance and reliability to run enterprise applications. The back office segment is highly contested with numerous UNIX solutions and Microsoft's Windows NT.
- *Internet service providers (ISPs).* ISPs are a newer segment that needs specialized software to deal with the rapidly changing Internet environment. Linux and Sun have carved out a strong niche in the ISP/Web server market because the Internet is based on widely adopted UNIX standards.
- *Power users.* Consumers in this segment include computer professionals who require a development platform. Linux is a favorite choice for price-sensitive users.
- *General users.* General users need a personal computer for business and entertainment. Microsoft dominates this category.

239

*CASE 5
Red Hat Software
and Linux Operating
System: Where Do
You Want to Go
Tomorrow?*

THE IMPACT OF LINUX ON THE COMPUTER INDUSTRY

The groundswell of support for Linux has caused industry leaders to consider this new operating system in their product strategies. Intel, IBM, Oracle, and SGI have developed comprehensive Linux strategies. Dell, Hewlett-Packard, IBM, and Compaq are offering to preinstall the Red Hat distribution of Linux on their low-cost servers. However, Sun Microsystems and Microsoft have done little publicly except talk about Linux.

In September 1998, Intel acquired a minority equity stake in Red Hat. "The investment largely fits with Intel's overall venture philosophy of using minority investments in small companies to expand the acceptance of the Intel platform," said Robert Manetta, an Intel spokesman.[4] Intel has also contracted to have Linux ported to its future 64-bit microprocessor architecture. This will ensure that Linux will run on the next generation of Intel chips. According to Tom Henkel, an analyst at the Gartner Group, "Clearly, Intel wants to expand its market share beyond the Microsoft-oriented desktops and servers. They seem to be willing to invest in anything that might foster that cause."[5]

IBM has publicly announced its support for the Linux operating system even though the company produces its own fully functional version of UNIX called AIX. IBM is preinstalling Linux on its low-end servers, porting its enterprise software (including DB2, Web Sphere, MQ Series, etc.) to run on Linux, and adapting Linux to run on its Power PC microprocessors. In addition, IBM is offering Linux support services in Japan. "Part of what we're trying to do here is help Linux become business as usual for business," claimed an IBM spokesperson.[6]

Silicon Graphics, Inc. (SGI), in a change from its recent NT focus, expects to showcase an Intel-based Linux machine in May 1999. According to SGI Technologist Dave McAlister, "SGI is making Linux part of our core engineering. SGI has about as many developers working on Linux as NT."[7] Oracle and Sybase have released database products that run on Linux. Even enterprise resource planning (ERP) companies like SAP are supporting Linux in their products. Industry support serves to add legitimacy to the Linux movement. Publicly, Sun Microsystems views Linux as an alternative to Microsoft's Windows NT products. According to Charles Andres, group manager for Sun's Market Systems Development, "Linux is hot because it offers low-end users the proven reliability of UNIX . . . Sun views Linux as an alternative to NT. It is a solid UNIX platform for traditional Microsoft customers."[8]

Some analysts, however, believe that Linux will cut into other UNIX deployment, like Sun's Solaris system, before they even come close to touching Windows.[9]

Furthermore, Sun has no plans to release Linux versions of its popular NetDynamics server software.[10] A Sun product manager believes that

> Linux will remain in strong demand for academic and price-sensitive customers, but corporate clients would rather spend the extra money for a company to stand behind its products. And Linux users are not going to spend money for proprietary software."[11]

Surprisingly, Microsoft holds the same sentiments. Bill Gates, the chairman of Microsoft, said the following: "Microsoft is taking Linux seriously. But ultimately we do not expect it to become a significant threat . . . The fact that you don't have a central testing point to control all the different incompatibilities probably means that the impact is fairly limited . . ."[12]

However, Ed Muth, Enterprise Marketing Group Manager of Microsoft, considers Linux a competitor:

> Linux is a competitor on the client and the server. My analysis is that Linux is a material competitor in the lower-performance end of the general-purpose server industry and the small- to medium-sized ISP industry. It is important to recognize that Linux, beyond competing with Microsoft, is also, and perhaps even more frequently, an alternative or competitor to other versions of UNIX. [13]

Some analysts believe that Linux could have even a greater impact on Microsoft, stating that it is twice as likely to replace Windows NT as it is to replace UNIX [14] (contrary to analyst comments on Sun). Even Microsoft engineer Vinod Valloppillil sees Linux and the open source software movement as a greater threat:

> OSS (Open Source Software) poses a direct, short-term revenue and platform threat to Microsoft, particularly in server space. Additionally, the intrinsic parallelism and free idea exchange in OSS has benefits that are not replicable with our current licensing model and therefore present a long term developer mindshare threat . . . The ability of the OSS process to collect and harness the collective IQ of thousands of individuals across the Internet is simply amazing. More importantly, OSS evangelization scales with the size of the Internet much faster than our own evangelization efforts appear to scale.[15]

THE LINUX BUSINESS: HOW TO MAKE MONEY FROM FREE SOFTWARE?

Bob Young wondered how each of these vendors would influence the Linux movement and Red Hat, especially since so many of them had an equity stake in the company. In addition to the major industry leaders, several start-up companies are also trying to devise Linux-based business models. Most of these new ventures have started as distributors. However, Bob Young had five other business models to choose from to determine their fit with Red Hat Software.

Distributor

While Linux is freely available on the Internet, it is not convenient for most users to download the entire product online. Distributors copy Linux onto a CD-ROM and sell the product for a nominal fee (see Exhibit 5.4). Red Hat, starting out as a distributor, developed a software program to aid in the complicated installation and upgrade

EXHIBIT 5.4 Retail Prices of Popular Operating Systems

CASE 5
Red Hat Software
and Linux Operating
System: Where Do
You Want to Go
Tomorrow?

Red Hat (Linux distribution)	$ 49.95
Slackware (Linux distribution)	$ 39.99
Caldera (Linux distribution)	
Windows NT Workstation	$230.00
Windows NT Server	$700.00
Windows 98	$200.00 ($86 for upgrade)
Solaris (binary)	$ 75.00

process. In addition, Red Hat developed installation manuals. Other current distributors include Caldera, Debina, Linuxware, SuSE Linux, and Slackware, to name a few.

Service

Many of the Linux distributors are also looking to provide postsales support services to each of their clients. Currently, one of the deterrents to the wide acceptance of Linux is the perception of a lack of service and maintenance support for such open source software. Currently, support for Linux is available through ad hoc communities on the Internet. This support mechanism is well suited for organizations or individuals with technical expertise, but may not be ideal for the less technical user.

Third Party Software

Other companies such as Corel, Oracle, and IBM are developing proprietary application software to run on top of the open Linux operating system. Examples of such applications include Word Perfect, DB2, and Oracle 8i. But there is a nagging doubt whether the open source software community will purchase proprietary software, given the possibility that it could undercut the very essence of the open source community.

Portal

Like Netscape and Yahoo! which provide content, there is the potential to create, aggregate, and exchange online Linux information. A "portal" site represents a fourth possible business model. Since most of the current Linux community is online and needs frequent upgrades and information, the advertising revenue generated from a Linux portal could be significant. However, there are already several online sources for Linux information and upgrades, including Red Hat, Linux Today, linux.org, Information Week On-line, slashdot.com, and Fresh Meat.

Training

Novell and Microsoft provided certification for their products, which in turn enhanced the perceived value of their products—certified engineers could claim expertise in that particular system. Linux-based distributors like Red Hat are already starting to provide these types of certification services. However, many competitors such as Learning Tree already provide these training services for Linux.

History of Red Hat

Red Hat was founded in 1994 in Research Triangle, North Carolina, by a group of UNIX enthusiasts led by Marc Ewing. Red Hat has been one of the distributors of Linux source code since its earliest days.

Because of the frequency of Linux's code revisions, upgrading the kernel of the operating system and the additional software packages was no small task. Recognizing this need, Red Hat developed the Red Hat Package Manager (RPM) that defines a distribution format and a tool to update packages easily. RPM was a huge success. As a result, Red Hat's popularity soared. Ease of installation became the distinguishing feature of Red Hat distribution. Even though RPM was released as an open source code and adopted by most competing distributors, it was clear that Red Hat had grabbed the leadership position in Linux distribution.

Despite popularity in niche markets and winning coveted industry awards, Red Hat was facing a hurdle getting its Linux used in the broader marketplace. Lack of support and absence of industry heavyweights behind Linux have often been cited as the reasons why corporate IT managers shy away from Linux. Linux was just as good as other UNIX variants in supporting the common Internet server applications (e.g., domain name server, telnet server, mail server, web server, ftp server), principally because all of them are open source applications. However, it needed the proprietary database servers that corporate IT departments use for e-commerce and internal business applications. While Red Hat could provide the Linux server, there was no way that Red Hat could develop a database server that corporations would use. The only option was to persuade the leading database server providers like Oracle, Sybase, Informix, and IBM to port their software to Linux. It also needed to win endorsement from at least one major computer vendor. Having Linux preinstalled would eliminate the complaints about its difficult installation. However, considering that most IT managers were planning to drop UNIX servers in favor of Windows NT, getting corporate support for Red Hat was a very challenging task.

Major Milestones

The wind started to change in late 1998 when Microsoft was under scrutiny by the Department of Justice. Its aggressive practices, exposed frequently in the media, fueled negative sentiment toward Microsoft. Windows NT servers did not live up to their expected performance and their upgrade was two years late, creating a window for other alternatives.[16] Several database server vendors pledged support for Linux. In October 1998 Intel invested in Red Hat along with the Silicon Valley venture capital firm Benchmark Capital. In the next few months, many more heavyweights jumped on the bandwagon, including computer vendors like Compaq, Dell, IBM, Sun, SGI, and Hewlett-Packard and software vendors like Netscape, Novell, Sybase, Informix, Oracle, and SAP. Many of these companies have taken a minority equity position in Red Hat as well.

As of April 1999, one can order a Dell Dimension PC preinstalled with Red Hat Linux directly from Dell's website. There is another handful of computer vendors offering complete Linux systems starting at under $500. The majority of these vendors are bundling Red Hat distribution and all the major media have paid ample press attention. There is no doubt that Red Hat is riding on the strong momentum behind Linux.

243

CASE 5
Red Hat Software
and Linux Operating
System: Where Do
You Want to Go
Tomorrow?

Competitors

Many competitors have cropped up in the Linux distribution and service business. In addition, there are no barriers to entry and the distribution market is getting crowded by many new entrants. Current competitors include Caldera, Debian, SuSE, Mandrake, LinuxPPC, Linux Pro, Linux Ware, MkLinux, Stampede, Turbo Linux, Yggdrasil Linux, DLX Linux, DOS Linux, tomsrtbt, and of course Red Hat. While some of them cater to niche markets, it is getting harder for new distributors to differentiate themselves from one another. Caldera, which has focused on the needs of the business segment, is currently seen as Red Hat's strongest competitor in that market. The company has announced plans to release its Openlinux suite in the second quarter of 1999. Caldera's CEO Ransom Love feels that Caldera has the infrastructure in place to service business customers as more businesses embrace Linux.[17]

Similarly, there is no barrier in providing Linux service. Linux Care is a new organization that aims to provide 24/7 technical support to corporations. Linux Care both threatens and complements Red Hat's business. Dell, for instance, bundles Red Hat's distribution, yet outsources support to Linux Care.

Current Issues

In spite of the rosy outlook for Linux, many concerns still remained. Linux was starting to run up against proprietary UNIX solutions in the server market and threatening some of its equity investors' revenue. In addition, the lack of standardization among Linux distributors was a big hurdle for third-party software developers. Clearly, there was a need for a leading voice in the Linux community to provide market leadership. Red Hat assumed this leadership role, but had met with resentment from some in the community.

Red Hat continued to recruit programmers to develop open source software to contribute back to the community. It was continuing to push for wider adoption by computer vendors and improving its service offering. It had started to offer training classes and certification tests. Lately Red Hat also embarked on a campaign to build a portal for the Linux community. To make Linux more viable as a desktop OS, it invested in developing Gnome, an open source graphical user interface.

Although Red Hat was becoming competitive in the server market, it still faced formidable barriers in the desktop market. The major hurdle was the lack of application software, where compatibility with Windows was, for all practical purposes, essential.

The most alarming news was the announcement from both IBM and Hewlett-Packard that they were starting to offer 24/7 Linux service in some areas. IBM had a global service organization with a reputation for excellent customer service. It already offered support services for Apache, the market-leading Web server, which was developed under an open source model. Under Louis Gertsner, IBM had been aggressively increasing the size of its service business. It clearly intended to enter Linux service if Linux became prevalent. What was stopping IBM from eating Red Hat's lunch? For that matter, what was stopping others—from Sun Microsystems to Andersen Consulting—from eating Red Hat's lunch? In such an environment, how far could "brand management" possibly take Red Hat?

REFERENCES

1. Interview with Bob Young on Screen Savers, Ziff Davis Net, April 1999.
2. Amy Harmon, "The Rebel Code," *New York Times Magazine,* February 2, 1999, p. 34.
3. Karlin Lillington, "Global Warning," *The Guardian On-Line,* October 8, 1999.
4. Tom Dunlap and Michael Kanellos, "Intel, Netscape Back Red Hat," CNET News.com, September 29, 1998.
5. Ibid.
6. Stephen Shankland, "Big Blue Gives Green Light to Linux," CNET News.com, February 16, 1999.
7. Nora Mikes, "SGI to Unveil Linux Machines This May: Looking into 'Rolling Its Own' Linux Distribution as Well," *LinuxWorld,* March 5, 1999.
8. www.sun.com/dot-com/realitycheck/headsup981008.html.
9. "Vendors are Driving This Leg of the Linux Movement," *Internet Week,* March 8, 1999.
10. Ibid.
11. Interview with Sun Microsystems Desktop Computing Line Manager, April 12, 1999, New York University.
12. "Gates Calls Linux Impact 'Fairly Limited,'" Reuters, April 14, 1999.
13. www.microsoft.com/NTServer/highlights/editorletter.asp, downloaded on April 15, 1999.
14. "Behind the Numbers: Momentum Builds for Linux," *Information Week Online,* March 15, 1999.
15. Amy Harmon and John Markoff, "Internal Memo Shows Microsoft Executives' Concern over Free Software," *New York Times,* November 3, 1998.
16. Steve Hamm, with Marcia Stpaneck, Peter Burrows, and Andy Reinhardt, "Microsoft: How Vulnerable?" *Business Week,* February, 22, 1999, pp. 60–64.
17. Nathan Cochrane, "Blue Moves, Caldera Stirs," *Fairfax IT,* March 2, 1999.

BEYOND INTERACTIVE: INTERNET ADVERTISING AND CASH CRUNCH

So how do you start a successful Internet business? Any MBA student might state the following success factors: an experienced management team, well-funded investors, technical employees, stock ownership plans, and a Silicon Valley headquarters. Jonn Behrman, CEO and founder of Beyond Interactive (BI), would have to disagree. In just over three years, Jonn had built a $4.6 million online advertising services firm with a management team all under 25 years of age. He had no outside investors, mostly non-technical employees, no employee equity program, and a headquarters in Ann Arbor, Michigan. Ask Jonn about the primary reason for BI's recent success, and he immediately answered "our people." John boasted, "We haven't lost a single employee since I started this business." However, when asked about the challenges facing BI, the big grin quickly disappeared . . . "Cash flow and competition are what keep me up at night."[1]

Behrman's strategy to combat the competition was simple. Grow—and do it fast! He realized the old method of slow growth through earnings was not enough to create a sustainable business model on the Internet. COO Nick Pahade agreed:

> We have more business than we can handle at the moment. We want to expand by hiring more people and opening more sales offices, but we just don't have the capital. We have no tangible assets, so our bank line of credit is just $50,000. Additionally, more and more customers are paying us later. Jonn and I agree that we need more money, but we're not sure which option is best. We're exploring the vulture [venture] capital route, alliances with traditional advertising agencies, and angel [private] investors. We're not interested in being acquired at this point. Our biggest concern is giving up equity and losing control of our business. Also, I know we need to get our bookkeeping in order before we attract investors. We're looking for a CFO right now![2]

On December 11, 1998, Jonn had more than the BI holiday party on his mind. Strong competitors in Internet marketing were entering the company's market space every day.

University of Michigan Business School MBA Candidates Charlie Choi, Patti Glaza, Ashesh Kamdar, Rich Lesperance, and Kevin White prepared this case under the direction of Professor Allan Afuah as the basis for class discussion rather than to illustrate either effective or ineffective handling of an administrative situation. © Copyright 2001 by McGraw-Hill/Irwin. All Rights Reserved.

Traditional agencies or well-funded start-ups could catch up to BI in months. BI needed to stay one step ahead of the rapidly changing environment in Internet marketing. His young but relatively experienced staff was being courted by competitors offering higher salaries. The list of expansion projects seemed to be growing daily, while the cash flow situation wasn't improving. As Jonn looked out from his new office, he thought hard about the right financing and growth strategy. He had to make the right decisions not only for his company, but also for his loyal and motivated "fraternity" at BI.

Background

BI had its beginnings in the undergraduate business program at the University of Michigan. After a summer internship in real estate, Jonn became interested in the real estate industry's use of the Web. This interest led to an academic project during the fall semester of 1995. During the project, Jonn became extremely frustrated with the time it took to find relevant information on the Internet. He saw a business opportunity for website promotion and in October founded Wolverine Web Productions (WWP). For over a year, the business focus was website optimization and targeted e-mail services. The company website, Web Production Resource Center (WPRC), not only promoted WWP but also provided general resources for Internet marketing. During this early phase of WWP, Darian Heyman and Nick Pahade joined the company as partners (see Exhibit 6.1). Heyman's enthusiasm and knack for selling helped WWP land its first large account: Ameritech. WWP stayed financially afloat through its clients who paid for marketing services up front, while BI's vendors required payment within 30 days.

In 1997 WWP added Internet media planning and buying to its portfolio of services. This decision spurred significant growth for the company. By the end of 1997, the company added another partner (Matt Day), employed 16 people, and billed clients $1.4 million for marketing services. Additionally, the company created a new business website separate from its resource site WPRC. The goal was to provide unbiased information about Internet marketing to the Web community.

In 1998 WWP changed its name to Beyond Interactive and continued its client-financed growth. By the end of November, billings reached $4.6 million with 42 full-time employees. The growth in revenue was the result of winning larger clients who could commit to larger Internet marketing budgets. Recently, BI instituted a policy of doing business only with clients that spent a minimum of $30,000 every three months. BI also opened a satellite sales office in San Francisco to build closer ties with potential West Coast clients. BI had learned that selling Internet marketing services actually required face-to-face selling. Finally, the company hired Kevin Hermida, a recent computer science graduate from the University of Michigan and Microsoft employee, as its chief technology officer (CTO).

The BI "Fraternity"

"It's like my college fraternity around here," Jonn commented with a smile as he observed the activity around his office. Rows of cubicles littered with huge toys were a short distance from the Ping-Pong room, the site of numerous company tournaments. Above an oversized gum ball dispenser hung a sign announcing a contest for employees. Employees at BI were 22 to 25 years old, had no dress code, and passed around bottles of beer in the office on Friday afternoons. Jonn is genuinely excited when talk-

EXHIBIT 6.1 The Founders of Beyond Interactive

247

CASE 6
Beyond Interactive:
Internet Advertising
and Cash Crunch

Jonn Behrman, CEO

Jonn Behrman was born in Venezuela and moved to the United States in the mid-1980s. He graduated from the University of Michigan's School of Business with an undergraduate degree in Computer Information Systems (CIS) and marketing in 1996. BI (then called Wolverine Web Productions) opened in 1995, when the industry was still in its infancy. Started without any external financing, the company's original focus was search engine optimization. Working out of his apartment, Behrman and his small team set out to make it easier to find sites on the Web. Within a short period of time, Behrman refocused the company toward online media buying and campaign management. Jonn Behrman is 25 years old.

Nick Pahade, COO

Nick Pahade graduated from the University of Michigan in 1996 with an undergraduate degree in biopsychology and marketing. Originally pursuing a career in medicine, he has been published in three Web medical journals and was a featured speaker at numerous premed symposiums. Pahade became involved with BI to develop a student housing locator. The relationship continued to grow until Pahade decided to commit to the company full-time in 1996. Shortly thereafter he was made both partner and vice president. As COO, Pahade is ultimately responsible for the company's profit and loss as well as operating budgets. He manages the financial and administrative personnel, develops operational processes, and ensures that they are deployed company-wide. He is also in charge of developing and managing relationships with outside vendors, suppliers, and clients. Nick Pahade is 25 years old.

Darian Heyman, VP Business Development

Darian Heyman has been vice president of business development at BI since he graduated from the University of Michigan in 1996 with a degree in international relations. He first turned down a business development opportunity with Procter & Gamble, as well as an opportunity to study in Mexico on a scholarship, to get involved with Internet advertising. Heyman has played a critical role in pushing the company's growth; in 1997 his efforts brought in $1.4 million worth of advertising sales. Darian Heyman is 25 years old.

---

ing about the environment he has created: "People are the key to success in this business. I am better at motivating people than any head coach you will meet. It's my gift. My people love me, they adore me. They love their jobs."[3] In stark contrast to other firms in the advertising industry, BI has had zero turnover since its founding in 1995.

To stay competitive, BI planned to grow from 42 to 100 employees within the next year. Employees were generally undergraduates with liberal arts degrees looking for their first job. Their qualifications? Passion and energy: "We often win business based on our enthusiasm."[4] This fun atmosphere was a big benefit to employees, who were willing to work for less than half the typical wages in the industry in order to support the company's aggressive growth. However, top management worried that rivals with far more resources, such as Avenue A, would lure away BI employees by offering fatter salaries and incentives. Employees in turn were becoming more concerned with the possible impact of growth on BI's culture. One employee complained that the Ping-Pong table might be removed to make room for more cubicles.

The Online Advertising Industry

In 1998 the opportunities for online advertising were staggering. E-commerce was expected to reach $425 billion by 2002. Ad spending was predicted to reach $2.3–3 billion by 1999 and as much as $25 billion by 2002. While online advertising in 1998 only made up 1.3 percent of all ad budgets, on average, this proportion was expected to increase rapidly as more users came online.[5]

Three forms of online advertising were dominant in 1998: banners, sponsorships, and interstitials. While these were the most popular, new forms were expected to emerge as a result of changing technologies.

Banners:	Rectangular ads that allow users to "click through" to advertiser's websites.
Sponsorships:	The advertiser is given a prominent position on a website, often on the top of the page, for its company name and logo, and usually given "sponsored by" credit. Content on the website is typically correlated with the advertiser's industry.[6]
Interstitials:	Ads that interrupt users, regardless of the users' actions. Similar to television ads that interrupt programming, users have no control over interstitials, which could take up the entire viewable area in the users' browsers. Users have to click on interstitials to close them.

How effective were these ads? Opinions varied. A study conducted by WebCMO found that the three most effective methods to generating sales and site traffic were (1) search engine submission, (2) solicited e-mail, and (3) off-line promotion. While banners were being used more frequently than off-line promotion in 1998, their value had increasingly come under attack.[7] In 1997 only 9.1 percent of online users said they looked at banner ads "very often" or "often," and the number of users that said they "never" looked at banners jumped from 38.7 percent to 48 percent between 1997 and 1998.[8] Martha Deevy, a senior vice president at Charles Schwab & Co., made a good analogy: "A lot of Internet banner ads are like billboards on the side of the highway. People drive right past them and don't bother to look."[9] An additional challenge facing advertisers was that looking at ads did not necessarily mean the user "clicked through."

One-to-One versus Mass Marketing

An important difference between traditional advertising media and the Internet was the capability for one-to-one targeting on the Web. Based on unlimited access to customer information, "the information superhighway is enabling direct marketing to fulfill its goal of nurturing that neighborhood-store feeling among customers."[10] No longer were companies forced to market general ads toward broad segments, but they could specifically target *you* based on where you lived, how much income you made, and what types of products you bought.

The key element for taking advantage of these trends was a company's ability to analyze and act on the information it gathered. For most companies, this gap was filled by third-party advertising and data-mining agencies.

While being able to offer personalized service was a critical requirement for advertising, a company's brand name also continued to play a major role. A recent survey showed that 69 percent of Internet buyers considered brand familiarity as critical to their buying decision. Unfortunately, in the race to get online quickly, many retailers, catalogers, and direct marketers forgot to leverage the branding that they worked so hard to create.[11]

Technology Trends Affecting Internet Marketing

Centralized Ad Serving

More and more Internet ads were being managed by third-party ad serving systems. These vendors managed customer ads from delivery to the destination website to reporting traffic statistics. The advantage of using a third-party ad server was consistent ad delivery and standard reporting for clients regardless of the chosen websites in the media plan. One company that provided this service was DART for Advertisers (DFA).

Internet Video Technology

Hardware limitations in processor speeds, monitor resolution, disk storage, and especially Internet connections led to software innovations in data compression and audio and video processing. For example, video "streaming" allowed users to download video clips in small data chunks in succession, so that the video could be viewed as it was being downloaded. In the past, the entire clip had to be downloaded (taking several minutes with a telephone modem) before it could be viewed. However, limited bandwidth (a measure of how much data could be sent simultaneously across a data line) on most Internet connections could still make online video slow, choppy, and grainy.

The typical modem used downloaded data at a speed of 56,000 (56K) bits per second (bps), but to get video approaching television quality required speeds of 1 million (1M) bps and higher. Two of the more promising technologies aimed at solving the bandwidth problem were cable modems and Digital Subscriber Line (DSL). Forward Concepts projects 9.6 million cable modems and 1.86 DSL modems in North America by 2003, less than 10 percent of U.S. households.[12] Given the rapid rate of innovation, it was almost impossible to predict with any accuracy where the next innovation would come from or what the online world would look like in the future. But as things stood now, due to the limited availability, high cost, and technological limitations, it did not seem likely that Internet connections of 1 Mbps and above would be commonplace for home users for at least another five years.

Boomerang Cookies

Many websites tagged visitors' computers with small files, known as "cookies," that helped identify users on return visits. With current technology, these data were useful only if the customer came back to that particular site. Starting in 1999 DoubleClick planned to introduce powerful software to let advertisers spot those visitors, even weeks later on other websites. Then those "visitors" could be greeted with more ads for the original merchant, and their surfing habits could be tracked for future targeting. DoubleClick called this boomerang technology.

Search Engine Submission Software

Most customers could not find a company's homepage/website if their address was not listed in the online "yellow pages"—the search engines. Posting addresses on these search engines could be extremely time intensive if undertaken manually. While most online advertising agencies assisted clients with this service, new software packages performed a similar function, all for under $100. CyberSleuth Internet Services' product offered fully automated submission to hundreds of search engines and directories, and also offered semiautomated support for hundreds of others.[13]

Media Convergence

In 1998 *The Wall Street Journal* reported: "Media companies are moving from the traditional analog to a digital environment."[14] Though high definition television (HDTV) was in its infancy, digital technology went far beyond simply better television pictures. Digital signals opened up the traditional world of "push" programming to "pull" scheduling. No longer would consumers be forced to watch specific programs or commercials at set times, but would instead choose what and when they watched.

Digital cable broadcasting would allow two-way, interactive communication through a television set, similar to what the Internet currently provided. This had two major implications for the advertising industry: (1) one-to-one marketing would become the dominant form of advertising,[15] and (2) advertising agencies could use digital technology to increase economies of scale by integrating television, print, and online media campaigns.[16]

Competition

There was no lack of available online agencies to take the growing ad dollars. Any search on the Web for "Internet advertising" brought back long lists of potential companies. These companies took all shapes and forms, but there were three typical models in 1998: traditional agencies, design shops, and specialty agencies.

Traditional Agencies (Integrating Print, Television, and Radio Campaigns)

While late to the game, traditional agencies moved quickly to develop expertise in online advertising. Either through hiring, buying small shops, or alliances, traditional agencies started to capture big accounts. Large portals that captured significant online viewership spurred the smaller upstart agencies to focus on developing integrated online and off-line campaigns. In mid-October, Excite hired Lowe & Partners/SMS, Geocities chose Young & Rubicam, and Snap released TV ads created by Saatchi & Saatchi. Though Snap had been open to nontraditional/specialty agencies, its final decision came down to "we needed an agency that could build a mass brand, and had experience with both television advertising and alternative media."[17]

Design Shops

Most of these companies were primarily focused on producing Web pages for clients. They assisted in the design and layout of the Internet site that the end customers visited. In order to offer a broader range of services to their clients, many of these design shops were "busy acquiring people, skills and companies with traditional media strengths such as brand strategy and media planning."[18]

Specialty Agencies

These companies focused on one or two types of advertising media exclusively. Instead of being a "one-stop shop," specialty agencies tried to maximize their value through dedicated resources. A large number of firms had entered Internet advertising to meet the growing needs of the marketplace for search-engine effectiveness, e-mail campaigns, and online ad creation. Specialty firms had survived intense competition in other media such as television, radio, and print.

With the rush to gain a piece of the online pie, companies spent a great deal of time trying to define themselves. "There is a pissing match going on over who offers the most services, not over who is creating the right model," stated the managing director of Grey Interactive. Mergers between technology and media companies, such as US Web/CKS Group and Sapient Corp./Studio Archetype blurred the lines between where technology ended and marketing services began.[19] How far clients would expect their ad agency to understand and handle the technology aspects of online services had not been established.

Not fitting into one of the standard company models, DoubleClick, Inc., offered standard creation and placement services, but also developed sophisticated tracking technologies. This allowed advertisers to target specific segments based on customers' country or metropolitan sign-in point. To expand its customer base, DoubleClick, Inc., sold its services and some of its technology to other ad agencies. For example, competitors could buy certain DoubleClick software tools to manage their own marketing campaigns.[20]

Back-end technologies also helped smaller specialty shops add value for their clients. Beyond standard offerings such as managing ad campaigns, conducting research on ad placement, negotiating prices, and delivering effectiveness reports, Avenue A Media used a proprietary planning system. This system contained performance and demographic information on tens of thousands of sites. Based on client objectives, budget, and product category, the system created a list of viable ad spaces that could be integrated into the media plan.

Customers

BI's client list contained a variety of both famous and less well known organizations. Some of the blue-chip companies include IBM, Ameritech, *The Economist,* and NextCard Visa. While these businesses are quite different, they all shared an interest in building their cyberspace brand. The following clients were recently added:

Fallon McElligott

Fallon McElligott (FM), a traditional advertising agency, needed an Internet marketing partner to assist with its client's cyberspace marketing needs. Its client, United Airlines, wanted to target business travelers on the Internet. BI won the contract on its ability to negotiate lower advertising rates on behalf of clients. BI also improved the media plan targeting. With BI's help, FM was able to concentrate on traditional media planning and still provide a complete marketing solution for United Airlines.

NextCard Visa

NextCard Visa (NV) wanted to attract prequalified traffic to its website. It hoped the Internet would enable the company to achieve aggressive customer sign-up goals. NV chose BI to assist with its Internet marketing plan. BI ran test campaigns on a variety of websites and established long-term relationships with the most effective sites. NV eventually reached its sign-up goals over the Internet and also locked up advertising on strategic websites.

Service Offerings and Operating Roles: Value Delivery at BI

Although BI began by offering limited online advertising services, by 1998 its service portfolio had matured to include search engine optimization, targeted e-mail, press release distribution, and interactive banner advertising.

Search engine optimization was initially provided to increase total traffic on client sites by using the many engines prevalent on the Internet. Not only did BI provide tips to optimize clients' pages for user searches, it also provided manual and automated URL submission services. Targeted e-mail and press release services were also used to promote client offerings. For e-mail advertising, BI aided clients in choosing the appropriate target audience and developing an advertising message that spurred consumer interest. Press release services were designed to communicate a client message through information releases in traditional media forms. Information had to be framed to interest not only the prospective end customer, but also the media channel used as the message conduit.

Although BI used these limited advertising solutions to expand the business, Jonn and his team knew that they had to provide greater value to customers to sustain growth. In early 1997 interactive banner advertising was identified as the engine that would power BI's growth. Partnerships were developed with vendors who could provide the services with less value added that had traditionally been the staple of BI's service offerings. The company began to optimize its systems and practices to efficiently provide services to its clients using this more sophisticated technique.

Interactive banner ads provided many advantages over their less sophisticated predecessors. Visual appeal, improved targeting, and customer-tracking options proved appealing to BI's growing customer base. Keys to banner advertising success were proper placement, design effectiveness, and cost, and BI's services addressed all three of these success factors. By using tools such as @plan media planning software, Inter-Watch AdSpend Report, and independent research, BI was able to identify advertising techniques and banner locations tailored for each customer. It also worked with clients to design the interactive banners and mediate appropriate vendor pricing options, including flat fee, CPM (cost per thousand impressions), and cost per click through.

BI charged clients through a service-specific compensation structure, as follows:

- A standard 15 percent agency commission for media buys and targeted e-mails.
- An hourly charge for strategic linking and nonmedia programs.
- A flat fee for search engine optimization, press releases, and/or copywriting.
- Varied fees for creative services.

Key Operating Roles

There were three primary functional roles that supported business development activities at BI: business developers (BDs), account managers (AMs), and media planners (MPs).

- *Business developers.* Primarily responsible for follow-up on initial business leads, these individuals screened potential customers and spearheaded the development of the marketing strategy overview (MSO). During the early days of BI, Jonn and Nick performed this function. As the number of customers grew, the business developer position was created to shoulder the initial screening and burden of MSO preparation. However, Jonn and Nick continued their involvement with large, strategic clients.
- *Account managers.* There were seven to nine account managers (AMs) at BI in November 1998 who managed the ongoing relationship with each client. AMs acted as the focus between the client and the vendors outlined in the media plan, providing ongoing campaign support throughout the duration of the advertising

initiative. AMs did not necessarily appear early in the history of BI; however, as BI's client list grew, it became increasingly important to have a single point of contact for the customer, and an internal expert who was familiar with that customer's expectations and idiosyncrasies. When describing the evolution of the position, senior AM Moses Robles commented:

> Early in the process, everyone was doing business development. The method for allocating accounts to people in the company was based primarily on who took the initial phone call. Our AMs were chosen based upon natural talent, not necessarily specific experience. Later on, we began to specialize in industry and vendor areas, with many of us developing strong working relationships with our vendors. In those cases, we were able to leverage such relationships to garner very competitive prices and offer them to multiple customers.[21]

AMs also acted as troubleshooters when things did not go as outlined in the media plan, managing vendor and customer expectations to arrive at reasonable conclusions. As client size increased, so too did the need to expand BI's services beyond an individual advertising campaign. It was the responsibility of the AM to set in motion repeat business from his or her clients, and to cross-sell or expand services into other divisions or business units within that client. Robles reflected:

> We need to maintain a good repertoire with our vendors for the long term, and we try not to overwork them on prices. On the same token, we feel that repeat client business will guarantee future revenue. Our [AM] #1 goal is to grow our existing client accounts and cross-sell services to other groups at that client. To do that, we rely not only on our knowledge of the client's industry, but also on our people skills.[22]

- *Media planner.* The backbone of the business development process, media planners (MPs) were responsible for much of the creativity in BI's client offerings. Although they were largely responsible for developing media plans for prospective clients, MPs also conducted vendor and industry research to support new or ongoing client needs.

Business Development Process

The business development process at BI consisted of five steps: lead follow-up and needs assessment, developing and submitting a marketing strategy overview (MSO), developing and presenting a media plan, project kickoff and campaign management, and cultivating future business opportunities.

Lead Follow-up and Needs Assessment

By November 1998 the flow of incoming business leads had evolved into three main sources. The bulk (about 50 percent) came from the websites, both WPRC and BI, which offered potential clients a free consultation on how they could benefit from online advertising. Although the highest volume of leads came through this channel, most of these were for smaller clients.

Another 20 percent of business leads came from trade shows, where BI employees gave ad technology seminars and descriptive presentations of BI services. The other main source of leads (about 30 percent) was through word-of-mouth referrals, either from past clients or companies who provided complementary services. BI had developed working referral relationships with a number of these companies, including traditional advertising agencies, design shops, and online media consultants. Overall, approximately 80 percent of customers contracted BI directly to provide services, while 20 percent came as subcontracts from traditional agencies or design shops. In that 20 percent, it was not uncommon for the end customer to have no idea that BI provided the Internet portion of its campaign.

These informal partnerships were reciprocal in nature. BI often referred new clients to these partners when it could not provide appropriate services to meet a client's advertising needs. According to Nick Pahade:

> Many traditional ad agencies do not have interactive [online] media departments. When their clients need those types of services, we want to be considered for such services. Unfortunately, it is often a catch-22 with these agencies—we can get referrals for large clients this way, but we may not get to pitch the client directly. In those cases, the client may not know who we are. What we really want to foster is relationships with traditional agencies where we can pitch the client with them, so that we can build our equity in the marketplace. Ultimately, we would like to be included directly on the RFP [request for proposal] lists of big customers.[23]

Once a lead had been identified, Nick, Jonn, or one of the two business developers took it and performed a needs assessment for the potential client, using a standard form and telephone or e-mail conversations. If the client had a clearly identified need and scope in mind, the BDs and MPs immediately began a media plan. If the client was unsure of its needs and budget, or if it was new to online advertising, an MSO was developed as an interim step to highlight BI's service offerings in the context of that specific client.

Developing and Submitting an MSO

The BD worked with the media planning department to create the initial pitch to the client. This pitch, termed the marketing strategy overview (MSO), outlined the services BI would offer the client, general advertising channels that would be pursued, the types of interactive advertising recommended, and estimated prices. The MSO was mailed to the client free of charge, and the BD, sometimes with the assigned MP, held a teleconference with the client to review it. A description of typical MSO content is shown in Exhibit 6.2.

EXHIBIT 6.2 Media Strategy Overview (MSO) Contents

- A typical MSO contains the following key elements:
- Overview of pricing models, including:
  - Cost per acquisition (CPA).
  - Cost per thousand impressions (CPM).
  - Cost per click through.
  - Flat fee.
- Description of online advertising opportunities, including:
  - Content site advertising.
  - Inexpensive run of network.
  - Search engines.
- Overview of Beyond Interactive skills, creative services.
- Overview of campaign performance tracking and analysis.

Developing and Presenting a Media Plan

255

CASE 6
Beyond Interactive:
Internet Advertising
and Cash Crunch

If a client was interested in employing BI, cash was requested to develop and implement a media plan. The commitment and payment typically covered the first three months of BI services. The MPs developed a detailed media plan which spelled out what types of ads would be designed for which websites, and how much they would cost.

The MPs used many complementary tools to develop this plan. AdPlan was an online service that reported (for a fee) which sites have worked best for different types of companies/industries advertising on the Internet. AdSpend was an online service that reported (for a fee) historical ad spending on the Internet by specific companies. Jupiter researched the effectiveness of different advertising techniques and shared the results of research for a fee. Various ad networks like doubleclick.net and 247media.com negotiated rights to vast networks of websites and could help prospective advertisers choose the sites frequented by customers in their respective target markets. In combination with these services, MPs used their personal experience and the group's collective experience to tailor a unique plan that best served a client's needs. Data acquired from the process was stored in a media plan database that housed valuable client, technology, and vendor information. This comprehensive database proved an invaluable resource to MPs and AMs as BI's client list grew, allowing new employees to leverage key lessons from previous campaigns. A description of typical media plan content is shown in Exhibit 6.3.

The finished media plan was then sent to the client for approval before ads were actually created and placed. A letter of engagement was also forwarded to the client. Upon receiving the signed letter, BI assigned an AM and proceeded with the campaign.

Project Kickoff and Campaign Management

Account managers (AMs) closely monitored campaign execution and tracked advertising performance using tools such as Doubleclick's DART for Advertisers. Through the use of such tools, BI could evaluate how well a campaign was reaching its target audience, and if that audience was following through to a purchasing decision. This information could be fed back to the client to modify or lengthen the ongoing campaign as necessary.

Cultivating Repeat Business Opportunities

During the client campaign, AMs attempted to make additional contacts at the client and leveraged those into new business opportunities. They also tried to develop a relationship with the client whereby they (AMs at BI) became the preferred online advertising provider for all future campaigns. Any new client work that entered the

EXHIBIT 6.3 Media Plan Contents

A typical media plan contains the following key elements:
- Online vendor information for any/all sources for the campaign, including:
  - Vendor name.
  - Flight dates.
  - Cost per thousand impressions (CPM).
  - Monthly/total impressions.
  - Monthly/total cost.
  - Site descriptions, URL, and creative specifications for each vendor.
- Special vendor notes (as applicable).

EXHIBIT 6.4 Income/Expense Structure

	% of Total Income
Income	
Media planning/buying	96.5%
Other services	3.5
Total income	100.0%
Expenses	
Ad placement costs	76.7%
Other services costs	.4
Wages & benefits	11.2
Travel & entertainment	1.2
Office & supplies	5.5
Marketing	2.3
Other expenses	2.2
Total expenses	99.5%
Net income	.5%

process through this channel usually skipped the MSO stage, and went directly into media planning. AMs were informally evaluated on their ability to drive repeat business with existing client organizations.

Looking to the Future

The management team at BI had a long list of growth projects for the company. Potential investments included new people, offices, and technology. Employees were needed in every area of the company. Additionally, BI was seeking an experienced chief financial officer (CFO) to improve its accounting and manage its financing. The management team was also committed to geographic expansion. Next year, Jonn planned to open offices in New York and London. Finally, BI would invest in the company's technological infrastructure in order to build their information-sharing capabilities, especially with other offices. Jonn summarized BI's strategy:

> We want to be the Rolls-Royce of the industry, both in the breadth of our online services and in their quality. We also want to grow the size of our accounts. To better serve our clients, we need to have offices in key areas around the U.S. and the world. We feel this expansion will help support, and actually drive, our revenue growth.[24]

These ambitious growth objectives required cash, which was in limited supply. Larger clients were demanding "net 30" payment terms, which meant that for the first time in BI's short history, it would need to rely on outside funding. Nick explained the following financing options:

- *Venture capital (VC).* BI started approaching VC firms in the fall of 1998. The management team was not excited about this option because they were afraid of losing management control. The team also knew that VC firms would probably pressure them into taking the company public within a couple of years. However, BI recognized that VC funding might be necessary as a last resort.
- *Acquisition.* BI had received several unsolicited offers from other advertising agencies to sell its business. These offers were turned down by the management

team who believed that they had the ability to develop BI into a premier digital advertising agency with a global reach.

- *Strategic partnerships*. A third option was to form an alliance with a traditional advertising agency. This option could increase the client list overnight, but the management team had some concerns. Would BI be able to pursue other clients or would the traditional agency demand exclusivity? Would the traditional agency eventually want management control?
- *Angel investors*. Another option would be to attract private investors into the business. This option sounded appealing to the management team. Angel investors might settle for a lower level of control in the business than professional VC firms, but they offered little or no management expertise.

Jonn was leaning back in his chair, thinking about these different financing alternatives. Even if BI was able to secure financing, how would BI best use the funds? He knew 1999 would be a very interesting year.

REFERENCES

1. Casewriters' interview with CEO Jonn Behrman, November 1998.
2. Casewriters' interview with COO Nick Pahade, November 1998.
3. Casewriters' interview with CEO Jonn Behrman, November 1998.
4. Ibid.
5. Jesse Berst, "Don't Be an E-commerce Victim," *ZDNet,* November 12, 1998; "Ad & E-commerce Revenue Streams Swell . . . ," *Min's New Media Report,* October 26, 1998; Jeff Lehman, "Bring TV, Radio Commercials to the Net," *Advertising Age,* September 28, 1998, p. 50.
6. Kate Maddox, "Sponsored Content's Next Level . . . ," *Advertising Age,* August 31, 1998, p. 23.
7. Nancy Dietz, "Survey: Banners Losing Effectiveness," *Business Marketing* 83, no. 9 (September 1998), p. 40.
8. Kate Maddox, "Survey Shows Increase in Online Usage . . . ," *Advertising Age,* October 26, 1998, p. S6.
9. George Anders, "Internet Advertising . . . ," *The Wall Street Journal,* November 30, 1998.
10. Lois K. Geller, "The Internet: The Ultimate Relationship Marketing Tool," *Direct Marketing* 1, no. 5 (September 1998), p. 36.
11. Ibid.
12. *European Broadband Networking News*, August 6, 1998.
13. Melissa Campanelli, "Hit List," *Entrepreneur* 26, no. 10 (October 1998), p. 49.
14. Raju Narisetti, "New and Improved," *The Wall Street Journal,* November 16, 1998.
15. Ibid.
16. John Owen, "The Interactive Future," *Campaign,* September 18, 1998, p. 41.
17. Randal Rothenberg, "Web Portals Invite Mad Ave to Spin Point of Difference," *Advertising Age,* November 9, 1998, p. 46.
18. Kate Maddox, "Online Agencies Seek Identity as Borders Blur," *Advertising Age* website www.adage.com/news.
19. Ibid.
20. *Hoover's Online,* December 8, 1998.
21. Casewriters' interview with Moses Nobles, November 1998.
22. Ibid.
23. Casewriters' interview with COO Nick Pahade, November 1998.
24. Casewriters' interview with CEO Jonn Behrman, November 1998.

HOTMAIL: FREE E-MAIL FOR SALE

THE PROPOSAL

Sabeer Bhatia and Jack Smith, cofounders of Hotmail, looked across the table at the six Microsoft managers dressed in suits. The cofounders listened with excitement as the Microsoft managers went through the terms of the offer for their young Silicon Valley company. Hotmail was the fastest-growing free Web-based e-mail system in the world. It had more than 9.5 million subscribers and was the 12th most visited website as of December 1997.[1] Microsoft's first offer of $200 million served as an appetizer for the discussion. Bhatia countered the offer by commenting that Microsoft must be "very poor" to make such a small offer. The room was filled with tension as Microsoft began to "pile cash on the table."[2] It made it difficult to avoid facing the decision: trade in the future potential of the company for immediate gains. Tempting as the offer was, was it enough to compensate Bhatia and Smith for the loss of independence and future gains?

THE FOUNDERS

Sabeer Bhatia, the CEO of Hotmail, was originally from India. He came to the United States in 1988 to attend Caltech and went on to receive a master of science degree from Stanford University in 1993. While at Stanford, Bhatia met many entrepreneurs and decided then that he eventually wanted to start his own company. After Stanford, Bhatia worked as a systems integrator at an Apple Computer subsidiary, Firepower Systems, where he met Jack Smith, Hotmail's current CTO. Bhatia and Smith saw their peers making fortunes on Internet ideas and decided that they wanted to do the same.

New York University Stern School of Business MBA Candidates Brian Faleiro, Dana Porter, Siddharth Rastogi, Vitaly Shub, Christine Stokes, and Lanchi Venator prepared this case under the supervision of Professor Christopher L. Tucci for the purpose of class discussion rather than to illustrate either effective or ineffective handling of an administrative situation. Copyright © 2001 by McGraw-Hill/Irwin. All rights reserved.

Bhatia said, "Here were all these young guys getting rich on Internet ideas and we started saying 'Hey, we could have thought of that.'"[3] With only their engineering backgrounds and no experience in management or starting companies, the two entrepreneurs set out to build the company that is now Hotmail.

THE CONCEPT

Bhatia and Smith originally thought their fortune was in writing a Web-based personal database tool called JavaSoft. Their concept was to build a relational database that was accessible through the Web. As they were both working full-time, they had to find time outside the workday to strategize, plan, and prepare for their database. This proved to be a challenge for both of them.

They were having difficulties effectively communicating and exchanging ideas with each other when they were in different locations. This problem led to an idea. One day while Jack Smith was driving to his home in a suburb of Silicon Valley, he came up with the idea to use the Web as a means for personal communication. At this point in its history, the Web was a directory of information more than a direct communication tool. He immediately called Bhatia, who exclaimed "Eureka! We found it!"[4]

Bhatia and Smith began to focus their energy on this new concept of allowing everyone to access e-mail from any Web browser. They recognized the huge potential demand for this product. The work world was gravitating toward a more global and mobile workforce. For people on the move, it would mean gaining access to e-mail from any portal, desktop, laptop, or dial-up. By removing the physical constraint of having to subscribe to an Internet service provider (ISP) or an e-mail provider, Bhatia and Smith's idea was poised to make messaging communication faster and more convenient.

Instead of making money on the service, Bhatia and Smith decided to provide the service for free. This was the best way to ensure that the service would catch on. Their money-making concept was to charge advertisers for access to their subscriber base. Not only would they provide access to subscribers but their ability to track subscriber's surfing habits and demographic information would allow advertisers to customize advertising information as well.

As they developed their new business idea, Bhatia and Smith never gave up on the relational database concept. They continued their work in this arena. In the meantime, the Hotmail concept crystallized. Bhatia and Smith realized that their next step was to raise capital. Their combined personal investment of $4,000 was not going to be sufficient to make their dream come true.

ENTER THE VCS

In December 1995 Bhatia and Smith approached the venture capital firm of Draper Fisher Jurvetson (DFJ) to sell their idea of a Web-based database. They originally had no intention of mentioning the free Web-based e-mail; they were afraid the venture capitalists would steal or exploit their idea. However, DFJ was unimpressed with the database idea. Recalls DFJ partner Tim Draper, "They were promoting a database product that other people already had. We were about to show them the door when they mentioned the free e-mail idea."[5] Forced to show their hand early in the game, Bhatia and Smith had to reveal their trump card. Once on board, DFJ granted Bhatia and Smith approximately $300,000 in funding in exchange for 15 percent of the company.[6]

Aside from monetary funding, DFJ gave Hotmail its start in what proved to be one of the most successful campaigns of "viral marketing." Viral marketing refers to product or service design that induces the users themselves to market the product (or service) simply by using it. The venture capitalists suggested that each Hotmail message should end with an "advertisement" directing recipients to the Hotmail site for their own free e-mail account. Recalls Draper, "When we first suggested it, they were taking the purist point of view, saying, 'We can't do that—it's spamming!' [delivering junk e-mail]. But by the end of the conversation, it dawned on them that it wasn't much different from running a banner ad."[7]

The result of this simple marketing device was an explosion of Hotmail's subscriber roster. Hotmail expanded its user base rapidly on very low advertising spending. Much later, *Red Herring* would write, "Draper Fisher Jurvetson came up with the concept of viral marketing, perhaps the most influential idea in the Internet Economy right now."[8]

IN THE BEGINNING

Success at gaining funding from DFJ allowed Bhatia and Smith to focus on their concept. They worked out of a two-room office all day and all night and took breaks only to go home and sleep. A lot of strategic decisions were made right there, in the initial stages of the business. Initially, they identified three marketplaces. One was the consumer market, which was huge. The second was the corporate market, which meant becoming an application service provider for e-mail over corporate intranets and extranets. And the third was to create a packaged Web e-mail product with Hotmail's software and actually sell it to corporations. Early on, however, Bhatia decided to stay away from the last two market areas because he did not feel they had the resources to build those, and decided instead to concentrate exclusively on the consumer market.

A month before the product launch, Hotmail's burn rate had eaten through all of its cash. But Bhatia persuaded the original 15 employees to stay with Hotmail for only stock options. At that time in Silicon Valley, jobs were instantly available and high salaries and stock options were used to attract employees from other companies. Bhatia commented later, "My greatest accomplishment was not to build the company, but to convince people that this is their company. I showed people how this would ultimately benefit them . . . We initiated the avalanche."[9]

The product was launched on July 4, 1996, operating on two primitive computers. That day, the founders constantly received the number of new subscriptions to the site by beeper. After starting with 100 subscribers in the first hour, Hotmail grew to 100,000 subscribers in a month, and reached a million in less than six months. Hotmail was universally and easily accessible because, like other websites, it could be reached through any Internet service provider.

GROWING PAINS

This explosive growth did not go completely without problems. Early on, Hotmail experienced intermittent service outages because of very high consumer demand. But unlike Juno, an early competitor, Hotmail never restricted how many users could adopt the service. Instead, Bhatia was continuously beefing up the service's networks, fire-walls, and security programs.

Bhatia understood that reliability and convenience of the service were the key ingre-dients of success and the creation of a powerful brand. In early 1997 Hotmail implemented a new, highly scalable and redundant architecture. This new architecture was capable of sustaining more than 50,000 new users a day, sending and receiving millions of e-mail messages daily, and achieving response time in less than a second regardless of system load. The system itself was outsourced to Exodus,[10] a leader in managing data centers for mission-critical Internet operations, to ensure constant uptime of all basic operations, including the Internet connection, server hardware, and power. Hotmail was trying hard to keep pace with the demands of its growth and to implement innovative technologies.

Hotmail's Web-based model and fault-tolerant system architecture were uniquely designed for high-volume traffic and reliability. Its system architecture featured dynamic load balancing and fully redundant storage, power, and processors that would allow the Hotmail system to scale well beyond the 10 million users it had in January 1997 and to provide a highly reliable and responsive service worldwide. "We're particularly excited about the load balancing design of this architecture," said Jack Smith. "When [users log] on to Hotmail, they get the least busy path to their e-mail, which dramatically enhances their online experience."[11] Hotmail's performance goals included providing millisecond system response time and delivery of Hotmail-to-Hotmail messages within five sec-onds. Every Hotmail Web server was backed up by hot standby and hot swappable servers that immediately would pick up the workload in case of a failure.

Indeed, Microsoft cited technology as the main reason for its interest in Hotmail. Hotmail had proven that its technology and systems could handle an enormous amount of e-mail, and could easily handle even more.

Another round of service slowdowns was caused by "vicious attacks from e-mail marketers using the service to deliver unsolicited electronic mail."[12] After numerous user complaints about junk e-mail, Hotmail developed several methods to help users deal with junk e-mail, or so-called spamming.[13] For example, users were provided with filters that redirected junk mail directly to the trash bin. Additionally, Hotmail installed automatic controls that observed the mailing behavior of individual customers.

GROWTH AND COMPETITION

Hotmail grew very quickly, attracting thousands of new users daily (see Exhibit 7.1).[14] By July 1997, Hotmail had over 5 million subscribers, making it the largest e-mail provider in the world after America Online (AOL). The site generated more than 8 million page impressions per day and had 30,000 new users sign up daily.[15] It was reported that 25 per-cent of free mail users logged on every day and 50 percent logged on every week, mak-ing the business even more attractive in terms of eyeballs for advertising dollars.[16]

While Hotmail was establishing its presence as a free Web-based e-mail provider, it had a number of competitors in the market who were segmented into Web-based e-mail providers and Internet service providers (see Exhibit 7.2).

Web-Based E-Mail Providers

Juno was a service launched in April 1996, just three months prior to Hotmail, and offered customers a free e-mail account.[17] This solution required users to install software

EXHIBIT 7.1 Subscribers

	Total Number of Subscribers	New Subscribers per Day
July 1996	20,000	
August 1996	75,000	3,000
October 1996	250,000	8,000
November 1996	500,000	10,000
January 1997	1,200,000	12,000
March 1997	2,000,000	20,000
July 1997	5,000,000	30,000
September 1997	6,500,000	40,000
October 1997	8,500,000	60,000

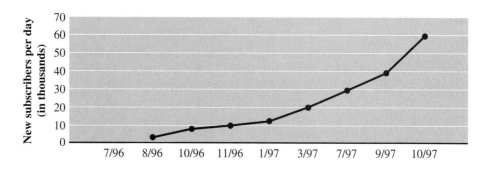

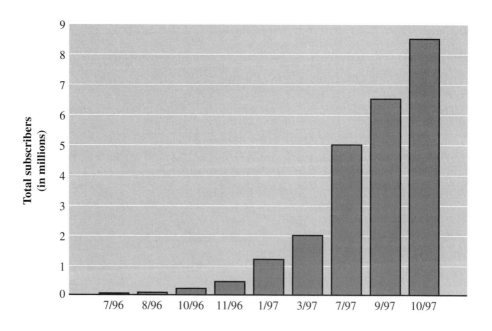

and use a dial-in modem in order to access the e-mail account. Therefore, unlike Hotmail users who were required to have their own Internet access, Juno users received the access as part of the offering, but this access could be used for e-mail purposes only.[18] In terms of user characteristics, 40 percent of Hotmail's users were international compared to Juno's strictly domestic user population. Demand for free e-mail was so great that in early 1997 Juno had to limit the number of new subscribers.[19] By October 1997 Juno had about 3 million subscribers. In November 1997 Juno struck a marketing alliance with Market Facts. Market Facts was attracted to Juno for one major reason. Juno claimed that its own subscriber base visited its site with more frequency than competing subscriber bases.

Four 11, an Internet white pages directory of e-mail addresses, launched a free Web-based e-mail service in March 1997.[20] The service was named RocketMail and had a user base of 700,000 by September 1997 with 7,000 new users a day. DFJ, the same venture capital group that sponsored Hotmail, supported the company. The service was acquired by Yahoo! in October 1997 for almost $100 million.

Other Web-based e-mail providers included iName, which began offering free e-mail in mid-1996.[21] WhoWhere launched its Web-based free e-mail in March 1997 and reported more than 1 million users by December 1997. WhoWhere partners with other websites, one of which is Excite. The Excite Web engine launched its own version of free e-mail, MailExcite, in July 1997 and had established a user base of 100,000 in just two months. USA.Net launched NetAddress, a Web-based e-mail service, in April 1996 and had almost 2 million members by December 1997. The NetAddress service also would forward messages to any other e-mail account, a feature not available on Hotmail.[22]

ISPs/OSPs

As of late 1997 AOL, Microsoft Network, and CompuServe were the largest e-mail providers. These companies were ISPs that allocated an e-mail account to any customer that purchased Internet access. Their revenue model differed since their accounts were based primarily on subscriptions that cost between $10 and $20 a month.[23] The service is also limited since a user can only access his account from a specific machine.

EXHIBIT 7.2 Competitors

Company	Product	Description	Revenue Model	Date Launched	Number of Questions New Subscribers Must Answer to Get an Account
America Online	ISP	ISP	Subscriptions + Ad	1985	(a)
CompuServe	ISP	ISP	Subscriptions + Ad	1979 (b)	(a)
Juno	Juno	Free e-mail	Ad	April 1996	20
USA.Net	NetAddress	Web-based	Ad	April 1996	None
Hotmail	Hotmail	Web-based e-mail	Ad	July 1996	5
Four11	RocketMail	Web-based	Ad	March 1997	5
WhoWhere	WhoWhere	Web-based	Ad	March 1997	(a)

(a) Information not available.
(b) Date when it began offering e-mail to personal computers.

With the free Web-based e-mail market heating up with an increasing number of competitors and consolidation in the industry, Hotmail had to figure out quickly how it should continue to grow and achieve profitability. One option was to merge with a large portal such as Microsoft's MSN. Microsoft had much to gain through a marriage with Hotmail. Up to this point, Microsoft had only 2.3 million subscribers and was one of the few portals without a free Web-based e-mail system. At the same time Microsoft offered services such as travel and car purchases for its customers. Hotmail's list of subscribers and market information would provide Microsoft with the ability to expand its market reach and tailor its services.

Hotmail's second option was to go public. Major e-mail competitors such as AOL and CompuServe were public and had deep pockets from the cash generated from the IPO and their own valuable stock currency to market their services and buy smaller companies. A third option was to remain private. Hotmail's competitors, Juno, USA.Net, and WhoWhere, each remained private and continued to thrive. The very independent Hotmail founders could continue to control and build their company.

Bhatia and Smith shifted in their seats. Should they consider Microsoft's offer of over $200 million and risk losing the company's independence? Or should they try to go public or remain private? For the company's very survival, they knew that they had to expand the firm quickly and either develop partnerships or risk giving away potential profits to the growing number of competitors.

REFERENCES

1. Steve Young and John Defterros, "President of Hotmail Discusses Recent Investor Interest," *Digital Jam,* October 16, 1997.
2. Po Bronson, "What's the Big Idea?" *Stanford Magazine,* September–October 1999, www. stanfordalumni.org/jg/mig/news_magazine/magazine/sepoct99/articles/bhatia.html.
3. Janet Rae-Dupree, "Everlasting E-mail Will Help Pitch Products," *San Jose Mercury News,* August 26, 1996.
4. Ibid.
5. Luc Hatlestad, "Free Mail Explosion," *Red Herring,* no. 55 (June 1998), www.redherring. com/mag/issue55/explosion.html.
6. Pramit Mitra, "A Capital Idea," *Far Eastern Economic Review,* September 17, 1998.
7. Hatlestad, "Free Mail Explosion."
8. Ibid.
9. Ibid.
10. Gregory Dalton, "Custom Web Service-Business Moves Beyond ISP to Specialized Hosts," *Information Week,* August 4, 1997, p. 73; John T. Mulqueen, "From Selling Web Access to Running Data Operations," *Communications Week,* April 21, 1997, p. 69.
11. Bronson, "What's the Big Idea?"
12. Lee Copeland, *Computer Reseller News,* January 12, 1998.
13. Sean Butterbaugh Wolfe, "Revamped Hotmail Hits 2 Million Users," *Media Daily,* February 28, 1997.
14. "E-mail Devotees," *Ad Week,* July 29, 1996, p. 94; "Hotmail Subscriber Base Doubles to 500,000 in One Month," *BusinessWire,* November 11, 1996; "Hotmail Corp," *InteractiveWeek,* July 14, 1997, p. 19; "Juno Survives Where Others Falter," *InteractiveWeek,* July 21, 1997, p. 28; "Hotmail Subscriber Base Tops One Million," *PR NewsWire,*

January 21, 1997; "Hotmail Is Now the Cyber Home to More than 2 Million Users: Popular Service Has New Architecture, Interface and Features," *PR NewsWire,* February 27, 1997; Young and Defterros, "President of Hotmail Discusses Recent Investor Interest"; Paul M. Eng, "E-mail: Fast, Fun and Now It's Free," *Business Week,* September 15, 1997, p. 68; Dupree, "Everlasting E-mail Will Help Pitch Products."

15. "Hotmail Celebrates One Year Anniversary and Five Million Users: Second Largest E-mail Provider in the World," *PR Newswire,* July 7, 1997.

16. Leslie Miller, "Supported by Ads, Free E-mail Is a Booming Business," *USA Today,* December 10, 1996.

17. Ibid.

18. Julia Angwin, "Another Free E-Mail Service Launched—Net Address," *San Francisco Chronicle,* December 3, 1996, www.sfgate.com/cgi-bin/article.cgi?file=/chronicle/archive/1996/12/03/ BU21357.DTL.

19. Joe Terranova, "Nielsen, Eat Your Heart Out," *Media Daily,* November 13, 1997; Wolfe, "Revamped Hotmail."

20. Eng, "E-mail: Fast, Fun and Now Its Free," p. 68.

21. Brian E. Taptich, "A Brief History of Web Mail," *Red Herring*, November 1998, www.redherring.com/may/issue60/mail.html.

22. Jamie Murphy, "Free E-mail Finds a Place on the Internet," *New York Times*, December 26, 1997, at search1.nytimes.com/search/daily/bin/fastweb?getdoc+site+site+126620+0+wAAA+netaddress.

23. Ibid.

GMBUYPOWER.COM: DEALER BEWARE

On May 29, 1997, Ann Blakney hung up the phone in her office in Thousand Oaks, California, and took a deep breath. She had faced many challenges in her 25-year career at General Motors (GM), including the last four years in California rebuilding GM's West Coast share. This latest assignment, however, could be her most challenging and highest profile project to date. She had just received a call from Ron Zarella, the VP of GM's North American vehicle sales, service, and marketing group. He had asked her to devise a way for GM to sell a significant volume of cars over the Internet, and had given her 90 days to have the service operational. Ann thought about the rapid growth of Internet-based automotive sales and information companies such as Auto-By-Tel and the threat they represented to the traditional way of doing business at the world's largest automaker. She also thought about the difficulties she would have convincing GM's dealers to support a sales tool that would effectively cut the average profit margin on each vehicle it sold.

GENERAL MOTORS AND THE AMERICAN AUTO INDUSTRY

The Origins of GM

The roots of General Motors can be traced back to 1886 and a ride hitched in a horse-drawn cart in a small Michigan lumber town. William Durant was so impressed with its innovative spring suspension that he bought the manufacturing rights and founded the Flint Road Cart Company. Thus were planted the seeds of what would eventually become the world's largest industrial corporation.

In 1903 troubled automobile manufacturer David Buick approached Durant for help. Always looking for new opportunities, Durant tested one of Buick's cars for three

---

months and subsequently bought the ailing company. Within three years, Buick's sales had risen from 37 to more than 8,000 cars per year.[1] This success cemented Durant's future strategy of aggressive growth through acquisitions and mergers.

By 1908 automakers were going in and out of business at a frenetic pace as tastes and technologies changed and standards emerged. Durant approached the heads of the other two major automotive manufacturers, Henry Ford and Ransom Olds. He proposed that the companies join together in a consortium as a buffer against the whims of the market. Henry Ford rejected a stock offer, preferring cash, but Ransom Olds accepted. The General Motors Company was incorporated with Buick and Oldsmobile as its first two divisions. Expansion continued over the next 10 years as GM acquired the Oakland Motor Car Company, Cadillac, and Chevrolet. By 1918 all of the modern-day divisions were in place, with the exception of Saturn. By 1927 GM was outselling Ford.[2]

The market for automobiles grew steadily over the next 50 years, and so did GM. The company expanded overseas, diversified its portfolio of businesses into radio and aircraft, and was a major contributor to the Allies' victory in World War II. The Big Three automakers, GM, Ford, and Chrysler, both fueled and prospered from the growth of the United States through the 20th century. As of 1997 General Motors was the largest company in the world by revenue, reporting $166 billion in sales and generating net income of $6.7 billion. The corporation employs 608,000 worldwide.[3] Exhibit 8.1 contains recent financial data.

EXHIBIT 8.1 Selected Financials of General Motors

	1997	1996	1995
	(in $ millions)		
Income			
Revenue	$166,445	$158,015	$163,861
Cost of goods sold	146,644	158,015	163,861
Gross profit	19,801	22,253	138,557
Gross profit margin	11.9%	14.1%	15.4%
SG & A expense	16,192	14,580	13,514
Operating income	3,609	7,673	11,789
Operating margin	2.2%	4.9%	7.2%
Net income	6,698	4,963	6,880
Net profit margin	4.0%	3.1%	4.2%
Full diluted earnings per share	8.62	6.02	7.14
Balance Sheet			
Cash	$ 11,262	$ 14,063	$ 11,044
Net receivables	66,363	66,614	68,720
Inventories	12,102	11,898	11,529
Current assets	101,449	100,774	96,892
Assets	228,888	222,142	217,123
Short-term debt	51,055	47,226	46,648
Current liabilities	66,837	61,447	58,547
Long-term debt	41,972	38,074	36,674
Liabilities	211,382	198,724	193,777
Common stock equity	17,505	23,417	23,344

Source: Hoover's Online.

Automakers Develop the Franchise System, 1900–1950

The original automobile manufacturers were small companies that applied their scarce capital to the development and manufacture of new products. Lacking the resources necessary to establish fully owned nationwide distribution networks, auto manufacturers turned to entrepreneurs to be the retail dealers of their products. What emerged was a franchised distribution system created out of a highly fragmented network of independent businesses.

The franchise system was based on loose sales and service agreements that gave dealers flexibility in the day-to-day operations of their businesses in return for a steady supply of vehicles to sell. The agreements gave automakers power over the dealers through the control of product supply, as well as the right to grant and revoke franchises. The system satisfied both sides as demand for cars grew steadily through the 1920s and 1930s.

Demand for new automobiles surged after World War II and by 1950, U.S. vehicle demand was at full production capacity. The Big Three were able to dictate terms to their dealers who complied to ensure a steady supply of new vehicles. Manufacturers used this power to force dealers to hold bloated inventories of cars and parts, purchase expensive repair tools, and contribute to national advertising funds that did little for local sales. Dealers that did not comply could be punished by having new competition licensed in their territories or their franchises canceled.

The Courts Shift Power to Dealers, 1950–1960

As the postwar boom subsided, it became increasingly difficult for dealers to pass on the financial burden of the automakers' demands to the consumer. The National Automobile Dealers Association (NADA), founded in 1917, intensified its government lobbying effort for a check on the power of the automakers. The Automobile Dealer's Day in Court Act of 1956 was passed after a U.S. Senate subcommittee investigation. This legislation outlawed many of the automakers' most aggressive tactics such as withholding product supply and dumping car and spare parts inventory. Perhaps more importantly, individual states were emboldened to pass their own acts expanding and refining their dealer franchise laws. One result of these legislative initiatives was that automakers in the United States are not allowed to sell their vehicles directly to end users. Even large fleet sales had to be channeled through dealers.

Under this new regulatory environment, dealers and manufacturers were bound by state and federal franchise laws, which superseded historic sales and service agreements. Automakers lost the power to strip dealers of their franchises and could no longer seriously punish dealers for low sales volume, poor customer service ratings, or substandard facilities. Automakers also lost the right to veto the sale or transfer of a dealership except to known felons.

The Industry Matures, 1960–1990s

Throughout the 1960s and 1970s, growth in overall demand buoyed dealer profitability, but by the 1980s, annual sales growth had slowed to 1.1 percent. Demand in the United States was expected to follow population trends as the U.S. market was mature and most households requiring a car already had one. As overall growth slowed, dealers turned to other methods to boost revenues. Many dealers entered new franchise agreements to represent additional brands.

The 1990s brought increased pressure on dealer and manufacturer margins, as it became difficult to differentiate between automobiles on quality or style. Quality had been improving across the industry since the mid-1980s. Accelerated design and development processes had greatly reduced the time period in which a company could enjoy an advantage from innovative technology and styling. In 1991 the Big Three's average model was over five years old. In 2001 the average model is expected to be just over three years old.

The automotive distribution system did not change significantly from 1960 to 1990, though the number of dealers declined. The decline in dealerships can be largely attributed to the marginalization of dealers in response to changing American demographics. By 1990, 80 percent of the U.S. population lived in metropolitan areas, compared with 63 percent in 1960.[4]

The Purchase Experience

Traditionally, purchasing a new car from a dealer involves going to several dealerships to compare models, test-drive cars, and negotiate prices. Customers generally work with a single sales representative at each dealer while choosing a model and options based on personal taste, availability, and price. The sales representative negotiates not only the car price, but also the trade-in price, financing fees, extended warranty or service contract costs, and other licensing and processing fees. It is common for a customer to obtain a rock-bottom purchase price only to have the dealer increase the margin on one of these other products. Customers often visit multiple dealers representing the same automaker in an attempt to get the car they want at the best price.

Although product quality has increased over time, customer satisfaction with the sales and service processes has not kept pace. Average car quality has improved by over 40 percent since 1989, while customer satisfaction with the purchase process has improved by about 20 percent.[5] Conventional wisdom has most consumers ranking purchasing a car right up there with a trip to the dentist. The largest contributor to this dissatisfaction is the negotiating process. Currently, 85 percent of franchised dealers still practice negotiated selling. Most of these dealers compensate salespeople heavily on the profit they are able to extract from the customer.

NEW DISTRIBUTION MODELS

CarMax

In 1991 the management at Circuit City Stores, Inc., began to contemplate ways in which the company could sustain growth once its electronics superstores business matured. They decided to apply the retail skills learned in the electronics business to another fragmented consumer durable goods market, automobile sales. Circuit City quickly found that state franchise laws and manufacturer relationships would inhibit them from dealing in the new car market. Based on market research indicating widespread dissatisfaction with the vehicle purchase process and the dealership experience as a whole, Circuit City developed a new sales model for used vehicles. The first Car-Max was opened in Richmond, Virginia, in 1993 and introduced the public to a new way of buying cars, the auto retailing superstore.

The CarMax model is different from the traditional dealership in several ways. CarMax stores are larger, offer a wider selection, and employ a no-haggle pricing strategy. Each car acquired by CarMax is reconditioned as necessary, is within a specified age and mileage range, and is guaranteed after purchase. CarMax sales representatives receive a salary and a bonus based on unit sales and customer satisfaction, not dealer margin.

CarMax planned to cover much larger territories with its superstores. For example, the entire Atlanta area supports 135 franchised dealerships and over 440 independent used car dealers, but was covered by only three CarMax superstores.

AutoNation

The most aggressive competitor to CarMax is AutoNation, a superstore chain started by Wayne Huizenga's Republic Industries. Huizenga is famous for his success in driving consolidation in the video rental industry with Blockbuster Video. AutoNation's business model is to establish a single retailer that provides the complete range of automotive products and services, including new and used car sales, finance, insurance, rental services, parts and accessories, and maintenance. Unlike CarMax, AutoNation plans aggressive growth through acquisition, and has purchased numerous new and used car dealerships, several car rental companies, and has formed its own finance company. AutoNation plans to have 2 or 3 used car megastores and 9 to 10 new vehicle superstores in each major metropolitan market. Responding to AutoNation, CarMax has also purchased several new car dealerships.

ONLINE AUTO RETAILING

A Challenge to the Dealer Model

Another more radical model for the sale of automobiles, online auto retailing, is having a profound effect on the industry. The detailed dealer cost data provided by these sites removes the asymmetry of information between buyer and seller that has for so long allowed dealers to extract the maximum economic rent from each customer. In the traditional process, the customer started at the vehicle sticker price and negotiated downward to his or her best price, unsure of the true dealer margin. The average buyer left the lot wondering whether or not he or she had obtained a fair price for the new car from a crafty and experienced sales staff.

The initial impact of the Internet was to provide shoppers with immediate access to information about the actual price paid by the dealer to the auto manufacturer for the automobile. Included on the sites were not only vehicle invoice costs, but also the arcane credits and rebates typically offered by automakers that determine the dealer's true cost. The customer was now armed to negotiate a fair margin above true cost with the dealer.

Newer, more sophisticated online models have further reduced the necessity to negotiate the sales price. The customer now can use these sites to receive price quotes directly from dealers. These sites also typically sell complementary products such as automotive financing and insurance. A buyer specifies the type of vehicle and the options he or she desires online and receives a best-price quote from a participating dealer. The customer then makes the trip to the dealer to execute the transaction and take delivery of the vehicle. The leading sites contain a comprehensive selection of vehicles from multiple manufacturers' product lines, allowing buyers to compare features and receive quotes on several types of cars. This process allows customers to feel confident that they have negotiated a fair price for the vehicle and eliminates the stressful and unpleasant good cop/bad cop negotiations with the sales representative and his offstage and perpetually displeased Loch Ness Monster, the "sales manager."

Online referral services offer various pay structures and levels of training to participating dealers. Many of these services sign an exclusive agreement with dealers in a particular region and charge start-up fees of up to $6,500, and monthly fees of $300 to $9,000.[6] Many also provide training in computer literacy and sales (see Exhibit 8.2). The auto manufacturer's margin is unchanged by this new structure. The online companies in effect return a portion of the dealers' profit margin to the customer and charge dealers a fee into the bargain. The dealer would rather book the sale at a reduced margin than see it funneled to a competitor. Additionally, the dealer does recoup some of the lost margin by realizing savings on sales commissions for these transactions. Finally, if the dealer has an exclusive referral agreement for his or her brand in a territory, a portion of the online customers are incremental to the dealership because otherwise customers would have bought their vehicles from a competitor's lot.

Dealer Margins Are Squeezed

The Internet reduces dealer control over vehicle purchases. Because consumers can more easily research dealer cost, dealers wind up with lower profit margins. On average, the gross profit drops to $100 to $200 when a customer has shopped the Internet. Some dealers feel that they are deriving significant profit from the Web despite a lower margin per unit. Bruce Bendell, president of Major Automobile Group based in Long Island, New York, says Internet shoppers represent 12 percent of the 400 new vehicles he sells each month.[7] He acknowledges that the Internet lowers gross profits, but these are offset by reductions in advertising costs. He pegs the cost of promoting cars online at $25 to $75 per unit, far less than the $300 to $500 it takes to market a car through conventional channels.[8]

For many dealers such as Pat Condrin, who owns a Cadillac-Oldsmobile-Subaru dealership in Altoona, Pennsylvania, new car sales were always close to a break-even proposition. He relies on his service department for the bulk of his profit. Pat feels that online auto sales have little value to his dealership: "You sell a car to a guy 200 miles

EXHIBIT 8.2 Online Referral Services Fees and Training, 1997

	Auto-By-Tel	AutoWeb	CarPoint	AutoVantage	CarSmart	Stoneage Corp.
Start-up fee	$2,500–6,500	None	$2,500	None	$800–1,500	$495
Monthly fee	$500–2,500	$475–975	$600–1,600	$6,000–9,000	$300–750	$20/lead
Training	2-day on-site 3-day at headquarters	Regional seminars, manual	Training thru Reynolds & Reynolds	On-site training by request, manual	On-site as needed, manual	No formal training

Source: Automotive News survey, 1997.

away for invoice and then never see the guy again. You are not really getting a customer. A lot of our future is in fixed operations." Although dealers may disagree on the benefits of online auto sales, none will disagree that the Internet will change their business. The top four online auto sales sites, Auto-By-Tel, AutoVantage, Autoweb.com, and Carpoint, estimate that they generate about 702,000 new vehicle sales a year; this already represents 5 percent of annual new unit sales volume.[9]

Auto-By-Tel

Auto-By-Tel was started in 1995 by Peter Ellis, a former automobile dealer who owned 16 dealerships throughout California and Arizona. Forced into bankruptcy during the automotive sales recession of the early 1990s, Ellis had a vision for a new type of automotive showroom on the Internet without the expensive overhead of traditional bricks-and-mortar facilities. He enlisted a partner, OSP Prodigy Services, Inc., and together they rolled out a site which generated 1,300 auto sales by its fourth day.[10]

In 1996 the company received 345,000 purchase requests through its site and had 1,206 subscribed dealerships. In early 1997 Auto-By-Tel was receiving 55 million hits a month on its site and had over 1.2 million unique customers. Auto-By-Tel provides training and support, real-time sales reports to dealer management, and requires dealers to contact customers within 24 hours of a purchase request. In addition to car sales, Auto-By-Tel partners with American International Group (AIG) and Chase Manhattan Bank to sell vehicle insurance and auto financing online. Despite the convenience of one-stop shopping and additional value-added services, Auto-By-Tel still has not shown a profit due to high expenditures in marketing and technology development (see Exhibit 8.3).[11]

AutoWeb.Com

AutoWeb.com is an online broker founded in Santa Clara, California, in 1994. AutoWeb allows users to research new and used cars for purchase, as well as advertise vehicles

EXHIBIT 8.3 Auto-By-Tel: Selected Financials

		Three Months Ended				
	December 31, 1995	March 31, 1996	June 30, 1996	September 30, 1996	December 31, 1996	Year Ended December 31, 1996
Revenues	$ 274	$ 436	$ 952	$ 1,434	$ 2,203	$ 5,025
Operating expenses:						
Marketing and advertising	476	475	678	1,247	2,039	4,439
Selling, training, and support	454	362	563	851	1,417	3,197
Technology development	99	67	78	294	954	1,393
General administrative	275	134	258	740	1,027	2,159
Total operating expenses	1,304	1,038	1,577	3,132	5,437	11,184
Other income (expense) net:	—	—	(6)	22	108	124
Net loss:	$(1,030)	$(602)	$(631)	$(1,676)	$(3,126)	$(6,036)

Source: Company financial statements and case writer estimates.

for sale. The company's "AutoWeb Affiliate" program pays participating online part-ners a commission for each customer sent by hotlink who either completes a purchase request or advertises a vehicle for sale. AutoWeb provides a fee-based service to par-ticipating dealers, allowing them to access data on the site's customers and receive sta-tistics on local demand for used vehicles. AutoWeb partners with State Farm Insurance and NationsBank to sell automotive insurance and financing. In 1997 AutoWeb had 750 participating dealerships and expected rapid dealer membership growth driven by a new "fee-per-lead" pricing structure.[12]

CarPoint

Microsoft Corporation founded CarPoint in 1995 as a feature site on its new Microsoft Network (MSN) portal. It was originally introduced as an informational website where prospective car buyers could see a 360-degree view of over 900 car models and check "spec sheets" provided by auto manufacturers.[13] Users could compare similarly priced cars, use the site's loan calculator to compute monthly payments, and locate dealers with a regional search feature. Customers were able to request detailed road test reports from partner IntelliChoice and were directed to partner Auto-By-Tel if they wished to purchase a vehicle. The disappointing initial operating results were attributable prima-rily to the low overall interest in MSN. In 1997 there were 560 new vehicle and 800 used vehicle dealerships participating in Microsoft's CarPoint service.[14] Subsequently, the site was redesigned in cooperation with Reynolds & Reynolds, a manufacturer of automotive dealer back-office software, into a stand-alone online buying service for vehicles, insurance, and financial services in the manner of Auto-By-Tel.

Kelley's Blue Book

Kelley Blue Book (KBB), the long-time publisher of automotive pricing guides, intro-duced an Internet site in July 1996. KBB online provides users with information on new car manufacturers' suggested retail prices and used-car retail and trade-in values. Users have access to the values of more than 15,000 types of cars, trucks, and vans covering most popular models of the past 21 years.[15] In the first six weeks of operation, the site received requests for over 1 million used-car reports from its database. The site generates revenue from advertisers and a fee-based service that allows customers to trace the title history of a car based on the vehicle identification number. KBB online has successfully levered the ubiquitous Blue Book brand to generate impressive traffic to the site.[16]

AUTO MANUFACTURERS ON THE WEB

Ford and Chrysler

Currently, neither Ford nor Chrysler offers buying services on their websites, follow-ing instead a strictly informational model. Ford encourages its dealers to use the Web as a supplement to traditional marketing efforts and provides technical and creative assistance to dealers in establishing sites.[17] Chrysler runs banner ads to promote its new car models and has recognized the value of Web advertising and promotions. Chrysler rewards its 5-star customer satisfaction dealerships with three free home pages on the

Chrysler.com website.[18] Customers visiting the corporate site are shown a list of the eight dealers closest to their location, highlighting the 5-star service award winners. Both Ford and Chrysler are experiencing heavy traffic volume on their corporate websites and are encouraging dealers to take advantage of marketing opportunities online.

Toyota

Foreign car manufacturers began to introduce multilingual online sites in late 1995. One of the pioneers was Toyota, the leading import brand in the United States, which offers its Toyota Internet Drive site in Japanese- and English-language versions. The site offers over 2,600 pages of information on Toyota's new vehicle models and data on Japan's automobile industry. Based on research indicating that over 56 percent of Toyota car owners and over 80 percent of luxury-division Lexus owners had access to a PC, Toyota has invested heavily in feature-rich CD-ROMs and online marketing campaigns to assist its dealers. In late 1996 a national Web development and corporate guideline training program was started across Toyota's 12 U.S. regions. As an additional feature, Toyota has partnered with international marketing and advertising giant Saatchi & Saatchi to add content on gardening, travel, sports, and other special interests in an effort to develop affinity groups centered around the @Toyota site.

Volvo

Swedish automaker Volvo has made the most innovative use of the Web. When the company launched its website in October 1994, it incorporated links from the corporate site to the Web pages of 50 of its 385 North American dealers. Volvo is a small manufacturer with an affluent, highly educated customer base that often uses the Internet. The company was a pioneer in adopting online content to complement and possibly reduce its reliance on expensive advertising. Sweden's lax dealer franchise laws have allowed Volvo to explore ways to eliminate costs by restructuring its traditional value chain using the Web.[19]

GM'S RESPONSE—GMBUYPOWER.COM

The Team

Ann Blakney began working for GM as a summer intern in 1974 while completing her MBA at Stanford and has spent the bulk of her career at the automaker in sales and marketing positions. Ann also has a bachelor's and master's degree in psychology. Charged with turning around GM's performance in California, which had long been a stronghold for imported cars, Blakney changed a number of long-standing dealer practices to improve the consumer purchase experience. She created the "Value Pricing" program to eliminate the unpopular haggling between the dealer and customer. Under this program cars are offered at a set price incorporating a moderate dealer margin (11 percent instead of 17 percent).[20] She also broke an industry taboo by putting independently compiled competitor price information in the showroom. This was a break with the existing unspoken rule to never say too much about the competition. These moves to develop a less adversarial purchase experience for the consumer have contributed to a 20 percent increase in sales and a 22 percent increase in GM's market share in California over the past four years.[21]

In the first days after Zarella's call, Blakney put together a team to undertake her new Internet assignment. She brought together six people with a variety of backgrounds to handle operations and technical issues, finance, field marketing (working with dealers), advertising, and public relations. It was decided to test the concept in four western states, California, Washington, Oregon, and Idaho. Technology development and website hosting was outsourced to former GM subsidiary Electronic Data Systems while website design was performed by Catalyst Resources.

The Process

The challenge of initiating GM's Internet sales program within 90 days meshed with Blakney's conviction that speed to market is critical for success in online sales. Blakney says of the Internet, "It's different from the traditional business model in which you evaluate all of the eventualities. You don't have time. You have to make a commitment of first to market, first to learn. It's much more aggressive."[22]

Blakney and her team envision one of the key roles of the site as providing an in-depth source of information about GM and competitor vehicles, allowing customers to research their options before entering the showroom. This concept differs from the accepted industry marketing philosophy, which seeks to entice the customer onto a dealer's lot where the sales department can close a sale. Blakney's goal was to empower online consumers with information that would streamline the buying process. She sought to create a competitive advantage for GM in attracting consumers who were using the Internet to escape the misery of the traditional vehicle purchase process.

Ninety-eight days into the project Blakney's team began the crucial process of enlisting dealer participation in the experiment. Blakney's team began an exhaustive road-show pitching to dealers across the four test states. It was very difficult to convince the dealers that it was a good idea to give your "best price" to consumers on the Internet. Each dealer that signed up had to have a salesperson trained in effective e-mail communication to handle the correspondence with customers. The team would eventually enroll dealers supplying 70 percent of GM's volume in the four-state region.

GMBuyPower.com was launched on October 27, 1997, just 137 days after its inception. The site was hyped with a blitz of Internet, print, radio, and TV advertising. The press had been introduced to the concept two weeks earlier, and GM set up a studio in Hollywood with a bank of PCs for reporters to try identifying, configuring, and pricing vehicles on the site.

The Website

GMBuyPower.com is currently active in four states: California, Washington, Oregon, and Idaho. GM's initial plan was to roll out the site to the rest of the country in the first quarter of 1999.

The website provides consumers with:

- Extensive vehicle information.
- Third-party competitive comparison.
- Access to dealer inventory.
- A personal message center to communicate with dealers.
- A "no-haggle" online list price good for 24 hours.
- GMAC financing options.

Consumers who visit the GMBuyPower.com site can browse through descriptions and specifications covering over 200 car models. Detailed information allows users to develop the option packages that they want to include on their target vehicle. The consumer can also view third-party competitive comparisons provided by the Automotive Information Center of their chosen car with similarly equipped cars from other manufacturers. Real-time inventory tracking allows buyers to locate dealers that have their ideal GM car in stock and then communicate with the dealer staff using online message forms. Finally, the consumer and the dealer can negotiate the terms of the transaction by e-mail. GMAC financing options are available and the customer can apply for credit online. The site even provides the buyer with directions to the dealer's showroom to pick up his or her new vehicle. "There's a very aggressive effort to give dealers the tools to meet the demands of customers in the Internet age," said Ann Blakney. "We offer dealers the ability to have a very sophisticated website and to be able to communicate in a way that customers have asked for." [23]

Results and Dealer Reaction

Many dealers and analysts have been disappointed with the performance of GMBuyPower.com. Only 60 percent of the total dealers in the four pilot states have signed on to the program and only 8,000 vehicle sales have been attributed to the website as of September 1998. [24]

One of the disappointed GM dealers who signed up for GMBuyPower.com has received eight leads which have generated only one sale in the 11 months the site has been active. This same dealer sells 15 cars a month through Auto-By-Tel. Jim Begier, general manager of Ben A. Begier Buick in San Leandro, California, believes that GM's long-term goal is to phase out privately owned dealerships in favor of company-owned facilities. However, Begier is convinced that car buyers prefer a more traditional approach. "BuyPower has been a failure. People still want to see, touch and feel a new car. GM is in denial on the whole thing." [25]

According to Boston Consulting Group consultant Oleg Khaykin, "GM is only recycling its existing customers on the Web. The only way that the website sells a car is if the consumer has already decided to buy a GM car." [26]

Whatever the reason, GM is underperforming its rivals online as evidenced by data provided by Auto-By-Tel (see Exhibit 8.4). Auto-By-Tel's founder Peter Ellis feels that GM needs the high-pressure sales techniques used by its traditional dealers to move GM products. A more charitable explanation may be that GM's traditional buyers are less likely to purchase cars over the Internet. Another faction of GM dealers believe that the company is not moving fast enough to capitalize on e-commerce opportunities. These dealers would prefer that GM satisfy its online customers with a corporate site rather than have these consumers give a piece of the margin to a third-party broker. They feel that developing online auto retailing in cooperation with GMBuyPower offers the best means to preserve their profit margins. [27]

EXHIBIT 8.4 Sales as a Percentage of U.S. Auto Market

	Toyota	Honda	GM	Chrysler
U.S. market	8.0%	7.0%	31.0%	16.0%
Auto-By-Tel sales	12.0	12.0	19.0	18.5

Source: "Can General Motors Learn to Love the Net?" *Business 2.0,* September 1998.

As Ann heads out of town for Memorial Day weekend, she is thinking about the whirlwind events of the past year. On balance she feels that the results to date have been inconclusive. Certainly the site has not been as effective as Auto-By-Tel, but the company has gained valuable online sales experience. Stuck in Los Angeles traffic, Ann has time to reflect on the big picture issues that surround her efforts. Should GM be developing its own site or working with existing brokers? What opportunities do online sales offer to restructure other areas of the business? Is an online auto store that offers only one automaker's products a compelling model for consumers? If online sales weaken GM's traditional dealer network, what will it mean for the company? Ann doesn't have all the answers, but she does know that the way the industry sells cars is being fundamentally transformed by this new technology. Unless changes are made to existing federal legislation, GM will continue to rely on dealers to retail its vehicles. However, the auto industry would dearly love to cut the estimated $100 billion tied up in new car inventory across the nation.

REFERENCES

1. www.gmcanada.com, accessed 1998.
2. Ibid.
3. www.gm.com, accessed 1998.
4. U.S. Census Bureau.
5. J. D. Power Associates.
6. *Automotive News,* January 12, 1998.
7. Ibid.
8. *Automotive News,* February 2, 1998.
9. *Automotive News,* January 26, 1998.
10. "Auto-By-Tel Drives Car Shoppers through the Internet," *Bank Technology News,* October 1998.
11. Ibid.
12. "AutoWeb Doubles Dealer Count with per Lead Fees," *Automotive News*, August 17, 1998.
13. "Microsoft Pitches Auto Mall on the Web," *Automotive News*, July 21, 1997.
14. "CarPoint Revs Up to Overtake Rivals," *Automotive News,* October 12, 1998.
15. "Smart Sellers, Buyers Use Kelley Blue Book in Their Automotive Dealings," *Sacramento Bee,* September 19, 1996.
16. "Kelley Blue Book Sets Up on the Internet," *Ward's Auto World,* January 1997.
17. "Court: Ford Had Right to Veto Dealership Sale," *Automotive News,* March 25, 1996; "Surf's Up: Ford Dealers Hit the Web," *Automotive News,* June 10, 1996.
18. "Chrysler Web Touts Best–CSI Dealers," *Automotive News,* February 24, 1997.
19. "Volvo Starts Selling on the Net," *Automotive News Europe,* May 25, 1998.
20. "GM on the Web," *San Francisco Chronicle,* September 9, 1998.
21. "Can General Motors Learn to Love the Net?" *Business 2.0,* September 1998.
22. Ibid.
23. "GM Revs Up Web Sales," *San Francisco Chronicle,* September 9, 1998.
24. "Heard on the Beat; GM Expands Online," *Los Angeles Times,* September 28, 1998.
25. "GM Revs Up Web Sales."
26. "Can General Motors Learn to Love the Net?"
27. Ibid.

*i*VILLAGE: INNOVATION AMONG WOMEN'S WEBSITES

Candice Carpenter, Cofounder and CEO of *i*Village, looked out the window of her New York City office and reflected on the stunning achievements of her company. The women's online network had experienced an extremely successful initial public offering (IPO), raising approximately $292 million in market value on its first day of trading in March 1999. *i*Village, having established a name for itself as the ultimate women's online resource, had reached a pivotal moment in its growth cycle. However, over the last four months, competition was heating up.

Three of the most powerful women in entertainment had teamed up to form Oxygen Media, a new company set up to offer integrated media and entertainment services by broadcasting over different channels. Launched in 1998 by Geraldine Laybourne, Oxygen, like *i*Village, recognized the value of this powerful and growing consumer audience. However, in addition to offering a stand-alone website, Oxygen planned to launch a cable station on January 1, 2000. Oxygen's long-term business model was highly innovative in that it revolved around convergence of the Web with television. The firm's website was slated to go online May 1, 1999.

Knowing that *i*Village's current business model would not create the sustainable revenues Carpenter needed, she speculated on what to say to the new stockholders at their first meeting the following morning. How should *i*Village innovate its product offering in the face of new competitive threats, notably Oxygen's arrival, and not alienate its current customer base? Carpenter started outlining ideas for product development.

THE CHANGING FACE OF THE MEDIA INDUSTRY

Since the Internet has infiltrated the home and become increasingly popular, it has redefined the role of media on a massive scale. The number of Internet users is estimated to

New York University Stern School of Business MBA Candidates Carol Foley, Falguni Pandya, Anne Shiva, Jonathan Singer, and H. Dassi Weinstein prepared this case under the supervision of Professor Christopher L. Tucci for the purpose of class discussion rather than to illustrate either effective or ineffective handling of an administrative situation. Copyright © 2001 by McGraw-Hill/Irwin. All rights reserved.

reach approximately 320 million by the end of 2002.[1] The widespread acceptance of the Internet, its low-cost infrastructure, and the nature of its interactivity have raised an uproar of excitement throughout the world by allowing anyone who has access to a computer and modem to establish a presence on the Internet. Moreover, worldwide commerce revenue on the Internet is expected to increase to more than $425 billion in 2002.[2]

In the wake of the Internet phenomenon, traditional media are going through a shakedown. Since the Internet can serve purposes that other media have served in the past, as well as offer entirely new functions of e-commerce, distribution, and interactivity, traditional media have had to refocus their approach in order to retain audiences. The Internet, however, has not managed to replace another media. Rather, it is blurring the lines between different forms of media, forcing traditional radio stations, magazines, newspapers, and broadcast TV stations to build a presence in other media channels. These traditional forms focus more heavily on the strength and "elasticity" (the suitability for different forms and end-user devices) of their content in order to retain their audiences.[3] In this respect, those who have a hold on a specific content niche are dominating the new paradigm. *i*Village has created a dominant brand that has a strong hold on a specific niche market—women aged 25 to 49.

WOMEN AS A MARKET

According to the Women's Consumer Network, women control 85 percent of all personal and household goods spending. Women also consume more media than men per day (8.8 hours versus 8.2 hours), and they currently account for 43 percent of Internet and online service users. In addition, women comprise 57 percent of new Internet service provider subscribers.

Moreover, according to an *i*Village Women's Net Monitor poll taken in February 1998, the Internet is no longer a place to gather information passively; rather, women are using it to actively solve real problems. The poll was conducted with 700 online respondents, split between men and women. Once on the Web, more women than men met and kept new friends. In addition, more women rated the online community as an important part of their lives.

An *i*Village online survey conducted in 1999 revealed that 77 percent of women go online primarily to explore, but 86 percent stay because they find information that helps them get through their daily lives. The survey results validated what *i*Village has believed from the beginning.

Bearing in mind these statistics, we can understand why women's websites have grown and flourished. In the last few years, three dominant players have emerged: *i*Village, Women.com, and the latest, Oxygen Media, Inc. Each company in its own way has attempted to capitalize on this powerful niche market.

THE COMPETITION

Carpenter is concerned about emerging threats from other online start-ups that are targeting women such as Oxygen Media, Inc., and Women.com. Allison Abraham, *i*Village's chief operating officer, commenting on the competition, said that "We must stay focused as opportunities are ours to keep."[4]

Women.com

Women.com, partly owned by Hearst New Media and Technology, a subsidiary of the publishing giant, was originally founded as a content site. During the creation of the Women.com site, the firm was able to exploit Hearst's rich database on women customers. Like other women's sites, Women.com evolved to have some community features, and most recently, has started a small commerce venture.

Oxygen Media, Inc.

Oxygen Media, Inc., backed by strong media personalities and heavy investors, has generated a wave of interest partly because of its innovative approach to satisfying women's needs. It is a multimedia company, aimed primarily at women, and combines the entertainment power of television with the power of the Internet to create interactive television. The combination of Oxygen online and Oxygen cable is a futuristic, visionary approach that will shape the future of the new media industry. Its vision is to create a comprehensive "Home Base" for women online, which would go beyond the offerings of *i*Village. Oxygen's model is innovative, more comprehensive, and hard to imitate.

Oxygen Media was founded by Geraldine Laybourne, one of the most powerful women executives in the television industry. The formation of the Oxygen network for women represents a partnership between Laybourne, Oprah Winfrey, and the Carsey-Werner-Mandach production company. Oxygen Media also acquired investments from America Online (AOL) and ABC, a Disney company. Oxygen plans to raise revenue through charging operators license fees per subscriber and by attracting a broad range of advertisers and e-commerce partners.

WWW.*i*VILLAGE.COM

History

Cofounders CEO Candice Carpenter and editor-in-chief Nancy Evans established *i*Village in June 1995. Carpenter began thinking about the idea for *i*Village while working as a consultant to AOL. As a single mother of two children, Carpenter knew that "women today are so pragmatic and time-pressed that they use the Web to find out how to get things done."

The company, headquartered in New York City, humanizes cyberspace by providing a relevant online experience for women. Carpenter and Evans originally created a one-stop destination for women looking for information on topics such as children, health, and family. They developed a site that was primarily a content site without any intercommunication. However, because of the way women use the Internet and the site's dynamic information, *i*Village then evolved into an online community where members exchange advice and develop relationships. In this case, the consumers drove the site's innovation. The firm had to respond by further developing its offering to fit the needs and wants of its users.

Target Market

*i*Village is one of the most demographically targeted online communities on the Web. The network of sites is tailored to the interests and needs of women aged 25 through 49. The average household income of the *i*Village customer is $55,000; most are married, employed full-time, and have attended college—an attractive market segment for potential advertisers and sponsors (see Exhibit 9.1). As such, the site is recognized as a leader in developing innovative sponsorships and commerce relationships. This leadership position has been vital to the company's revenue growth to date.

Product

*i*Village.com is the world's largest online destination for women. By actively participating in the network's communities, members learn from experts and from each other, gain empowerment to find solutions, and inspire fellow members to handle everyday challenges more effectively. Candice Carpenter summed up the goal of *i*Village's offerings: "We strive to help women navigate through increasingly busy lives and maximize their potential in their various roles as parents, friends, spouses, partners, career women, breadwinners, employees, and individuals."[5]

*i*Village was the first company to offer this type of online product to women. Moreover, the firm has innovated its product offering into what could be called the "un-content" provider. The firm has developed its site into a community-oriented site from its original content-only product. Offering support groups, bulletin boards, and buddies, *i*Village has developed a community for every interest. *i*Village's current channels and sites include: Better Health, Career, Relationships, Food, ParentsPlace, Shopping, Fitness & Beauty, Work From Home, Travel, Pets, Astrology.net, Book Club, and Money Life. Also, *i*Village and Intuit, the makers of Quicken, launched Armchair Millionaire in an online partnership.

Beyond Armchair Millionaire, *i*Village offers little information on finance or world news, although it does offer a group of experts available for consultation on many topics. At any one time, there are some 1,400 ongoing discussion boards which bring together groups of like-minded women who share experiences or help each other solve problems. For example, the Work from Home section offers a software library filled with bookkeeping, billing, legal, payroll, and sales-lead shareware. From the Health page, members can access the huge store of medical information in its database. In contrast,

EXHIBIT 9.1 *i***Village Demographic Profile**

Gender	Female/Male	80%/20%
Age	Average	33.7
Household income	Average	$54,744
Marital status	Married	59.6%
	Living w/ partner	7.6%
	Single	21.7%
	Separated/divorced/widowed	11.2%
Employment status	Full-time	55.0%
	Part-time	9.7%
	Work from home	9.3%
	Unemployed	5.6%
	Full-time parent	8.7%
	Student	9.1%
	Retired	2.7%
Education	Attended/graduated college	61.2%
	Attended graduate school	6.4%
	Postgraduate degree	12.7%

competing aggregate sites tend to resemble traditional women's magazines, carrying mostly articles and lacking in any chat or message board functions.

Traffic

In terms of traffic, *i*Village is the most successful women's website. Traffic flow is vital because it is a concrete definition of success and future potential in current Internet business models. According to Relevant Knowledge, a Web measurement company, more than 2 million different visitors visited *i*Village sites during June 1998 alone. This was more than twice the traffic of its nearest competitor, Women.com. April 1998 statistics revealed that *i*Village has the largest reach (3.8 percent) of any women's site and it claims 65 million page views a month. Traffic to the site continues to increase exponentially.

Financial Issues

> A growing number of industry watchers and executives have begun to question how a volume-driven Internet can survive, let alone grow, when its native businesses can bring themselves to utter the "P" word only in the negative. "No profit for the foreseeable future" is now a boilerplate disclaimer in the prospectus of an Internet company preparing an initial stock offering.[6]
>
> — Susan Karlin, *Upside Magazine*

Like many companies based on the World Wide Web, *i*Village has yet to turn a profit. Indeed, it has accumulated a substantial deficit; the company is still spending more money than it brings in. Analysts surmise that the company's profitability is not a near-term goal; losses grew in 1998 to $43.7 million from $21.3 million in 1997 (see Exhibit 9.2). Clearly, accumulating losses are a consideration when reviewing and restructuring *i*Village's current business model.

*i*Village's Business Model

Like many new sites based on content and community, *i*Village generates most of its revenues by selling banners, text-links, and sponsorships from other business. As traffic, or volume, is the key to attracting advertising clients, this business model has become known as the "volume-based" model. This model, however, may not be sustainable. According to Jupiter Communications, Internet advertising is expected to total only $1 to $2 billion, or roughly 1 percent of the total advertising spending in the United States. Combined with this fact, more and more websites are competing for the same revenue dollars from advertisers. Along these lines, advertisers have become less willing to post ads on pages that are increasingly congested with other sponsors' banners and links. As such, pages are limited in the number of ads they can post, which in turn caps their ability to generate revenues.

This trend has forced most online companies to experiment with other revenue-generating models such as e-commerce. However, the e-commerce business model, too, has yet to be proven as a reliable means for generating profits. For instance, Amazon.com sells 2.5 million books over the Internet, yet it closed 1998 with $124.5 million in losses. However, in venturing into e-commerce, *i*Village maintains a distinct advantage. Whereas Amazon had to spend vast amounts of money marketing its product and service, *i*Village was able to launch *i*Baby with little or no promotion due to its existing customer base and online community. *i*Village should be able to capitalize on this advantage in future e-commerce ventures.

EXHIBIT 9.2 *i*Village Financials

	Income Statement		
	1998	**1997**	**1996**
Revenues:			
Sponsorship, advertising and usage	$ 12,450,620	$ 6,018,696	$ 732,045
Commerce	2,561,203	—	—
Total revenues	15,011,823	6,018,696	732,045
Operating expenses:			
Production, product and technology	14,521,015	7,606,355	4,521,410
Sales and marketing	28,522,874	8,770,581	2,708,779
General and administrative	10,612,434	7,840,588	3,103,864
Depreciation and amortization	5,683,006	2,886,256	108,956
Total operating expenses	59,339,329	27,103,780	10,443,009
Loss from operations	(44,327,506)	(21,085,084)	(9,710,964)
Interest income (expense), net	591,186	(215,876)	28,282
Loss on sale of website	(503,961)	—	—
Minority interest	586,599	—	—
Net loss	$(43,653,682)	$(21,300,960)	$(9,682,682)

	Balance Sheet	
	1998	**1997**
ASSETS		
Current assets:		
Cash and cash equivalents	$ 30,824,869	$ 4,334,721
Accounts receivable	3,147,561	2,199,520
Other current assets	715,161	153,985
Total current assets	34,687,591	6,688,226
Fixed assets, net	7,380,366	3,802,823
Goodwill and other intangible assets, net	4,535,148	5,598,233
Other assets	187,860	146,801
Total assets	$ 46,790,965	$ 16,236,083
LIABILITIES AND STOCKHOLDERS' EQUITY		
Current liabilities:		
Accounts payable and accrued expenses	$ 11,559,711	$ 3,989,945
Capital leases payable	136,573	247,943
Deferred revenue	2,909,740	1,004,199
Other current liabilities	162,859	332,531
Total current liabilities	14,768,883	5,574,618
Capital leases payable, net of current portion	—	139,346
Total liabilities	14,768,883	5,713,964
Stockholders' equity:		
Convertible series	21,851	9,486
Common stock	21,133	18,197
Additional paid-in capital	112,848,505	43,180,649
Accumulated deficit	(76,274,895)	(32,621,213)
Stockholders notes receivable	(565,000)	(65,000)
Unearned compensation and deferred advertising	(4,029,512)	—
Total stockholders' equity	32,022,082	10,522,119
Total liabilities and stockholders' equity	$ 46,790,965	$ 16,236,083

Source: Company SEC filings.

The Shift to E-Commerce

In March 1998, *i*Village ventured into electronic commerce with the acquisition of an online store, *i*Baby, a one-year-old online commerce success. This shift in revenue generation marked a milestone for *i*Village. The company began as a content site, evolved into a community site, and, with this latest move, has further developed its product to include e-commerce. *i*Village's latest product development was a clear response to heightening competition for sustainability and revenue.

*i*Baby delivered the most extensive selection of baby products and gift services worldwide. *i*Village was striving for a quick and convenient shopping experience for its consumers, offering more than 14,000 baby-related products, access to over 800 vendors, and a baby gift registry. Already, *i*Baby had a unique position as a young venture touting $1 million in sales and a database filled with thousands of loyal customers.

In the agreement, *i*Village offered *i*Baby more than 65 million page views per month, the ability to strategically target segments of its online communities to market *i*Baby's products, and an expertise in building compelling and functional online environments. *i*Baby brought to the table complementary areas of expertise such as product sourcing, established vendor relations, warehousing, inventory control, and customer service.

As a stand-alone business, *i*Baby would retain control of the inventory management and shipping operations to guarantee a top-quality experience for customers. This gave *i*Baby the ability to track both inventory and shipping flow precisely, efficiently, and effectively. Considering that e-commerce was outside of its original model, *i*Village's venture with *i*Baby was a first step toward further product innovation.

Carpenter viewed *i*Baby to be a strong step toward innovation into e-commerce. But how far should her company venture? Was *i*Village ready to make such a sharp turn in product development into a new area of business? Would it affect the existing community experience? How would its business model have to change? Carpenter knew that all of these issues had to be viewed in light of the competition. Every day new players were encroaching on *i*Village's territory.

LOOKING TO THE FUTURE

As Carpenter outlined her thoughts for the stockholders the next morning, she considered the events over the last four months. She needed to consider how growing competitive threats and dynamic customer needs would reshape *i*Village's revenue stream. The decision regarding product development into electronic commerce needed to be made soon.

REFERENCES

1. *i*Village website statistic: www.corporate-ir.net/ireye/ir_site.zhtml?ticker=IVIL&script =2100.
2. Ibid.
3. Lisa Allen, Bill Bass, Chris Charron, and Jill Aldort, "Old Media's New Role," *The Forrester Report,* vol. 3, no. 5, January 1999, p. 6.
4. Allison Abraham, "Internet Communities," Presentation in Electronic Commerce class, New York University, Stern School of Business, April 12, 1999.
5. Heather Green, "For Women, *i*Village is a Site of Their Own," *Business Week,* businessweek.com/1998/29/b3587126.htm, July 20, 1998.
6. Susan Karlin, "It Takes an *i*Village," *Upside Magazine,* www.upside.com/texis/mvm/ story?id=3665bcf40, December 2, 1998.

eBAY, INC.: DIVERSIFICATION IN THE INTERNET AUCTION MARKET

"eBay Agrees to Buy Butterfield & Butterfield"
—eBay press releases, April 26, 1999

"eBay Purchases Respected Automobile Auctioneer"
—eBay press releases, May 18, 1999

"eBay Halts Auction of Human Kidney; Bidding Had Reached $5.7 Million"
—CBS MarketWatch, September 2, 1999

"eBay Comes to Tampa-St. Petersburg With New Local Web Site"
—PR Newswire, October 27, 1999

"eBay Starts Business-to-Business Auctions"
—Reuters, November 4, 1999

Nineteen ninety-nine was a tremendous year for eBay, the champion of the person-to-person online auction business. Gross merchandise sales rose 280 percent, to $741 million from $195 million a year ago, and registered users jumped 509 percent, to 7.7 million from 1.3 million.[1] eBay has emerged as one of the leading Internet companies among online giants such as Amazon and Yahoo! However, given the increasingly competitive online auction market, Margaret C. Whitman, the CEO of eBay, knew that the battle ahead would not be easy. As she retraced the events that happened in the last six months, she pondered eBay's strategy to manage both the external competitive situation and the internal hypergrowth of the company.

Several issues were troubling Whitman. eBay had always focused on the person-to-person auction market. But given the recent hype about the growth prospects in the business-to-consumer (B2C) and business-to-business (B2B) markets, was eBay missing out on these opportunities? Besides, this year the company started pursuing a regional and international expansion strategy as well as an off-line strategy by purchasing two auction houses. Even if eBay did enter the new markets, would it be spreading itself too thin? How could it integrate these different ideas without losing focus on the core business? eBay's revenue model was another concern. Some competitors were relying on their retail revenue and offering auction services for free. Was eBay's main revenue stream from placement fees and commissions on transactions sustainable?

THE HISTORY OF eBAY

> We started with commerce, and what grew out of that was community.[2]
>
> —Meg Whitman, CEO of eBay

eBay was conceived initially as a result of a conversation between Pierre Omidyar, an engineer at General Magic, and his fiancée. His fiancée was an avid Pez collector and trader. She commented to Omidyar how great it would be if she were able to trade dispensers with other collectors over the Internet. As an early Internet enthusiast, Omidyar knew that people needed a central location to buy and sell unique items and to meet other users with similar interests. He started the first online auction website to fulfill this need.

With a BS in computer science from Tufts University and years of experience running start-ups, Omidyar was not a newcomer to the Internet industry (see Exhibit 10.1 for company biographies). He brought in his friend Jeff Skoll, a Stanford MBA, as the company's first president. Together, they wrote the company's first business plan and launched the first online auction service, Auction Web, on Labor Day in September 1995. Within a few weeks, buyers and sellers began flocking to the service as news of it spread by word of mouth. A few months of heavy traffic later, Omidyar realized he had a company on his hands and quit his job.[3]

Auction Web was incorporated in 1996 and changed its name to eBay in 1997, when it began promoting itself through banner ads and advertising. By the middle of that year, eBay was boasting nearly 800,000 auctions each day. eBay was profitable from the beginning and unsolicited offers from venture capitalists began to pour in. It secured a

EXHIBIT 10.1 eBay Management Biography

	Pierre Omidyar	**Jeff Skoll**	**Margaret C. Whitman**
Title	Founder	First president	Current CEO
Education	BS, computer science, Tufts University	MBA, Stanford University	MBA, Harvard University; BA, economics, Princeton University
Experience	Engineer, General Magic; Cofounder, Ink Development (online shopping)	Founder, Skoll Engineering (computer consultancy); Founder, Micros on the Move, Ltd. (computer rentals)	General manager, Hasbro; CEO, Florists Transworld Delivery (FTD); President, Stride Rite; Senior VP, Disney's Consumer Products unit; VP, Bain Consulting; Brand manager, Proctor & Gamble

Source: Red Herring.

$3 million round of venture financing from Benchmark Capital that it put in the bank and never touched. "We wanted a good mentor, not money," explained Jeff Skoll.[4]

In early 1998 Omidyar turned over the CEO position to Margaret ("Meg") Whitman, formerly of Bain Consulting, Procter & Gamble, Disney, StrideRite, FTD, and Hasbro, so he could concentrate on strategy. eBay's highly successful IPO occurred in September of that year. With heavy marketing through national advertising campaigns and alliances with America Online and WebTV, eBay had become a household name identified with the largest online auction trading community. The number of registered users had grown to more than 6 million (see Exhibit 10.2) and eBay was deemed the "stickiest" site on the Internet, according to the Nielsen/NetRatings research in the first quarter of 1999 (see Exhibit 10.3). One year after its initial public offering (IPO), eBay now had a market capitalization of $19 billion. Unlike most of the Internet start-ups, eBay was actually making a profit—$2.4 million on sales of $47.3 million in fiscal 1998 (see Exhibit 10.4 for eBay's quarterly financial statements).

287

CASE 10
eBay, Inc.:
Diversification in
the Internet Auction
Market

HOW DOES eBAY WORK?

Online Auction Mechanism

Functioning as an Internet-based garage sale, consumers participate in eBay's online trading community for four main reasons: It's fun, you meet people with similar interests, you get a great deal (most of the time), and you find valuable collectibles. Goods are sold through an auction that lasts several days. Many bids are usually garnered for each item. Each day, more than 2 million new auctions are conducted and over 200,000 new items are listed.

EXHIBIT 10.2 Number of eBay Registered Users

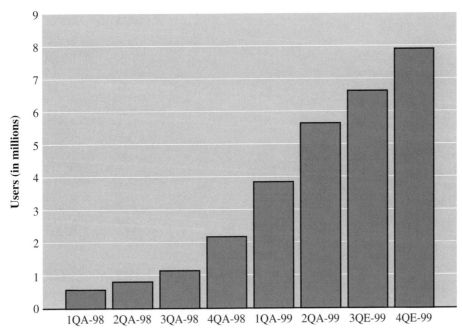

Source: Deutsche Banc Alex. Brown estimates; company reports.

EXHIBIT 10.3 "Stickiest" Online Activities

Property	Type	Monthly Rank Time Spent (hours:minutes:seconds)	By Unique Audience	Pages per Person
eBay	Auction	3:08:19	17	233
Yahoo!	Portal	1:02:34	2	75
MSN	Portal	1:00:03	3	48
Uproar	Gaming	0:44:21	65	33
The Excite Network	Portal	0:33:10	7	30
AOL sites	Portal	0:32:01	1	24
Prodigy	Portal	0:31:47	56	11
Knight Ridder Real Cities Network	Newspapers	0:29:18	59	22
GO Network	Portal Plus	0:27:46	5	27
CNN	News	0:26:43	20	25

Source: Nielsen/NetRatings, March 1999.

EXHIBIT 10.4A eBay, Inc., Annual Financials

eBAY INC.
CONSOLIDATED STATEMENT OF INCOME
(in thousands, except per share amounts)

	Year Ended December 31,		
	1996	1997	1998
Net revenues	$ 372	$ 5,744	$ 47,352
Cost of net revenues	14	746	6,859
Gross profit	358	4,998	40,493
Operating expenses:			
Sales and marketing	32	1,730	19,841
Product development	28	831	4,606
General and administrative	45	950	9,080
Amortization of acquired intangibles	—	—	805
Total operating expenses	105	3,511	34,332
Income from operations	253	1,487	6,161
Interest and other income, net	1	59	908
Interest expense	—	(3)	(39)
Income before income taxes	254	1,543	7,030
Provision for income taxes	(106)	(669)	(4,632)
Net income	$ 148	$ 874	$ 2,398
Net income per share:			
Basic	$ 0.02	$ 0.04	$ 0.05
Weighted average shares—basic	6,375	22,313	49,895
Diluted	$ 0.00	$ 0.01	$ 0.02
Weighted average shares—diluted	$42,945	$82,660	$114,590

Source: eBay 10-K filed on March 29, 1999.

EXHIBIT 10.4B eBay Quarterly Financials

eBAY INC.
CONDENSED CONSOLIDATED STATEMENT OF INCOME
(in thousands, except per share amounts; unaudited)

	Three Months Ended September 30,		Nine Months Ended September 30,	
	1998	**1999**	**1998**	**1999**
Net revenues:				
Fees and services	$ 20,816	$ 57,632	$ 52,143	$147,827
Real estate rentals	915	893	3,056	2,978
Total net revenues	21,731	58,525	55,199	150,805
Cost of net revenues:				
Fees and services	3,947	16,687	8,635	34,821
Real estate rentals	420	394	1,509	1,182
Total cost of net revenues	4,367	17,081	10,144	36,003
Gross profit	17,364	41,444	45,055	114,802
Operating expenses:				
Sales and marketing	9,414	27,230	21,317	67,104
Product development	1,514	6,851	3,062	14,490
General and administrative	4,249	11,779	11,049	29,481
Amortization of acquired intangibles	327	328	477	983
Merger related costs	—	—	—	4,359
Total operating expenses	15,504	46,188	35,905	116,417
Income (loss) from operations	1,860	(4,744)	9,150	(1,615)
Interest and other income, net	190	7,524	686	14,880
Interest expense	(351)	(449)	(1,279)	(1,491)
Income before income taxes	1,699	2,331	8,557	11,774
Provision for income taxes	(1,238)	(979)	(3,923)	(5,841)
Net income	$ 461	$ 1,352	$ 4,634	$ 5,933
Net income per share:				
Basic	$ 0.01	$ 0.01	$ 0.12	$ 0.06
Diluted	0.00	$ 0.01	$ 0.04	$ 0.04
Weighted average shares:				
Basic	48,385	115,980	39,002	105,864
Diluted	113,619	140,082	109,625	135,358
Supplemental pro forma information:				
Income before income taxes	$ 1,699	$ 2,331	$ 8,557	$ 11,774
Provision for income taxes as reported	(1,238)	(979)	(3,923)	(5,841)
Pro forma adjustment to provision for income taxes	274	—	(1,239)	(677)
Pro forma net income	$ 735	$ 1,352	$ 3,395	$ 5,256
Pro forma net income per share:				
Basic	$ 0.02	$ 0.01	$ 0.09	$ 0.05
Diluted	$ 0.01	$ 0.01	$ 0.03	$ 0.04

Source: eBay 10Q filed on November 15, 1999.

Conceptually, the online auction is similar to that of physical auctions. In a nutshell: Items are listed and viewed, bids are entered, and items are purchased and delivered (see Exhibit 10.5 for the eBay trading community). Since only very expensive rare items are typically sold at physical auctions, an online auction fills the void for all other goods.

Before bidders can bid and sellers can list items for sale, each must register with eBay, indicating some personal contact and credit card information, and acknowledging acceptance of disclaimer and disclosure rules. Like the off-line world, a bid invokes a legally binding contract.

To list an item for sale, a seller must choose which category to list it under. Categories include antiques, collectibles, sports memorabilia, dolls, jewelry, pottery, toys, and so forth. Each category is divided into more specific subcategories. For example, the computer category is broken up into hardware and software; the hardware subcategory is divided into areas such as modems, printers, monitors, and so on. Once selected, the seller indicates the duration of the auction (three days minimum), lowest bid acceptable, purchase description and photo (if available), payment (currency specified), and delivery terms.

During the auction period, eBay updates bidders about the status of their bid—whether they are high or have been outbid. To avoid having to monitor an auction continuously, bidders can invoke the "bid proxy." Here, bidders specify up front the maximum they would pay for an item; eBay then monitors the auction and adjusts the bid as needed without exceeding the maximum level. Upon auction closing, eBay sends e-mail messages to seller and bidders notifying them of the results and reminding the high bidder of the need to contact the seller within three business days to claim the item.

EXHIBIT 10.5 eBay Trading Community

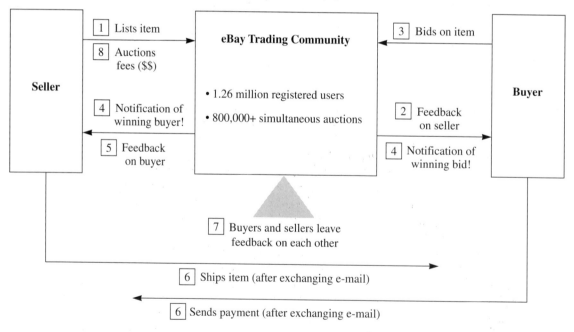

Source: eBay and BT Alex. Brown Research Report, October 27, 1998.

Security and Technology Issues

291

*CASE 10
eBay, Inc.:
Diversification in
the Internet Auction
Market*

Trust is an important element in the online auction environment. eBay addresses fraud and unscrupulous deals in two primary ways: a feedback system that encourages users to rate each other and indicate comments regarding the reliability and credibility of the buyer or seller, and an optional escrow system (i-Escrow) through which payment will be released to the seller only when the buyer gives approval. With these additional value-added services, eBay is able to address consumer concerns about security and to attract more users to its site.

Another factor vital to eBay's existence is technology. In the second and third quarters of 1999, eBay experienced several outages that resulted in the company's loss of millions of dollars in revenue. While eBay has traditionally relied chiefly on internal resources to maintain and service its technology infrastructure, it recently announced that it would outsource its back-end Internet technology to Abovenet Communications and Exodus Communications. Thus, the maintenance and performance responsibilities for Web servers, database servers, and Internet routers will switch to an external provider. As eBay continues to grow, it hopes these measures will help ensure success.

INDUSTRY OVERVIEW

The public has embraced online bidding ever since eBay pioneered person-to-person online auctions. The Internet has collapsed the distance between buyers and sellers, thereby creating a dynamic marketplace where prices are more fluid than ever. Now, the market has evolved to include not only personal collectibles, but also surplus inventory offered by retail merchants. The auction market has become increasingly crowded because barriers to entry are very low. Auction technologies such as LiveExchange and AuctionNow are readily available, essentially allowing any online merchant to offer these services. In the consumer auction space, eBay competes with many players, including Amazon, Yahoo!, and FairMarket.

Amazon.com

Amazon.com is the largest and broadest online consumer retailer, with close to 12 million registered customers as of the second quarter of 1998. The company's mission is to help people find almost anything they want to buy online, including books, toys, pets, and furniture. In March 1999 Amazon moved into the online auction space to compete head-to-head with eBay. Its online auction house is called "zShops" and it conducts both person-to-person and business-to-consumer auctions.

To distinguish its auction services, Amazon provides a $250 guarantee for consumers, and a $1,000 guarantee if the transaction is conducted through its 1-Click ordering capability. These guarantees address the fraud issue. The well-known brand name, an established customer base, and the ability to cross-market its retail and auction merchandise certainly helps Amazon build a strong presence in the online auction world.

Yahoo!

Yahoo!, founded in 1995, is currently the most popular Internet portal site. It offers a branded network of comprehensive information, communication, and shopping services to millions of users daily, and it boasts more monthly usage hours than any other site on the Internet. To start its own auction service, Yahoo! first licensed Onsale's technology and then took over Exchange, Onsale's person-to-person auction service. The Yahoo! auction is free and is supported only by advertising revenues.

FairMarket AuctionPlace

FairMarket, founded in 1997, represents the newest competitor in the online auction market that poses a significant threat to eBay. In September 1999 it announced a plan to aggregate the bidders and sellers across about 100 portal, retail, and community sites, including MSN, Excite, Lycos, Dell, and Ticketmaster Online, and allows goods to be shared among these member sites. This means that someone listing a used Palm Pilot for sale on Lycos, for instance, will automatically have the gadget posted on the auction sites of Microsoft and Excite as well.[5] Pulling together an instant critical mass of a combined 50 million users, FairMarket is helping companies to extend their reach to consumers and challenge the leading auctioneer eBay.

STRATEGY FOR GROWTH

As the pioneer of online person-to-person trading, eBay has been able to leverage its first-mover advantage into the creation of critical mass. With roughly 80 percent of the person-to-person auction space on the Internet and the largest offering of individual auctions (over 3 million items), eBay has created a solid brand name and a loyal customer base. Over the last year, the company has employed an aggressive growth plan to solidify its leadership position in the auction market. This includes a focus on product and service offerings, and regional and international expansion.

Product and Service Offerings

Since eBay is a virtual company—one that never actually physically handles merchandise—the company believes that it must offer better customer service and marketing than most. To foster a stronger community, eBay offers a number of venues such as News Features, Library, and Charity to help users meet and exchange information. Additionally, the company has forged innovative partnerships with companies like Kodak (for digitizing customer photos), Mailboxes Etc. (for shipping), i-Escrow (for releasing funds after items are received), and Collectors Universe (for authenticating auction items) to improve its customer service. In 1999 the company acquired Billpoint to enable customers to pay with credit cards.

To expand its product portfolio, eBay took an unprecedented step in April 1999 to acquire Butterfield & Butterfield, the 134-year-old auction house, for approximately $260 million. A month later it bought Kruse International, the high-end automobile auction house.[6] Before these acquisitions, eBay had focused on collectibles that were worth less than $500. These new businesses signaled eBay's drive in hosting higher-value auctions. But more importantly, they also marked the beginning of the company's off-line strategy.

Regional Auction Strategy

In October 1999 eBay shocked the market again by creating yet another source of new revenue. It rolled out regional auctions in 10 new markets and the list continues to

293

*CASE 10
eBay, Inc.:
Diversification in
the Internet Auction
Market*

grow. For example, "the San Francisco site has a Grateful Dead section, bundled-up Minneapolis residents can buy ice-fishing equipment, and Atlantans might bid on Braves paraphernalia."[7] Through further segmentation of the auction market, eBay attempts to reach more customers and capture the share from smaller regional and niche market players.

International Expansion

As eBay continues to penetrate the auction market in the United States, it also plans to leverage its knowledge in this core market across international borders. In June 1999 eBay purchased alando.de, a German online trading community. In addition, the company has developed separate Web pages for several communities abroad and mechanisms to allow cross-border trading. eBay has been building up its management team according to specific markets, including (1) Germany, Switzerland, and Austria, (2) the U.K., France, and Scandinavia, (3) Asia (Japan and Korea), (4) China, and (5) Australia and New Zealand.[8] It is expected that eBay will invest aggressively in these target markets to secure a leadership position in the online auction market.

THE FUTURE?

With the person-to-person auction market becoming increasingly competitive, Meg Whitman wonders what should be the next step for eBay. Although she has repeatedly told the press that the strategy for eBay is to focus on the person-to-person (P2P) market, the opportunity to bring in name-brand partners to offer business-to-consumer (B2C) auctions certainly sounds attractive. Forrester Research predicts that while P2P auctions constituted 70 percent of 1998 online auction sales, B2C auctions will gain momentum and generate 66 percent of total online auction market revenues by 2003.[9] Competitors such as Amazon and FairMarket are already entering that market. Should eBay follow the lead?

Another opportunity for eBay is business-to-business (B2B) auctions. This fall, eBay started offering a B2B sales category on its German auction site alando.de. In addition, eBay recently made a capital investment in a U.S. privately held company, Tradeout.com. Tradeout.com provides auctions for corporate surplus materials, a fast growing segment of the B2B auction revenues. These two investments provide eBay with a foothold into this new market, but the plan to aggressively pursue this business is still questionable.

Whitman also wonders about the sustainability of eBay's revenue model. With competitors like Yahoo! offering their auction service for free, can eBay justify its placement fees and commission on sales? How should eBay integrate its product and service offerings in the person-to-person market, and regional and international sites?

REFERENCES

1. Carolyn Koo, "eBay Beats Estimates But Stock Takes a Bath," www.thestreet.com/_yahoo/brknews/internet/805387.html.
2. Linda Himelstein, "eBay vs. Amazon," *Business Week,* May 31, 1999, p. 128.
3. Cate T. Corcoran, "Does eBay Represent a New Way of Doing Business?" *Red Herring,* www.redherring.com/mag/issue69/news-auctions.html.

4. Ibid.
5. Jon G. Auerbach, "Internet Giants Pool Their Bids for Auction Site to Rival eBay," *The Wall Street Journal,* September 17, 1999, p. B1.
6. Christina Stubbs, "Internet Upstarts Are Acquiring Complementary Real-World Operations to Expand Their Markets," *Red Herring,* www.redherring.com/mag/issue70/news-physical.html.
7. Adam Lashinsky, "eBay's Not-So-Secret Strategy for World Domination," www.thestreet.com/comment/siliconstreet/805456.html.
8. Research on eBay Inc., Deutsche Banc Alex. Brown, August 11, 1999.
9. Evie Black Dykema, Kate Delhagen, and Carrie Ardito, "Consumers Catch Auction Fever," *The Forrester Report,* March 1999.

MICROSOFT: BREAKING UP IS HARD TO DO

To the detriment of consumers, however, Microsoft has done much more than develop innovative browsing software of commendable quality and offer it bundled with Windows at no additional charge. As has been shown, Microsoft also engaged in a concerted series of actions designed to protect the applications barrier to entry, and hence its monopoly power, from a variety of middleware threats, including Netscape's Web browser and Sun's implementation of Java. Many of these actions have harmed consumers in ways that are immediate and easily discernible. They have also caused less direct, but nevertheless serious and far-reaching, consumer harm by distorting competition.[1]

—U.S. District Judge Thomas Penfield Jackson

On November 5, 1999, William (Bill) H. Gates III, chairman and chief executive officer of Microsoft Corporation, read these words from the recently issued findings of fact in the ongoing antitrust trial filed by the Department of Justice (Justice). In it, Judge Thomas Penfield Jackson dealt a striking blow, declaring that Microsoft used its monopoly power to crush competitors. Based on the recently issued findings, antitrust experts believed that a breakup of Microsoft had become more likely. Justice antitrust chief Joel Klein confided to millions of Sunday morning talk show viewers that a breakup is now squarely "in the range" of potential solutions. While a final decision was not due until next year, Gates knew that now was the time to begin contemplating options for Microsoft.

Both he and Steve Ballmer, president of Microsoft Corporation, were unwilling to yield from their core belief that government may not supervise what can and cannot be included in Microsoft's products. "The software industry's success has not been driven by government regulation, but by freedom and the basic human desire to learn, to innovate, and excel," claimed Gates. "We are not going to compromise on the freedom to

University of Michigan MBA candidates Andrew Aronson, Robert Moore, Min Park, and Christina Strader prepared this case under the supervision of Professor Allan Afuah as the basis for class discussion rather than to illustrate either effective or ineffective handling of an administrative situation.

innovate," Ballmer had said to the press.[2] To avoid this type of government intervention, many experts proposed a "structural remedy" of breaking up Microsoft into several piecemeal companies, as happened earlier to AT&T and Standard Oil. With this option in mind, Gates looked across the Redmond, Washington, campus and began considering his options for dividing the company should such drastic action become necessary.

MICROSOFT OPERATING SYSTEMS HISTORY

Bill Gates founded Microsoft (originally Micro-soft) in 1975 after dropping out of Harvard at age 19 and teaming with high school friend Paul Allen to sell a version of the programming language BASIC. While Gates was at Harvard, the pair wrote the language for Altair, the first commercial microcomputer. Microsoft was born in an Albuquerque, New Mexico, hotel room and grew by modifying BASIC for other computers. Gates moved Microsoft to his native Seattle in 1979 and began developing software that let others write programs. The modern personal computer (PC) era dawned in 1980 when IBM chose Microsoft to write the operating system, Microsoft Disk Operating System (MS-DOS), for its new machines. Because other PC makers wanted to be compatible with IBM, MS-DOS became standard on PCs. Microsoft retained licensing rights and began making compatible software. Appendix 11.1 (see page 308) presents a definition and description of operating systems.

On November 10, 1983, at the Plaza Hotel, New York City, the Microsoft Corporation formally announced "Microsoft Windows," its next generation operating system that would provide a graphical user interface (GUI) and multitasking environment for IBM-compatible personal computers. Microsoft promised that the new program would be on the store shelves by April 1984, and it might have been released under the original name of "Interface Manager," if Microsoft's marketing whiz Rowland Hanson had not convinced Bill Gates that "Windows" was the better name. On November 20, 1985, Microsoft finally shipped "Windows 1.0" almost two years past its promised release date. On April 6, 1992, "Windows 3.1" was released; 3 million copies were sold in the first two months. "Windows 3.x" became the number one operating system installed in PCs until 1997, when "Windows 95" took over.[3]

In 1995 Microsoft began buying the technologies of leading-edge start-up firms, investing heavily in their development and underpricing the resulting products. When the Internet began transforming business practices, Gates embraced the medium and assigned the Internet the highest priority for Microsoft's product development. The next year Microsoft licensed the Java Web programming language from Sun Microsystems and introduced its Internet Explorer Web browser as part of the Windows operating system. Microsoft now owns over 95 percent of the PC operating systems market.[4] Appendix 11.2 (see page 309) summarizes the Windows product road map. Exhibit 11.1 contains Microsoft's recent income statements. Exhibit 11.2 presents the revenue and stock price growth to date.

MICROSOFT'S LEGAL HISTORY

Microsoft has been the subject of antitrust investigation and courtroom battles since 1990. Based on investigations from 1990 to 1993, the Federal Trade Commission (FTC) concluded Microsoft had engaged in anticompetitive behavior. At the heart of this early investigation was the way Microsoft sold its previous operating system, MS-DOS.

EXHIBIT 11.1 Microsoft Financial Statements

| | Fiscal Year | | | |
	1998A	1999A	2000E	2001E
Last Revised October 20, 1999	(in $ millions)			
Revenues				
Windows platforms	$ 6,279	$ 8,504	$ 10,251	$ 12,800
Productivity applications and development tools	7,041	8,816	10,348	10,950
Consumer, commerce, and other	1,942	2,427	3,185	3,700
Total revenue	15,262	19,747	23,784	27,450
Cost of revenue	2,460	2,814	3,141	3,623
Gross profit	12,802	16,933	20,643	23,827
Operating Expenses				
Research & development	2,601	2,970	3,975	4,750
Sales & marketing	2,828	3,231	4,103	4,225
General & administration	433	689	713	815
Total operating expenses	5,862	6,890	8,791	9,790
Operating income	6,940	10,043	11,852	14,037
Interest income & other	473	1,688	1,597	1,600
Pretax income	7,413	11,731	13,449	15,637
Extraordinary credit/charge	296	160	156	0
Taxes	2,627	4,106	4,626	5,316
Preferred stock dividend	0	0	0	0
Net income	4,490	7,785	8,667	10,320
Earnings per share	0.84	1.43	1.57	1.83
Earnings per share (operating)	0.89	1.40	1.61	1.83
Shares outstanding (Th)	5,360	5,443	5,513	5,632
Revenue Breakout				
Platforms (% of revenue)	41%	43%	43%	47%
Applications & tools (% of revenue)	46%	45%	44%	40%
Consumer/commerce (% of revenue)	13%	12%	13%	13%
Margin Detail				
Product license gross margin	83.9%	85.7%	86.8%	86.8%
Total gross margin	83.9%	85.7%	86.8%	86.8%
Research & development	17.0%	15.0%	16.7%	17.3%
Sales & marketing	18.5%	16.4%	17.3%	15.4%
General & administration	2.8%	3.5%	3.0%	3.0%
Operating margin	45.6%	50.9%	49.8%	51.1%
Pretax margin	48.6%	59.4%	56.5%	57.0%
Tax rate, fully taxed	35.5%	35.0%	34.0%	34.0%
Net margin	29.4%	39.4%	36.4%	37.6%
Quarter-to-Quarter Growth				
Windows platforms	27.7%	35.4%	20.5%	24.9%
Productivity applications and development tools	25.4%	25.2%	17.4%	5.8%
Consumer, commerce, and other	38.3%	25.0%	31.2%	16.2%
Total revenue	27.9%	29.4%	20.4%	15.4%
Operating income	35.3%	44.7%	18.0%	18.4%
Pretax income	39.5%	58.2%	14.6%	16.3%
Net income	30.0%	73.4%	11.3%	19.1%
Earnings per share (operating)	35.5%	57.0%	14.9%	13.8%

Source: Microsoft Corporation. Financial statement October 20, 1999; Robertson Stephens, "Internet and e-Commerce Applications Research," November 22, 1999.

EXHIBIT 11.2 Revenue and Stock Price Growth

Historical Financials and Employees

Year	Revenue ($ millions)	Net Income ($ millions)	Net Profit Margin	Employees
1999	$19,747	$7,785	39.4%	31,396
1998	14,484	4,490	31.0%	27,055
1997	11,358	3,454	30.4%	22,232
1996	8,671	2,195	25.3%	20,561
1995	5,937	1,453	24.5%	17,801
1994	4,649	1,146	24.7%	15,257
1993	3,753	953	25.4%	14,430
1992	2,759	708	25.7%	11,542
1991	1,843	463	25.1%	8,226
1990	1,183	279	23.6%	5,635

Stock History

| | Stock Price ($) | | | P/E | | Per Share ($) | | |
Year	Fiscal Year High	Fiscal Year Low	Fiscal Year Close	High	Low	Earnings	Dividend	Book Value
1999	$95.63	$43.88	90.19	67	31	1.42	0	5.57
1998	54.28	29.50	54.19	65	35	0.84	0	3.35
1997	33.73	13.44	31.59	51	20	0.66	0	2.22
1996	15.73	9.98	15.02	37	23	0.43	0	1.45
1995	11.55	5.86	11.30	40	20	0.29	0	1.13
1994	6.83	4.40	6.44	28	18	0.24	0	0.98
1993	6.13	4.09	5.50	31	20	0.20	0	0.72
1992	5.55	2.52	4.38	35	16	0.16	0	0.50
1991	3.27	1.41	2.84	30	13	0.11	0	0.32
1990	2.19	0.72	2.11	31	10	0.07	0	0.22

Source: "Microsoft Financials," *Hoover's Online,* December 14, 1999, www.hoovers.com.

Microsoft offered personal computer makers a variety of ways to buy the software, one of which is a license that provides significant discounts to original equipment manufacturers (OEMs) who pay for a copy of DOS for every PC that they ship—whether or not the PC comes with MS-DOS. Investigators believed this practice discouraged PC makers from buying competing software.[5]

In August 1993 the FTC commissioners deadlocked and closed their probe without acting on Microsoft and passed the files to Justice. Justice broadened the investigation to include charges that Microsoft's near monopoly in operating systems gave it an unfair advantage in applications that run on those systems. In July 1995 Justice reached a consent decree with Microsoft to end specific anticompetitive practices in its licensing policy.[6] Specifically, Microsoft was not allowed to require PC makers to license one Microsoft product in order to obtain another Microsoft product.

Justice continued to be involved in Microsoft's affairs by suing to block its attempted merger with personal finance software maker Intuit, Inc., in May 1995.[7] Peace with the legal process lasted only a summer for Microsoft. In October 1995 Justice accused

Microsoft of violating the consent decree by forcing PC makers that license its Windows operating system to also install Microsoft's Internet Explorer on every machine.[8]

Justice's suit against Microsoft again revolved around anticompetitive practices. Microsoft's argument was that integration made technical sense by telling the story of how memory management, printer drivers, graphical user interfaces, and other once-independent software features have been integrated into the operating system over the years. Thus, Internet Explorer was simply an incremental improvement, not a distinct technology to be marketed separately.[9]

Despite the specifics of Microsoft's browser argument, Justice conducted a thorough investigation that included several other examples of where Microsoft threatened to withdraw its software if an OEM used another software package. Justice sought to show a pattern of anticompetitive behavior by a monopolist. The initial findings of fact released on November 5, 1999, unambiguously showed that Justice's argument was convincing. See Appendix 11.3 (page 310) for a chronological listing of the essential events in Microsoft's legal history.

MICROSOFT'S CULTURE

I just don't think they can change their behavior. This is a 20-year-old culture. There the first thing they think about each morning is how to leverage the business. What are they going to do—send all the executives to class, like this was sexual harassment? It won't work. The nation will spend the next 20 years trying to enforce it.[10]

—Anonymous computer maker CEO

In a word, "competitive" best describes the Microsoft culture. Alternatively, according to the Jackson court ruling, Microsoft's culture may actually define the word "competitive"; that is, competitive to the point of unfair, anticompetitive business tactics. Microsoft has a pervasive paranoia about the competition, a constant mistrust and anxiety about market opponents. Perhaps that apprehension is a result of its own devious competitive tactics. If you believe the above quote, the competitive nature of the company is innate within the organization and its people—there is no means of treating the symptoms without killing the patient. Healthy competition among businesses is the heart of the American capitalist system. How then did Microsoft get to be this monopolistic evil to be slayed by the Department of Justice? How did it get to be so brutally competitive that America had to put a stop to it? It might have something to do with the environment that Microsoft has created. It hires the brightest, most successful candidates (read competitive) that apply. Microsoft can afford to be selective. It gets over 12,000 resumes a month but hires only 0.1 percent of those applicants.[11]

Bright, aggressive, and fiercely competitive not only define the Microsoft organization, but also its chief executive officer. It has been said that the corporate culture of Microsoft seems almost inseparable from its founder and CEO, Bill Gates. Being almost synonymous with the organization and deeply vested both personally as well as financially, Gates is intensely defensive and passionate about the company and its business tactics. The employees (also driven by stock options) are ardently loyal to the company; there is a less than 1 percent turnover of the MBAs hired since 1995.[12] This loyalty and competitive drive translate into long hours at the Microsoft campus. One recent MBA hire commented that it was not uncommon to see sleeping bags hanging on the back of office doors.[13] There is a joke around the Redmond campus that goes, "There are no set hours at

Microsoft . . . You can work any 12 hours of the day you want!" The competition to be the best and excel in every market is said to be all-consuming in the Microsoft culture.

Highly intelligent, talented, driven, passionate, dedicated—all lead up to another major characteristic of the Microsoft culture: arrogance. Microsoft's arrogance is said to have contributed to the legal problems that it faces today. Microsoft knows how to play only one way: to win. Everything else is a loss.[14] This approach to market competition is echoed in its legal strategy. Even after consent decree violations and investigations going as far back as 1991, Microsoft has yet to implement an internal antitrust screen for its actions.

KEY COMPETITORS

Below is a description of Microsoft's key competitors and their product focus. Exhibits 11.3 and 11.4 show a more complete list of Microsoft's competitors.

Netscape

Netscape introduced the Internet browser Navigator, which brought Microsoft into the market (with its competing product Internet Explorer). Justice has charged that Microsoft deliberately damaged Netscape by bundling its Internet Explorer with its Windows operating system. Microsoft allegedly first tried to keep Netscape from competing in the market, and offered to orchestrate a deal where it would take a 20 percent stake in Netscape if it would stay out of the Windows market. (Navigator can be used as a platform to run software and thus competes directly with MS operating systems.)

EXHIBIT 11.3 Microsoft's Competitors

Adobe	Software
AOL/Time Warner	Online, content development, and acquisition, and cable and online news and entertainment
Apple Computer	Computer hardware, peripherals, and software
Auto-By-Tel	Online car sales
Bell Labs	Networking systems, interactive communications
Borland	Desktop applications
Broderbund	Software games, home-entertainment products
CompuServe	Online systems, content development, and acquisition
CNN	Cable News service
Computer Associates	Database management
IBM	Hardware, OS2 operating system, peripherals, desktop applications
Informix Corp.	Database management for networks
Intuit	Personal finance and online banking applications
Novell/Word Perfect	Networking systems and desktop applications
Netscape	Internet browser and applications software
Oracle	Database management for networks
Red Hat	Operating systems, Linux
Silicon Graphics	Servers and workstations
Sun Microsystems	Servers and workstation, Java Internet software
Sybase	Database management for networks
Walt Disney/ABC News	Online news service

Source: "Microsoft Competition," *Hoover's Online,* December 14, 1999, www.hoovers.com.

Sun developed Java, the Internet software programming language that is designed to function with any operating system. It is a multiplatform structure that breaks up into "applets" that allows for swift Internet transmission. This allows central servers to do much of the work currently handled by installed software. Sun sued Microsoft over the company's use of Java in its 4.0 version of Internet Explorer, arguing that Microsoft's program is not compatible with Java.

EXHIBIT 11.4 Competitors' Financials

Income Statement and Balance Sheet (all figures in $ millions)

Company	Ticker Symbol	Revenues	Net Income	Cash	Total Assets	Long-term Debt	Total Equity
Microsoft, Inc.	Nasdaq:MSFT	$19,747.0	$7,785.0	$4,975.0	$37,156.0	—	$28,438.0
Operating systems							
Apple Computer	Nasdaq:AAPL	$5,941.0	$309.0	$1,481.0	$4,289.0	$954.0	$1,642.0
Red Hat, Inc.	Nasdaq:RHAT	$10.8	$(0.1)	$10.1	$15.3	$0.4	$12.1
Sun Microsystems	Nasdaq:SUNW	$11,726.3	$1,031.3	$1,089.0	$8,420.4	—	$4,811.8
Applications							
Adobe Systems Inc.	Nasdaq:ADBE	$894.8	$105.1	$110.9	$767.3	—	$516.4
Corel Corporation	Nasdaq:CORL	$246.8	$(8.7)	$24.5	$140.2	$16.1	$28.6
Oracle Corporation	Nasdaq:ORCL	$8,827.3	$1,289.8	$1,785.7	$7,259.7	$304.1	$3,695.3
IBM	NYSE:IBM	$81,667.0	$6,328.0	$5,375.0	$86,100.0	$15,508.0	$19,433.0
Internet/consumer							
America Online	NYSE:AOL	$4,777.0	$762.0	$887.0	$5,348.0	$348.0	$3,033.0
Yahoo!	Nasdaq:YHOO	$203.3	$25.6	$125.5	$621.9	—	$536.2
Novell, Inc.	Nasdaq:NOVL	$1,083.9	$102.0	$1,007.2	$1,924.1	—	$1,493.5

Financial Ratios

Company	52-Week Earnings per Share	60 Month Beta	P/E Ratio	Shares Outstanding (in millions)	Market Cap (in $ Billions)	Financial Information Dated
Microsoft, Inc.	1.51	1.3	69.87	5,160,022	$544.4	June 99
Operating systems						
Apple Computer	3.61	0.5	26	160,880	$15.1	Sept. 98
Red Hat, Inc.	n/a	n/a	n/a	68,795	$15.8	Feb. 99
Sun Microsystems	0.73	1.4	102.57	1,573,432	$117.8	June 99
Applications						
Adobe Systems Inc.	1.48	1.3	41.98	120,198	$7.5	Nov. 98
Corel Corporation	0.30	1.2	89.79	64,131	$1.7	Nov. 98
Oracle Corporation	0.96	1.4	90.79	1,423,672	$124.1	May 99
IBM	4.23	1.1	25.22	1,802,604	$192.3	Dec. 98
Internet/consumer						
America Online	0.34	2.4	252.39	2,235,486	$191.8	June 99
Yahoo!	0.25	3.1	1296	263,240	$85.3	Dec. 98
Novell, Inc.	0.55	1.6	38.75	333,066	$7.1	Oct. 98

Note: All market information dated as of December 15, 1999.

Source: Hoover's Online, December 15, 1999, www.hoovers.com.

Novell

Novell is one of the leading producers of networking systems and desktop applications. It provides network software by directory services. Novell also provides Internet solutions through worldwide channel, developer, education, and technical support programs.

Oracle

Oracle is the largest provider of database software and information management services. Oracle is now targeting the emerging Internet market by developing software for low-cost network computers, as well as taking steps to compete directly with the Windows PC operating system. Oracle and Microsoft got into a bidding war over Time Warner's broadband Internet service, Roadrunner. Oracle placed a bid for $300 million, and Microsoft came in $100 million higher.

America Online (AOL)

AOL is the world's most popular online service provider, and a potentially formidable competitor for Microsoft on the Internet. In a move to become an all-in-one hardware and software powerhouse, it purchased Netscape for $10.2 billion, formed an alliance with Sun, and invested $800 million in an alliance with Gateway. It also merged with Time Warner.

Red Hat

Founded in 1994, Red Hat is a market leader in open source operating system software, services, and information. It is well known for its open Linux operating system (it has more than 15 million users), which is MS Office compatible. The Official Red Hat Linux OS and related services are available directly from the company and through its partner, distributor, and reseller programs, which include top PC and server manufacturers such as Compaq, Dell, Gateway, IBM, Hewlett-Packard, and Silicon Graphics. Red Hat is seen as the most likely threat to Microsoft's long-lived dominance in that market.

PRODUCTS

Microsoft is a major high-tech player in a variety of markets, and it continues to reinvent itself and expand to new segments of the industry. It has a wide array of products from office applications (MS Office) to interactive media.[15] A description of its product segments follows.

- *Business Software.* Windows, Excel, Outlook, PowerPoint, Access, Word, Office (Office now accounts for 30 percent of the company's revenues[16]), FrontPage, MS Project, MS Publisher.
- *Operating Systems and Servers.* Personal computer operating systems (Windows 98), handheld device operating systems (Windows CE), databases (SQL), servers (NetShow, Proxy), server operating systems (Windows NT), management tools (Systems Management Server), and server suites (BackOffice Server).
- *Developer Tools.* Software to help you develop your Microsoft databases, develop Internet tools, scripts, programs, and animation.

- *Internet/Web Products.* More development tools specifically for the Internet, browsing tools (Internet Explorer, WebTV), Internet commerce server, and intranet and Internet servers (Roadrunner), as well as online databases (Sidewalk.com), e-mail (Hotmail).
- *Games.* Adventure games, classic games (Dilbert's Desktop Games), online games, sports, strategy (Chaos Island, Age of Empires), and simulations (Monster Truck Madness).
- *Home Productivity.* Buying guides (CarPoint), desktop publishing, personal finance (Money), home office products.
- *Reference.* Development reference, educational reference (Encarta, Bookshelf).
- *Hardware.* Products include gaming devices and mouses.
- *Macintosh Products.* Microsoft offers a host of business software for the Macintosh, including Excel, Office, Word, and PowerPoint. Microsoft also has development tools, games, and reference software for Macs.
- *Books.* MS press publishes books on business software, operating systems and servers, development tools, Internet products, games, home productivity, reference, and hardware.

STRATEGY

Microsoft's culture of fierce competition is perfectly suited for one of its core strategies: rapid market share growth with a take-no-prisoners approach, in an all-out effort to achieve total market domination. This tactic may result in initially sacrificing profits during the growth phase, but it reaps huge margins when successful in monopolizing the market.

Sheer marketing and financial muscle are the keys behind Microsoft's rapid share growth. Microsoft's marketing machine is well known in the industry to have a superior marketing machine—it conducts intensive consumer research to develop new products and upgrade existing ones. Additionally, Microsoft spent $2 billion on R&D; to put this sum in perspective, that is a little less than four times Netscape's 1998 total revenues.[17] With assets worth over $30 billion—$5 billion in cash—and no long-term debt, Microsoft is able to acquire any company competing for its market share. See Exhibit 11.5 for Microsoft's balance statement.

Another core strategy for Microsoft has been rapid product evolution and aggressive innovation. Microsoft has historically not been as much an innovator as a masterful synthesizer—able to improve products with each successive launch. It buys or "borrows" product concepts from other industry competitors and improves on the product and launches it under the Microsoft name. For example, in January 1996 Microsoft acquired Vermeer Technologies for its Web-authoring product, FrontPage, for a rumored $130 million.[18]

Not to be underestimated, an essential strategy of Microsoft is its powerful culture. We mentioned earlier that the company attracts some of the best and brightest talent in the industry and fosters an atmosphere of passion, drive, competition, and dedication to Microsoft's all-out success. This of course is fueled by the personal financial stake that the employees have in seeing the company succeed. It has delivered a strong record performance and has made Microsoft employees some of the wealthiest people in Seattle: More than 2,000 Microsofties are millionaires and six are billionaires.

EXHIBIT 11.5 Microsoft Corporation Balance Sheets

	June 30,	
	1998	**1999**
	(in $ millions)	
Assets		
Current assets:		
Cash and short-term investments	$13,927	**$17,236**
Accounts receivable	1,460	**2,245**
Other	502	**752**
Total current assets	15,889	**20,233**
Property and equipment	1,505	**1,611**
Equity and other investments	4,703	**14,372**
Other assets	260	**940**
Total assets	$22,357	**$37,156**
Liabilities and stockholders' equity		
Current liabilities:		
Accounts payable	$ 759	**$ 874**
Accrued compensation	359	**396**
Income taxes payable	915	**1,607**
Unearned revenue	2,888	**4,239**
Other	809	**1,602**
Total current liabilities	5,730	**8,718**
Commitments and contingencies		
Stockholders' equity:		
Convertible preferred stock —		
shares authorized 100;		
shares issued and outstanding 13	980	**980**
Common stock and paid-in capital —		
shares authorized 12,000;		
shares issued and outstanding, 4,940 and 5,109	8,025	**13,844**
Retained earnings, including other comprehensive		
income of $666 and $1,787	7,622	**13,614**
Total stockholders' equity	16,627	**28,438**
Total liabilities and stockholders' equity	$22,357	**$37,156**

Source: Microsoft Corporation, *1999 Annual Report.*

POTENTIAL REMEDIES FOR THE CURRENT SITUATION

At the time of Judge Thomas Penfield Jackson's "Finding of Fact," Microsoft had several different options available. Differences of opinion exist on whether "breaking up" Microsoft makes sense. Eric Schmidt, CEO of Novell, a competitor of Windows NT, dislikes Microsoft's business tactics but feels, however, that "the likely consequence is a lot of confusion." On the other hand, James Barksdale, former CEO of Netscape Communications, feels that "a breakup is not necessarily bad for Microsoft. The companies that have been broken up in the past have done better for their shareholders."[19]

In considering a possible breakup, the interested parties (Bill Gates, Microsoft, and the Court) have several questions to consider. These include:

1. What would the resulting structures be?
2. Who would orchestrate the breakup process?
3. Who would head the resulting companies?
4. Where would Bill Gates end up?
5. How should the intellectual property be divided?
6. How should the assets and liabilities be divided?
7. What would be the value of the resulting companies?
8. What would be the effect on customers, shareholders, the competition, and the industry?

"Horizontal" Breakup Structure

One option is to pursue a "horizontal" breakup into three separate companies. The three focuses would be on Operating Systems, Office Applications, and business related to the Internet and e-commerce. The difficulties would be determining the boundaries between the OS and applications, especially since Windows 98 incorporates the browserlike functionality of Internet Explorer. Several combinations of a horizontal breakup are also possible.

"Vertical" Breakup Structure

A second potential restructuring is a "vertical" breakup into identical "Baby Bills," mimicking the breakup of AT&T into "Baby Bells." Each of the "Baby Bills" would duplicate Microsoft's Intellectual Property and would get an equal share of its assets. This option would increase industry competition, but would be logically and logistically difficult to implement, in particular, the equitable reallocation of the workforce, division of profits from licensing contracts, and redistribution of employee shares to avoid conflicts of interest created by owning shares in newly formed competitors.

Releasing the Source Code

Another alternative addresses competition in the applications market but not Microsoft's monopoly in the operating systems market. An application programming interface (API) is a set of functions that allows software to operate properly with a given operating system (such as Windows) or hardware device. In other words, an API provides programmers an easy way to ensure that their software can use the functionality of the hardware or operating system, without needing to know the inner workings of the device. By publishing the APIs (source codes) for Windows, Microsoft would make it easier for other companies to create Windows-compatible application software.

A similar or related approach to the above option is to force Microsoft to integrate widely accepted protocols such as Java. Currently, Microsoft uses DirectX, its own proprietary protocol, instead of Java. The implication of forcing Microsoft to use standard protocols would be to further enhance the cross-compatibility of application software.

An option that does not include a breakup is to put Microsoft under close governmental scrutiny. The current legal situation arose because of the alleged previous predatory and anticompetitive practices of Microsoft. One way to prevent further monopolistic behavior would be for the government to impose and enforce stringent rules rather than pursuing a restructuring action. These rules could also include specific actions that would inhibit interference tactics previously exhibited by Microsoft, such as buying and shutting down competitive technologies. These governmental actions consist of rules aimed at curbing Microsoft's anticompetitive behavior.

Additional government rules could address technological limitations for Microsoft. For instance, the government could require Microsoft to unbundle Windows and Internet Explorer. This would help address the concerns of Netscape, which filed an anticompetitive complaint against Microsoft. Similar to the open API solution, the government could impose a technology quarantine on Microsoft. This would consist of a requirement to stop free-release of new features for Windows and require full disclosure of its technology road map. The government overseers would have to approve any enhancements. This option raises many antientrepreneurial and anticonsumer concerns and is rife with "Big Brother" undertones.

CONCLUSION

As Bill Gates looks at the analysis made by his business advisors and ponders his options, he is sure of one thing: regardless of the outcome, Microsoft needs to continue moving forward to avoid losing focus, being surpassed by the multiple competitors, and losing employee morale. As a business manager of the Developer Tools Group at Microsoft noted, until the dust settles, "it's business as usual around here."

REFERENCES

1. *USA v. Microsoft,* "Findings of Fact," United States District Court for the District of Columbia, November 5, 1999.
2. Mike France, "Does a Breakup Make Sense?" *Business Week,* November 22, 1999.
3. About.com, *Inventors of the Modern Computer: Microsoft,* December 15, 1999, inventors.about.com/education/inventors/library/weekly/aa080499.htm.
4. *USA v. Microsoft,* November 5, 1999.
5. "The FTC vs Microsoft. The Software Giant May Be Forced to Change," *Business Week*, December 28, 1992.
6. "A Hard-Line Judge for Microsoft?" *Business Week,* February 6, 1995.
7. "Oh Microsoft, Poor Microsoft," *Business Week,* June 26, 1995.
8. "Microsoft Goes Low Tech in Washington," *Business Week,* December 22, 1997.
9. "Oddsmakers Bet on Bill," *Business Week,* June 29, 1998.
10. "Does a Breakup Make Sense?" *Business Week,* November 22, 1999.
11. "Wet Feet Reports," *Microsoft,* 1999.
12. Ibid.
13. Interview with anonymous Microsoft employee, 1998.

14. David Thielen and Shirley Thielen, *The 12 Simple Secrets of Microsoft Management,* New York: McGraw-Hill, 1999, p. 175.
15. Vault Reports, *Microsoft,* 1998
16. Vault Reports, *Microsoft,* 1998.
17. "Wet Feet Reports," *Microsoft,* 1999.
18. Don Clark, "Microsoft to Buy Maker of FrontPage, Software to Create Internet Web Pages," *The Wall Street Journal,* January 16, 1996.
19. John R. Wilke and Lee Gomes, "Assessing Microsoft's Options in a High-Stakes Antitrust Endgame," *The Wall Street Journal,* November 10, 1999.

Operating System

An operating system (OS) is an interface between the user and the hardware components in a computer. There are two types of operating systems, based according to their user interface:

1. *Character User Interface (CUI).* This type of OS needs the particular user to type in a command in a specified format in order to perform the required task. Once the command has been entered, the OS will process the command and produce a corresponding computer instruction. Examples of a CUI operating system are MS-DOS and UNIX.
2. *Graphical User Interface (GUI).* This OS uses graphical objects, such as drop-down menus, dialog boxes, and pop-ups. Users are able to perform a number of tasks by simply clicking on these graphical objects with a mouse. This makes things very easy for users because they do not have to type commands to get the computer to perform a particular task. Examples of GUI Operating System are Windows NT, Windows 98, Windows 95, and Apple Macintosh System 8.

In addition to classifying operating systems according to their user interface, OSs can also be classified according to the number of users that it can support at any given time. An operating system can be classified as:

1. *Single-User.* A single-user operating system can only process instructions from one user at a time. This means that only after one user has completed his or her tasks on the system will another user be able to work on the system. Examples of single-user OSs are MS-DOS and Windows 95.
2. *Multiuser.* A multiuser operating system means that the particular system can support more than one user at a time. It can simultaneously process instructions from multiple users. The single computer that is running the multiuser OS will handle all the processing. Examples of multiuser OSs are Windows NT and UNIX.

Functions of an Operating System

1. *Peripheral Management.* The OS manages the basic input and output operations to and from peripherals such as the mouse, keyboard, printer, and monitor.
2. *Storage Management.* The OS manages files and folders by allocating space on the disk for the particular file or folder created by the user.
3. *Security.* The OS helps prevent any illegal access to the computer and files. Only authorized personnel or users will be able to view or make changes to any files.
4. *Failure and Recovery.* The operating system will detect if there is any hardware or software failure and will try to establish methods of recovery (if possible) or it will inform the user about the particular failure.
5. *Networking.* Some operating systems are able to provide multiuser support. With networking features in the OS, users can communicate and share resources such as printers and files.
6. *Executing Applications.* The OS works as a platform for executing applications. It takes the particular application from its source and loads that particular application into the random-access memory (RAM).
7. *Memory Management.* The OS allocates memory space for tasks performed by the user. When there are two or more operations being performed at the same time, the OS will manage the systems memory to ensure that no clashes occur.

The Windows Family

Microsoft Windows is a graphical user interface (GUI) operating system. There are many versions of Windows in the market, for example, Windows 3.11, Windows 98, and Windows 2000. Some of these products are just simply add-ons to MS-DOS while others are true operating systems that replace DOS.

MS-Windows 3.x

There were three versions in the MS-Windows version 3.x family: Windows 3.0, 3.1, and 3.11. Windows 3.11 was also known as "Windows for WorkGroups" because it had computer networking capability built into the product. None of the three are true operating systems. Each is installed with MS-DOS to provide a complete operating atmosphere. The Windows/DOS operating system is a "16-bit" platform, meaning that it cannot take advantage of the enhancements of newer Intel processors.

MS-Windows 95

Windows 95 was designed to replace the Windows/DOS combination, which was not very stable. The main reason Windows 95 is more stable is that it has the ability to run both 16-bit and 32-bit applications. The two basic requirements of Windows 95 compared to Windows 3.11 are more memory and a higher-speed processor. A new object-oriented user interface was also introduced in Windows 95.

MS-Windows 98

Windows 98 supports the latest Internet, graphics, and multimedia technologies while providing better performance and easier maintenance. A few improvements were made in Windows 98 with respect to Windows 95 in order to enhance the entertainment experience with a new generation of technologies and to save hard-disk space with an improved file allocation table (FAT).

MS-Windows NT

Windows NT, which stands for Windows New Technology, is well designed and is targeted at corporate users. Windows NT is a true 32-bit operating system. In addition to being a GUI operating system, it is also a multiuser operating system. Windows NT is often used as the operating system for Network Servers because it has built-in network capabilities.

MS-Windows CE

Microsoft Windows CE is an operating system for handheld devices. It makes possible new categories of business and consumer devices that can communicate with each other, exchange information, synchronize with Windows-based computers, and connect to the Internet.

MS-Windows 2000

Windows 2000 combines the ease of using Windows 98 on the Internet, at work, or on the road, with the manageability, reliability, and security of Windows NT.

Sources: John R. Wilke and Lee Gomes, "Assessing Microsoft's Options in a High-Stakes Antitrust Endgame," *The Wall Street Journal,* November 10, 1999; Mike France, "Does A Breakup Make Sense?" *Business Week,* November 22, 1999.

APPENDIX 11.3 Legal Events, 1990–1999

The Federal Trade Commission (FTC) Investigation Begins, 1990–1993

The FTC begins investigating Microsoft for possible antitrust violations based on its massive market power in operating systems. Competitors believe that Microsoft has an unfair advantage because it sells operating systems and applications. In 1992 the FTC concludes that Microsoft engaged in uncompetitive behavior. The FTC investigators file a report with its commissioners stating that Microsoft maintained its market dominance with overly aggressive licensing arrangements, and that the company has unfairly used the stranglehold to gain an edge in the development of word-processing programs and spreadsheets. In August 1993 FTC commissioners hand the case over to the Department of Justice.

Microsoft Prevails in Apple Lawsuit, 1993

On June 1, 1993, Microsoft announces that Judge Vaughn R. Walker of the U.S. District Court of Northern California ruled in Microsoft's favor in the Apple v. Microsoft and Hewlett-Packard copyright suit. The judge granted Microsoft's and Hewlett-Packard's motions to dismiss the last remaining copyright infringement claims against Microsoft Windows 2.03 and 3.0, as well as Hewlett-Packard's NewWave.

Microsoft and Intuit End Merger Agreement, 1995

On May 20, 1995, Microsoft and Intuit announce that they have agreed to terminate their planned merger, rather than appeal and pursue months of litigation with the Justice Department at the trial and appellate court levels. These litigation delays would have followed the months of delay already caused by the Justice Department's unusually lengthy Hart-Scott-Rodino Act review.

Antitrust Settlement Reinstated, 1995

On June 16, 1995, the U.S. Court of Appeals reinstates a 1994 antitrust settlement between Microsoft and the Justice Department that was rejected by U.S. District Judge Stanley Sporkin in February 1995. The 26-page opinion of the court delivers a harsh rebuke to the judge and grants Microsoft's request to remove him from the case.

Justice Department Files Action against Microsoft, 1997

In October 1997 the Justice Department files a motion in Federal District Court, alleging that Microsoft had violated a 1994 consent decree dealing with certain aspects of licensing the Windows operating system to computer manufacturers. Specifically, the Justice Department asked the court to stop Microsoft from tying the use of its Windows 95 operating system to the use of its Internet browser, a tool to navigate the Internet.

Source: Microsoft's World Wide Web site, www.microsoft.com, December 1, 1999.

SUN MICROSYSTEMS: JUMPING FOR JAVA

In the past, power and success in the computer industry all boiled down to who controlled the key technological choke points . . . Customers don't want that kind of industry domination anymore . . . That's why Java is different. Sun is leading it, but by design nobody really owns it.

—Irving Wladawsky-Berger, IBM's Internet czar and chief Java strategist

Scott McNealy, CEO of Sun Microsystems, was thinking about the future as he walked back to his office. He had just met with Alan Baratz, president of Sun's Java-Soft subsidiary, to discuss Sun's next move regarding Java, the company's platform-independent programming language. Since its launch in May 1995, Java had been a rousing success. It was adopted more quickly across the software industry than any other new technology in computing history. Realizing its potential, many of Sun's competitors, including Microsoft, had rushed to license Java. Sun currently had over 200 licenses outstanding and 900,000 software developers working on new applications.

Java's proliferation had quickly convinced Microsoft that the "write once, run anywhere" software represented a real threat to its entrenched Windows monopoly. McNealy had boasted about the demise of Windows and how Java would be running on everything from cell phones to household appliances. Sun held to the belief that large networks of Java-enabled devices powered by massive servers would someday render the PC obsolete. Microsoft began to move aggressively to counter Sun's every move. They were able to persuade thousands of software developers to use Microsoft's version of Java. Sun continued to win the battles, but who would win the war?

As McNealy sat down in his office, he contemplated Sun's next move. Java represented a major part of Sun's future success. Its continuing development would spur sales growth for Sun's Internet servers, software tools, and microchips. In the past

---

Sun's tall promises, late releases, and tight grip on Java development had allowed Microsoft to counter Java. Now other partners were beginning to follow suit. What began as collaborative agreements with partners to make Sun's Java the standard programming language was quickly evolving into a struggle for control over development. McNealy considered the consequences of giving up some of this control.

SUN MICROSYSTEMS

Sun is regarded as "the last standing, fully integrated computing company, adding its own value at the chip, [operating system], and systems level."[1] The company first made a name for itself by making high-powered computer workstations, but is now better known for building the servers and software that power the Internet. Sun's major products include the UltraWorkstation, Solaris Operating Environment, Sparc Microprocessor, and Java and Jini Connection Technologies (see Appendixes 12.1 and 12.2 on pages 320 and 321). In 1996 Sun was generating nearly $1.3 billion in revenues from server sales. Driven by the rapid growth of the Internet and increased demand for networked systems, the server market reached quarterly sales of over $16 billion in 1998 (see Exhibit 12.1). As Sun's server business flourished, intense competition and shrinking margins began to erode the company's core workstation business. Despite these pressures, the company still managed to increase product revenues by $856 million or 11 percent in 1998, following a 21 percent growth year in 1997 (see Exhibits 12.2 and 12.3).

Sun was founded in 1982 by a group of four young pioneers brought together by a shared vision of decentralized, heterogeneous computing systems. In 1987 Sun adopted the slogan, "the Network is the Computer" to promote this open-systems philosophy. McNealy described Sun's vision as:

> a networked computing future driven by the needs and choices of the customer. It is a vision in which every man, woman, and child has access to the collective planetary wisdom that resides on the network . . . Our role is to make the most of opportunity, by delivering open, affordable, and useful products to help as many people as possible share in the power of the network around the world.[2]

EXHIBIT 12.1 Server Industry Market Share

Vendor	4th Quarter 1997	Market Share (%)	4th Quarter 1998	Market Share (%)	Growth
IBM	$ 5,234	31%	$ 4,553	28%	−13%
Compaq	1,430	8	2,072	13	45
Hewlett-Packard	1,782	11	1,886	12	6
Sun Microsystems	**1,275**	**8**	**1,508**	**9**	**18**
Fujitsu	766	5	776	5	1
NEC	630	4	638	4	1
Dell	319	2	603	4	89
Siemens	381	2	599	4	57
Hitachi Ltd.	693	4	500	3	−28
SGI	392	2	271	2	−31
Others	4,038	24	2,796	17	−31
Total market	**$16,940**	**100%**	**$16,202**	**100%**	**−4%**

Source: IDC Research, 1999.

EXHIBIT 12.2 Sun Microsystems Revenues

Sun Revenues (Products), 1996

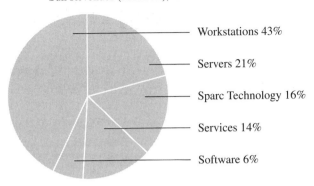

- Workstations 43%
- Servers 21%
- Sparc Technology 16%
- Services 14%
- Software 6%

Source: Business Week, January 22, 1996.

EXHIBIT 12.3 Abbreviated Financial Statement

	Years Ended June 30,		
	1998	**1997**	**1996**
	(in $000s)		
Net revenues:			
Products	$8,603,259	$7,747,115	$6,392,358
Services	1,187,581	851,231	702,393
Total net revenues	**9,790,840**	**8,598,346**	**7,094,751**
Growth	13.9%	21.2%	N/A
Cost of sales:			
Products	3,972,283	3,790,284	3,468,416
Services	721,053	530,176	452,812
Total cost of sales	4,693,336	4,320,460	3,921,228
Gross margin	52.1%	49.8%	44.7%
Research and development	1,013,782	825,968	653,044
Selling, general, and administrative . . .	2,777,264	2,402,442	1,787,567
Purchased in-process R&D	176,384	22,958	57,900
Operating income	1,130,074	1,026,518	675,012
Margin	11.5%	11.9%	9.5%
Gain on sale of equity investment	—	62,245	—
Interest expense, net	(46,092)	(32,444)	(33,862)
Income before income taxes	1,176,166	1,121,207	708,874
Provision for income taxes	413,304	358,787	232,486
Net income	**$ 762,862**	**$ 762,420**	**$ 476,388**
Other data:			
Total assets	$5,711,062	$4,697,274	N/A
Total debt	$ 47,169	$ 100,930	N/A
Total stockholders' equity	$3,513,628	$2,741,937	N/A
Estimated number of stockholders . .	341,000	289,000	N/A
Total employees at year end	26,343	21,553	N/A

Source: Company SEC filings.

McNealy's pugnacious attitude helped define Sun's culture in its early years. He promoted a coach/team-like atmosphere in which head-to-head competition was encouraged, and was quoted as saying, "If everyone believes in your strategy, you have zero chance of profit." Those who worked for him saw him as an inspirational corporate rebel who "made you want to win one for the gipper." Those who competed against him recognized his belligerent charm; one anonymous competitor told an industry publication, "Sun sells UNIX, a boring techie thing. You think if not for McNealy they'd be so successful and have so much name recognition?"[3]

THE BIRTH OF JAVA[4]

With the technology market booming in the early 1990s, a group of Sun's top computer programmers grew restless and thought about leaving the company. Included among them were programming gurus James Naughton and James Gosling. Keenly aware of their value to Sun, McNealy sat down with the two and made them an offer they couldn't refuse: The company would give them a team of top software developers with the freedom to pursue whatever they wanted. The only requirement was to make something "cool."

Rising to the challenge, Naughton and Gosling went into self-imposed exile with their new team, code-named Green, at a site miles from Sun's headquarters in Palo Alto, California. There they were no longer distracted by the everyday workings of Sun's office. The team was referred to as a modern-day version of the scientists on the Manhattan Project. They were intrigued with potential opportunities in the consumer electronics market that could make it possible for household consumer devices to communicate with each other. With this in mind, they set to work trying to create a language that would allow TV devices, such as a universal remote control and an interactive set-top box, to interact seamlessly. Meeting with little success, Gosling realized that the usual computer languages were too bulky and unreliable to program these types of devices. He began to develop a new, streamlined language called Oak, named for a tree outside his window. The Green project continued to evolve into a Sun-owned company called FirstPerson.

In 1993 the National Center for Supercomputing Applications introduced Mosaic, and the World Wide Web was born. FirstPerson recognized that the seamless programming language it had been unsuccessfully trying to apply to consumer electronics was well suited for online media. Sun began to market the product as a "language-based operating system," meaning the system itself became the product instead of part of a device. By March 1995 Oak had become known as Java.

WHAT IS JAVA?

Java is software for writing programs that can run on any device connected to a network. Unlike other programming languages such as C, C++, Pascal, or BASIC, which depend on an underlying operating system, Java can run on any operating system and on any computer. This unique versatility means that people working on completely different operating systems can work on the same document or play the same game as long as the program is written in Java. This is a fundamentally different vision of computing from the PC, and fits perfectly with the World Wide Web's way of doing things.

In essence, the Web is what Java was designed for—to be a network application—fitting into Sun's vision of the network as the computer (see Exhibit 12.4).

JAVA IN THE MARKETPLACE

Java was poised to affect the technology market in four important ways:

Versatility

Java's "write once, run anywhere" capability would enable programmers to create a single piece of software that could be understood by any major operating system. This would significantly cut development time for individual programs and expand the market potential of a program. From a programmer's perspective, this meant that all operating systems would be equal. Computers would interpret each line of Java code separately and translate it for the operating system. In turn, the operating system would translate the code for the microprocessor chip.

Savings

Java would not only cut development time, but also help users save money. Java would significantly reduce creative, distribution, and transfer costs because its applications run on any kind of computer.

EXHIBIT 12.4 An Architectural View of Java and Jini Technology

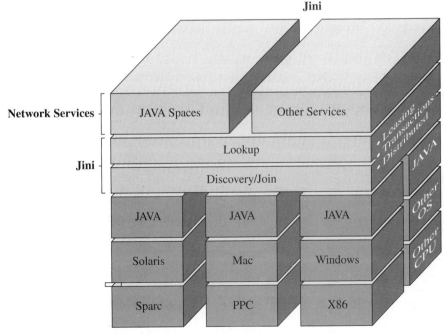

Source: www.sun.com.

Competition

Java would make it possible for a new class of cheap network computers to compete with the elaborate Wintel operating system. According to McNealy, this was a pipe dream come true: "We always thought we were onto something with Java — that it was our one big chance to challenge Microsoft and change the economics of the business."[5]

Providing "the Dot in .Com"

With the dawning of the Internet age, perhaps the most important implication of Java is that it would adopt the role of the language best suited to the Internet. By nature, Java doesn't discriminate against specific machines and is inherently virus proof.

EXPLOITING JAVA

If the standard gets fragmented then Java fails.[6]

—Ken Morse, chief technology officer of Power TV, Inc.

Alliances and Partnerships

To exploit Java's full potential, Sun entered into a series of alliances and partnerships. In its quest for ubiquity and market acceptance, rather than profitability, Sun killed its own HotJava browser to enter a licensing agreement with Netscape. In September 1995 Netscape launched Navigator 2.0 with support for Java applets, giving Java unprecedented market penetration and a major presence on the Web. Several companies, including Oracle, Novell, and IBM, recognized Java's potential for network computing in the Internet age, and embraced Java, hoping it would blunt Microsoft's hegemony. Appendix 12.3 on page 321 lists the strategic alliances in which Sun was engaged.

Microsoft had initially dismissed Java's potential as overblown, but quickly reversed its position. In March 1996 Microsoft licensed Java for its Internet Explorer 3.0, which touted the best Java performance of any browser at the time. However, Sun's victory was limited. When Microsoft launched Internet Explorer 4.0 in 1997, it contained a Java source code optimized for Windows. This meant that certain Java applets would run smoothly only on Internet Explorer. Java as a standard universal language was under fire.

The Creation of JavaSoft

In January 1996 Sun announced the development of a new strategic business unit named JavaSoft. Its mission was "to develop, market, and support Java technology and products based on it." The overarching goal was to work toward building Java into an OS. This involved decreasing Java's association with UNIX and making it "cross-platform" as the architecture promised. JavaSoft was staffed by 100 people broken into developer services, products, and marketing. They received additional help from 200 volunteers working on developing the Java platform. By 1998, however, JavaSoft began to turn its sights away from platform development, moving to office application development, much to the chagrin of large and small third-party developers such as IBM and WebLogic.

Sun's vision for the office application market was that all kinds of programs written in Java would reside on networks. Instead of a PC, offices would use bare-bones network computers. When employees needed to use an application, such as a word processor, they would download the application from the network, use it, and then the program would disappear. By centralizing software rather than duplicating it on individual terminals, businesses would reduce the costs of upgrading and fixing mismatched or corrupted systems.

Implementing this vision was not easy for Sun. Customers found that Java office applications had limited functionality and were unstable. The Java Virtual Machine, an "environment" that sat between the Java program and the machine it was running on, did not behave consistently across all computing platforms. This made it difficult for Java to live up to its versatility and speed claims. Java's "write once, run anywhere" technology meant that applications catered to the lowest common denominator. Thus, Java applications tended to run slower than programs honed for platforms like Macs or Windows. Additionally, many companies had already made a significant investment in the Windows platform and were not receptive to rewriting all of their software to be compatible with Java.

THE FUTURE OF JAVA

The WebTone

Sun continues to pursue its mission to make Java the platform for a "platformless" technology. The company's future strategy is to supply all of the hardware and software necessary to build a 100 percent reliable Internet system—much like the dial tone offered by telecom companies. McNealy explains this concept of "WebTone":

> Information will become a utility, rather than people having a mainframe on their desk . . . That's why so much of our effort this year has been directed toward what we call the WebTone—computing that's as powerful as a supercomputer, yet as reliable and as easy to use as a telephone.[7]

Open Licensing Agreements

Sun has maintained its philosophy to offer open licensing for Java. This means that other technology companies can develop their own versions of Java, provided that it passes the "100 percent Pure Java test." Open licensing agreements have spawned more than 900,000 third-party software developers including IBM and Borland. These 100 percent Pure Java programs compete directly against Sun's package, the Java Development Kit. In 1998, Sun's revenue from licensing had reached $130 million.[8]

Internet Alliances

Sun continues to promote Java as the language of the Internet. In November 1998 the Internet community was rocked by news of a merger between AOL and Netscape.

Behind the deal was a strategic alliance between Sun and AOL. Barry Schuler, president of America Online Interactive Services, explained:

> There are two big phenomena that make this strategic alliance a compelling opportunity. First, consumers are coming online in droves, accelerating e-commerce. Second, businesses are embracing network computing on top of Internet standards as the architecture for all of their back-end systems. That's what this strategic alliance will do: enhance the value chain all the way from silicon to eyeballs.[9]

Microsoft

> In a world of manias and emotions, I have to make rational decisions. Someone who thinks that because a language is magic, these guys can overthrow the world — that person can't even think two chess moves ahead. You're not even in the game I'm playing.

> —Bill Gates, on the possibility that Java
> will make Windows obsolete, 1996.

Scott McNealy's continuous belittling of Windows NT has added fuel to the competitive fire between Sun and Microsoft. Microsoft has begun an all-out assault against Java, influencing thousands of software developers to use its Windows-optimal version. Moreover, Microsoft Research has developed its own Windows-optimal virtual machine based upon technology acquired through its purchase of Colusa Software.

In 1997 Sun sued Microsoft, alleging that the company had violated Sun's license to use Java and was "polluting" the technology by distributing incompatible software tools and systems, including versions of Windows. In October 1998 Sun won the first round of the legal dispute when a federal judge issued a preliminary injunction ordering Microsoft to make its Java products compatible with Sun's Java. However, the victory was limited. The court ruled that Microsoft could still ship versions of its development tools to third-party developers and was still free to distribute Java versions developed independently from Sun's technology.[10]

SUN'S DILEMMA

While McNealy continued to pitch Sun's audacious "WebTone" vision to Wall Street analysts, the standard that Sun had worked so hard to develop themselves seemed to be slowly slipping away:

- In November, Sun archrival Hewlett-Packard (H-P) announced the creation of the Real-Time Java Working Group (RTJWG) consortium of Internet companies to develop real-time application program interfaces (APIs). RTJWG's claim was that Sun was tardy in developing Java's real-time capabilities and that Sun's licensing fees were excessive.[11]
- Longtime allies IBM and Novell began to complain that Sun's licensing restrictions were too tight. IBM specifically wanted more control over how Java interacts with its own legacy systems. Frustrated, Novell teamed up with Intel to develop an "optimized" version of Java.
- Microsoft enlisted the aid of Hewlett-Packard to codevelop its own version of Java. Shortly thereafter, Microsoft and H-P targeted Sun's Jini by developing a Java-based version of Microsoft's Universal Plug and Play (UPNP) software. Jini

is a Java-derivative programming code that enables "dumb" devices like cell phones to communicate with a network.

With Microsoft building momentum and longtime Sun allies growing impatient, McNealy knew that Sun had to act decisively. He also knew that Sun could not win the Java war alone. There was no doubt that Java's future was uncertain and Sun was vulnerable. McNealy kept thinking of the popular film *The Godfather* and the infamous words of wisdom spoken by Don Corleone to his youngest son. "Keep your friends close, *but your enemies even closer.*"

REFERENCES

1. John Doerr of Kleiner Perkins, quoted in David Kirkpatrick, "Meanwhile, Back at Headquarters," *Fortune,* October 13, 1997, p. 82.
2. www.sun.com/aboutsun/investor/faq.html.
3. Darryl K. Taft, "Top 25 Executives: Scott McNealy," *Computer Reseller News,* November 17, 1997, www.crn.com/sections/special/comdex97/764_25top1.asp.
4. The story of Java's birth taken from the following articles: Jason English, "The Story of the Java Platform," November 16, 1998, java.sun.com/nav/whatis/storyofjava.html; Kevin Maney, "Sun Rises on Java's Promise," *USA Today,* February 28, 1999, www.usatoday.com/life/cyber/tech/cta838.htm; John Clyan, "Your Guide to Java for 1998," *PC Magazine Online,* April 7, 1998, www.zdnet.com/pcmag/features/java98/index.html; "Where Did Java Technology Come From?," www.sun.com/java/comefrom.jhtml.
5. Brent Schlender and Eryn Brown, "Sun's Java: The Threat to Microsoft Is Real," *Fortune,* November 11, 1996, p. 165.
6. Power TV, Inc., is a consumer software toolmaker.
7. Robert D. Hof, Steve Hamm, and Ira Sager, "Sun Power," *Business Week,* January 18, 1999, p. 64.
8. Sun Microsystems, Inc., *1998 Annual Report.*
9. Sun press release, March 30, 1999, www.iplanet.com/alliance/press_room/press_releases/strategy. html.
10. Steven Shankland, "HP Works to Reverse Sun Java Victory," *CNET News,* March 26, 1999, aolsvccomp.cnet.com/news/0-1003-200-340418.html.
11. Mary Jo Foley and Deborah Gage, "Vendors Wrestle to Control Java," *Sm@rt Reseller,* April 2, 1999, www.zdnet.com/sr/stories/news/0,4538,2236254,00.html.

The "Virtual Machine"

The breakthrough application of Java was its capability of creating a "virtual machine" (VM). In essence, the VM is an abstract computer that sits between the Java program and the computer it operates on, executing Java code and guaranteeing certain behaviors regardless of the underlying hardware platform.

100% Pure Java

100% Pure Java is Sun's Java language without the embellishment of other companies' designs. The 100% Pure Java initiative was formed as a reaction to competitors like Microsoft who made versions of Java that ran better in certain environments and on certain platforms. 100% Pure Java stands for Sun's commitment to a platformless Java that treats all systems equally.

Jini

Jini is a Java-based language that allows computers and devices to quickly form impromptu systems unified by a network. The system is a federation of devices, including computers, which are simply connected. Within a federation, devices are instantly on—no one needs to install them. Similarly, you simply disconnect devices when you don't need them.

Solaris

Solaris is a 32-bit and 64-bit UNIX operating environment for enterprisewide computing. For users who value distributed network computing, Common Desktop Environment (CDE) for Solaris offers a high-performance, industry-standard desktop environment.

SPARC Technology/SPARC Families

SPARC is the flagship processor family for Sun. SPARC is characterized by design simplicity, allowing shorter development cycles, smaller die sizes, and ever-increasing performance. The SPARC architecture enables a unique combination of semiconductor and design scalability. With its multiprocessor capabilities, high bandwidth support, and register window design, the SPARC design allows implementations through a range of price/performance levels. SPARC processors achieve a higher number of instructions per second with fewer transistors.

Source: www.sun.com.

Management Solutions
- System Management
- Intranet Management

Support Solutions
- Educational Services
- Professional Services
- Online Support Tools

Development Solutions
Workshop Development Products
- Java WorkShop
- Sun Visual Workshop for C++
- Project Studio
Java Products
- Java Developer's Kit (JDK)

Deployment Solutions
Desktop Computers
- JavaStation Network Computer
- Ultra Family of Workstations
- Creator and Creator3D Graphics Stations
- Sun Elite3D High-end Graphics Station
Servers
- Sun Enterprise family of servers
- Sun Enterprise Starfire data center
- Netra family of dedicated file servers
Storage
- Sun StorEdge family of mainframe class and desktop storage products
- Components and Boards
- UltraSparc
- picoJava

Source: www.sun.com.

APPENDIX 12.3 **Strategic Alliances and Licensing Agreements**

Computers/Information Services
- IBM

Consumer Electronics
- Sony
- Samsung

Digital and Wireless Communications
- Alcatel
- Nortel
- Motorola
- Ericsson
- Siemens-Nixdorf

Electronic Commerce/Internet
- AOL/Netscape

Enterprise Resource Planning
- Baan
- Oracle
- PeopleSoft
- SAP

Interactive Television
- OpenTV
- Scientific Atlanta

Java Development Tools
- IBM
- Symantec/H-P
- Borland
- BEA Systems

Network Software
- Novell

Source: www.sun.com.

DIAMOND MULTIMEDIA AND THE RIO: DAVID'S INNOVATION IN THE FACE OF GOLIATH

THE DILEMMA

It was late October 1999. With the imminent end of the 20th century as a backdrop, Diamond Multimedia's chairman and CEO, William Schroeder, pondered the rapid pace at which his company's hot new product, the Rio, had swept his company headlong into a pending hardware war with some of the music industry's largest players. As the various purveyors of competing digital audio formats raced to develop an industry standard, Diamond sought to position the Rio as the portable digital audio device "du jour" for early adopting "audiophiles." The objective was early market domination of this burgeoning space in anticipation of mass-market product adoption.

Throughout 1999 Schroeder's focus had been on continuous improvement of player storage, replay capabilities, and ancillary aesthetic product features in order to remain one step ahead of a mounting list of formidable competitors. In addition, his Internet music "vortal"[1] play, RioPort.com, continued to take on increasing strategic importance in his consideration set. While the introduction of the Rio PMP500 in August 1999 had been a consumer and critical success, Schroeder's task at hand remained twofold:

1. Maintain the lead that the Rio device range and RioPort.com had established within the digital audio market.
2. Establish the resources required to appropriate sustainable financial returns from these innovations.

Further, Diamond's acquisition by S3, Inc., was completed in September 1999. Although the stated and implied strategic imperatives behind this transaction had minimal direct impact on Diamond's digital audio aspirations, whose management and operations had been separated from the rest of the firm,[2] Schroeder felt he must maintain his focus while effecting the implementation of postmerger integration.

New York University Stern School of Business MBA candidates John Aisien, Paul LeBlanc, Kathryn Nelson, Miri Polachek, and Emmanuelle Skala prepared this case under the supervision of Christopher L. Tucci for the purpose of class discussion rather than to illustrate either effective or ineffective handling of an administrative situation.

CASE *13*
*Diamond
Multimedia and the
Rio: David's
Innovation in the
Face of Goliath*

Diamond Multimedia is a leader in accelerator interactive multimedia, communications technologies, and portable digital audio hardware. The company has essentially grown organically since it was founded in 1982, although it has also judiciously used acquisitions to bolster its product portfolio. The company is headquartered in San Jose, California, and has been publicly traded since it raised $120 million in a high-profile initial public offering (IPO) in 1995.[3]

Diamond's accelerator solutions allow users to design, deliver, and display media content through the Internet at an accelerated rate by speeding data transfers to and from the hard drive of a personal computer (PC). Its communications technology product range includes internal and external modems that allow Internet connectivity at various speeds. Appendix 13.1 on page 330 gives a comprehensive listing of Diamond's product range.

The Diamond Rio product range consists of portable audio playback devices for digital files of competing formats, typically downloaded over the Internet. They enable convenient, skip-free playback of music and spoken word by consumers "on the move." The devices' main drawback at this stage is their relatively low music file capacity, up to 2 hours compared with 32 hours for spoken word files. However, these products address one of the three main impediments in the way of large-scale adoption of digital audio distribution—"music by the bit"[4]—by a mass audience: (1) lack of portability, due to previous dependence on the PC as the hardware medium, (2) bandwidth, and (3) legal limitations. The last precludes the digital distribution of music content from most established artists.[5]

Diamond's products are distributed through computer retailers, so-called original equipment manufacturers (OEMs), and various other distributors worldwide. Diamond also has an e-commerce site that serves as an increasingly important distribution channel.

Prior to its acquisition by S3, Diamond was in the throes of a cash flow and valuation crisis. It had yet to turn in a profitable year since going public in 1995 and had lost more than $65 million from operations in 1997 and 1998 as its core modem and multimedia products have turned into low-price commodities. Its lack of quarterly earnings repeatedly disappointed Wall Street, triggering the gradual erosion of shareholder value.[6] Exhibits 13.1 and 13.2 provide a summary of Diamond's financial and market performance since its initial public offering.

Despite its financial woes, Diamond's recent track record of innovation has led to widespread critical acclaim (see Appendix 13.2 on page 330 for a summary of recent industry awards). The challenge that the firm now faces involves creating the context required to profit sustainably from its hot new product range.

WILLIAM SCHROEDER

Schroeder, 54, became CEO of Diamond in 1995, just prior to the initial public offering of the 13-year-old privately held firm. He has deftly shifted Diamond's investments away from PC products toward information appliances like the Rio. "See, you can teach an old dog new tricks," he remarked at a press conference in March 1999.[7]

A key additional component of Schroeder's strategy was the launch in January 1998 of RioPort.com, a vertical Internet portal targeted at music fans and Rio owners. Diamond describes RioPort.com as an integrated platform for acquiring, managing,

EXHIBIT 13.1 Diamond's Financial Performance

	Selected Financial Data		
	1998	**1997**	**1996**
	(in $ millions, except per share data)		
Net sales	$608.6	$443.3	$598.0
Gross profit	66.7	55.8	112.8
Operating expenses	133.1	123.5	90.1
Income from operations	(66.4)	(67.7)	22.7
Net income	(39.5)	(45.6)	16.3
Net income per share	$ (1.13)	$ (1.33)	$ 0.46
Total assets	$306.9	$337.6	$332.4
Total liabilities	160.5	157.0	108.1
Total shareholders' equity	146.4	180.6	224.3

Source: Company SEC filings.

EXHIBIT 13.2 Diamond's Stock Performance from 1995 to Its Acquisition by S3, Inc.

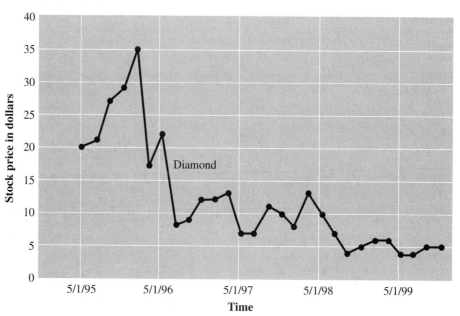

Note: Price data smoothed between bimonthly dates.
Source: Bloomberg.

and experiencing music and spoken audio programming from the Internet. Schroeder clearly sees it as a very important element of his tactical mix.

"We want to extend out of the hardware-only model." He compared Diamond's new approach to the razor market, where Rio represents the razor and RioPort the blades. "Razor manufacturers make far more money on the blades than the razors," he added.[8]

CASE 13
Diamond
Multimedia and the
Rio: David's
Innovation in the
Face of Goliath

The PMP500, Diamond's latest Rio product, is a portable digital audio player that stores up to 2 hours of music and 32 hours of spoken audio programming. Its successful launch in September 1999 provided additional respite to the firm, subsequent to the great success of its precursor, the PMP300. This trendy $199 device has attained unit sales of 100,000 since its launch in November 1998, contributing over 20 percent of Diamond's revenue over the same period.

The PMP500 is a greatly enhanced device whose retail price is $269.00. It features a USB port connection, allowing for compatibility with both Microsoft Windows and Apple (iMac) formats (the Rio was the first player for Macintosh users) and connection speeds five times faster than those allowed with the conventional parallel port connection. The PMP500 is also compatible with numerous digital audio formats including MP3, VBR, MPEG 2.5, and ADPCM. Diamond has deftly broadened its appeal by enabling third-party access to the Rio's source code. This has encouraged alliances with other trendy device manufacturers like Handspring, whose Visor (next-generation handheld PC) can be employed as a portable audio device by means of an additional module from Diamond at minimal cost to the consumer.[9]

The Rio is primed for use by following a three-step process:

1. Load CD and launch Music Match's encryption software.
2. Encode songs in MP3 format.
3. Launch Rio Manager and copy songs to the Rio.[10]

In addition, MP3 (or other format) files from a PC's hard drive (files previously downloaded from the Internet) can be copied directly to the Rio.[11]

While new product features such as size, color, and multiplatform compatibility are essential to the Rio's short-term success, the significance of the Rio's support of the numerous digital audio formats is central to its long-term survival. As the standards war is waged over digitally downloadable music, the Rio continues to support most formats—and to preclude the potential for obsolescence—until a dominant design emerges.

STRATEGIC ALLIANCES

Diamond has demonstrated a consistent history of entry into strategic alliances as an essential part of its product development arsenal. Appendix 13.3 on pages 330–332 illustrates in tabular form the recent alliances involving the Rio and RioPort.com.

Alliances with software and content providers have expanded the breadth of services and features that the Rio PMP300 and Rio PMP500 support. Since September 1998 Diamond has allied with Xing Technology (MP3 Jukebox software), GoodNoise, MP3.com, Audio Explosion, and Sonic Foundry. These alliances have allowed Diamond to expand the Rio's scope of offerings to include, for example, jukebox and digital audio software that allow musicians to create, post, and play back new music over the Internet. Rio's customers can also access and download audio content enablers such as Audible's AudibleManager software which, when bundled into the Rio, will allow customers to buy, download, and transfer spoken audio content to the Rio.

Another key alliance was driven by the need to extend the Rio's appeal to users who seek to play content from their existing CD collection of mainstream artists

(MusicMatch's Jukebox software can "rip" tracks off audio CDs placed in a PC's CD-ROM drive and store them as MP3 files). This of course led to a dispute with record labels over copyright concerns, so Diamond promptly entered into an alliance with the Recording Industry Association of America (RIAA), the trade association representing the major and independent record labels. The RIAA is leading a Secure Digital Music Initiative (SDMI), which is charged with developing a music delivery technology aimed at becoming an industry standard. The goal is to bring the worldwide music community and the technology companies together in an open forum to develop a standard for digital music security through the creation of new architecture and specifications.

Other industry forums in which Diamond holds memberships include the MP3 Association and the Digital Media Association. Diamond has also announced a strategic agreement with Liquid Audio (a competing digital audio format provider) in which the two companies are working cooperatively to bring Liquid Audio's secure music delivery system to RioPort.com and, by extension, to the Rio.

Finally, Diamond has used alliances to effect hardware manufacture and distribution. These alliances have, in general, provided Rio customers with additional services and access to a wide array of legally available content over the Internet. Potential foes have been deftly co-opted into mutually beneficial partnerships. However, it still remains questionable whether Diamond's plethora of alliances has adequately positioned the company to compete with large, vertically integrated players such as Sony, Samsung, and RCA.

DIGITAL AUDIO FORMATS

Digital audio technologies have reached new heights over the last few years. The essential premise behind these technologies is to compress audio files to a size practical for transfer over the Internet, without any perceived loss of quality. Various formats have proliferated, including:

- Windows Media Audio (WMA files are half the size of MP3 files)
- MPEG Audio Layer Series (MP2.5 and MP3)
- Liquid Audio
- Real Audio

These formats are locked in a keenly fought race for adoption as a digital audio standard.

MPEG AUDIO LAYER-3 (MP3) HISTORY[12]

The MPEG Audio Layer-3 (MP3) technology was invented in 1987 at the Institute for Integrated Circuits (Institut Integrierte Schaltungen) (IIS) in Germany. Working in joint cooperation with the University of Erlangen, the IIS devised a very powerful algorithm that is standardized as ISO-MPEG Audio Layer-3.

Without data compression, digital audio signals usually comprise 16-bit samples recorded at a sampling rate of more than double the actual audio bandwidth (e.g., 44.1 kHz for compact disks), ending up with more than 1.4 million bits to represent just one second of stereo music comparable in quality to a CD. By using MPEG audio coding, one can shrink the original sound data from a CD by a factor of 12 without losing sound quality. This makes it feasible to reduce CD-quality music to a compressed size that would allow for efficient distribution over the Internet and the storage of audio files on PCs and audio devices.

327

*CASE 13
Diamond
Multimedia and the
Rio: David's
Innovation in the
Face of Goliath*

The popularity of MP3 among Internet-based music lovers has been made possible by its open standard; that is, it is not the patented property of any company. The MP3 is thus particularly well received by audio software developers, driving the rapid proliferation of content based on this format.

SECURITY AND BANDWIDTH ISSUES[13]

The delivery of audio by means of digitized formats over the Internet is clearly an important new channel, but the technology needs a major overhaul before it achieves mass appeal. A new pirate minimization code (such as a digital watermark) needs to be adopted by the industry and incorporated into any digital audio format with aspirations of becoming the standard. This will be the trigger that the major labels—with their promotion and distribution clout—require to permit access to the content of mainstream recording artists. The RIAA, along with various corporate stakeholders, including Diamond, has made great strides with the formation of the Secure Digital Music Initiative (SDMI). (See Appendix 13.3.)

Lack of sufficient bandwidth also poses a hurdle in the path of large-scale adoption of pure-play digital audio delivery. With a 56K modem, which is typically found in most homes, MP3 files can download at about 1 MB per minute of music. It thus takes about four minutes to download a typical music track. This conveys significant disadvantages to the consumer. It is thus likely that the importance of digital audio formats (and by extension, the importance of the Internet as an audio distribution channel) will follow the oft-predicted explosion in bandwidth of the "Last Mile" to individual households.

COMPETITION[14]

RCA LYRA RD2201

The LYRA retails for $199.99. It is compatible with both the MP3 and Real Networks G2 technology and can be upgraded with future downloads from the Lyrazone website. The LYRA uses an external compact memory card to connect the device to PCs for file transfers. Additionally, the LYRA has numerous ancillary product features such as auto power down and auto resume that have been popular with consumers. Perhaps the most significant asset of the LYRA is the backing of its corporate parent, RCA, given its rich endowment in financing, marketing, and distribution.

Creative Labs NOMAD II

The NOMAD II retails for $229.99. It is compatible with both the MP3 and Windows Media format. It also features upgradeable firmware that can be downloaded from its website, allowing the player to continuously adapt to the evolving formats and standards of digital audio. Like the Rio, the NOMAD II features a USB port for faster download times. Ancillary features include an FM tuner, voice recording capabilities, and a wired remote control. The NOMAD II is also SDMI compliant.

Saehan MPMan

Saehan was the first to market, in February 1998, a portable MP3 digital download audio player. The company has since come out with numerous product upgrades, the most recent in September 1999. Like Sony and RCA, Saehan is a large consumer electronics company and therefore owns the necessary resources to compete effectively in this market.

Sony Memory Stick Walkman NW-MS7

Retail price: $449.95. The Memory Stick Walkman marks the anticipated entry of Sony, which created and dominated the "off-line" tape cassette and CD format Walkman. The Memory Stick Walkman features a USB port, compatibility with both MP3 and PCM formats, and a rechargeable battery. The player utilizes Sony's own proprietary storage system, MagicGate. Like the NOMAD II, it is also SDMI compliant.

The Memory Stick's most significant feature, however, is its maker. Sony is the innovator and indisputable leader in the off-line portable music market and is a fully integrated entertainment conglomerate whose activities encompass the creation and distribution of content. It is therefore well positioned for long-term survival in the digital audio hardware marketplace, endowed as it is with financial resources, distribution and marketing strength, and access to talent and proprietary music sources that most of its competitors lack. Additionally, Sony's technological leadership in video games, PCs, and other electronic devices indicates an R&D expertise that will probably be brought to bear quickly within this nascent space.

Samsung YP-E32 and Philips

Although not as technically complex or oriented toward product features as the other players in the market, the entrance of these two large, experienced players in the electronics and entertainment industries further muddles the competitive landscape for Diamond. Because they are also armed with the resources required for long-term success in this market, these two competitors add to the sense of urgency that Diamond faces. Appendix 13.4 on page 332 provides a tabular summary of the quickly evolving competitive landscape for the Rio player.

AFTER THE PARTY WAS OVER

As William Schroeder struggled to create the Rio Division's list of New Year's resolutions, he was cognizant that the forthcoming holiday season would be his last without competition from formidable players like Sony, which recently celebrated the 20th anniversary of the Walkman by announcing its own digital audio delivery player. Additionally, he must brace himself for the inevitable and rapid technological strides that would be made in the coming year by other consumer products rivals like Samsung, RCA, and Philips. After a year marked by a long list of judicious strategic alliances, countless industry awards, and Diamond's recent acquisition by S3, Schroeder pondered the further steps he must take as he aimed his slingshot at the menacing suite of "goliaths" lumbering across the horizon.

REFERENCES

1. *Vertical portal* is a term coined by *The Economist* magazine to describe an Internet portal that serves a singular purpose.

329

CASE *13*
Diamond
Multimedia and the
Rio: David's
Innovation in the
Face of Goliath

2. www.diamondmm.com/companypress_centerpress_releases.asp?ID=326.

3. Ibid.

4. Mihir Parikh, "The Music Industry in the Digital World: Waves of Changes," working paper, Institute for Technology and Enterprise, 1999.

5. Mark E. Hardie, John C. McCarthy, Eric Schmitt, and Joseph L. Butt, Jr., "Music's Internet Era," *The Forrester Report,* January 1998, pp. 1–2; Mark E. Hardie and Joseph L. Butt, Jr., "Road Testing Diamond's Rio," *The Forrester Brief,* February 22, 1999.

6. Amey Stone, "Can New Facets Make Diamond Shine Again?" *Business Week Online,* February 26, 1999, www.businessweek.com/bwdaily/dnflash/feb1999/nf90226a.htm.

7. Peter Burrows, Andy Reinhardt, and Heather Green, "Trailblazers: The Company Man," *Business Week,* March 8, 1999, p. 78.

8. Ibid.

9. "Diamond Multimedia Announces Support for Handspring's Springboard Platform," Handspring Press Release, September 14, 1999, www.handspring.com/company/pr/pr_rio.asp.

10. Paul M. Eng, "Diamond's Rio: The Little Music Player That Could," *Business Week,* December 3, 1998, www.businessweek.com/bwdaily/dnflash/dec1998/nf81203a.htm.

11. Maria Seminerio, "Stop the Music! Diamond Multimedia Faces Lawsuit over its Rio Player," *ZDNet News,* October 9, 1998, www.zdnet.com/zdnn/stories/zdnn_smgraph_display/0,4436,2147735,00.html.

12. www.iis.fhg.de/amm/techinf/layer3/index.html.

13. Jennifer Jones, "MP3: Is It Time to Play?" *Equip Magazine,* equip.zdnet.com/gear/mp3/feature/2a52/.

14. www.wearablegear.com; hardware.mp3.com/hardware/.

APPENDIX 13.1 Diamond's Product Portfolio

PC Subsystems—Multimedia Accelerators
- Viper Media Accelerators (High End)
- Stealth Media Accelerators (Lower End)
- Monster Entertainment 3D & Audio Accelerators
- Fire Professional 3D Graphics & SCSI Accelerators

Communications Products—Modems
- Supra Internal/External Modems (up to 56 Kbps)
- Supra NetCommander ISDN Digital Modem

Downloadable Digital Music Hardware Devices
- Rio PMP300
- Rio PMP300 Special Edition—Additional Memory Capabilities
- Rio PMP500

Source: www.diamondmm.com/products.htm.

APPENDIX 13.2 The Rio: Summary of Recent Awards

Date	Award Provider	Purpose
August 3, 1999	Macworld Expo 1999	Rio PMP500 portable digital audio player was awarded "Best of Show" at Macworld Expo '99, held July 21–23 in New York. "Best of Show" awards are presented for the hottest new products introduced at Macworld Expos every year.
April 29, 1999	*Discover* Magazine	Rio PMP300 selected as finalist in the Personal Entertainment category of the 1999 *Discover* Magazine Awards for Technical Innovation. Past nominees and winners include the NASA Jet Propulsion Laboratory, MIT, Mercedes-Benz, and IBM.
November 11, 1998	*Popular Science* Magazine	Rio PMP300 selected for "Best of What's New" award, awarded to 100 of the most important and innovative products introduced to the world during the year.

APPENDIX 13.3 Tabular Representation of Recent Alliances Involving the Rio and Rioport.com

Timeline	Partner(s)	Purpose
September 14, 1999	**Handspring, Inc.** (handheld computing device provider)	Diamond is developing an expandable hardware module that enables Handspring's Visor (handheld computer) to be expanded into a portable MP3 player.

CASE *13*
*Diamond
Multimedia and the
Rio: David's
Innovation in the
Face of Goliath*

Timeline	Partner(s)	Purpose
April 13, 1999	**Sonic Foundry, Inc** (developer and marketer of digital audio software)	Sonic Foundry is developing a complete solution to enable musicians to create, post, and play back new music on the Internet. The software will be the premier audio creation tool offered with the Rio.
June 24, 1999	**Amplified.com** (business-to-business provider of Internet services to the music industry)	Amplified will provide a service by which Rio users (and RioPort.com customers) can order custom-burned CDs containing both promotional and for-purchase digital audio files for a small fee.
June 24, 1999	**Audible, Inc** (provider of Internet-delivered spoken audio content)	Through this partnership, 15,000 hours of audio from Audible's content library (Stephen King, John Grisham, Harvard Management Update) has been made Rio-ready and available for purchase and downloading by RioPort's customers.
June 24, 1999	**GVC Corporation** (Taiwan-based electronics manufacturing giant)	GVC will handle assembly for hardware licensee production of the next generation of Rio portable digital audio players. GVC is the manufacturer of the new Rio PMP 500 and the PMP 300.
June 24, 1999	**Microsoft Corporation** (uber-monopolist, misunderstood behemoth)	Future Rio-brand digital audio players will incorporate support for Microsoft's Windows Media Audio, a key feature of its Windows Media Technologies.
February 8, 1999	**Independent labels and artists**	To offer an expanded collection of MP3 music and audio files on the Internet through RioPort.com, Diamond signed distribution agreements with a suite of "independents" designated as site partners.
December 15, 1998	**Record Industry Association of America** (association representing major and independent record labels)	As a means of settling the pending lawsuit brought by the RIIA, Diamond entered into a Secure Digital Music Initiative, charged with developing a digital music standard that addresses security and copyright protection considerations.
November 2, 1998	**Liquid Audio** (provides software for digital audio distribution)	Diamond released its Media Device Manager API to Liquid Audio to enable the support of audio files in Liquid's format by future Rio portable devices.

(continued)

APPENDIX 13.3 (*continued*)

Timeline	Partner(s)	Purpose
November 2, 1998	**Audio Explosion** (closely held San Francisco start-up that provides music on demand over the Internet)	Agreement to copromote and market Internet music. Audio's Mjuice Music Card allows Rio customers to purchase $5.00 worth of songs from the Mjuice.com site, which contains more than 200 licensed songs, priced at $1.00 per download, from various genres including hip-hop, alternative rock, and acid jazz.
September 14, 1998	**MusicMatch** (MP3 solutions provider) and **Xing Technology** (digital audio software provider)	Exclusive, six-month licensing agreement with MusicMatch Corporation and Xing Technology Corporation to bundle their Jukebox CD conversion and MP3 encoding software with the Rio.
September 14, 1998	**GoodNoise** (pioneer Internet record company)	Copromotion and marketing of MP3 audio content through sample distribution and cross-advertising.
September 14, 1998	**Z Company** (founders of MP3.com)	Strategic partnership to comarket licensed MP3 content. Diamond will bundle MP3.com content with Rio player, while each entity cross-advertises its services on their respective sites.

APPENDIX 13.4 Tabular Representation of Competitive Landscape for the Rio

Product	Exp. Launch Date	Price	Feature Summary
RCA Lyra RD2201	October 1999	$199.99	• Supports myriad formats • Expandable memory • SDMI compatible • Very small—cell phone sized
Creative Labs NOMAD II	September 1999	$225.99	• Only supports MP3 format • FM Tuner • Handy desktop cradle for downloads • Voice recorder
Sony Memory Stick Walkman NW-MS7	January 2000	$399.95	• Supports myriad formats • Magic Gate Memory Stick • SDMI Compliant • Lightweight silver casing • 80–120 minutes of digital audio
Saehan MPMan	February 1998	$199.00	• Only supports MP3 format • Expandable • SDMI compatible
Samsung YEPP	Available in the U.K. in December 1999	$169.00–$249.00	• Voice recording • Memory expansion with card slot
Philips	Not yet announced	To be determined	Not yet available

Source: hardware.mp3.com/hardware/.

MERRILL LYNCH: FINANCIAL PORTAL STRATEGY

The do-it-yourself model of investing, centered on Internet trading, should be regarded as a serious threat to American financial lives.[1]

—John "Launny" Steffens, vice chairman,
Merrill Lynch, Summer 1998

As John "Launny" Steffens read the latest investment research report on Merrill Lynch, he was pleased to see that the company was receiving favorable comments from the investment analysts who covered Merrill's stock, including staunch rival Morgan Stanley Dean Witter. The transformation of the largest brokerage house in the United States was under way, and presiding over the transition to a more nimble and more effective firm that embraced technology and the Internet promised to keep Steffens and his management team quite busy.

The big question now was whether the new financial portal strategy was the right way to go. Did it go too far? Did it not go far enough? Accused by some of having underestimated the power of the Internet once before, Steffens wanted to make sure that this time Merrill was making the right moves not only to compete, but to win in the marketplace of the future—a marketplace that now included competitors such as eBay and Amazon.com as much as American Express and Morgan Stanley Dean Witter.

MERRILL LYNCH CORPORATE HISTORY

Merrill Lynch, the largest brokerage firm in the United States, with 8 million customer accounts and more than $1.5 trillion in assets, was founded as a bond underwriting firm in 1914 by Charles Merrill. With his friend and partner Edmund Lynch, the new firm catered to small, individual investors. During this period Merrill Lynch developed its famous catch phrase and unique philosophy of "Bringing Wall Street to Main Street."

During the Great Depression, Merrill thought it best to divest the retail brokerage arm of the company, which he sold to the largest brokerage firm in the country—E. A. Pierce. In 1940 Merrill Lynch merged with Pierce and continued to execute its strategy of pursuing individual investors, a group that powerful banks such as J.P. Morgan dismissed as inconsequential. The general disdain that the large banks had toward the average American provided Merrill Lynch with an untapped client base.

Throughout the second half of the 20th century, Merrill continued to find success with innovation. For example, during the 1970s Merrill was the first investment bank to go public and it also introduced the now common "central account." This new product, the "cash management account" (CMA) allowed investors to keep track of their securities, write checks, and make deposits. This revolutionary centralization of all financial activity in one account, combined with Merrill's ability to pay money market rates on deposits, brought clients to Merrill Lynch offices in droves. In the 1990s Merrill Lynch extended its global reach through acquisitions, including some major overseas purchases such as Mercury Asset Management and Yamaichi Securities.

Until recently, the competitive landscape was clear and could be characterized by the major global investment banks on one side and by brokerage houses on the other. Many attempts by other firms to mimic Merrill's successful model of combining the investment bank and brokerage had failed in the past, although more recently, the Morgan Stanley/Dean Witter and Salomon Brothers/Smith Barney combinations proved that Merrill's business model could be successfully copied. Another key area of competition that emerged, credited mainly to the pioneering efforts of Charles Schwab, was the discount brokerage firm. Citing that "you get what you pay for," Merrill dismissed the discount brokerage organizations and continued to focus on building its full-service brokerage client base and capabilities.

THE RISE OF ONLINE TRADING

The origins of online trading actually date back to 1987, but as recently as 1992 only about 400 trades a day were processed.[2] In the mid-1990s, the Internet emerged as a tool for investors to gather information, research companies, and trade stocks. Merrill, confident in its strategy and position in the market, largely ignored this trend toward online trading. Investors, however, were not so confident. With standard commissions at Merrill Lynch reaching into the hundreds of dollars, new competitors such as Ameritrade and E-Trade emerged, offering free research, access to up-to-the-minute trading information, and a price advantage that was hard to ignore. At Merrill, for example, a purchase of 100 shares of IBM could cost an individual investor $175 in commissions. The same trade at an online discount broker could run as low as $8. Today, 12.5 percent of investors trade online, and that number is expected to climb to 29.2 percent by 2002.[3]

"WORK WITH MERRILL: ANY WAY YOU WANT TO"

The rise of the Internet and online trading was impossible to ignore, even for the traditional brokerage houses. One by one, firms were developing their own online trading capabilities and adding this capability to their portfolio of offerings. Many investors found this to be an effective means to manage their finances, and the growth of online trading was rapid.

In early 1999 Merrill announced that it would offer online trading capabilities for individual investors. Pushing the concept to the next level, Merrill claimed its desire to be a financial portal—a one-stop shop for investing, shopping, information, and even auctions. Many point to the day that Charles Schwab surpassed the market capitalization of Merrill Lynch as the catalyst for such a drastic reversal in strategy. Indeed, as an example of how quickly the brokerage landscape had changed, the day that Merrill announced its online plans, Merrill's market capitalization was $27.6 billion. Charles Schwab's was $40.7 billion.[4]

However, the 15,000 traditional brokers at Merrill were not all sure that they supported their leader's new strategy. Stockbrokers rely on commissions for at least part of their income, and the new online trading threatened the way that they conducted their business. In September 1999 four brokers in Detroit, Michigan, defected to the PaineWebber Group, taking over $2 billion in customer accounts with them.[5] Attrition among the top 40 percent of Merrill brokers in 1999 was up 27 percent compared with 1998.[6] There were several other high-profile defections to other brokerage firms soon after the online trading announcement, but many of the brokers accepted the Internet as a new medium that they must incorporate into their already competitive client management process.

Senior management at Merrill acknowledged the broker defections, realizing that they may be a fact of life in the new competitive landscape. However, they saw the online offering as providing another opportunity to manage the entire customer relationship. Allen Jones, director of marketing for retail brokerage said that, "Pure online will end up being a niche business. Most people are going to want a combo of online, discount, and full service." And CEO of Schwab, David Pottruck, agreed, saying, "Customers want a variety of distribution channels … face to face. The mail. The telephone. And the Web. We have to match up the right medium with the right interaction so that customers feel most comfortable."[7]

FROM TRADITIONAL BROKERAGE TO FINANCIAL PORTAL

> I want to have the ability to deal with our clients anywhere along the spectrum of financial services.
>
> —John Steffens, Merrill Lynch Vice Chairman

The key components of Merrill's strategy to execute the Financial Portal included both the online trading component, as well as the actual portal. The portal was designed to be a sophisticated means of interaction for a variety of financial and e-commerce needs.

A portal is a "website or service that offers a broad array of resources such as e-mail, forums, search engines, and online shopping malls." The most commonly known Internet portals were Yahoo!, Excite, and Infoseek, which were designed to be "familiar, useful places to enter the Web every time a person connects to the Internet."[8] The competition in this space was intense, and Merrill must contend with the established brands of the above portals, as well as the myriad of other portal sites that litter the Internet.

Merrill Lynch was clearly betting that the winner in the online investing and servicing battle could not win on price alone. Instead, Merrill believed that the winner would be the company that complements its brand equity with products and services to provide a unique value proposition for customers. In addition, through the use of loyalty plans, incentives, and convenience, Merrill hoped to establish substantial switching costs, essentially locking in its customers.

In addition to offering basic online trading for a fixed commission, Merrill leveraged its extensive financial planning services. A staff of 835 certified financial planners (more than any other firm) and 683 analysts offered immediate or same-day access to research reports and specific investment recommendations. Merrill also offered clients more personalized portfolio tracking programs. Convinced that its clients had a higher propensity to transact business and shop online, Merrill even extended its reach into e-commerce and auctions by taking on formidable contenders such as Yahoo! and Amazon.com.

With its new financial portal in hand, Merrill hoped to enhance customer loyalty with existing subscribers and establish high switching costs for new clients. According to chief executive officer David Komansky, "We are trying to build different mechanisms to be able to attract people to the portal—our clients predominantly—and to strengthen the overall relationship."[9] Indeed, Merrill Lynch was striving to manage the total financial relationship with its customers, not just their investments.

FINANCIAL PORTAL COMPONENTS

Unlimited Advantage[10]

A key element of the strategy to provide unique value to customers was Unlimited Advantage, a program offering virtually unlimited trading of stocks for a minimum fee of $1,500 per year, or 1.0 percent of assets for equities and 0.3 percent for bonds. Steffens believed that this cost structure would soon become the industry standard. Merrill's 1.0 percent fee was significantly less than Morgan Stanley Dean Witter's 2.25 percent fee. The Unlimited Advantage program was extremely successful, boosting assets in fee-based accounts by $16 billion in the third quarter of 1999, of which 20 percent was new money to the firm.

ML Direct[11]

Merrill Lynch Direct [ML Direct], an online trading account offering Internet trades for a $29.95 commission each for stocks, mutual funds, and bonds, was launched December 1, 1999. Other securities such as options, high-yield debt, and mortgage-backed securities were also expected. However, the ability to simply trade stocks was enough to make everyone take notice. On the eve of the rollout, one analyst exclaimed, "The big gorilla is about to do a cannonball in the pool! Merrill will definitely make a big splash online."[12] Although the program could cost the firm approximately $1 billion in lost equity commissions, Merrill executives were confident that this loss would be more than offset by increased client assets.

ML Direct was somewhat different than the programs of the competition in terms of the ability to have access to discounted commissions. To be eligible for a $29.95 commission on trades, investors must open an account of at least $20,000, compared with $5,000 for Charles Schwab and $1,000 for E-Trade (with commissions of between $14.95 and $19.95 per transaction respectively.)[13]

E-Shopping (shopmerrill.com)

At shopmerrill.com, clients could shop from several hundred online merchants offering over 4 million products. Categories included apparel, books and magazines, computers and video games, computer hardware, computer software, consumer electronics, family and lifestyle, health and beauty, movies and video, music, office supply, toys and games, travel, and weddings. This site also offered product and price comparison features, merchandising capabilities, and purchasing recommendations. Points were rewarded for online purchases made with Merrill's Visa Signature card.

Analysts looked at shopmerrill.com as another tool for Merrill to replace the lost commission revenues from stock trades. Specifically, shopmerrill.com allowed the firm to earn additional revenues through revenue-sharing arrangements with product manufacturers, and gain valuable insights about consumer shopping behavior. In addition, shopmerrill.com was a key launching pad for new products and services of companies which Merrill underwrites or has strategic partnerships. And with 8 million customer accounts, Merrill already had the customer base from which to work.[14] It just needed to convince investors that they should do their online shopping with Merrill as well.

Merrill Institutional Internet Site

Merrill Lynch released the first version of its institutional site at the end of 1999. The site combined more than 50 products for its 3,500 large institutional customers, including corporations, governments, mutual funds, and pension funds. Merrill hoped that access to this website would lead to an institutional account expansion of more than 20,000 middle-market corporations. The site's features included the ability to personalize and consolidate positions and exposures, analytical functions, research and investment advice, and the ability to view daily offerings.

Other Services

Merrill Lynch offered additional online links to complement its existing product and service mix:

1. Business Center (businesscenter.ml.com): interactive tools to explore financial solutions for small-business owners.
2. Benefits Online (benefits.ml.com): access to 401(k) program performance.
3. AskMerrill (askmerrill.com): visitor registration for Merrill research for a 30-day trial period.
4. Auctions (merrillauctions.com): special auctions for clients, who can redeem Merrill Visa card points. Merrill arranged discounts for small-business owners and helped auction excess inventory over the Internet.
5. CMA Visa Signature card (signaturerewards.com): Clients could redeem points for numerous products and services, including travel on any airline at any time, hotel stays, access to sporting and cultural events, high-tech electronics, and for payment of fees and commissions.
6. Global Investor Network (GIN): in-house video news service. Merrill hired broadcast journalists to anchor news reports and conduct business segments for online viewing.

Alliances

Merrill Lynch actively formed strategic alliances to complete its financial portal infrastructure. It joined forces with companies such as Microsoft Network, Multex, Thirdage, and Medialink.com to drive additional traffic to its website. Service partnerships with companies such as works.com automated purchasing capabilities for small businesses. AT&T, Cisco, IBM, Microsoft, and Sun provided technology and outsourcing applications. Standard and Poor's, Dow Jones, and Intuit provided news and data content. More recently, Merrill formed an alliance with Inktomi to implement back-end Internet infrastructure software.

Merrill invested heavily in building a solid online trading platform. A licensing agreement with StarQuest extended applications, increased speed, and reduced complexities associated with transaction processing. Merrill invested in alternate trading systems from Primex and Bloomberg. In addition, Merrill bought a 14.3 percent stake in Archipelago, an electronic communications network (ECN), to offer after-hours trading. Merrill also owned stakes in three other ECNs, OptiMark, Primex, and Brut. Participation with TradeWeb allows corporate clients to see Merrill's offerings as well as those of its competitors. Merrill even partnered with academic institutions such as MIT to research and develop technologies affecting financial services in 2002 and beyond. A growing client base may also be found internationally as partnerships with foreign media, technology, and financial services companies help Merrill establish an overseas online presence in countries like Japan and Australia.

THE NEW COMPETITIVE LANDSCAPE

The financial portal opened Merrill up to an entirely new and mostly unfamiliar and hostile competitive environment. Modifications to the Glass-Steagall Act of 1933, the Depression-era law prohibiting the interaction between commercial and investment banks and insurance companies, promised to increase the pace of change in the investment industry. In addition, new competitors, some known and others unknown, had to be reckoned with. These competitors include the following firms:

Charles Schwab & Company

Charles Schwab founded his brokerage firm in 1974, hoping to capitalize on investors' frustration with full-service traditional brokerage firms (e.g., PaineWebber, Smith Barney, and Merrill Lynch). In 1975 Schwab capitalized on changes in SEC regulations that eliminated fixed fees for executing stock trades. Schwab also introduced the following:

- Created the OneSource mutual fund supermarket, making no-load mutual funds available to the general public.
- Opened the industry's first 24-hours-a-day, seven-days-a-week (24/7) order entry and quote service.
- Developed publications and seminars to teach people about buying and selling stocks and mutual funds.
- Launched a marketing campaign that emphasized consumers' ability to manage their own investments.[15]

Schwab believed he was helping give the individual investor more power. In return they would reward him for providing that value. In addition, Schwab felt that information technology could facilitate this belief and in 1979 brought all of the firm's data processing in-house. In 1984 Schwab introduced online trading with a simple software program called Equalizer. A Windows-based version, called StreetSmart, was introduced later. However, the number of investors using these services was never greater than 4 percent of the total Schwab customer base.[16] In 1995 the number of personal computers sold in the United States exceeded the number of televisions sold for the first time, and the Schwab team determined that the opportunity existed to dominate the market for computer-based trading. The company now has more than 2.8 million active online accounts and handles one-third of all online trades.

Schwab continued to exploit its first-mover advantage as the first established broker to provide online trading capabilities. As both established bricks-and-mortar firms and pure Internet companies continued to invade the online trading space, Schwab differentiated itself based on service. Schwab planned to increase the amount of tools and research available to clients, and to attract wealthier customers by offering special, enhanced service accounts to investors who carried at least $100,000 in assets and made at least 12 trades a year. In addition, Schwab experimented with ways to let its clients trade using personal digital assistants (PDAs) with wireless connectivity.

In late July 1999 Schwab announced a partnership with Fidelity Investments and Donaldson Lufkin & Jenrette to join Spear Leeds & Kellogg in an electronic communications network to let users trade stocks around the clock. This partnership furthered Schwab's position as a financial portal with full dedication to making its customer's financial lives as easy as possible.

What did Schwab think about electronic commerce beyond its core financial services businesses? Apparently, not much. According to a key strategist at Schwab, the company had no plans to extend its capabilities in this area; "we think that begins to dilute what the brand means to people. I don't think anyone wants to come to Schwab for an auction of . . . Beanie Babies."[17]

Amazon.com

Jeff Bezos founded Amazon.com, originally an online bookstore, in 1994. In July 1995 Amazon's website went live and by September of that year had sales of over $20,000 a week. Bezos and his employees continued to improve the site by introducing many features such as one-click shopping, customer reviews, and e-mail order verification. Amazon went public in 1997 and became the sole provider of books for both America Online customers and Netscape's portal site. In 1998 the company launched music and video "stores" and also began selling toys and even electronics. Bezos expanded the company's base of online services, buying Junglee, a comparison-shopping service, and PlanetAll, an address book, calendar, and reminder service. By mid-1998, Amazon.com had attracted so much attention that its market capitalization equaled the combined values of profitable bricks-and-mortar rivals Barnes & Noble and Borders, but Amazon's sales were far below these competitors.[18]

To expand Amazon beyond investors' wildest dreams, the firm then raised $1.25 billion in a public bond offering in early 1999. Amazon used these funds to buy all or part of drugstore.com, HomeGrocer.com, Pets.com, Gear.com, Web-use tracking firm Alexa Internet, rare book and music marketplace Exchange.com, e-commerce systems firm

Accept.com, and wedding-gift registry Della & James. It also bought the catalog business of Tool Crib of the North, expanding into home improvement products, and added software, video games, and gift sections to its store offerings. In addition, Amazon began conducting auctions in early 1999 and soon partnered with auction house Sotheby's to offer live auctions for rare collectibles. It also bought auction site LiveBid.com. Later in 1999 Amazon.com introduced its zShops program, allowing other companies to sell products from travel packages to maternity clothes through Amazon.com.

Many people (even loyal investors) had a hard time guessing what Amazon would do next. While currently focused on selling to its customers, it would not be out of Amazon's scope to offer basic financial services as well. This would only serve to make its customer's purchasing even easier. This could be as simple as an Amazon.com credit card, or more robust financial services such as stock trading. Founder Bezos said he wants Amazon to be the place people go on the Internet to buy anything. He believed in putting the customer first. While this may not sound out of the ordinary, it was practically a religious belief at Amazon. By offering its already huge customer base (over 13 million in 1999) anything a customer might ever want to buy online, Amazon may live up to its founder's statement.

American Express

Broadly defined, American Express is a diversified services company. Founded in 1850, American Express (AXP) provided travel, financial, and network services. Within financial services, American Express's businesses included credit cards, traveler's cheques, financial planning, insurance, mutual funds, and stock brokerage. American Express provided accounting and tax preparation for small businesses and banking services to wealthy individuals, corporations, retail customers, end users, and financial institutions in the United States and around the world.[19]

American Express maintained a unique relationship with its customers by marketing combinations of various service offerings. For example, customers who owned American Express credit cards received discounts on travel services. American Express also linked its brokerage and banking services.

Membership B@nking, American Express's online banking service, was founded in August 1999. It expected to open 200,000 accounts by August 2000 and 1 million accounts within five years. To attract customers, Membership B@nking offered free electronic bill payment and rebates for automated teller machine (ATM) service charges. Accounts were linked to American Express Brokerage's online service.

Through American Express Brokerage, customers could buy and sell various types of securities for very low transaction fees. American Express was the first discount broker to offer free trades (buys only) to customers with accounts valued at $25,000 or more. For these accounts, sell transactions carried a $14.95 fee. Customer accounts valued over $100,000 were allowed free buys and sells as long as the customer did not buy and sell the same security on the same day (same-day trades carried the $14.95 fee). The cost of these trades to American Express was estimated to be at least $8 per transaction, but the company believed profits would come from other areas such as interest on margin lending.

American Express Brokerage customers were given access to other services as well. Account owners could access free research from American Express, Zach's, Standard & Poor's, SmartMoney, and Street.com. In addition, the website offered online tools to assist with tasks such as financial planning, asset allocation, and equity evaluation. Personal service from American Express's 9,300 financial advisors was also available. One website linked the various online offerings from American Express. Available services included online brokerage, Membership B@nking, retirement services, credit card services, online shopping, and travel and entertainment services.

Morgan Stanley Dean Witter

The 1997 merger of Morgan Stanley and Dean Witter and Discover & Co. created a global financial services firm with core businesses in securities, asset management, credit, and transaction services. With more than 45,000 employees and total assets of $38.9 billion on November 30, 1998, Morgan Stanley Dean Witter (MSDW) was a full-service financial powerhouse. Full-service brokerage had long been a core business for MSDW.[20]

Founded in August 1995, Discover always was a discount online brokerage business. Dean Witter purchased the Discover business from Lombard Brokerage only months before the merger with Morgan Stanley. Renamed Discover Brokerage Direct (DBD), Discover's online model competed with traditional, full-service brokers such as those working for MSDW. Although part of the same parent company, DBD and MSDW's full service brokers did not work together. Customers maintaining accounts at both DBD and MSDW received separate statements. In a study of online trades per day in the first quarter of 1999, CS First Boston ranked DBD ninth (2.8 percent) in market share.[21]

In October 1999 MSDW announced it would migrate DBD customers to a new service called Morgan Stanley Dean Witter Online, phasing out the Discover Brokerage Direct name. MSDW Online offered accounts at $29.95 per trade, annual flat-fee accounts, and accounts with fees based on a percentage of the assets. Account holders were given access to MSDW research, shares of initial public offerings underwritten by MSDW, mutual funds, extended hours trading, and wireless trading on a Palm Pilot.

CONCLUSION

Steffens was still thinking about the financial portal when the telephone rang. A group of successful Merrill brokers had arrived for a meeting to discuss the potential implications of the financial portal on the way they did business. As Steffens headed for the meeting, he could not help but wonder if the investment analysts were right about his strategic moves over the past year.

REFERENCES

1. Charles Gasparino, "Internet Trades Put Merrill Bull on Horns of a Dilemma," *The Wall Street Journal,* February 12, 1999, p. C1
2. Christine Chen and Angela Key, "A Nation of Traders," *Fortune,* October 11, 1999, p. 116.
3. Ibid.
4. Charles Gasparino, "Merrill Faces a Challenge with Web," *The Wall Street Journal,* November 4, 1999, p. C1

5. Charles Gasparino, "Some Top Bankers at Merrill Are Jumping Ship as Company Prepares to Enter Online Waters," *The Wall Street Journal,* September 15, 1999, p. C2.

6. Ibid.

7. Christine Chen and Angela Key, "A Nation of Traders," p. 116.

8. "Net Rewards Await Firms That Choose the Right Portal Strategy," *South China Morning Post,* November 2, 1999, p. 6.

9. Leah Nathans Spiro, "Merrill's Battle," *Business Week,* November 15, 1999, p. 260.

10. Ibid.

11. Ibid., p. 264.

12. "Merrill Jumps into Online Brokerage Battle," *The Standard,* November 30, 1999, www.thestandard.com.

13. Ibid.

14. Henry McVey, "Merrill Lynch (MER): Can You Say Portal?" *US Investment Research Report,* September 29, 1999, Morgan Stanley Dean Witter, "Clicks and Mortar," *Upside*, November 1999, p. 209.

15. www.schwab.com.

16. "Reboot," *Wired,* November 1999.

17. Patrick McGeehan, "A Traditional Brokerage Firm Spouts the Online Gospel," *New York Times*, October 8, 1999, p. 1.

18. www.amazon.com/exec/obidos/subst/misc/news.html/102-5734195-8674463.

19. www.americanexpress.com. Patrick McGeehan, "Latest Lure on the Web: Free Trades," *New York Times,* November 14, 1999, p. 7.

20. www.msdw.com.

21. Leah Nathans Spiro, "Morgan for the Masses," *Business Week,* November 1, 1999, p. 180. Ruth Simon, "Full Service Brokers Complicate Online World," *The Wall Street Journal,* October 19, 1999, p. C1.

EXHIBIT 14.1 Merrill Lynch Consolidated Statement of Earnings

	Fiscal Year Ended December		
	1998	**1997**	**1996**
	(in $ millions, except per share amounts)		
Revenues			
Commissions*	$ 5,799	$ 4,995	$ 4,085
Interest and dividends	19,314	17,299	13,125
Principal transactions	2,651	3,827	3,531
Investment banking	3,264	2,876	2,022
Asset management/portfolio service fees	4,202	3,002	2,431
Other	623	500	519
Total Revenues	35,853	32,499	25,713
Interest expense	18,306	16,243	12,092
Net revenues	17,547	16,256	13,621
Noninterest expenses			
Compensation and benefits	9,199	8,333	7,012
Communications and technology	1,749	1,255	1,010
Occupancy and related depreciation	867	736	742
Advertising and market development	688	613	527
Brokerage, clearing, and exchange fees	683	525	433
Professional fees	552	520	385
Goodwill amortization	226	65	50
Provision for staff reductions	430	—	—
Other	1,057	1,098	834
Total noninterest expenses	15,451	13,145	10,993
Earnings before income taxes and dividends on preferred securities	2,096	3,111	2,628
Income tax expense	713	1,129	980
Dividends on preferred securities	124	47	—
Net earnings	$ 1,259	$ 1,935	$ 1,648
Net earnings to common stockholders	$ 1,220	$ 1,896	$ 1,602
Earnings per common share			
Basic	$ 3.43	$ 5.57	$ 4.63
Diluted	$ 3.00	$ 4.79	$ 4.08

Source: EDGAR 10-K

EXHIBIT 14.2 Merrill Lynch Commission Breakdown

	1998	**1997**	**1996**
	(in $ millions)		
Listed and over-the-counter	$3,185	$2,759	$2,207
Mutual funds	1,871	1,594	1,302
Other	743	642	576
Total	$5,799	$4,995	$4,085

Source: Merrill Lynch, EDGAR 10-K

EXHIBIT 14.3 Growth Rates on the Internet, July 1998–July 1999

	1998	1999	Percent growth
	(in millions)		
Online consumers	53.5	65.4	22%
Online purchasers	14.5	24.4	68
Online banking	6.2	6.3	2
Online trading	4.0	6.1	53

Source: Cybercitizen Finance.

EXHIBIT 14.4 U.S. Top Four Discount Securities Brokers, October 1999

Firm	Total Number of Accounts	Number of Online Accounts
	(in millions)	
Fidelity	10.8*	2.8
Merrill Lynch	8.0	n/a
Charles Schwab	6.3	2.8
TD Waterhouse	2.1	1.0

* Includes mutual-fund accounts.
Source: Putnam Lovell De Guardiola & Thornton, Inc.; Goldman Sachs & Co.; US Bancorp Piper Jaffray; company reports.

EXHIBIT 14.5 Assets Invested Online [in $ Billions]

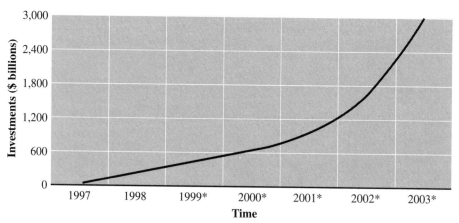

* Year-end projections as of March 1999.
Source: Fortune; Forrester Research, June 1999.

Index